Football League

GROUNDS
FOR A CHANGE

Published By:

Dave Twydell
12 The Furrows, Harefield,
Middlesex. UB9 6AT.

Printed By:

JUMA. Tel: 0742 720915.

ISBN 0 9513321 4 7.

Cover acknowledgements:
Front:
(Top) A painting showing action at the Newcastle Road Ground, Sunderland, in 1895.
(Reproduced by permission of Sunderland A.F.C.)
(Lower) The Leamington Street Ground of Blackburn Rovers, how it might have looked (based on written information) in 1882.
(Dave Twydell)

Rear:
(Top) The Crystal Palace pre-First World War home at Herne Hill Cycle Track.
(Dave Twydell)
(Lower) Fellows Park, Walsall versus Bristol City in 1989.
(Reproduced by permission of Walsall F.C., copies of this painting, by Peter Watson, are available from the Club.)

CONTENTS:

Acknowledgements:

A book such as this which covers such a wide area of research depends so much on the help and co-operation received from many people. For those that provided the occasional fact or pointed me in the right direction I offer my appreciation. I am particularly grateful to the following who went out of their way to ensure that different aspects were covered in detail (names in alphabetical order):
Chris Ambler, Stewart Beckett, Tony Bluff, Bill Gibbs, Graham Haynes, George Higham, Bryan Horsnell, David Howgate, Mike Jay, Paul Joannou, Colin MacKenzie, Roy King, Mr Lindsay, Rob Marsden, Kevin Powell, Stan Searl, Les Triggs, Mr R.Weller and David Woods.

Also to Walsall Football Club and Sunderland A.F.C. for permission to reproduce the illustrations of their former Grounds.

My travels throughout the Country have brought me into contact with countless Public Libraries (normally in the Local History or Reference sections), and my thanks to those Librarians. My special thanks for the help provided at the following:
The British Museum: Reading, Map and Newspaper Libraries.
The Public Libraries at:
Carlisle, Nottingham and Stratford (London)
Grange Museum (London Borough of Brent).
Greenwich Local History Library.
Luton Museum and Art Gallery.
Southend Central Museum.
Walsall Local History Centre.

The Principal sources of reference were made to innumerable (mostly Provincial) newspapers, plus the following books:
The Book of Football (Published 1905).
Association Football and English Society 1863 - 1915 (Tony Mason).
History of the Lancashire Football Association 1878 - 1925.
Football in Sheffield (Percy Young).
Hotbed of Soccer (Athur Appleton).
'The Footballer' Magazine.
The Association of Football Statisticians reports.

Plus, in varying degrees of detail, the Club History and Stat- istical Books (both old and modern) from many Clubs, too numerous to mention individually.

Every effort has been made to acknowledge the source of specific illustrations and photographs, and to ensure that copyright has not been infringed.

Introduction:

The majority of active football followers are supporters of one Club. Regularly they make a pilgrimage to watch their team, yet over the years many aspects change. The team itself is composed of ever changing individuals. the Managers come and go with frequency. The Directors and Chairmen of the Club are replaced. Even the supporters themselves must inevitably change over the decades. Yet the one normal unchanging facet of football is 'The Ground'. There cannot be a true fan who does not get a thrill when they enter 'their' Ground, or fulfil an expectation when seeing for the first time a 'new' one. The growth of the 'Groundhopping' spectator who will often go to extraordinary lengths to attend a match at a new venue confirms the fascination that the actual Grounds themselves have for most supporters. Yet this is an aspect of the game that has been almost totally ignored over the years.

For most Clubs there was a changing of venues before a final settlement at a permanent base, and although until recently further moves were very rare, economic and óther pressures in the modern age has made further upheavals more frequent. But the Grounds have been almost totally ignored by football history; Team groups, Individuals and action photographs are fairly common and date back well into the 19th century, yet a specific portrayal of where these events all happened are frustratingly rare indeed.

Even Club Histories, with notable exceptions such as 'The History of Sunderland' and 'Millwall Lions of the South', rarely give more than a casual mention or glimpse of the Grounds. But there is now a new awareness of this important aspect of Football History that has been, in the main, previously ignored. Therefore, I hope I have carried on, in a sense, from where Simon Inglis left off with his book, 'The Football Grounds of Great Britain'.

Perhaps a definition of a 'Football Ground' of yesteryear would not go amiss. We are used to well enclosed stadiums, with walls and barriers that not only exclude the free viewer but also the vandal. These contain within, the banks of concrete terracing, comfortable (and otherwise) seated Stands, executive boxes, floodlights, toilet and refreshment facilities, etc. While in many cases some of these amenities still appear to date back to the dark ages, radical changes are afoot to make the lot of the football supporter a better one. But what facilities did our Grandfathers, and their Fathers have?

There was never in the past, no more than there is in the present, a 'typical' Ground, but there were certain aspects that gradually changed over the decades, which can give an insight into the football spectating venues of yesteryear.

Influenced principally by the Public Schools who had their own separate forms of 'Football' that would be unrecognisable in todays game, the pupils took back to their homes the rudiments of the sport. The formation of the Football Association brought together a uniform set of rules which made the playing of matches between different organisations feasible. But in the early days, two diverging paths resulted which led initially to two different types of Ground.

In the Midlands and North of England, (and particularly noticed in the Industrial Lancashire towns), the former Public school pupils introduced to the working man a game that provided an interest and relief from the long hours and drudgery that were experienced in the Mills and Factories. The Industrial Overlords soon saw the value of such enthusiasm, not always from an altruistic viewpoint since a happy employee is more likely to work harder! What started as informal challenges played on reasonably flat areas of grass, quickly developed into a passion and support for individual teams. With the introduction of knockout Cup Competitions and then to League football, the interest grew to such a degree that the number of spectators increased dramatically. It soon became necessary to regulate such crowds in properly defined areas, but such developments cost money. There was also the payment for travel to matches that also had to be made, and so the enclosed Football Ground came upon the scene, with the payment of a fee for entry. But many of those spectators that were now being attracted from a wide spectrum of society also expected certain basic facilities. Those that could afford it were willing to pay extra in order to sit in a degree of covered comfort, although the vast majority of the populace was only able to afford the minimum, and hence continued to accept standing in the open. Football became more than just a sport it became a challenge, and in order to ensure that any one team was able to provide an advantage over their opponents, the better Players had to be induced to play for that team. Professionalism was born. Bigger crowds were attracted, and the Grounds became more developed and larger.

Initially in the South of the Country, the development of the game followed a less radical path. The Public Schools themselves, and other similar institutions, were for many years committed to retaining a purely amateur status.

The playing members paid for the privilege, and such spectators as there were, could freely watch the proceedings. Without the need for additional finance, the Clubs neither needed to enclose the open playing areas nor charge a fee to spectators. Since spectators were not a necessary factor, then provision for them was not considered necessary. Such fields (for they could hardly be termed 'Grounds') were used until the late 19th century, by which time professionalism had spread to these Southern counties. With 'The North' having had a head start, it remained for the South to fall in line and develop fenced venues on similar lines.

From the open fields in the earliest days, enclosed pitches first developed along the lines of Cricket Grounds, due in no small measure to the fact that many teams owed their origins from such Clubs. The Pavilion started appearing at Football Grounds. Initially this was almost invariably a timber structure that usually provided dressing room accommodation for the Players, and some comfort for the select few - the Committees of the competing Clubs. Those teams without pavilions continued to rely on local establishments (usually Public Houses) for the provision of changing rooms, and the Proprietors would often provide an area as a Clubroom; the increased custom no doubt more than made up for this service provided by the Publican! But the pavilions only catered for a small number of spectators and so they were enlarged and incorporated banked seating, the Grandstand was born; but in many instances it was still referred to as a Pavilion until well into the 20th century.

Reserved enclosures became a feature. This was an area for the exclusive use of the likes of vice-Presidents plus Club members, and eventually those prepared to pay for a year's viewing in advance, the season ticket holder. Such areas were initially little more than a fenced off standing area (plus the seated Stand) to segregate the 'haves' from the 'have-nots'. But probably the greatest discomfort for the non-seated spectator was the standing on wet grass and mud. Duckboards (open slatted timber pallets) became popular, first in the Reserved enclosure, and eventually around the complete pitch perimeter. Flat standing areas were hardly conducive to a good view in a packed Ground, and therefore either natural or man-made embankments were utilised. These were initially of grass covered soil or waste material, but as time progressed these were often reinforced with timber planks forming vertical steps and ash laid down on the surface as steps. Other improvements to the spectator's lot was the provision of unroofed timber 'Stands' (on which to sit), and finally open sided roofs over the standing areas.

Perhaps the greatest innovation (around the dawn of the 20th century) was the laying of raised concrete steps - the terraces. The football spectator could now choose to stand in relative comfort (without an obscured view or getting his wet feet), and often in areas protected from the elements, i.e. under cover. For an extra premium (and in the early days a large one), covered seating was possible with the provision of timber planks laid on the raised steps of the Grandstands. The timber stands became concrete and steel, the planks were replaced with individual and backed seats, and the column obstructions gave way to cantilevered roofs.

Contrary to popular misconception, football violence and hooliganism was prevalent even in the earliest days. Perhaps wanton damage was not so rife, and therefore the Ground enclosure fences were usually only flimsy timber fencing, around three metres high, that were installed solely to prevent free viewing. Whereas high perimeter pitch fencing is only a modern phenomena, it has always been considered necessary to provide a barrier against encroachment onto the field. The earliest barriers were no more than ropes tied between posts that had been driven into the Ground. But enthusiasm (and sometimes riotous behaviour) soon made it necessary to provide a more substantial barrier. Timber picket fences and finally sturdy masonry walls became the 'norm'. The provision of refreshment facilities is perhaps the one aspect of a Ground that has not greatly changed. Refreshment bars, cabins, rooms, booths were some of the names given to the buildings that provided this service. And even in those far off days, it was not unusual for alcohol to be sold on the Ground. Until the 1950's, 'Bovril' and 'Oxo' were synonymous with the game, but are less obvious now; enter the berger and the hot-dog, the coke and the crisps.

Hopefully this has served as a brief introduction to Football Grounds over the decades. But remember the 'Ground' could refer to an open field, or a covered Stadium, the following pages I trust will define and illustrate these varied venues of yesteryear.

Footnote: The reader may be critical regarding the extent of content (or lack of it) that has been devoted to individual Clubs. But please remember that the amount of information available varies greatly, and therefore this factor has dictated the extent of my text and illustrations. Unfortunately due to their antiquity, the quality of many of the illustrations is below the standard that would have been liked.

ARSENAL

June 1989. The site of the former Manor Ground from the Southern Outfall Sewer embankment.   (Dave Twydell)

Being formed in 1886, the Club can hardly claim to be one of the oldest in the South, yet their rapid rise in status led to them being the first to adopt professionalism, and their lead in this field has ensured that they have remained one of the premier Clubs in the Country.

Although now based in North London, their origins and early years were centred some miles away, to the South-east, in Kent. For a short period the Arsenal were known, unofficially, as Dial Square and were created as a works team by a small group of Scots working in a Woolwich Foundry. Their first properly organised match was played on the 11th of December 1886, North of the Thames on the Isle of Dogs, when Eastern Wanderers were thrashed 6-0. The conditions at this first (away) game were appalling since the the back gardens of houses lined one side of the pitch, and recovery of the ball had to be frequently made from a ditch, which was more accurately described as an open sewer. The team used the local Public House as a changing room, but the players were in such a filthy state after the game that the Landlord considered that he was due a fee for clearing up after them! The Club formerly adopted the name of 'Royal Arsenal' following a meeting that was held later that month at the Royal Oak.

PLUMSTEAD COMMON.

The second game was undertaken on the 8th of January when Erith were entertained 6-1, by which time not only had the Club's name been changed, but a home Ground on Plumstead Common was used. For the remainder of the 1886/87 season, four more home matches were played on the Common, but this could only be loosely described as a 'Ground', since it was, as it is now, nothing more than a large open grassed area. The surface was very poor since it was uneven and deeply rutted (the horses of the Royal Artillery were also exercised here), and one of three Public Houses - of which only the much altered 'Star' remains - were used as Dressing Rooms. Goal posts had to be erected for each game, and these were stored in one Fred Beardsley's back garden! The initial season went well for of the total of ten games played, seven ended in victory with only one defeat.

SPORTSMAN'S GROUND.

For a Club with ambition, it was apparent that a more suitable Ground had to be found, and a move was made about a mile to the North, to a field known as the Sportsman's Ground. Such a title was something of an exageration, for this former pig farm, that was leased by the War Department to Mr. Walton, was located on the edge of the Plumstead Marshes and frequently became waterlogged! Mr. Walton was also the Landlord of the 'Sportsman' Beerhouse in Griffin Manor Way which this was demolished around 1905. It is probable that the Ground was enclosed, but most unlikely that any facilities were provided for either Players or spectators. The first match was played at this second location on the 30th of September when Alexandria United were entertained and beaten 5-1. The Club struggled through the 1887/88 season at this unsatisfactory location, with the final match being played on the 11th of February. Already the team were attracting considerable interest from the general public, and this Good Friday match, when Millwall were beaten by 3-0, was watched by several thousand spectators. But the game was something of a farce since the pitch was, in part, under several inches of water, and an immediate move was made to the Manor Field next door. Although so close to the former, it was less susceptible to waterlogging, and this Ground remained as the Club's home until the end of the 1889/90 season.

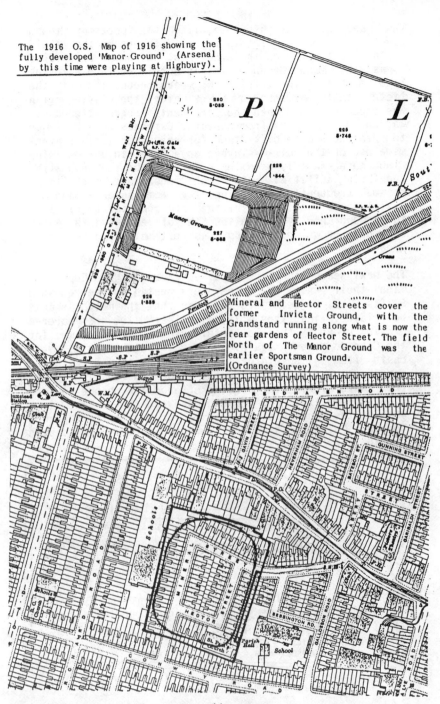

The 1916 O.S. Map of 1916 showing the fully developed 'Manor Ground' (Arsenal by this time were playing at Highbury).

Mineral and Hector Streets cover the former Invicta Ground, with the Grandstand running along what is now the rear gardens of Hector Street. The field North of The Manor Ground was the earlier Sportsman Ground.
(Ordnance Survey)

-11-

MANOR FIELD.

The Manor Field at this time, like it's Sportsman Ground counterpart, offered little for the players on the field or those attending on the sidelines, but some years later - as the Manor Ground - it was developed into a worthy Stadium. During the (first) two years occupation of the field, that was owned by a Mr. Cavey, the playing pitch was roped off, and when the frequent large attendances warranted it, wagons from a nearby Barracks were borrowed to provide a makeshift Stand for spectators; the Players made use of the Railway Tavern as a Dressing room. The Club were rapidly becoming a force to be reckoned with, and their abilities were soon recognised with large crowds frequently attending the home games - when Old Westminsters were beaten by the only goal in the Final of the London Charity Cup on the 5th of April 1889 - an enormous crowd of 10,000 was estimated to have been present.

The next season the Club first entered the F.A.Cup, but made their exit when they were beaten by the renowned Swifts Club. So keen were the fans that the match should be played, that they willingly cleared the snow covered playing area. By the end of this season, it was time for the Club to move on again. The Manor Field was still very basic from a spectators point of view, and with the continuing and greater interest shown towards the Club, they were fortunate in being offered the chance to move into a properly fenced and equipped enclosure. The last game at the Manor Field was played on the 3rd of May when London Caledonians were entertained in a Clapton Combination fixture.

1891 drawing from the Press Box at the Invicta Ground.
(Penny Illustrated)

Part of the concrete terracing to the (East) Stand, side of the Invicta
Ground still remains in the back gardens of the houses in Hector Street.
(Kentish Independant)

INVICTA GROUND.

George Weaver owned an area of land that was ideally
situated on the other side of the railway station from
the Manor Field, and just South of Plumstead High Street.
He created a Sports Ground, probably with the main
intention of letting it out to the Royal Arsenal Club.
Although compact and hemmed in by schools and the rear
gardens of houses, it provided, on the East side, a
narrow but near full pitch length seated and covered
Stand that held around 1,500 spectators, and was built
upon concrete steps. There was a flat standing area in
front of the Stand and elsewhere, plus a long length of
open concrete terracing on the West side that could
accommodate about 3,000 fans. The Ground was far superior
to any other football enclosure in the South (and better
than most elsewhere), and was innovative in the use of
concrete for terracing. The entrances to the Ground were
directly off the High Street together with a wider route
via Butcher's Lane. A Press Box was provided in the
North-east corner, and the overall playing area was 130
yards long by 90 wide. One can well imagine the prestige
gained and delight felt by the Club when they moved into
the newly built Invicta Ground for the start of the
1890/91 season.

The Club's occupation of the Invicta Ground only lasted for three years, but during this time they embarked on a career that was to shake the Football World. The North had already appreciated the possibilities of professional football where the rich Indutrialists were able to provide an interest, at low a relatively cost for their workers, whereas the more affluent South had remained purely amateur. After continually losing good Players to other Clubs, the Royal Arsenal decided to turn Professional in 1891 (following a well attended meeting that was held at the Windsor Castle Music Hall), a move which shook and horrified the "conservative in outlook" South of England. This drastic step could have sounded the death knell for the Club, for they were banned from playing matches with Southern Clubs (other than F.A.Cup-ties), and with the Football League already in operation, they had to principally depend on Friendly games with Clubs from Birmingham and further North. But this rejection of the Amateur code only helped to create even greater interest in the Club, and with the visit of the Scottish Club, Hearts, on Easter Monday in 1891, 12,000 enthusiasts packed into the Ground. At this juncture the Club was renamed 'Woolwich Arsenal'.

Consistent good play and support led to the Club becoming the first from the South to be elected into the Football League in 1893. This elevation also had big repercussions, for the owner of the Invicta Ground decided to raise the rent form £200 to £350 per annum. The Club considered such an enormous increase quite unacceptable, and the 1892/93 season became the last at the Ground. The Invicta Ground was opened with a match versus the 93rd Highlanders on the 6th of September 1890 (two goals were shared), and the last match was lost to Stoke by the only goal of the game on the 29th of April 1893.

An artists impression of the match at the Invicta Ground (the North-west corner), on the 2nd of October 1899. Hunt scores the only goal versus Aston Villa.

-14-

BACK TO THE MANOR FIELD.

By now the Club was quite affluent, and it took the opportunity to purchase the Manor Field for £4,000 from Mr.Cavey. The full implications of a businesslike approach were realised when the Club became a Limited Company around this time. With the help of the supporters the fenced, but basic Ground was transformed into a 20,000 capacity Stadium during the summer of 1893. A narrow but full pitch length covered and seated Iron Stand (capacity for 2,000) was built on the North side, which left a wide flat standing area in front. Opposite the Stand a slightly - earth banked - terrace was created, and in the early years military wagons were again utilised to provide additional viewing platforms on the flat surrounds of the pitch. During the Club's twenty year occupancy of the Manor Ground it changed dramatically, and became one of the largest and best equipped Football Grounds.

The raised embankment of the Southern Outfall Sewer outside the Ground, to the South, provided a free viewing area. To counteract this potential loss of revenue a full pitch length seated Stand was built opposite the early Stand and a wide expanse of concrete terracing was introduced beind the East end goal, both of which effectively masked the view of non-paying customers! A new seated Stand replaced the original, and further concrete terracing was built behind the Manorway goal. Support continued for the Club as they gradually established themselves in the ranks of the Football League Second Division. After eight years of moderate placings in the table, they gradually became a real force to be reckoned with and at the end of the 1903/04 season they were promoted to the First Division. Little progress was made in the F.A.Cup - although support for the competition was always high with the visit of Sheffield United in February 1903 attracting an attendance of 25,000 and match receipts of £1,000 - until two semi-final appearances in 1906 and 1907.

Their elevation to the First Division should have signalled the start of a new era and continued success, but after a period of regular attendances of 10,000 or more, near disaster soon hit the Club. The Club had been an essentially working-man's organistaion, but the outbreak of the Boer War in 1899 had led to increased work in the muitions factories, and less time was left to spend on leisure activities.

Support for the team slumped as did the finances. After five mediocre seasons, the Arsenal only just avoided relegation at the end of the 1909/10 season, and the consequent loss of support led to debts of £3,000 and bankruptcy. The Fulham F.C. Chairman, Henry Norris, took over the Club, and if it hadn't been for the vociferous ojections that were raised from all sides, would have amalgamated the two teams. The new Management intially revitalised the Club and a recovery was made over the next two years, but the 1912/13 season became the Club's worst - they won only one home game - and they were relegated.

With support at an all time low and the consequential finances going from bad to worse, Norris decided to re-establish the Club on the North side of London! The Club's programme editor of the time was said, during that last fateful season at Plumstead, to have stood outside the Ground on a matchday and implored the locals to pay and watch the game! Plumstead was not the ideal site from an access point of view, whereas the more populated North of London did not suffer from this problem. Despite the vociferous objections from nearby Tottenham Hotspur and Clapton Orient, a move was made at the end of the 1913/14 season to Gillespie Road, and a Stadium was built that was later to become Highbury. The last first team match at the Manor Ground was played on the 26th of April 1913, when Middlesbrough shared two goals. This was a benefit game for Joe Shaw, and the poor match receipts of only £130 were boosted by £120 from the Directors own pockets!

The damaged Refreshment Room at the Manor Ground after a Munitions Factory explosion in February 1907.   (Daily Graphic)

THE GROUNDS TODAY.

The Invicta Ground disappeared soon after Arsenal moved, and the houses of Mineral and Hector Streets now cover the site. One intriguing remainder, is part of the concrete terracing to the Stand that runs along the bottom of the back gardens to some of the houses in Hector Street. The Manor Ground now consists of an Industrial estate, located to the East of Griffin Manor Way and between Hatton Road and Natham Way. A climb to the top of the embankment that still serves the Southern Outfall Sewer reveals a view over the Industrial site, and proves that the building of a Stand and high terracing was necessary to prevent a free view! The site now occupied by a Government Department immediately to the North of this estate was the location of the Sportsman's Ground.

Action at the Manor Ground, versus Preston in 1903.

ASTON VILLA

In 1874, a number of members of the Villa Cross Wesleyan Chapel in the Birchfield District, decided to add football as a winter sport to their cricketting pursuits that they had started playing around two years earlier. But the footballers beginnings were of a very low key, and suitable opposition proved to be hard to find.

Within Birmingham itself the Soccer form of Football was rarely played at this time, but instead a mixture of both codes was the popular pastime. Slightly further afield, there were a number of Clubs that had adopted the 'round ball' sport - notably Wednesbury Old Athletic and Stafford Road (from Wolverhampton), but as established Clubs they would not have considered this new team as worthy enough opposition. Therefore after the reputed first competitive match of Aston Villa in March 1875, it was not until the Autumn of that year before the next match against another team was played. The first game was against Aston Brook St.Mary's - a Rugby team - and a compromise had to be reached, with one half of each code being played! Jack Hughes was the historical scorer of the Villa's first goal, in the 1-0 victory. A suitable Ground was a problem, but a site on or near the present Wilson Road was used on probably just this single occasion, and a crowd of 250 was said to be present.

ASTON PARK AND LOWER ASTON GROUNDS.
The Club's opponents in the 1875/76 season included the likes of St.George's Excelsior and Aston Unity, with home games being played either in Aston Park, or at the Lower Aston Grounds Meadow. The Lower Aston Grounds were, at this time, public pleasure gardens, and other sports included Athletics and Cricket. There was also an aquarium, a boating lake, a skating rink, a restaurant, a concert hall and a theatre. Birmingham Cricket and Football Club were amongst other users of the Grounds, and were probably the Villa's closest rivals in these early days. Within a very short time, Football began to become a stronghold in the area, and was aided by the arrival of the Scotsman George Ramsay (who was to become a prime mover in the Club's rise in stature). It soon became apparent that a more suitable home venue would be required for the rapid increase in interest as a spectator sport.

PERRY BARR.

The search for a new Ground ended when Ramsay, and fellow Scot John Lindsay, settled upon some grazing land near Wellington Road in the rural, Perry Barr District. And so in 1876, an agreement was reached with a local Butcher, who was the tenant of this chosen land (it was owned by the Bridge Trust School), and it was sub-let at a rent of £5 per annum. This figure rose to £8 the next year, and a demand for £10 twelve months later. The Club eventually managed to secure a three year lease direct from the owners, but at an initial cost of £60 per annum, and this rose to £175 by 1891! Although the Ground was enclosed to enable an entrance charge to be made, it was a far cry from the much later Villa Park, since there were no facilities for either Players or spectators. In the early days, a hayrick had to be moved from the middle of the pitch before each game and a hump near one end of the playing area had to be contended with! A line of trees on one touchline remained for several years before their removal, but did at least provide back supports for the local Press! The changing rooms consisted of a Blacksmith's shed, and the Club's headquarters were established at The Crown and Cushion, a Public House that was situated at the nearby junction of Birchfield and Wellington (where the latter becomes Aston Lane) Roads.

During the 1888 F.A.Cup tie versus Preston North End at Perry Barr, police and mounted soldiers hold back the crowds.

Although the principal reason for establishing an enclosed Ground was in order to take gate money, the first match must have been a bitter disappointment when an attendance of only 21 who each paid 3d. (a little over 1p) to see the locals play against Wednesbury Town! But the rapid rise of the Villa soon led to much larger crowds at Wellington Road, Perry Barr. An early acquisition for the the Committee was William McGregor, who was no doubt attracted to the Club by his own Wesleyan upbringing, and the fellow Scots that were members of the Club. McGregor was later to go down in history as the prime mover in the formation of the Football League in 1888.

But the early years of the Club were very much a struggle, and at one time the bailiffs were called in and seized all of the Club's possessions. The 1879/80 season saw the Club enter for the F.A.Cup the first time, and a measure of their stature can be judged from their 1-1 draw with the renowned Stafford Road Club, and subsequent replay victory at Perry Barr, before a record crowd of 4,000. This works team from Wolverhampton, came from the Engine Sheds of the same name. The next round in the Cup decreed a visit to the former winners, Oxford University, yet for an undisclosed reason the Midlands team withdrew from the Competition - perhaps the long journey with little prospect of success (the University team eventually reached the final) - deterred them. One season later their F.A.Cup run took them through to the 4th round when they again met Stafford Road at Perry Barr. There was great interest shown in the game, and a large crowd was present, but the locals narrowly lost by the odd goal in five. The Club's extended Cup run produced an average attendance of around 5,000 for their home games, but one year later crowds rose considerably, with a peak of nearly 12,000 for the Cup-tie visit of Notts. County. But this number was dwarfed in the third round match with West Bromwich (second replay), when 22,088 were present on the 3rd of January 1885.

By the mid 1880's, from it's humble beginnings, the Perry Barr Ground had been developed to a reasonable degree. On the East side a Grandstand had been built which extended about one third pitch length, and two pavilions were located, one opposite the Stand and another smaller one in the South-east corner. Although there was plenty of room around the pitch, standing spectators had little more than flat areas from which to view the games.

By this time the Club had joined the professional ranks, and support continued to grow. On the 29th of January 1887, with the visit of Wolverhampton Wanderers in a 3rd round, 3rd replay match in the F.A.Cup, an estimated crowd of 12,000 was present. Villa finally won this marathon tie, and went on to shock the football World by winning the trophy by eventually beating fellow Midlanders, West Bromwich Albion, in the Final.

The Midlands had become a strong footballing centre, and the Villa, along with Wolverhampton Wanderers, Small Heath (later Birmingham City) and most powerful of all - the West Bromwich team - dominating the scene. Following Aston Villa's Cup success in the Final, support had never been stronger, and on the 7th of January 1888, a staggering attendance of 26,849 crammed into the Perry Barr enclosure to see the Cup holders against the mighty Preston North End. This match became the first at which serious crowd disorders were experienced at a football match. The massive crowd broke through the barriers and spilled onto the pitch, and it required the combined efforts of police and soldiers mounted on horseback to restore order. Preston triumphed by 3-1 (in an earlier round they had beaten Hyde United by the all time record score of 26-0), and went on to lose to West Bromwich in the Final. Such crowd numbers were reserved only for big cup-ties, and in an attempt to generate greater support for other matches, the inspiration of Aston Villa's McGregor, led to the formation of the Football League.

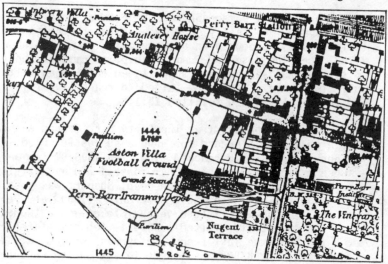

The Perry Barr Ground in 1886. (Ordnance Survey)

Quite · inexplicably regular competitive matches did not initially become the crowd-pullers for the Villa that had been expected. The first such match, on the 15th of September, attracted only 2,000 to see Stoke beaten 5-1, and far worse, on the 27th of October there was only a paltry attendance of 600 for Accrington's visit. It was obviously the quality of opposition that created the interest, for when eventual Champions Preston North End came to Parry Barr the numbers had risen to 12,000. Despite claiming the runners-up position in this, the inaugural season of the first ever season of League football, a season's average crowd at home games of only 4,800 must have been a big financial disappointment.

One year later, and with a final league placing of 8th of 12, the average crowd had risen to just over 5,700. This was to signal a fairly rapid rise in interest, for succeeding seasons saw the averages rise to over 5,800, 6,500, 7,500 and finally 10,600 at the end of the 1893/94 campaign. The large increase for this latter season was not surprising since this coincided with the Club's first Championship win. On the 17th of September 1892, a best League crowd to date of 16,000 was present for, reigning Champions, Sunderland's visit - an embarrassing 1-6 defeat. Five figure crowds had become commonplace during the Championship season, although the last League match, at home to Nottingham Forest, only attracted 4,700 to Perry Barr.

Although the 1894/95 season saw the F.A.Cup come to Aston Villa again, a fairly poor season, by their standards (third place), produced an average gate down to around 8,700. The Club's second Championship win came at the end of the 1895/96 season, and support had never been better. Only two home attendances failed to reach five figures, and the final average totalled 13,143.

By now it was apparent that the Perry Barr Ground was not of a high enough standard for such a successful Club, and the annual rental had reached £200. The 1896/97 campaign - when a second successive Championship win was attained - became the last at Wellington Road. Support was poor at the season's start when there were only 6,000 at Perry Barr for the opening fixture versus Stoke, and a thousand less for Sheffield United's visit ten days later. On March the 22nd the last League match was played at the old Ground, and 8,000 were there to see Bolton Wanderers defeated 6-2 (there was a crowd of 18,000 for Liverpool's visit just nine days earlier). The curtain was finally pulled down at Perry Barr on Good Friday, when the Reserve team met Shrewsbury Town in a Birmingham League fixture. The last two home Football League fixtures of the season were played at the Club's new ground, to the East of Wellington Road.

The move was made back to the area of the Club's much earlier days, with the development of the Lower Aston Grounds into what was eventually to become Villa Park. These Grounds had already been honoured with 'big' football matches, notably the F.A.Cup semi-finals of 1884 and 1890. By the turn of the Century all traces of the Perry Barr enclosure had disappeared, for by then, as now, the Ground had been replaced with the rows of terrace houses of Willmore and Leslie Roads.

A contemporary Artist's impression of the Perry Barr Ground - match versus West Bromwich on the 2nd of September 1893.

BARNSLEY

In Barnsley, in the 1880's, there was a great rivalry between footballers and those teams that played the Rugby code. Also in common with a number of Clubs, football came to the town via the Church. It was the Reverend Preedy - the Curate of St.Peter's Church - who founded the Barnsley team in 1887, after several earlier abortive attempts by others to popularise the sport. The first meeting of Barnsley St.Peter's (they didn't drop the suffix until 1897, after the initial proposal two years earlier) took place on the 6th of September 1887.

DONCASTER ROAD, WORSBORO BRIDGE:

Just eleven days after that inaugural meeting the Club played their first match when they entertained Manor House, and beat them by four unopposed goals. A rudimentary Ground was used as the home venue that was situated in Doncaster Road, Worsboro Bridge (near the Dove Inn), and since this was nothing more than an open field, a local Pub was used for changing rooms. But within weeks, Arthur Senior was approached with a view to the Club making use of his field, that was more suitably located for the fledgling team. But the request was turned down. The Club made several more approaches to Mr.Senior before he finally agreed to their wishes, but only on the understanding that the team's presence would not cause any troubles! This simple field was first used before the end of this, the Club's first season, and from that moment on the venue, which was later to be known as Oakwell, was to become the Barnsley Club's permanent home Ground.

To identify the location of the initial Ground of the Club now, is all but impossible. At the time of Barnsley's formation, the first field used could have been one of many that lay off of the Doncaster Road, a main route which leads East from the town centre. One other puzzle that concerns the whereabouts of this first Ground, is the fact that Worsborough Bridge itself is far removed from the Doncaster Road, as it lies some two miles South of Barnsley! Of course there may have been a Doncaster Road leading from Worsborough Bridge, but even so the area at the time was very variable and the Ground, if here, could once again have been one of many fields.

Unfortunately there would appear to be nothing suitable to illustrate Barnsley's short stay at Doncaster Road.

BIRMINGHAM CITY

As is the case with so many Clubs, the origins of Birmingham City can be traced back to a Cricket Club, and in this instance also a religious institution. In 1875 the young men of the Holy Trinity Cricket Club, Bordesley, sought a winter activity, and under the name of 'Small Heath Alliance' obtained the rent free use of a field in Arthur Street to pursue the sport of football.

ARTHUR STREET.

Unlike many Clubs of this era, a suitable venue was not difficult to find, and the pitch was said to be well turfed. After a few practice games, the Club's first proper match was played against Holte Wanderers, a team from the Aston district, although being somewhat football pioneers in the Birmingham environs, suitable opposition was not always easy to find.

LADYPOOL ROAD, SHARPBROOK.

The Club must have had early ambitions, since for the 1876/77 season an alternative home venue was obtained, which being enclosed, enabled them to charge entrance money. The Ground was in Ladypool Road, Sparkbrook, and the first gate achieved a total of 4/3d. (21p). With the Club being one of the first in the area, support was good, and crowds numbering several hundred were not uncommon. The stay at Sparkbrook lasted for just one season, for the Club had already decided that with an ever growing body of fans, a better enclosure was required. Both the Arthur Street and Ladypool Road Grounds could have been any one of a number of fields that existed at that time, and have long since disappeared.

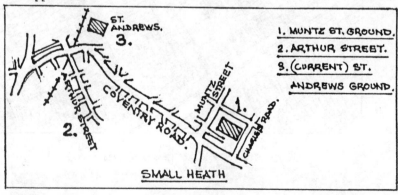

ST. ANDREWS.
3.

1. MUNTZ ST. GROUND.
2. ARTHUR STREET.
3. (CURRENT) ST. ANDREWS GROUND.

SMALL HEATH

MUNTZ STREET.

A move was made to the area of their name, Small Heath, and a suitable site was found in the strange sounding Muntz Street, or Coventry Road as it was also referred to. Although the situation may have been suitable, the condition of the pitch was far from good. The ground surface was marked with many potholes and a number of pronounced furrows, facts which were later to provoke opposition Clubs into offering money to reverse the venue for important Cup-ties! But with the rent initially at only £5 per annum, the Club developed the Ground into a neat, but limited, enclosure and remained there until 1906.

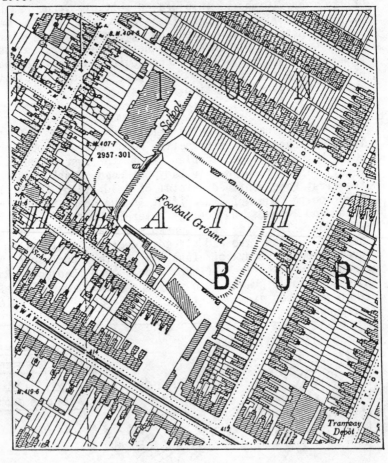

The Muntz Street Ground in 1904.
(Ordnance Survey)

The first gate taken at Muntz Street was little more than their previous 'first' (6/8d. - 33p), but with a successful team - they were undefeated in their first twenty two games there - this figure rose dramatically. A year or so later, when another Birmingham team, Calthorpe, were the visitors for a cup-tie, the takings were nearly £3-00. Opponents in the early years included the likes of Coventry, Walsall Swifts and Redditch, but it was not until the 27th of September 1879, that the Midlands 'Giants', Aston Villa, put in an appearance. With a weaker than normal team, the visitors were defeated by one goal (and one disputed) to nil, a rare reversal for the Club from the other side of Birmingham.

The Ground was located between Muntz Street and Charles Road, and North of Coventry Road. Apart from the enclosure fencing, the only early development consisted of a small timber Stand that ran approximately quarter pitch length along the South side. Further development was not long coming, and by the turn of the century it had become one of the better equipped Grounds. Open concrete terracing was built on the narrow South side (West of the Stand), and a substantial area introduced behind the goal at the West end. Also at this end an ornate timber, seated Stand was built. Embankments (probably unconcreted) were formed on the other two sides, the North being very wide, and it was on the top of the slope on this side that two small buildings were built which probably provided refreshment and toilet facilities. The main entrance was at the end of Wright Street, and on entering the Ground (behind the Stand) to the left were two more small buildings which were probably the Club Offices. Another narrow entrance passage gave access to the Ground off of Muntz Street, and possibly a third by way of Somerville Road, adjacent to the School.

One month after the first Aston Villa match, Wednesbury Old Athletic (the Holders) gave the Alliance Club £5 to reverse the venue for a Birmingham Senior Cup match, and became the losers on two counts for they were defeated at their own Oval enclosure! But this shock victory did not lead to any success in the competition, and it was not until 1907 that the Birmingham Club finally captured the trophy. However, this surprise victory gained for the Club a reputation that ensured them of worthwhile future opposition.

In 1879 the Club first entered the F.A.Cup and the second
round was reached in 1881. Only four years later (the
1885/86 season) the Club reached the semi-finals. The
Club were fortunate in the early rounds for all the games
were played at Muntz Street, but the last game, played at
Aston Villa's Ground, was a poor match and the team lost
to West Bromwich Albion. In 1885, the Club adopted
professionalism - paying Players on the basis of the size
of each home gate - and three years later became the
first football Club to become a Limited Liability
Company, with only 216 shares. At the same time the
'Alliance' was dropped from the Club's name, a change
that was generally not popular with the supporters. The
first season as a professional Club saw them pay out £71
in wages, and gate receipts continued to rise, from £299
in 1884 (of which a third went to the visiting teams) to
£3,971 only twelve years later.

The Club were elected into the Football Alliance for the
1889/90 season, and after finishing as runners-up in the
third, and last season, were elected with most of their
competitor Clubs into the Football League Division 2 for
the 1892/93 season. Despite the Club's continual rise in
stature, and increasing income, the early 1890's were not
successful in financial terms, and although the Muntz
Street Ground had become a good enclosure for spectators,
opponents did not relish playing matches on the still
uneven pitch. When Sheffield Wednesday were due to play
an F.A.Cup tie in Birmingham during the 1891/92 season, a
staggering £200 was offered to Small Heath for the match
to be played in Sheffield. In the circumstances it was an
offer that could not be refused, and much to the
annoyance of the local supporters the game was played in
Yorkshire, where the Birmingham Club lost.

Relegation followed a brief appearance in the First
Division, but the Club bounced back to join the elite in
1901. Once again another drop and another rise resulted
in the team finishing their days at Muntz Street as a
First Division Club, and a name change (in 1905) to plain
'Birmingham'. But by now three factors led to the Club
making a move to the current St.Andrews enclosure. After
a number of lean years, by 1905 the Club were back in the
black, and the ever increasing annual rent was increased
to £300. But success on the field also brought large
gates - the record was achieved during the 1903/04 season
when Aston Villa as opponents attracted a capacity
attendance of 29,000 - and by 1906 the Club had simply

outgrown their Ground. Lastly, the lease was due to run out in June 1907! The last League match on December the 22nd resulted in a 3-1 victory over Bury. It was a nostalgic moment as the Band played 'Auld Lang Syne' at the end. Two days later the Reserves beat the Wst Bromwich second eleven in a Benefit match for Dorrington.

And so a move was made from the attractive but somewhat compact Muntz Street Ground that had served the Club for nearly thirty years. On Boxing Day 1906, despite the cold and snow, Middlesbrough were the visitors to the new Ground at which there was an attendance of 32,000. Nothing remains of the Muntz Street Ground now, for within a few years the area was developed and houses built. Swanage Road now runs between Muntz Street and Charles Road, and along the centre of the former pitch. In the North-west corner however a school is still to be seen, as it was back in the late 19th century.

The ornate Grandstand at the West end of the Muntz Street Ground in 1905. (Book of Football)

BLACKBURN ROVERS

Alexandra Meadows In 1911 (After the Club had moved to Ewood Park). Higher Bank Street bisects the former Leamington Street Ground.
(Ordnance Survey)

In 1874, there were several Football teams in the area, and towards the end of that year two ex-Blackburn Grammar Schoolboys, along with several friends, decided to form a new Club. Blackburn Rovers were formed, but with no funds - and having to provide money for their own kit - there was nothing left to hire a suitable field for home matches. But undeterred the members immediately set about arranging matches, and during the latter half of the 1874/75 season played several. All of these games had to be played on their opponents Grounds, yet not a match was lost.

The next season was completed once again with all 'away' games, although their opponents were to become some of the leading teams in these early days of organised football. Amongst these teams were Darwen, Church and Park Road (Blackburn), in addition to the less familiar Cob Wall and St.Marks. The first - reported - match of the Rovers was on the 18th of December 1875, when the match with Church was drawn 1-1.

OOZEHEAD.

For the 1876/77 season the Club at last acquired the use of a field for home matches. It was conveniently situated at Oozehead, near to St.Silas' School, just to the West of the town, and off Preston New Road. But the venue was very rudimentary, certainly had no facilities for either Players or spectators, and had a pond located within the playing area which had to be covered with wooden planks and covered with grass turfs! Despite the lack of amenities, gate money was taken, which totalled just over £9 for the season, and after all expenses the Club were left with a positive balance of 2d. (1p)

PLEASINGTON CRICKET GROUND AND ALEXANDRA MEADOWS

This Ground was to last for only one season before the Rovers moved to the more presitigious Pleasington Cricket Ground, where it was hoped that they could broaden their horizons. But within a few months they were on the move again, this time to Alexandra Meadows. This was also a Cricket Ground, which was enclosed and had the luxury of a pavilion. The enclosure also included a seated Stand, if not at first, at least before the Club's departure.

By now the status of the Club was such that on the 2nd of January 1879 they entertained the Partick Club from Scotland in the first match at their new home. The match ended as a 2-1 victory to the homesters, and two players of particular significance took part in the game. A.N.Hornby, the Rovers half-back was an International Player, but for Rugby Football, while the Scots had in their line-up Fergie Suter, a man who after signing for Darwen (ironically at one time he played also for Blackburn) became, it is believed, one of two, of the first professional Players in England.

During the Club's stay at the Alexandra Meadows, which was for less than two years, they entered the F.A.Cup for the first time, and reached the third round. After a 5-1 win over Tyne Association, Darwen were beaten, and in the next round they were matched with Nottingham Forest. It was only after a replay that the Rovers bowed out of the competition. The Club also had a taste of floodlight football, when Darwen were the visitors on 4th of November 1879. Gramme lights were erected on high scaffolding at each end of the Ground, which provided a total of 12,000 candlepower. A crowd of nearly 6,000 packed the Ground, plus many who watched from the hilly park to the North. The experiment was a resounding financial success, and the match was won by 3-0. Darwen met the Rovers, in the pre-League days on numerous occations, and with both vieing for the accolades, such encounters were not always played in the most sporting of attitudes! There was no more a competitive match than that staged at Alexandra Meadows on the 27th of November 1880. An estimated crowd of 10,000 had crammed into the Ground, and as well as the packed Grandstand, twenty lorries provided raised viewing platforms. The bulk of the spectators were massed around the touchlines, and hard up against the ropes. During the first half a goal from each side was scored, and on two occasions the crowd broke through the ropes. Eight minutes into the second period, Marshall of Darwen was robbed of the ball, whereupon he grabbed his adversary and threw him down near the touchline. This was the signal for a mass pitch invasion, and the game had to be abandoned!

On the 26th of February, the Club were honoured with an International match - England versus Wales - being staged at their headquarters, before an attendance of 3,000. As football rapidly gained popularity in the area, crowds of over 5,000 were not uncommon, it soon became necessary for the Rovers to consider an enclosure for their own exclusive use. In October 1881, a move was made to Leamington Street (now 'Road'). But before the end of the 1880/81 season the Club played at another new location. The last match at Alexandra Meadows was probably that versus Nottingham Forest on the 12th of March, before an attendance of over 4,000.

EWOOD - A TEMPORARY HOME.
On April the 9th, Sheffield Wednesday were entertained at 'Ewood Bridge' (an excellent 7-3 victory in front of 4,000 spectators), followed one week later when a similar sized crowd saw the locals beat Edinburgh Hibs. by 4-2; the venue of the latter match was described as the "Ground of the Rovers at Ewood Bridge". On April the 18th, Aston Villa were entertained at 'Ewood', with between five and six thousand in attendance, and finally four days later Glasgow Dumbarton were beaten by four unopposed goals - at 'Ewood'. The Glasgow match was in aid of the 'Working members of the Club', but heavy rain before and during the match resulted in a crowd of no more than 1,000. These four matches at Ewood almost certainly referred to a field, possibly even enclosed at that time, that was to formally become a Sports Ground one year later. This Ground was located exactly where the later Ewood Park home of the Rovers is now, and therefore the fact that the team played, in effect, at 'Ewood Park' in 1881 may well have been previously overlooked by Football Historians.

LEAMINGTON STREET.
The move to Leamington Street was just a few hundred metres to the West of Alexandra Meadows, and in just a few months an impressive enclosure was created. The Ground was situated at the top of Leamington Street, no doubt the area that was bounded by Revidge and New Park Roads, and later Lynwood Road and the extended St.Silas's Road. It was well enclosed and well drained and had a

slight fall (from Revidge Road towards St. Silas's Road). A "Handsome" and spacious Grandstand was built, painted in the Club colours (blue and white) and was 152 feet long with seating for 600. A substantial area around the touchlines was covered with footboards, and the large enclosure had "every accomodation for players and spectators", which included a pavilion, plus a large refreshment pavilion which measured 52 by 16 feet and contained a 38 foot long counter. This structure was also painted in blue and white. The main, and possibly only, entrance was off of Leamington Street, at which point a large arch was built which was later inscribed with the name of the Club and of the Ground. Six pay boxes, three each side of the entrance gates were also installed, and the total cost of the work amounted to £500.

Large crowds gathered on the 15th of October 1881, long before the kick-off, for the first game at the new venue. A local derby match versus Blackburn Olympic was played, and won 4-1 by the hosts, before an attendance of around 6,000. This first season at Leamington Street was to become the Club's best to that date, for after thrashing Park Road 9-1 in the 1st round of the F.A.Cup, they caused a football sensation by becoming the first Northern Club to reach the final, when they lost by the only goal of the game at the Oval, to the renowned Old Etonians.

The Club's stay at Leamington Street lasted for nine years, and this represented one of the most successful in the Club's history. Their honours included their winning of the F.A.Cup in three consecutive seasons, and their entry in 1888 to the first Football League in the World. Their prowess waned immediately after their last F.A.Cup success, in 1886, and during the next season they made their exit in the first round. During that campaign more games were lost than won, although the next year the balance was redressed with 29 victories and only 13 defeats in the 48 matches that were played. This general downturn in the Club's abilities in the mid-1880's was reflected in their financial affairs and two significant steps were taken. Entrance charges were halved at the start of the 1885/86 season to 6d. (2½p) and 3d, and during that same season an ambitious sweepstake was held. With a top prize of a house (valued at £150!), there were thousands of tickets sold at a cost of 6d. each.

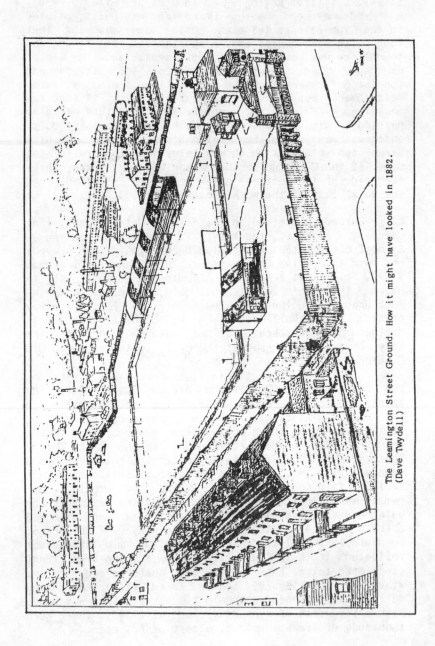

The Leamington Street Ground. How it might have looked in 1882.
(Dave Twydell)

The Club's earlier successes made them an obvious choice to become one of the twelve founder-members of the Football League in 1888. In early August an Athletics Festival was held at Leamington Street, and attracted a crowd of 5,000, which was followed in the next few weeks by several Friendly fixtures. Things did not start well for the Rovers, since all of these pre-League matches ended in defeat.

On September the 15th, the League campaign started for the Club, at home to near neighbours Accrington. A large crowd was present, who witnessed an amazing five-all draw. Fortunately for the team they had a good season and finished 4th in the final League table. The next season a third final placing was achieved, and the last League match which, as things transpired, also became the last at the Ground, occurred as early as January the 4th, when Stoke were crushed 8-0. A number of Friendly games followed which culminated in a single goal home defeat to, old (but still non-League) rivals, Darwen, on the 17th of May 1889. There was no announcement that this was to be the Club's last season at Leamington Street, and, since it was reported that the Ground was 'lost', it can be assumed that a move was not instigated by the Club. The rapid building of houses was taking place, and it appears that this was also to happen at the Leamington Street Ground. The Club had no debts, they were one of the lowest wage payers in the League, and had assets of £500 at the Ground. Therefore, although rapid plans had to be made for the move during the summer, it would seem to have been no financial hardship. The fact that they "succeeded in obtaining a splendid new Ground at Ewood..." tends to confirms that this move was to the Sports Ground that they had temporarily used some years earlier.

THE GROUNDS TODAY.

Alexandra meadows still exists in total, although now solely for the use of the East Lancashire Cricket Club, who were founded in 1864. The current pavilion, although not the original, is located in the same position as the earlier one, and the open seated Stands on the West side of the Ground, may well have existed in the days when the Football Club played there. No traces of the Leamington Street Ground remain, it having been built over with houses many years ago, probably soon after the Club's departure in the summer of 1889.

BLACKPOOL

Map of 1893 of Raikes Hall –
like a miniature Crystal Palace
of the day.   (Ordnance Survey)

The modern Club bearing the name of 'Blackpool F.C.' were
not founded until 1887, but prior to that year at least
three Clubs existed in the town. Blackpool St.Johns (who
played home matches at Masheter's field off of Caunce
Street) were originally formed in the early 1870's as
were, around this time, a Club by the name of 'Blackpool
F.C.' The latter Club soon became extinct, and while the
St.Johns Club continued, South Shore came upon the scene.
A number of Blackpool St.Johns members first mooted the
desire to change the name of the Club to plain
'Blackpool', which would be more representative of the
town as a whole. However, the Vicar and Club Chairman,
refused to sanction this title. Four days later, on the
26th of July 1887, a large number of Club members held a
meeting at the Stanley Arms Hotel (which eventually
became, for many years, the Headquarters of Blackpool
F.C.), and decided to form a separate club.

RAIKES HALL.

An entrance fee to join the new Club was set at 3/6d. (17p), and at the end of the 1887/88 season the Club gained it's first major honour by winning the Lancashire Junior Cup. Initially a field off of Bloomfield Road was used as a home venue, following the first match which produced a 2-1 win at Chorley. A more suitable Ground was soon secured at Raikes Hall (or Royal Palace Gardens as it was also known), an enclosure within a Pleasure Grounds complex which also included a Theatre, a Skating Rink, facilities for other sports and - immediately adjacent to the Football Ground - a Lake. The Ground, which was also used, during the summer, for Cricket, consisted of a (probable) enclosure fence and a two thirds pitch length covered and seated Stand on the North (lake) side.

After the first season, the new Club made a satisfactory profit of nearly £20, and with a membership which contributed £66 from subscription fees. On the 5th of November 1888, a notable victory of 12-0 was achieved over Little Hulton, and on the 28th of that month, the Club's first visitors of note were entertained at Raikes Hall - Bolton Wanderers. Although this match was lost 2-4, the homesters were far from disgraced. Such was Blackpool's early success, that at the end of this second season, the total receipts over the year doubled to £480, and a profit of £60 was made.

1890. The Raikes Hall Ground (top right). Some people are content to mess about in and around the lake while a football match goes on!
(Blackpool Public Library)

The rapid rise of the Club continued for several years, for after becoming founder-members of the Lancashire League in 1889, they soon became a force to be reckoned with being runners-up on three separate occasions from 1891. This was followed by the Championship in the 1893/94 season. Inexpicably, and after such a noteworthy quartet of gratifying seasons, interest waned the following year, despite the team finishing second in the final table once again. Entrenched in an area where most members of the Football League were based, perhaps the Club's followers found their team were nothing more than 'also-rans'. They had strong local opposition in South Shore - more or less a southern suburb of Blackpool - but the older Club never aspired to such heights as their near neighbours. Whatever the reason, Blackpool's support declined, and in 1896, they became a Limited Company with capital of £2,000. But this move did not halt the slide, and one year later an enormous loss of £1,183 was announced, although in their bid to maintain their prowess, wages accounted for £1,470 of the Club's income. During the 1896/97 season gates averaged around 2,000 at home matches. An agreement was made on the 18th of April 1896, when the two local Clubs agreed to pool their resources, and amalgamate. But South Shore, probably unwisely, cancelled the arrangement, and the two continued as separate Clubs.

ATHLETIC GROUNDS, STANLEY PARK.
Despite the Club's financial problems, they were elected into the Football League for the 1897/98 season.

But after nine years at Raikes Hall, the Club were forced to seek a new home, since the Pleasure Grounds were earmarked for future housing. The Club moved, somewhat prematurely, in August 1897, when a five year lease was taken out on the Athletic Grounds, that were located within Stanley Park. The first home Football League match was played on the 11th of September, when Burnley were the visitors, and two goals were shared. On a sunny afternoon, the Mayor ceremonially 'kicked-off' in front of an encouraging attendance of 4,000.

It had been a rush to make the Ground playable, and much labour had been used draining and levelling the pitch. The Athletic Grounds were not so conveniently situated as Raikes Hall, being further from the centre of town (a 3d. bus ride away), and the overall layout of the venue was far removed from their former compact arena.

A Racecourse ran around the perimeter of the overall 24 acre enclosure, with much of this area taken up by a Cricket Ground - complete with pavilion and open seating areas. At the West end there was an elongated oval shaped, cinder covered, trotting and cycling track, by then disused and rapidly decaying. On the West side there was a covered Stand and a short length of uncovered seating (but not, initially, an enclosure for the Press!). The spectators were somewhat removed from the action, and cover and seating were very limited. The first match ended as a 1-1 draw,

Initially attendances rose, but this uplift in the Club's fortunes was shortlived, and by the season's end the financial situation forced the Club into selling several promising players. Games versus Manchester City and Newton Heath both attracted tradionally good crowds of around 3,000, but for some games, barely four figure gates were achieved (Small Heath's visit produced only £27 in match receipts). The Club also attracted unruly elements, and the bad language frequently heard in the Stand caused many complaints. On December the 31st 1898, a 1-2 defeat in pouring rain was conceded to Glossop, and two days later a Friendly match with South Shore ended goalless in front of no more than 300 spectators, who had to brave the elements once again. These two games were the last played at the Athletic Grounds, for after a stay of only eighteen months a move was made, back to Raikes Hall. The expected redevelopment of the site had not started, and for just under one year the Club were able to play at this preferable enclosure.

BACK TO RAIKES HALL.

The first game back at the old home not only produced an encouraging three goal defeat of Burton Swifts (on the 14th of January), but also a rise in the normal attendance, to around 1,000. It was by now appreciated that the Club's premature move to the Athletic Grounds had been a bad mistake! Rumours abounded with regard to Blackpool and South Shore amalgamating, and this now seemed a distinct possiblity with both team floundering in the League, and each accompanied by poor attendances for home matches. The season finished with the Club placed 16th in the League, and although only third from bottom they were somewhat surprisingly not re-elected. Fortunately the attendances had improved back at Raikes Hall, with 3,000 present for the Newton Heath match and the match receipts for this game and the other home

fixture over Easter totalling £200. The 1899/1900 season
started in gloom once again. Back into non-League
football plus the announcement that 71 plots on the
Raikes Hall Estate had been sold. It was obvious that
Blackpool F.C. would soon have to move on again. On
September the 2nd a good crowd saw the team thrash
Rochdale 8-1 in their first fixture back in the
Lancashire League.

SOUTH SHORE'S COW GAP LANE.

Meanwhile for their neighbours things had not been
particularly bright. South Shore joined the Lancashire
League in 1891, playing their home games at the Cow Gap
Lane (later Waterloo Road) Ground, which was located
about a quarter of a mile South of Bloomfield Road. The
entrance to the Ground was off of Cow Gap Lane, and
contained a small covered seated Stand on the West side,
with narrow standing areas alongside and at the Cow Gate
end, plus a wider expanse opposite the Stand. It was a
small, compact Ground, yet despite being the underdogs to
their more illustrious rivals, it was South Shore who
managed to secure the Bloomfield Road Ground. Financially
it had been far more of a struggle for South Shore, with
attendances normally only in the hundreds, although in
September 1899, a crowd of 2,000 were present for
Blackpool's visit for a Lancashire Senior Cup-tie. South
Shore upstaged Blackpool F.C. when they moved to
Bloomfield Road and played their first match there on
October the 21st when the First South Lancashire regiment
were beaten 6-3. The Ground was unfinished for there was
no rope enclosure to the pitch and the Grandstand had not
been built. A Bar plus two Dressing tents were planned
for. The formal Ground opening coincided with the perhaps
the team's finest victory when they beat Newton Heath in
the F.A.Cup. In the next round Southport were entertained
before a very large crowd, and a few more attendances of
this size would have removed the financial worries from
the Club. But after a draw, they lost the match in the
replay, and dreams of Cup glory, and more money, were
dashed.

On December the 9th Blackpool were the hosts to South
Shore, a game which attracted one of the best attendances
of the season. However, their time at Raikes Hall had
nearly come to an end, and that same evening it was
finally decided that the two Clubs should merge.

c.1890. An excellent view of the Cow Gap Lane Ground of South Shore - the Stand
was later moved and re-erected at Bloomfield Road (Note the apparent same design
as the Stand at Raikes Hall)   (Blackpool in old Picture Postcards)

The site of the old Cow Gap Lane Ground of South Shore, now partly a car park.
Note the Tower and the floodlights at Bloomfield Road in the background.
(Dave Twydell)

With Blackpool F.C. being the more successful of the two, they continued in the Lancashire League, while South Shore resigned. The last game at Raikes Hall, on December the 16th 1899, produced a good crowd - despite the poor weather, and Darwen were beaten by three unopposed goals. Seven days later, the 'new' Blackpool crushed Horwich in their inaugural match at Bloomfield Road.

THE GROUNDS TODAY.

The three former Grounds of the two earlier Clubs have all disappeared. The Raikes Hall Ground is now covered principally by Leicester and Longton Roads; the formerly named 'Athletic Grounds' remains a sporting area, and still contains the Cricket Ground. But the former Football enclosure is not the current Athletic Ground, which is now covered mainly by West Park Drive. The old Cow Gap Lane Ground which was nearly opposite the modern Blackpool South Railway Station is currently part of the enormous Summer Coach and Car Park.

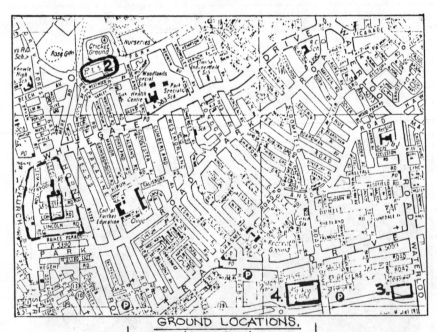

GROUND LOCATIONS.
1. Raikes Hall.
2. Athletic Grounds.
3. Cow Gap Lane.
4. Bloomfield Road.

BOLTON WANDERERS

Near the end of the Club's stay at Pikes Lane (c.1895), new building work is fast approaching the Ground.
(Bolton in 1926 It's Trade, Sport and Industry)

In view of the Club's early formation, in 1874, it is not surprising to find that they also had several Grounds before finally settling at Burnden Park in 1895. It is equally predictable that, save for one of these venues, they were all little more than open fields.

A VARIETY OF GROUNDS.

During the first few years of the Wanderers - perhaps indicative of their name - they switched home Grounds quite frequently. The first game played by the Club, in July 1874, was a trial match which was held at 'Bob Wood's' field on what is now the East side of Heaton Cemetery. This was followed by an encounter at Smithfield, located between Green Lane and Plodder Lane, on the Farnworth boundary of the town; since the opponents of Christ Church - as Bolton Wanderers were initially known - was played against Farnworth, this initial contest could perhaps be more accurately considered as an 'away' fixture.

The style in which the Club's early matches was played has been stated in one reference as the Rugby code for the first two years, and in another as both Rugby and Football. But whatever form these matches took, it was certainly in a minor and almost totally non-reportable form. During the first seven years of the Club's life, probably three different venues were used for home matches, but all were near to Pikes Lane (later Wigan Road). The Park Recreation Ground was first used, followed by Dick Cockles Field (opposite the Cross Guns public house), and Bankfield was also referred to.

A track led off of Pikes Lane to a farm by the name of 'Bankfield', and continued on, passing various fields en route. It is not easy to identify the exact field, but, if as is reasonably likely the 'ground' was near the farm, then this overlay the later, and far more pretentious Ground, known as Pikes Lane. The track later became a road, with the name of Bankfield Street. In the Club's early days Christ Church School was used as a headquarters, until the insistance by the Vicar that he should be present at all meetings which led the fledgeling Club to seek pastures new! The Gladstone Hotel, was followed by the Brittania Hotel as an H.Q., with the latter occupation lasting until 1895.

PIKES LANE.

As they rose in stature so did their ambitions, and a more suitable name for the Club was decided upon in August 1877, with the adoption of 'Bolton Wanderers'. Eventually, around 1880, as spectator interest in the game became more popular, the Club settled and developed their first true Football Ground. This Ground became known as Pike's Lane, due to its close vicinity to this road.

The Pike's Lane Ground was at the foot of a hill, and despite the spending of £150 on improved drainage and other general improvements to the pitch that were carried out in the early days, it remained a notoriously muddy venue. The entrances to the Ground were by way of the later road - Bankfield Street - and Oriel Street. The complete enclosure of over four and a half acres, was almost square in shape, with the pitch running East to West. Shallow grass embankments existed or were created on all sides, with the most notable - and widest - being on the South side, which was in effect the start of the hill. Eventually, spectator accommodation was added in the form of a rickety (as described at that time) timber Grandstand - about ten rows deep - that ran for approximately two thirds pitch length, and two raised timber 'terraces' at the Eastern end of the pitch. In the early days entry into the Grandstand cost 4d. and 6d. (2½p) and a Ground season ticket cost £1-05. But the majority of the crowd was content to stand to see the match, with those in the front few rows sitting on the grass. Additional 'terracing' and enclosure covers were temporarily commandeered for 'big' matches. Dressing rooms were located on the Ground - probably behind the East 'terrace' - and a refreshment bar was quite likely to have been located alongside. It is perhaps something of a surprise to find that the Club remained at this Ground for fourteen years, but with the money spent over the period on other improvements, and the likely difficulty of finding a better and equally economic alternative, the Wanderers ceased to wander.

c.1885, Pikes Lane Ground looking North.
(Bolton Public Library)

The Club's debut at the Pike Lane Ground was suitably crowned with a nine goal thrashing of Great Lever on the 10th of September. Other early visitors were Blackburn Rovers, in the Wanderers first season of entry into the F.A.Cup, which attracted an attendance of some 3,000, and around 5,000 were present when Derby County came to play the Wanderers in the first Football League match staged in Bolton on the 8th of September 1888. But a crowd well in excess of these was present when the Club was engaged in one F.A.Cup (replay) match. On the 2nd of February 1884, there were between twelve and eighteen thousand paying customers (to see a 2-2 draw in the 4th round game with Notts.County). An enterprising farmer who owned one of the fields that overlooked the Ground from the South, charged half the entrance price to over 4,000 fans, who viewed the contest from this more distant vantage point!

Not only was Pikes Lane uncomfortable for spectators, but also the atmosphere did not suit visitors! Glasgow Celtic made their first ever appearance in Lancashire at the Ground, and were greeted with hoots of derision by the 7,000 crowd. While back in 1883 the Club was nearly expelled from the Lancashire F.A. following the booing of the crowd, and later assault, towards referee Sam Ormerod!

Probably the most memorable match at the Ground occurred on the 1st of February 1890, when Sheffield United were pursuaded to reverse their home drawn tie, and play, instead, at Pikes Lane in the second round of the F.A.Cup. The condition of the pitch was in a very poor state - a common condition - and after taking a 90 second lead, the Wanderers went on to a five goal interval lead. The homesters ran riot in the second period, to record a final 13-0 victory, which had been watched by around 4,000.

Although the rental, in the late 1880's, was only a modest £35, by 1893 this had risen to £175 per annum, and with the Club's lease drawing to a close, an alternative Ground was enquired after in August of that year. The Club no doubt reasoned, anyway, that with the sprawl of Development that was gradually surrounding them, a renewal of the agreement was unlikely. On the 24th of February 1894 a record attendance was established at Pike's Lane, when an estimated 20,000 crammed into the enclosure to see the Wanderers defeat Liverpool by three unopposed goals in the F.A.Cup quarter final (They went on to make their first appearance in the final). Although the Club were never honoured with the staging of a F.A.Cup semi-final at Pike's Lane, they did play host to the Football League team when four goals were shared with the visiting Scottish team in April 1892 before a 9,500 crowd. Capital was raised when Club shares were sold in October 1894, which provided the means for their impending move.

The last Football League game was played at the Ground on the 13th of April 1895, when West Bromwich Albion attracted 12,000 fans, and were thrashed by 5-0 (the Wanderers last League game that season resulted in a reversal of that scoreline at Sheffield United). Earlier in February a massive 15,000 (official) crowd attended the F.A.Cup tie - but more was estimated - when Bury came to Bolton, and in the Lancashire Senior Cup, that same month, the attractive Everton team in opposition produced a crowd of between ten and twelve thousand. The last match played at the Ground occurred on the 20th of April, when 6,000 fans came to see Halliwell Rovers and Edgeworth Rovers fight it out in the Bolton Charity Cup Final.

The far from attractive, but ideally situated patch of
land, one mile to the East (and located off of the
Manchester Road), was made available to the Wanderers at
an annual rent of £130. This was the site that caught the
Club's eye two years earlier. They moved from the not
much-loved Pike's Lane and set out to create Burnden
Park.

Within ten years, houses had been built on the site of
the former Ground, and then, as now, Alice and Jessie
Streets plus the continuation of Bankfield Street covers
the area.

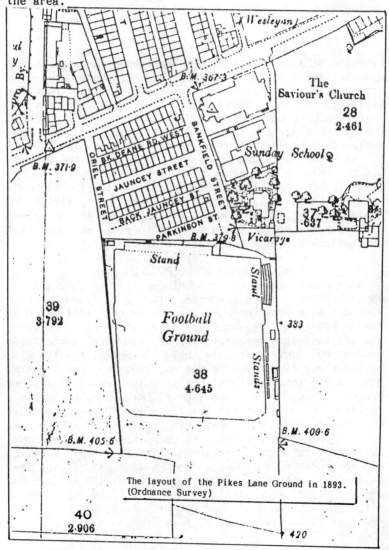

The layout of the Pikes Lane Ground in 1893.
(Ordnance Survey)

A.F.C. BOURNEMOUTH

The Club was founded as Boscombe St. John's in 1890, but the Hampshire and Dorset area was somewhat barren in respect of football, and for some years the Club existed in near obscurity. The game had been played in the town from the 1870's, mainly through the efforts of Bournemouth Rovers, but they like several other minor teams in the area were formed and disappeared frequently and with little reference made to their existance! Bournemouth F.C. were founded in 1875, and still exist today.

KINGS PARK.

Boscombe St.John's were created from the members Church associations, and initially played their home matches in Kings Park. The Park still exists in the Boscombe District, wherein Dean Court is situated. For several years the Club rarely received a mention in the local Press, playing as they were at a very minor level, and achieved no honours of note. It was not until the summer of 1899 that a reformation of the Club under the name of plain 'Boscombe', gained them more attention. The majority of the Players remained with the new Boscombe team, although they had strong local competition in Bournemouth F.C. who were by now playing in the Dorset and District League. Boscombe were to play in only the Bournemouth and District Junior League!

CASTLEMAIN ROAD, POKESDOWN.

A real home Ground was spought for, rather than a pitch amongst others, and a suitable site was found, albeit some distance from Boscombe itself. In the first match of the 1899/1900 season, on the 23rd of September, Heathfield Rovers were entertained, and were comfortably beaten by four goals to nil. One week later the Club played their first ever League match when Christchurch R.A. were the visitors, but the Club soon fell foul of Winton United, who accused them of bribing the United's Captain to play for the seaside team! The new Ground in Castlemain Road, Pokesdown was rented for £5.50 per annum. This thoroughfare is now known as Castlemain Avenue and is built up residentially. The exact location of the Ground could have been one of many fields that existed at that time, but was probably at the western end of the road and possibly opposite Pokesdown Farm. Although an undoubted improvement over Kings Park, it is doubtful if the field was at first enclosed.

By 1906 the Club's status had risen, and by then they had won all of the local, albeit minor, football honours that were available. But the Hampshire League was reorganised for the 1903/04 season, and Boscombe were admitted into the Second Division (Western Division) alongside Bournemouth. Boscombe became Champions at the end of the 1906/07 season, and repeated this feat in 1911. There was no automatic promotion, and the Club dominated the Division with five Championships to 1920. As the team became more successful they attracted greater support and by 1910 it was time to move to better pastures. The rent at Pokesdown had now risen to over £13 per annum, but as an entrance charge was now made, the Ground must have at least been enclosed by this time. The latter matches of the season saw the team's return to Kings Park,

TEMPORARY RETURN TO KINGS PARK.

The choice for a permanent new Headquarters was an area of waste ground that was owned by the Club President Mr. Cooper Dean. The Club paid only a peppercorn rent, but they repaid their benefactor by naming the Ground in his honour. Voluntary work by the supporters undertook to create a Football Ground from the wilderness, and a Grandstand was built to seat 300. However the work was not completed in time for the start of the 1910/11 season, and continued use of Kings Park had to be made. But where possible early season matches were played 'away', and an F.A.Amateur Cup game was undertaken at a neutral venue.

The second home game drew a large crowd for the local derby with Pokesdown - a 6-1 victory to the homesters. The final match before the big move was played versus Cowes, on the 10th of December. Dean Court was due to be opened on the 26th of December when Bournemouth Wanderers were to provide the opposition, but this was delayed until five days later, when a large crowd saw the prestigious encounter with Southampton Reserves in the first round proper of the Hampshire Cup.

1910 Map. There is nothing to suggest that any of the 'Football Grounds' were enclosed. The Dean Court Ground was then part of a gravel pit (top of map). (Ordnance Survey).

BRENTFORD

The original idea of the formation of a football team in
Brentford was first publically voiced at a meeting on the
10th of October 1889, and was quickly followed with a
search for a suitable field on which to play home
matches. An application was made, on the 17th of October,
to the Local Board (the Local Council) for the use of the
new Recreation Ground that was about to be opened. This
Recreation Ground, sandwiched between Lateward and Albany
Roads, still exists today. By the time of the next
meeting of the Club, seven days later, it was stated that
no answer from the Board was received, although there are
reasons to believe that the request was in fact rejected
or that the Local Board decided to defer a decision for
three weeks. In any event a supporter, Mr. Montgomery,
offered the use of a field that he owned, which was
located in Windmill Road. The rent would be nominal, and
the field was situated a distance far enough away from
the town to be free of the roughs of the area, but not
ideally near enough for spectators from the town. This
offer would appear to have been a reasonable compromise,
but the Club effectively turned it down. No reason has
been recorded, therefore this rejection can only be open
to conjecture. The size and surface of the field must
have been acceptable, for in the final event, the
Brentford Reserve team was to make use of it. Therefore
there must have been other circumstances regarding the
Club's final choice of a home Ground.

The Brentford decision to look for an alternative home
Ground - whether it was forced upon them by rejection, or
time, or by their own choice - may well have been decided
and based upon the football climate of the day. The
Club's Officials may well have been sufficiently
ambitious, even at the time of the Club's formation, to
opt for an enclosed Ground, rather than accept whatever
field became available regardless of it's lack of
provision for paying spectators. In any event, the
alternative offer for the use of the land located behind
the Wesleyan Chapel in Windmill Road offered several
advantages over the Recreation Ground and the somewhat
distant Montgomery's field.

CLIFDEN HOUSE GROUND:

The land was owned by Edwin Underwood, who had been elected as the Club President, and at a Dinner to celebrate the opening of the Recreation Ground, he made the offer of the use of his field at a nominal rent to Brentford F.C. The 'Ground' today consists of Clifden Road plus the houses each side, and was located directly behind the Brook Road end of the later Griffin Park. In 1889, Clifden Road did not exist, and the present entry of the road, off Windmill Road, was occupied by Clifden House - coincidently the Offices of the Local Board - and the Weslyan Chapel. The back gardens of the houses in Hamilton Road, together with the rear of Clifden House and the Chapel, provided ideal enclosed boundaries to two sides of the Ground.

Brentford were able to use the Griffin Public House as a Clubhouse and Changing Rooms, which was situated, as it is today, at the junction of Braemar Road and Brook Road, and was almost adjacent to the Clifden House Ground. The use of the Griffin, was not only convenient, but the Landlord at this time was Frederick Allen, a supporter of the new Football Club.

A local reporter stated on the 6th of November 1889 that: "The Ground on which the club is situated at the rear of the Local Board offices has a private entrance near to the 'Griffin' - the Club house - and is fenced in thereby being excellently adapted for gate money." This entrance was either at the end of the housing in Brook Road - at the present junction with Clifden Road - or was by way of an opening in Brook Road, directly opposite Braemar Road, which led around to the Ground. The newspaper report went on to say that the grass on the field was long and rank, and therefore it was not all plain sailing for the new Club! At the start of the 1889/90 season, the Club's capital was no doubt minimal, and therefore the provision of any form of cover or seating at the Ground was out of the question.

The first competitive match for the Club, at home, was on November the 23rd, when half-a-crown (12½p.)was taken at the gate. A 1-1 draw with Kew ensued. The total for the season amounted to nine pounds and fifteen shillings (£9-75p.)

During the Club's three seasons use of the Clifden House Ground, Mr. Montgomery's Field (previously occupied by, and known as George Clarke's) was also use for occasional

reserve team fixtures and pre-season trial matches. This
field could well have been the later named Shotter's
Field (Brentford's third Ground) since in 1889 George
Clarke occupied Boston Lodge which was located
immediately adjacent to this field. Once again the Club
was dependant on Club supporters for permission to use
this field; there were two Montgomerys who were
vice-President's of the Football Club. Brentford ceased
to use Clifden House at the end of the 1891/92 season
(Loyola of Westminster being the last visitors on March
the 12th). The Ground's location so close to the town and
its enclosed nature had suited the Club well, and it was
with great reluctance that they had to move on due to the
termination of Mr.Montgomery's lease. The land was
earmarked for development, and house building commenced
there in 1894. The Club was in a desperate plight, for
although there were plenty of fields in the area, not all
were suitable for enclosure, but more importantly there
were few owners willing to allow the Club usage. This
reluctance was probably brought about by the team's
undoubted popularity and the consequent unruly element
amongst 'fans'.

The Plough Inn, Little Ealing c.1900. The entrance to Benn's
Field was through the gates on the left.

BENN'S FIELD, LITTLE EALING:

It was not until after the start of the 1892/93 season that an alternative could be found and its suitablility was open to question. A move had to be made to Little Ealing, and although only one mile away from Brentford, at this time of non-existant public transport, the Club ʰad fears – which were later pᵣoved well founded – that this would have an inevitable effect on support for the Club. On the 15th of October 1892, Clarence were beaten 2-1 in the first match at Benn's Field. For Dressing Rooms, use was made of The Plough Inn, that had supposedly been frequented by Dick Turpin the highwayman (as most Inns in the area claimed!).

Members Ticket of
the 1897/98 season.

It was, as now, located opposite Windmill Road (Ealing) where it joins with Little Ealing Lane. Earlier in 1880, a field adjacent to The Plough, had become the outdoor entertainment centre of the district, when an ornate arch, proudly proclaimed the entrance to the "Bowling Greens and Pleasure Grounds". The continuation of the public footpath that ran across the Pleasure Grounds led to Benn's Field. Brentford were able to use the Inn, but were faced with a long walk of several hundred yards along the footpath to their Football field. Although the Club was fortunate in that the field was large enough to contain two separate pitches – and occasionally both Brentford teams would be in action at the same time – preventing unpaying spectators from watching the matches was difficult. It can be assumed that some form of fencing was used to screen the Ground from the footpath and the adjacent fields, but the nearby bridge at the North end, which spanned the railway lines, gave a good free vantage point, the 'cheap gallery' as it was described in a local newspaper. As with the Clifden House Ground, it is doubtful if the field catered for spectators comfort, and it's distance from Brentford ensured that it was an unpopular venue with most of the Club's followers.

Brentford felt that they could command even better support than the five or six hundred that regularly trekked to Benn's Field, but with such a large following for the Club, the owners of fields nearer to the town were still reluctant to lease them out. Benn's Field was never regarded by the Club as a permanent home, and an alternative venue, at Ealing Park, which was slightly nearer Brentford (South-east of the Plough) was used for the first match of the 1894/95 season on September the 15th. However this Ground, which had previously been used by the St.Paul's Club, was quite unsuitable since the pitch was not wide enough, and for two more months a reluctant move had to be made back to Benn's Field. Darfield were beaten 5-0 in the last game on December the 15th.

SHOTTERS FIELD, WINDMILL LANE:

Negotiations had taken place to move at last to a better suited venue in Windmill Lane, Brentford, and known as Shotter's Field. This field was now owned - as was much of the Land in the area - by Colonel Clitheroe who also now resided in the adjacent Boston Lodge. The field was leased to Messrs. Shotter and Veysey. On the 22nd of December 1894, the first game was played at this new Ground (a three goal defeat to the 8th Hussars) with the venue being described as being very dry and level, and grandly referred to as one of the best in Middlesex. Shotters Field was bounded by Windmill Lane and The Ride, and was adjacent to Boston Lodge. The field contained a pond in the North-west corner, which on occasions gave rise to matches being stopped whilst the ball was retrieved!

The venue was completely lacking in facilities for spectators and initially had no proper enclosure fencing. But in respect of the latter, the private lane - The Ride - which ran between Boston Road and Windmill Lane (passing Boston Lodge) provided a form of barrier from non-paying spectators, as did the adjacent fields. Windmill Lane presented far more of a problem as it ran immediately adjacent to the Ground, and it was not until early April 1896, that measures were taken to prevent this potential loss of revenue. At this time, large hoardings were erected along the roadside, but even then the more adventurous spectators would get a free view by climbing the nearby trees!

By the start of the 1895/96 season, a Reserve Enclosure had been formed, but it is doubtful if there was any protection from the weather. One cause for concern was the high cost of the hire of the Ground, which was created by the Club having two Landlords, the owner and the occupier. The latter, by now a Mr. Beldam, let it out to the Club, although strictly speaking such sub-letting was not allowed. There was still a dearth of suitable fields from willing Landlords in Brentford, and if Shotter's Field had not been available, the Club would have had to move out of the district again.

But by the end of the 1895/96 season, some animosity appears to have developed between the Club and Mr. Beldam, and despite the Bees offering 'over the odds' for the field's continuous football use, Mr. Beldam steadfastly refused to back down. With Brentford steadily attracting more support, these noisy crowds were not welcomed in this quiet rural neighbourhood, and Mr. Beldam's complaints became more frequent. With Brentford in a desperate situation once again, it would seem that they managed to pay and/or talk Mr. Beldam around, for in the final event they remained at this Ground until the close of the 1897/98 season. By now Brentford F.C. had become a big attraction for local football followers, with frequent attendances of around 3,000. A record crowd - at an increased admission charge of 6d. (2½p.) - was present when the Grenadier Guards were in opposition at the Bees first ever F.A.Cup tie. Such prosperity did not go unnoticed, and in early 1898, Mr. Beldam decided to further increase the rent for the lease of the field.

'The Ride' from Boston Manor Road c.1900. The Shotter's Field Ground was to the right of this lane.

This demand did not please the Committee of the Football Club, and with the chance to play at a proposed brand new Sports Ground nearer the town, they informed Mr. Beldam that they would not require the use of Shotter's Field after the end of the season. The creation of a Sports Ground on the site of the Boston Park Cricket pitch in York Road had been under negotiation for two years, but then to Brentford's consternation, they were informed that this was not to proceed after all. The Club were quite unprepared for this set-back, for they had by now moved out of Shotter's Field, and consequently had no home venue for the coming, 1898/99 season.

Until recent years, Shotter's Field became a recreation ground, but currently the site is occupied by the Gunnersbury Catholic Boys School, although The Ride still exists.

No doubt, in something of a panic, the Club had to search around yet again for a suitable alternative venue, and eventually one was found. But this latest proposed move had the draw-back that it meant a move back into 'foreign' territory again, this time to South Ealing. The new Ground, known as Cross roads, was literally situated at the cross-roads in South Ealing, at the North-west corner of the intersection of Ealing Road with Little Ealing Lane and Popes Lane. This venue was again a good distance from Brentford, some fifteen minutes walk, although horse-drawn buses from Kew Bridge and Ealing which passed the Ground could now be used. Alternatively the District Railway trains stopped conveniently just a short distance along Ealing Road, at South Ealing Station. By mid-August 1898, work was well underway in levelling the field, and some basic facilities were provided. A corrugated iron Pavilion with dressing rooms was completed by mid-September, and a refreshment bar was also provided, but the venue noticeably lacked any cover for spectators. Although the surface of the pitch was somewhat uneven and full of little dips, the Club were ready to play their first match there on September the 1st, a game which attracted all of 2,000 fans, but was well down on the support that could have been expected had they been playing nearer the centre of Brentford. The distance factor was to have a disastrous effect on the Club, for by the season's end attendances had dropped alarmingly, and even an attempt to attract more support by lowering the entrance charge to 4d had little effect.

The start of the 1899/1900 season started in poor spirits with gate receipts that were now averaging only some £8 (approximately 500 spectators). A total of £172 was taken at the gate during that season, whereas the previous campaign at Shotter's Field had grossed £525.

Despite all the work that was undertaken, it was not surprising that the stay in South Ealing was to be for only two seasons. What with the lost support, a rather poor pitch (complete with a very pronounced slope) and the lack of spectator facilities, a move back to Shotter's Field was strongly preferred, and attempted. Negotiations for this move were made in August 1899, but the Club were presumably still considered to be undesirables, and their hearts sank when the talks came to nothing.

The site of the former Cross roads Ground is now part of the housing development that also encompassed Benn's Field. Temple, Creighton and Netherby Roads now disect the former Cross Roads Ground.

BOSTON PARK CRICKET GROUND:

However, the Club's constant search for a suitable Ground, with good facilities for themselves and spectators, and located near their Town, at long last was realised. Mr. Underwood who had remained a loyal supporter over the decade or so of the Club's life, managed to pursuade the Boston Park Cricket Club to Ground-share. Way back in the Clifden House days, Mr. Underwood had expressed the hope that Brentford Football Club and the Boston Park Cricket Club could combine; although there was no question of a merger, at least the two could at last come together for hoped-for mutual benefit. Edwin Underwood was a renowned Cricketer, but had developed an interest in the winter sport and had attached himself to Brentford F.C. from their earliest days. He was, at one time, to keep the Club alive, virtually single handed, when the Club were suspended for paying players. In this era, many a football club's very formation was created from the local cricket club and the footballers shared use of the ground, Brentford's twist in the usual story had seen them move to the local cricket club, eleven years after their own formation!

In suitable recognition of his support Mr. Underwood was elected President of the Club, and Brentford set out in determined fashion, not only at a new Ground, but also as a Professional Football Team. The first game at the Cricket Ground drew a 3,000 gate for Chesham Generals visit on the 15th of September. Despite a vast improvement over the Cross roads Ground, the Cricket Ground was lacking in many respects for it contained only two pavilions, and no real spectator facilities. Initially the Cricketers were against a plan to erect covered enclosures, but with the expected big crowds, the Football Club considered that their progress was being inhibited. After persistant approaches, the Cricket Club finally agreed to the request of Brentford F.C., and during the season the Club took steps to raise money for these improvements.

A seated stand was eventually built that held around 800 spectators, but as the interest in the team increased - the 7,000 present for Woolwich Arsenal's appearance in the F.A.Cup in 1902 was easily surpassed a year later with a 12,000 crowd for Fulham's visit. But frustration built up, for by now the Football Club were clearly the premier Club (of the two sports) in the district, and yet they were dependant on the Cricket Club for the use of the Ground, and the leasing arrangement meant that football in Brentford was not possible after the 1st of April each year.

The Boston Park Cricket ground remained until after Brentford's election into the Football League in 1920, but with the building of the Great West Road and the Industry that came to the area, factories were finally built on the site. This former ground is now occupied by the Alpha Laval Company.

After nearly four years of uneasy occupation, in May 1904 a Public Meeting was called for at the Vestry Hall. It was formally announced then that Brentford F.C. were to move a few hundred yards down Ealing Road, to a former orchard owned by the Chiswick Brewers - Fuller, Smith and Turner. The intention was to use the new Ground for bowls, cricket and other sports, in addition to its main football programme, a move that at least would put the Club in a favourable light with the locals. The Club were fortunate in only having to pay £40 per acre (the Ground occupies some five acres) for the 21 year lease, and this cost included the turfing of the pitch. It was rather unfortunate that the team's fortunes on the field by now were poor, for when at the beginning of the 1903/04 season the Club had started negotiations for this new enclosure - and despite very reasonable support even during these low days - the Committee were very apprehensive, as a considerable sum of money would be required to fully prepare and equip the Ground. The large support and enthusiasm at the Meeting convinced the Club that they had been right to ambitiously proceed with the project.

On the 1st of September 1904, after a day of drizzle and at the unusual time of 5.30 p.m., the fans were ready for the kick-off at Griffin Park, for the game versus Plymouth Argyle. A draw ensued, before an attendance of 5,500 for this Western League fixture.

March 1921. A match is on at Griffin Park (top right) - the first season in the Footbal League. At the extreme top left is part of the Boston Park Cricket Ground. (Aerofilms)

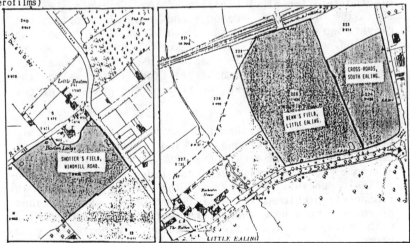

The grounds of Brentford F.C. in 1894.
(Ordnance Survey)

-59-

BRIGHTON & HOVE ALB.

In football terms, the South coast was a late developer! In Brighton, until 1898, the game was confined to local amateur teams who normally played their matches in the large open spaces of Preston Park, which still remains today, on the Northern outskirts of the town.

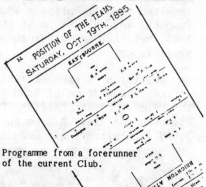

Programme from a forerunner of the current Club.

THE COUNTY CRICKET GROUND.

But in 1898, John Jackson - the former trainer at Wolverhampton, West Bromwich, Liverpool and latterly Leicester - became one of the enthusiasts behind the formation of the first professional team in the area. The inaugural match for Brighton United was played at Southwick, when, before a crowd of 2,000, the fledgling Club hammered the locals with a 8-1 scoreline. Although the Club made a low-key start to their playing days, the F.A.Cup competition was entered, and an encouraging home record saw Romford beaten by 8-2, and Ashford by five goals, before bowing out to Thames Ironworks - in a replay. As a home Ground, the Northern part of the County Cricket Ground was used. The Club was surprisingly elected into the First Division of the Southern League, for the 1899/1900 season, and several professional players were enticed down South from their Scottish homeland. Although the Cricket Ground provided an enclosed arena, they were unable to use this venue for the first and last months of the season, since the Cricketers would not take the risk of the grass being cut up.

The United had the honour of being the first visitors to Southampton's new Ground at The Dell, when they were beaten 1-4 before a crowd of 8,000. The lack of playing at home for several weeks coupled with an eight match initial run of reverses in the League resulted in financial problems. Defeat followed defeat, and the lack of cover - when home encounters were often accompanied with rain, at the Cricket Ground, discouraged good crowds.

In March 1900, after completing only 22 Southern League matches, the Club folded. Despite several Public Meetings and appeals, the Club had little choice, with enormous liabilities of £1,200 and assets of only £65.

HOME FARM, WITHDEAN.

But the indomitable Jackson did not remain inactive for long, and with players from the earlier United Club, supplemented by several from the North End Rangers team, a senior Club was reformed in 1900, under the name of Brighton and Hove Rangers. A 'home' was sought, and following an amicable arrangement with Mr. Hampton, a Farmer, the Club commenced their playing days to the North of the town, at Home Farm, Withdean. Home Farm was probably enclosed, although presumably lacking in any facilities for spectators or players. However, gate money was taken at the Ground, normally by the Players themselves who, after this duty had been performed, would hurriedly change in time for the kick-off! Season tickets cost five shillings (25p), or an individual entrance charge of 6d. was levied. The first game for the new Club attracted around 400 spectators scattered around the roped off pitch, and a scoreless draw was played with Clapton. This first season saw the Rangers playing Friendlies and Cup matches only, and an encouraging year was concluded with the newcomers reaching the final of the Sussex Senior Cup, when they lost to Eastbourne. With a wages bill of £11 per week, but encouraging numbers at the home games, the 'new' Brighton were confident that the same fate would not befall them as it did their predecessors.

BACK TO THE COUNTY GROUND.

In April 1901, the Club were invited to join the Southern League Division 2, but by now they had serious local competition in Hove F.C. The Hove Club, an Amateur team, had been playing their matches in the unenclosed Hove Park. This was, and still is, located just North of Old Shoreham Road. However, they were ambitious enough to seek something better, and managed to negotiate

1899 Map. The Withdean Ground.
(Ordnance Survey)

-61-

a three year tenancy of a suitable field, at a not insubstantial rent of £100 per annum. The land was known as Goldstone Bottom, and formed part of the Stanford Estate. The field, which was later to become the current Goldstone Ground, was leased to Alderman Clark, who in turn sub-let it to the Hove F.C., and the Club had an agreed useage for two days a week. Meanwhile the Rangers returned to the more centralised County Cricket Ground, the former home of the earlier professional Club.

The 1901/02 season commenced with the Rangers playing their first match on the 9th of September, but at the Dyke Road enclosure (to the West side of Brighton). The two rival Clubs were in close proximity to each other, once the Rangers took up residence back at the County Cricket Ground again. A fairly good season was enjoyed with the team finishing third (of nine) in the League and three victories in the F.A.Cup before defeat to Clapton. However, it was recognised that Hove F.C. had by far the more convenient of the two Grounds, and the Hove Club were approached with a view to amalgamation. Unlike so many other teams, there appears to have been a perfectly amicable arrangement, for in early 1902, the new combined Club were formed into a Company, and in August 1901, the combined Clubs took the name of 'Brighton and Hove Albion'. The last game at the County Ground, a 2-3 defeat, was played against Tottenham Hotspur, and on the 22nd of February, Brighton and Hove Albion F.C. played their first match at the Goldstone Ground, when Southampton Wanderers were beaten 7-1, in a friendly game.

Hove Park, the County Cricket Ground and, of course, the Goldstone Grounds still remain. The Withdean enclosure was probably a field (which, as yet, has not been built upon) set just off to the East of the main Brighton to London Road.

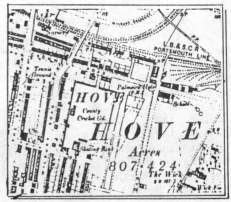

1899 Map. The County Cricket Ground. (Ordnance Survey)

BRISTOL CITY

Football was flourishing in the area well before the
Bristol South End F.C. came into being in 1894. Warmley,
Bedminster and Eastville Rovers (the former name of the
other Bristol Club that has lasted the pace) were the top
dogs. Earlier the Bristol South Club were the challengers
to Bedminster in the immediate area, but · with their
demise at the end of the 1893/94 season, Bristol South
End came into being. This new outfit had grand ideas and
were determined to eventually adopt professionalism. They
were in reality a breakaway group from Bedminster F.C.

Artist's impression of the match versus Notts. County at St. John's Lane in
February 1895 (looking West) - from the 'Press Box'. Note the duckboards for
feet protection. The structure in the background on the right is the Gasholder
which still exists today.   (Bristol Observer)

ST. JOHN'S LANE, BEDMINSTER.

The new Club chose as it's home Ground, an enclosure at
St.John's Lane, leased to the Club by the Trustees of the
Ashton Gate Estate, a name that was to have a great deal
of relevance some years later. The enclosure was in the
Bristol suburb of Bedminster while Bedminster F.C.
itself remained at the Cricket Ground in Greenway Bush
Lane, a short distance to the North-west. The first
season for the newcomers, one of Friendly matches, kicked
off with additional entertainment provided by the Bristol
South Brass Band and a visit of Swindon before a crowd of
3,500 on the 1st of September 1894. Entrance cost 3d. (a
little over 1p) and double this amount for the enclosure.
Boys paid 1d. while Ladies were admitted free, and it was
not long before the new Club could boast 400 members.

Other visitors included Hereford Thistle, London Welsh, Tottenham Hotspur, Cardiff, and most prestigious of all, Preston North End. Expecting good support for the visit of the latter, the homesters offered their Lancashire visitors a £40 guarantee, but the day was nearly a disaster. Due to torrential rain the total gate only realised £50 and the South End lost by 0-6. But overall this first season was a success for total gate receipts realised £400, and the Ground rent only amounted to £20. The St. John's Lane Ground was at this time surrounded by fields, with Mutton Hill to the South. It was enclosed, but it was not long before a method had to be devised to prevent hundreds of spectators getting a free view from the hill. The solution was to erect 30 foot high poles, and with a system of pulleys, a large canvas sheet was hoisted during matches to block the view. This contraption was doubly beneficial since not only did attendances rise - many of the free viewers paying up - but also the large screen was used as an advertisement hoarding which brought in extra revenue! Facilities were somewhat limited for spectators, but during the early years, a Pavilion (seated stand) was built on the West side of the pitch which held around 500 spectators, and substantial earth banks were formed at both ends; the Press of course could not be ignored, but they were no doubt unhappy with only their small open seated area opposite the Stand. The dressing rooms were located at the St.John's Lane end of the enclosure, and the only entrances were positioned off this thoroughfare. In 1899 further improvements were made with substantial white painted railings being erected around the pitch, the banks were increased in height, and the ends of the Stand were enclosed with glass for better weather protection. For the Players, hot baths were made available at the end of matches.

In 1896 the Club's great rivals, Bedminster, moved to a new Ground at Ashton Gate (a quarter of a mile to the South-west), and one year later the South End Club fulfilled their avowed intentions, turned Professional, and were renamed 'Bristol City'. The Club's changes coincided with their entry into the Western League (the Professional section - Bedminster chose the Amateur division 1) and their election into the Premier Competition in the South of England, the Southern League Division 1. A remarkable rise in status for the young Club, and glories that did not end there. On September the 11th, at the first home game of the season, Wolverton were beaten by 7-4 in the Southern League before a crowd of 4,000. In their eight team League, the City became the Western League Champions, whilst in the more prestigious Southern League they finished as runners-up to the all powerful Southampton. Support was gathering momentum, and the season's best gate of 12,170 (at that time a record attendance for any match in the South-west, and far in excess of the previous best of nearly 9,000 in 1894 for a Bristol and District X1 match with Sunderland), was recorded on January the 15th, for a visit from the Saints; the gate receipts amounted to £400. Attendances varied enormously - from as little as 1,000 to a second highest of 10,000 for the Western League local derby with Warmley in April. But with an average of around 3,500, the Club proved that the support was there for a professional Club. Bristol City were by now the undisputed Senior team in the area, for although Bedminster joined them in the Southern League in 1898, their final eighth placing fell short of the City's second Runners-up position. A new record attendance was reached on the 29th of April when 13,000 fans packed into the St.John's Lane enclosure for the Championship decider with Southampton, an exciting 3-4 reverse for the homesters. Once again the crowd numbers varied enormously over the season from a low of 1,500 for Sheppey's visit, to a second highest gate, which amounted to 10,250, for the local derby with Bedminster.

(Top): Action at St. John's Lane versus Woolwich Arsenal, 26th October 1901. Note the canvass screens that were raised at home matches to prevent the free view for those spectators on the hill!   (Black and White Budget)
(Bottom): A rare photograph of the St.John's Lane (looking South) taken in 1895, probably versus Preston North End.

The 1899/1900 season produced something of a reverse with Bristol City dropping to ninth, while Bedminster rose to sixth. The relative poor form of the City took it's toll when the October visit of Queens Park Rangers attracted the largest number of fans - of 7,500 - and other games only averaged between two and three thousand. But a sensible compromise was reached with the City's greatest rivals, when the two Clubs from the South of the town amalgamated at the season's end. The two however still functioned separately, for just one year, with Ashton Gate and St.John's Lane being used by both. In an improved season for the City, the gates rose again - to an average of around 5,000 - with the Bedminster Ground proving to be generally the better supported venue of the two.

The 1901/02 season provided the Club with it's greatest honour with their election into the Football League Second Division, and with the City being the more dominant of the two, the two teams were finally fused into one, and Ashton Gate as a home venue was abandoned in favour of St.John's Lane. On September the 14th, Stockport County became the first opponents in the Football League, when the visitors were beaten by three unopposed goals before a crowd of 7,000. During the following months, average gates of around 4,000 were realised, with the best of 14,175 who packed into the Ground when West Bromwich were the visitors in the Football League. A creditable sixth place in the Second Division was achieved.

St. Johns lane was used for just two more seasons, as the support for the team steadily rose. During the 1902/03 season, 12,024 were present for Woolwich Arsenal's visit and approximately 13,000 for the Manchester City game; this period saw the average attendance rise to over 6,000. One year later the figures were similar, with the top crowd pullers being Woolwich Arsenal, with a crowd on this occasion of 14,000. But the all-time record attendance at St.Johns Lane was for an F.A.Cup-tie with Sheffield United, with a figure of 17,909 (£750 receipts). Although the last Football League match at this venue only attracted 4,000 for Burslem Port Vale's visit on the 23rd of April 1904, it had become apparent that the Club had by now outgrown the Ground, and they moved to the most recent home of the former Bedminster team, to the Ashton Gate Ground.

The earlier Greenway Bush Lane enclosure of Bedminster was a Cricket Ground, and was situated at the corner with North Street. The venue offered little more than just a Pavilion, although temporary Stands were used for important matches. The Ground, which had a pronounced slope, is now the site of the large Imperial Tobacco Building (formerly W.D. and H.O.Wills). Opposite the Ashton Gate Ground of Bristol City, is the large Greville Smyth (Public) Park, which was the former home of Southville F.C., who were at one time another notable Club in the City.

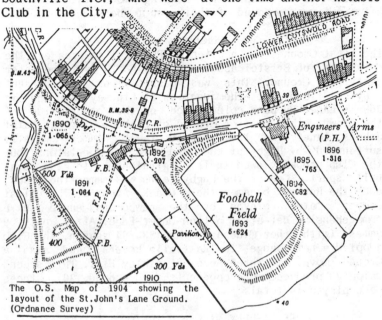

The O.S. Map of 1904 showing the layout of the St.John's Lane Ground. (Ordnance Survey)

THE GROUND TODAY.

St.Johns Lane, despite the long period since being an enclosed Football League Ground, is one of the rare venues which still exists in a similar form today. The Stand and embankments have long since gone - although there is the remains of one slope alongside St.Johns Lane. But the Ground has not lost it's football connections, since it is now known as the Robinsons DRG Sports Ground, and the team of that name now play there before crowds of 200 to 300. Albeit the pitch - situated at the far end of the field - has been turned at ninety degrees to the former direction. The prominent 'Engineers Arms' Public House still lies adjacent, as it did a century ago.

BRISTOL ROVERS

When the Rovers were founded in September 1883, they were somewhat footballing pioneers, since Rugby was the popular Winter sport in the area. There were only three or four other Association Clubs and for some while, opponents were scarce, therefore, many of the Club's earliest of matches were nothing more than contests between teams composed of their own members.

PURDOWN.

The first Ground, was a pitch at Purdown, an area on the outskirts of Bristol about one mile North from the later Eastville Ground. This was possibly on the current playing fields at the junction of Lindsay Road and Sir John's Lane. By pure coincidence, on the other side of the town, the earlier Ground of Bristol City was Saint John's Lane! The team played their games usually surrounded by Rugby pitches and with few spectators, but the Club probably owed their original name to the oval ball sport. One of the Rugby teams was named the Arabs, and, the Rovers became the 'Black Arabs'. The first proper match played by the newcomers ended in a comprehensive defeat at Wotton-Under-Edge. After only 9 games (with other Clubs) in the 1883/84 season, the Club adopted a namechange, to 'Eastville Rovers', and also a Ground move, to Three Acres at Ashley Hill. This second campaign produced more opponents, and around 20 matches were played in total.

THREE ACRES, ASHLEY HILL AND THE DOWNS, HORFIELD.

The location of this second Ground is once again difficult to pinpoint. There was a large field at Ashley Down (of 8 acres), and adjacent to the County Cricket Ground, which was later developed and noted as a 'Football Ground', but in 1884, this was nothing more than an open field. Alternatively there were at this time two fields of the approximate correct acreage off Muller Road and adjacent to Narrowby Hill Footpath, now the site of St. Thomas More School and Allfoxton Road. But in the early years the efforts of the Club were rarely reported, and it can be safely assumed that this 'Ground', and the soon to follow next one, were no more than open fields with no facilities for spectators or players.

Suitable opponents were still quite scarce, and the season proper did not begin until the 1st of December, when a home Friendly match was played against Bristol Wagon Works. The next venue was at the Downs, Horfield, and although this again cannot be precisely located, there is currently a Downend Road in the general area (a little further North of Eastville), which joins with Ashley Down and Purdown Roads. This brings us back, at least in name, to the first two Grounds!

THE RIDGEWAY GROUND.

The early 1890's brought about innovations that began to firmly establish the Club on the football map. In 1892, the Rovers became founder-members of the Bristol and District League (later to become the more widely supported Western League). Two years later they moved about one mile to the East of Eastville, to the Ridgeway area, with a new venue that was probably at least enclosed. The Rudgway (sic.) Ground was probably one of two fields that were flanked by Fishponds Road and Crooked Lane (later named Ridgeway Road). The Club's Headquarters at this time was the Star Inn, which still exists - in a rebuilt form - opposite Star Lane. The first visitors to the Rudgway Ground were Staple Hill on the 6th of October 1894. In 1896, the Club turned professional, but realised that something better than the Rudgway Ground would be required for matches at which paying gates would now become a necessity. A search started for a suitable site, and eventually a Ground at Stapleton Hill and previously used by the Harlequins Rugby Club was acquired. After becoming a Limited Company in March 1897, the new Ground was christened with a visit from Aston Villa on the 3rd of April, who spoiled the party by winning the game by five unopposed goals! One week later Bedminster were entertained in a Bristol Charity Cup match and a crowd of 1,500 saw the homesters lose again, this time by two goals to nil.

A name change, to Bristol Rovers, was made which suited the wider support that they could now attract. The 1897/98 season saw the Club entering both the Birmingham & District League and the Western League with them now playing at Stapleton Hill, which later became known as Eastville Stadium. On the 1st of September, the first League match was played (in the Birmingham competition), when the Reserve Eleven of West Bromwich Albion attracted a crowd of 1,200.

Eastville from the air in 1969.
(Aerofilms)

EASTVILLE.

The full trials and tribulations of the Rovers and
Eastville have been well documented elsewhere. But to
summarise: The 20,000 capacity Stadium, was later
increased by 50%, although in 1960 a record crowd of
38,472 crammed into the enclosure. Having brought the
Ground for £150 in 1897, in a bankrupt state it was sold
43 years later for £12,000, to a Greyhound Company. The
two sporting persuits ran side by side for many years,
but the latter ones were fraught with antagonism. Unable
to agree the terms of a new lease, arrangements were made
for them to share with Bristol City (where they had
earlier played several home matches, following the fire
and total destruction of the South Stand and Offices at
Eastville). However, Bristol City had their own problems,
for after going out of business in 1982, the new
Management wanted to double the Rovers rental!

For five more years the Club remained at Eastville in a
strained and unhappy relationship with the Greyhound
Authority, before their final game on the 26th of April
1986. Before a crowd of 3,576 they fought out a 1-1 draw
with Chesterfield, to bring down the curtain on their 89
year stay at the Stadium.

A new home had to be sought, and after several suggestions - principally the Gloucestershire County Cricket Ground at Ashley Hill and the Memorial Ground of Bristol Rugby Club - they finally opted to move to the nearby town of Bath and play at non-League City's Ground at Twerton Park. A Groundshare at the fine Ashton Gate enclosure of Bristol City would appear to have been the best option, but the fierce partisanship between two teams in the same town is particularly apparent in Bristol, and such a move on paper, could well have turned out to be a disaster in practise!

Eastville still exists, tight up against the Motorway but for how long? A Superstore and a gradual encroachment of other developments elsewhere have left the Ground with little more than the North Grandstand and some remaining terraces at the East end.

Eastville in 1989. Little is left of the Stadium (now used solely for Greyhoun Racing), apart from the main Stand, and adjacent terrace.   (Dave Twydell

CAMBRIDGE UNITED

The unpretentious 'Celery Trenches' Ground; The First Round F.A.Amateur Cup match versus Soham Rangers. R.Ding scores the winner. (1928/29 season)

In recent years, the United have been the dark horses of the two teams in the University town, for over the far greater period of their parallel existence, it was Cambridge City (formerly 'Town') who were the more Senior, and hence more likely Club to progress. Cambridge United are one of the most recent additions to the Football League, yet looking back to the earliest of days of football, this City had perhaps the greatest influence regarding the formulation for the rules of the game. This influence came from the University rather the the town itself, despite the 16th century ban of playing football due to it's unlawful and hurtful consequences! The generally acknowledged first ever set of Laws for the Game were devised by the University around 1848, and these 'Cambridge Rules' as they became to be known were first posted up on Parker's Piece, a playing area that much later became, for one year, the home 'Ground' of Cambridge United.

Cambridge Town who were founded in 1908, were followed four years later by Cambridge United under their former name of Abbey United. Between times a 'Cambridge United' was created in 1909, became defunct at the start of the First World War, were reformed in 1918, but then faded way again. The current Football League Club have no connection with this earlier 'United', and in fact have generally operated from outside the town boundaries (to the East of the City Club), in the Abbey district. Supposedly Abbey United were formed after a meeting between several enthusiasts under a street lamp in Stanley Road. Their formation has also been linked with the Abbey Rifle Shooting Club, but regardless of their creation they started life in a very minor fashion; the first season, 1913/14 consisting of unreported friendly games at an unknown home Ground.

MIDSUMMER COMMON.

The first reported match of Abbey United took place on the 22nd of November 1913, when M.J.Drew's X1 were met on Midsummer Common, a large open area of land, ironically just to the South of the Cambridge Town Ground. Twelve days later, St.Phillip's were beaten 4-0 at the same venue, and this location became the home Ground of the new Club throughout the 1913/14 season. The Club were still playing at only a very minor level, and with the advent of the First World War they ceased activities until 1919, when they were in effect reformed.

STOURBRIDGE COMMON.

On the 20th of September 1919, and at a new home venue, on Stourbridge Common (once again an unfenced large open area, to the East of the former Ground), Ditton Rovers were beaten 6-3. Just seven games were played that season, and the minor nature of the Club - and near lack of activity - continued with only an entry into a 6-a-side tournament during the next year. The 1921/22 season saw the Club enter a League for the first time - the Cambridgeshire Division 3 - and on the 10th of September Chesterton Rovers Reserves were played in the initial game of the season. Stourbridge Common continued to be used, with the Mission Hut in River Lane being used as a headquarters.

STATION FARM, BARNWELL - THE CELERY TRENCHES.

As the Club's status rose in the County League it was realised that a more appropriate Ground was required, and for the 1923/24 season a move was made to a field at Station Farm, Barnwell. The three acre field, behind Aviation Hall, was located just to the South of the Newmarket Road, and in later years became part of Marshall's Aerodrome. The Ground was very basic as it contained no spectator accommodation or facilities for the Players, and a new headquarters was made use of at

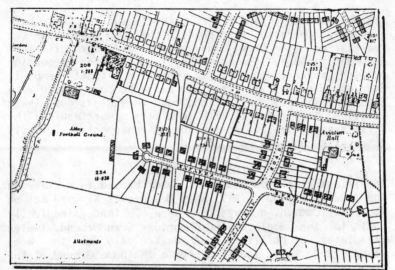

Map of 1927. The Celery Trenches Ground was (prior to the development shown) little more than a field at the rear of 'Aviation Hall'. The current Abbey Stadium at this time was virtually undeveloped. (Ordnance Survey)

the nearby 'Dog and Pheasant' Public House. The field was probably enclosed since paying spectators of upto 300 attended the early matches at the Club's new home, but the surface of the pitch was very poor and contained long furrows running lengthways, which led to the Ground being known as 'The Celery Trenches'. As the team continued to thrive during the 1920's the far from satisfactory Ground, continued to be hired from Bert Rayment, while the Club's rivals (Cambridge Town) were enjoying the use of a better home in Milton Road, and were rising to a higher status than the United. Even so the team was not lacking in support, for they had 300 fans amongst a crowd of over 2,000 when Cottenham were played in a local Cup competition at Chatteris.

In the 1926/27 season the F.A.Amateur Cup was entered for the first time (Norwich YMCA were beaten in the first game, at home), and one year later the Club were considered good enough to compete in the F.A.Cup; the first match at Great Yarmouth was lost before an attendance of 3,000. Two years later the team reached the 2nd round proper of the National Amateur competition, and that same season the County League was split into two geographical sections, with the United in the Southern Division. Abbey United clinched the title in the League on the 18th of April when, before one of the biggest

crowds ever at a home match, near neighbours Cambridge
Town (who also played in the Southern Amateur League at
this time) were beaten by the odd goal in five. It was
not until the 1929/30 season that the team won its first
F.A.Cup tie, with their victory at Newmarket Town.
Wisbech were then surprisingly overcome by four goals,
followed by a home game versus Crittall Athletic. In the
League it was a poor season, and dogged by many injuries
the United were thrashed by five unopposed goals, but
before a crowd of 1,200.

PARKER'S PIECE.

There had been many complaints over the years regarding
the poor state of the Celery Trenches pitch, and after
just one match at the start of the 1930/31 season, the
Club were compelled to move on. After the early poor
playing season, and now no proper home venue, several of
the best players left to join up with Cambridge Town.
This resulted in another unhappy period, with home
matches being played on the wide open spaces of Parker's
Piece in the town centre. It was apparent that this venue
was totally unsuitable since it was not possible to make
an entrance charge, and after this stop-gap year, a
suitable and permanent ground was at last soon to be
available.

During the summer of 1931, the Club President, Henry
Clement Francis met the United's Officers and generously
offered them a plot of land at the rear of Mr. Sindall's
old works. There were two options open to the Club, the
first being the entire area of land, or alternatively a
smaller acreage but with the additional incentive of Mr.
Francis providing a three to four hundred seated Stand,
plus ground enclosure fencing. The Club gratefully
accepted the second offer with the intention of building,
at their own expense, dressing rooms either side of the
Stand. The arrangements and preparation were going to
take some time, therefore it was decided that the United
should return to the Celery Trenches for one more year.
After only a moderate season, the new Ground was ready
for the first match at the current Abbey Stadium, when
the University Press were beaten 2-0 in a friendly match
on the 31st of August 1933.

Letterhead from the Abbey United days.

THE GROUNDS TODAY.

The former large open space Grounds at Midsummer and Stourbridge Commons plus the ancient Parker's Piece all still exist in the same form. The access to Stourbridge Common (which to this day is still used, apart from public recreation, as land for grazing animals), is approached via Stanley Road - the street where supposedly the Club was originally conceived. The Celery Trenches Ground first became part of the Marshall's Aerodrome, but later housing developments created Elfleda Road, the East end of which bisects the area of this former venue. Modern housing now covers most of the site, with Whitehill Road (only about 200 hundred metres from the current Abbey Stadium) lying close to the old Celery Trenches.

March 1934, and the Stand nears completion ready for the first game at the Abbey Ground.
(Cambridge Evening News)

CARDIFF CITY

In the South of the Principality, Football was a slow starter, Clubs of any consequence being formed some years after their counterparts in the North. Rugby was always the more popular of the two sports, as it is now, and it was only for a number of years around the turn of the Century and for some time afterwards, that the round ball sport really captured the imagination.

No more was this more apparent than in the Capital of Wales itself, for the present City Club were not formed until 1899. There were some earlier Clubs in and around the town, notably St.Margarets (founded in 1888) whose home matches were played at Claude Road. The first Cardiff Club were formed in 1890, and for a number of years they played at Tyn-y-coed Farm in the Roath area of the town, with their dressing rooms at the Royal George Hotel, but like St.Margarets they soon disappeared from the scene.

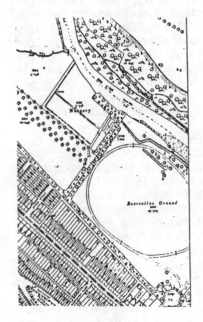

O.S. Map c.1900. Riverside Cricket Club (and Sophia Gardens Ground?). Part of this large recreation ground later became the Glamorgan County Cricket Ground.
(Ordnance Survey)

RIVERSIDE CRICKET CLUB GROUND.

When the current Cardiff City Club came upon the scene, they were created from, and played at, the Ground of the Riverside Cricket Club. At this time the Ground, was probably that known as the Recreation Ground, which was spread over nearly 28 acres and was located on the west banks of the River Taff, just North of the still existing Sophia Gardens. Although principally used for Cricket, the venue offered no facilities for either players or spectators, although it was enclosed principally by virtue of the River and the avenues of trees that elsewhere lined the boundaries. The main entrance to the Recreation Ground was via the Lodge that was located in the South-west corner, and at the end of Talbot Street.

ROATH AND SOPHIA GARDENS.

The early years of the Riverside team were played at a minor level, although they struck out in the 1902/03 season in an independant fashion, when they made use of a Ground at Roath - possibly the same venue as the team's forerunners. But like those forerunners their stay was but for a short time, and they were soon to disband. In November 1905 they re-emerged on the scene, and played at Sophia Gardens, either within the same named public park, or at the adjacent, and previously used Recreation Ground. Around this time two other Clubs were founded, Riverside A.F.C. and Riverside Albion, but both failed to make the grade. With the town elevated in status, the Cardiff Club, in 1906, tried to do the same, by adding 'City' to their name. But such a name was considered only worthy of a team that could truly represent the Town, and so the Welsh F.A. ruled that such a suffix could only be awarded to the first team that turned professional.

CARDIFF ARMS PARK AND THE HARLEQUINS RUGBY GROUND.

Although the Cardiff Club had little opposition, they were reluctant to take such a drastic step so soon after their reformation, but in order to judge the response from the general public, three exhibition matches were played against professional teams. Properly enclosed Grounds were used, and Crystal Palace and Bristol City (a draw and a defeat respectively), were played at Cardiff Arms Park. This now famous Rugby Stadium was sparsely equipped at this time, having only - on the South side - a Grandstand with open seating each side. The response from the public was favourable after these two contests in November 1909, therefore a third match which finally tipped the balance was played, at the Harlequins Rugby Ground in Newport Road.

A move was made to the Council owned Ninian Park for the start of the 1910/11 season, when the Club's rapid progress gained them entry into the Southern League. The City's rise to Senior status was celebrated with their first game at Ninian Park, when Aston Villa were the visitors. The Sophia Gardens Ground, albeit much reduced in size, became the home of Glamorgan County Cricket Club, whilst other areas within the boundaries of the earlier Ground now include a Sports Centre and Tennis Courts.

The first match at Ninian Park.

CARLISLE UNITED

Although something of a soccer outpost (at present the nearest possible local derby match is sixty miles away at Newcastle), the area was active around the turn of the century. The Cumberland League provided a reasonable level of football for teams in the County. As well as the more familiar Workington team, Carlisle was rep- resented by Red Rose and Shaddongate United.

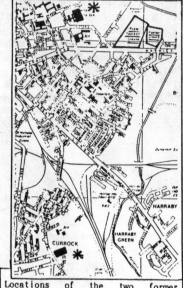

Locations of the two former Grounds. Note the Rugby Ground (adjacent to the current Brunton Park) which was used for big matches in the early days.

MILLHOLME BANK, BOUNDARY ROAD:

Shaddongate played at Mill- holme, whilst Red Rose were based at Boundary Road. These 'Grounds' were to the South of the town, and it is possible that they ground- shared, since the 'Mill- holme' and 'Boundary Road' Grounds were sometimes ref- erred to as one and the same). Red Rose were the League Champions in the 1901/02 season, but the end of the following campaign saw a close fought fight for the lead between Shaddongate and Workington. The last home match at Millholme, on the 21st of April, brought these two contestants together, before a large crowd. After the game and with a lead in the table of six points Workington claimed the title. This was disputed by Shaddongate since two of their matches remained unplayed, plus the return fixture with Workington; this game was to have been played on the 30th of April but was cancelled due a Cup Final on the Ground that day! It was argued that if Workington's four points that were obtained against the teams that Shaddongate had not played were deducted - and assuming a victory to the Carlisle team in this unplayed match - then Shaddongate would be the new Champions. The fixtures remained unplayed and Workington were awarded the Championship!

Interest in football continued to rise in the area, and by 1904 matches between Red Rose and Shaddington United were always well supported. On the 18th of May 1904, at the A.G.M. of Shaddongate United which was held at the Temperance Hall in Caldergate, a resolution was passed that ensured the name of Carlisle in the Football World. Although the Club was solvent, there was a balance in hand of £24 (compared with £35 a year earlier when many matches were played in bad weather), and it was realised that for greater support the Club should be more representative of the town. The seventy to eighty members present voted on the proposal th change the Club's name to Carlisle United, and this was passed with a 3:1 majority. A number of members objected to the proposal, claiming that as there had been no full notice of the Agenda for the meeting, then such a name change could not legally be taken. The majority had won the day, but on the 20th of July there were repercussions!

The section of dissatisfied supporters held their own meeting at the Duke of York Inn. The forty or so present considered that a name change was not necessary as the Club had money in hand and felt that change for changes sake was unnecessary. The meeting resolved to form a breakaway Club under the old name and find a field from which to play home games. But it would seem that the name of Shaddongate United never re-appeared!

On the 1st of September, Carlisle United played their first match, a Friendly against Victoria Wanderers. A large crowd saw the homesters win by 2-1 at the Millholme Ground. Two days later another encouragingly big attendance saw Carlisle win at home again, this time versus Hexham in another Friendly encounter. The 1904/05 season was very successful for the Club won the double, the Cumberland League and Cup. Millholme Bank although being enclosed and having a Grandstand was now insufficient for some of the Club's major attractions, and occasionally the Rugby Club Ground in Warwick Road (that was immediately adjacent to the later Brunton Park) was used. This enclosure was bigger and offered better facilities (there were two Grandstands) than Millholme Bank. The Cumberland Cup Final was held at Warwick Road, and the two contestants - Carlisle United and Red Rose - attracted the biggest crowd ever seen in the town for a football match. Several thousand were present and the match receipts amounted to over £106. Over Easter another game was played at the Rugby Ground, when Glasgow Rangers were entertained (who won by only the odd goal in three), at which the crowd numbers exceeded 3,000.

The last match of the 1904/05 season, and the last for
the United at Millholme, was played on the 6th of May
against their old foes Red Rose, for Carlisle Hospital
Cup. A very large crowd was once again present, many of
whom did not normally watch either of the Clubs, but the
United surprisingly lost the encounter by the only goal
of the game. Even so, Carlisle United had undoubtably
become the top Club in the town, and were elected into
the Lancashire Combination Division 2 for the 1905/06
season.

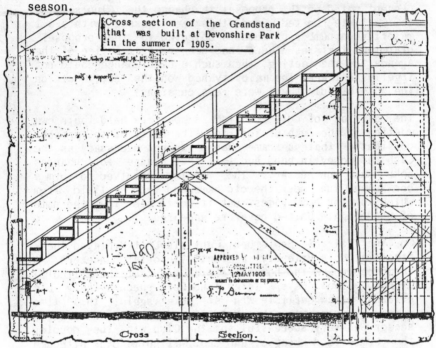

Cross section of the Grandstand
that was built at Devonshire Park
in the summer of 1905.

Cross   Section.

DEVONSHIRE PARK:

The United's new Ground was at Devonshire Park, which was
situated in the Northern part of the town. It had the
benefit of a covered Stand, including a Press Box, and
presumably a degree of raised embankments since it was
reported that standing spectators were able to enjoy a
good view. The large sum of £1,200 had been spent on
preparing the enclosure. On the 2nd of September 1905, St
Helens Town were entertained at Devonshire Park, for a
Lancashire Combination fixture. It was not a very
auspicious start for after going in two goals down at
half time, the final result was a 2-3 defeat. The Club
finished in a low mid-table position, but the lot of the
Red Rose team was even worse.

The Millholme Ground was used by this Club, but in July 1905 they resigned from the Cumberland League. Although they were subsequently reinstated in the League, they soon faded from the scene. The Millholme Ground, just off of Boundary Road, is remembered in name alone, by Millholme Avenue which was built across the site of this former enclosure.

On the field, the Carlisle United team enjoyed something of a meteoric rise! They were Lancashire Combination Division Two Champions for the 1906/07 season, and subsequently promoted. In their first season in the First Division they finished as runners-up to Everton Reserves - two places and seven points above the Liverpool Second Eleven! In the F.A.Cup the Club fought through to the 2nd round proper during the 1907/08 season. In the first round they first drew with Southern League Brentford before a record Devonshire Park attendance of 5,068, and won the replay in London, before losing to Grimsby Town in the next round. Sixth place in their League was achieved at the end of the 1908/09 season, but in early April they were delivered a bombshell.

The Club were told that they must vacate the Devonshire Park Ground, a directive which did not make the Duke of Devonshire very popular! Despite their success on the pitch, the financial side of the Club was not very healthy, and now they needed to raise around £1,000 for the costs of purchasing and preparing a new home Ground. Fortunately a Public Appeal was fairly successful, and was sufficient to secure a plot of land off of Warwick Road. Supporters were urged to buy £1 shares of the Club in order to raise the final £200 or so, with the grim warning that if this was not realised then the Club would fold!

Meanwhile the season's fixtures had to be completed. Workington were beaten in the Cumberland Cup Final, and over Easter the two matches (versus Bolton Wanderers Reserves and Atherton) produced home crowds of about 3,000 at each. On the 29th of April, Accrington Stanley were entertained in the last game to be played at Devonshire Park. This League match was won by 4-0, but there were only a few hundred enthusiasts present, as the proceedings were accompanied by rain, thunder and lightening! Devonshire Park remains today, but only as an open sports field to the adjacent Trinity Comprehensive School.

Sufficient capital was raised, and the five acres of land adjacent to the Rugby Ground was purchased. H.Foxall was appointed as Architect, and a basic Ground with an estimated capacity for 30,000 was created. On the 2nd of September, the Newcastle Reserve team (the First Eleven were expected) beat Carlisle United in the first match at Brunton Park.

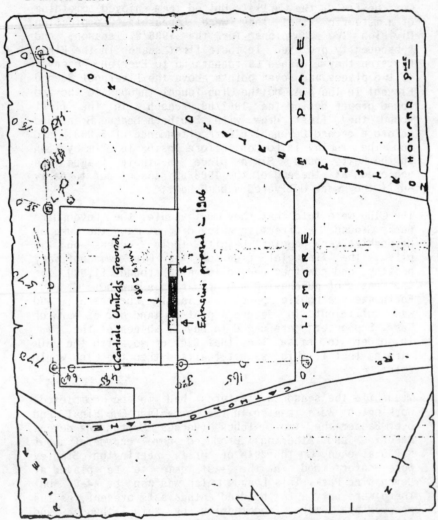

Block Plan of the Devonshire Park Ground - part of the details submitted for permission to enlarge the Stand, that was passed on the 20th of July 1906.

CHARLTON ATHLETIC

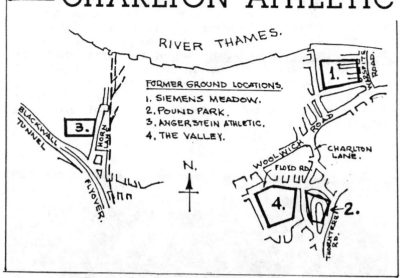

RIVER THAMES.

FORMER GROUND LOCATIONS.
1. SIEMENS MEADOW.
2. POUND PARK.
3. ANGERSTEIN ATHLETIC.
4. THE VALLEY.

The location of the former Grounds, (Ringstead
Road was some miles away, in Catford).
....

When Charlton Athletic moved from the Valley to Selhurst
Park - some miles away - early in the 1985/86 season, it
was an undesirable upheaval. Yet this was not the first
time that the Club had left their home environment, and
rumours of even more unlikely moves had been previously
mooted!

Not formed until 1905, the Club could hardly expect to
flourish with the two Southern pioneers of
professionalism in close proximity. Just to the East lies
Plumstead, still inhabited at that time by Woolwich
Arsenal (who were to move to the North of London eight
years later - ironically because they were unable to
attract sufficient support), and just to the West,
Millwall, a team from the other side of the River, who
were in five years to move to the South bank! Within this
environment it is little wonder that the Charlton Club
remained as just another amateur organisation for a
number of years.

SIEMENS MEADOW.
The first 'Ground', was at Siemens Meadow, close to East
Street (now Eastmoor Street), the area in which many of
the young founders of the Club lived. The meadow, nothing

more than a large, flat, open space lay between Westfield Street, Yateley Street (later Hardens Manor Way) and extended almost to the River Thames. But the stay was to be only a short one, and after one year these amateurs had to move on. Around the start of the First World War the meadow was built upon, but Westfield Street still exists, as does Siemens Road which runs East to West across the site of the earlier meadow. Today the area is a mixture of drab, but functioning Industrial Buildings, and of dereliction.

The Siemens Meadow Ground (in front of the buildings), c.1905. Close to the River Thames.   (Greenwich Local History Library)

WOOLWICH COMMON AND POUND PARK.

The second Ground was on Woolwich Common, some mile or so South-east of Siemens Meadow. The common still exists, and no doubt provided a suitable venue for the Club to stage their, minor, Lewisham League matches. Their stay on the Common was also shortlived, and so, in 1908, another move was made, this time to Pound Park. This was not a Park in the true sense of the word, since it was a privately owned piece of land. The Ground was not truly enclosed, although it was surrounded by a hedge, and the Club's slightly elevated status meant that they were able to supplement their meagre funds with a collection box that circulated amongst the handful of fans that watched the team.

Playing by now in the First Division of the Lewisham League, the first match at Pound Park resulted in a 3-1 victory over Wellcome Institute. The Club's stay at this, their third home, lasted for five years, and during this time they developed into a force to be reckoned with. The Championship of the League was won in the 1908/09 season, and they also captured the Woolwich Cup. The next two seasons saw them as Champions of the Woolwich League, and, in 1911 they recorded a hat-trick of Woolwich Cup successes. In the 1911/12 season, an entry into the South Suburban League (Junior Division) proved no obstacle to the Club, and by 1913 it was decided that the Club's ambitions should be aimed at a higher level.

At the Club's A.G.M. on the 14th of May 1913, which was held at the Bugle Horn Public House, it was decided that the team should adopt Senior Amateur status, for which another Ground would be necessary. The sloping pitch of Pound Park was developed in the 1920's, and became, as now, Coxmount Road and Wolfe Crescent.

ANGERSTEIN ATHLETIC GROUND.

A more suitable Headquarters was easily found, and for the 1913/14 season the Club moved a little under a mile West to the Angerstein Athletic Ground. The Ground was shared with Deptford Invicta - fellow members of the South Suburban League. This Ground was adjacent to Horn Lane, just North of Aldeburgh Street, and in a currently rapidly developing Industrial area building work is likely to engulf this site. The Club's rise to a Senior level saw them also play in the London League First Division, a much respected combination that had seen other teams from the Capital enter before their eventual moves into the Southern League. The Athletic Ground had a supposed capacity for 4,000, but apart from being enclosed, had only dressing room facilities that were located on the Horn Lane side. The first competitive match played by Charlton on their new pitch was a South Suburban League fixture on the 6th of September, versus the Army Ordnance Corps - a 5-1 victory - and it wasn't until late November 1913 that the first London League match was played, which resulted in a single goal victory over Hampstead Town. The team's progressive rise continued for they finished as runners-up in the London League, with only one defeat. Champions West London Old Boys - whose home was at Loftus Road in Shepherds Bush - pipped the Athletic on goal average.

By now the Club had a reasonably well supported team, but
the outbreak of War took it's toll, and the 1914/15
season was to be the last for several years. But the
period was notable for the Club's first F.A.Cup and
Amateur Cup entries, reaching the 1st round in the
latter, but being defeated by Dartford in the first game
of the former. The last match of the season, and - as it
transpired - the last at Horn Lane was a Friendly versus
a Charlton Charity team. But the fans were not very
charitable and a pitifully small crowd of only 56
attended, which produced receipts of less than £1!

THE VALLEY.

As the War drew to a close, the Club reformed, but were
unable to return to Horn Lane due to it's War use as a
Petrol storage depot. In any event past successes
prompted them to seek their own true 'home' Ground,
despite their having total assets of just 2/3d. (11p)! A
move was made back East to a site between Siemens Meadow
and Pound Park. This choice was known locally as 'The
Swamp', a large disused chalk and sand excavated pit with
ponds in it's base. At £6 per annum, the venue was a
snip, but required a vast amount of voluntary work to
create a large enough flat and grassed playing area for
the start of the 1919/20 season, just three months away.
Post-war enthusiasm for football produced plenty of
support for the Club, and one of it's biggest supporters
was the local M.P., Sir Ian Hamilton Benn. By September
the 13th the Club were ready to play their first home
game, but at this time the venue had little to offer
spectators or players alike. The steep sides could give
ample, if slippery, vantage points for the fans, but
there was no cover whatsoever. The roughly fenced-off
venue's only amenities were a few old army huts which
were converted for use as changing rooms and
accommodation for Officials. This Ground became known as
The Valley.

The first match, a South Suburban League fixture resulted
in a two goal victory over Summerstown. Professionalism
soon followed with the Club's entry into the Southern
League, and the final accolade, acceptance in to the new
Third Division South of the Football League in 1921. This
accelerated rate of progress was repeated with respect to
the Ground, since in June 1921, The Valley was purchased
for £3,000. With the Club's imminent debut in the
Football League, the facilities had to be improved, and
the Contractors - Humphreys of Knightsbridge (this

Company became the financial benefactors to the Club for over a decade) - set about building a Grandstand, Dressing rooms and construct terracing, at an incredible cost (for the period) of £14,000. In fact by the time of the first Third Division game (a single goal defeat of Exeter City on August the 27th), the Grandstand was far from complete, and the eventual cost amounted to a total expenditure of over £20,000!

The Valley in 1920 - little more than a vast open bowl.
(Sports Pictures)

Even with the Grandstand completed, there was precious little else in the way of facilities for spectators, but the potential for such a vast arena was soon realised, and The Valley as a venue for future Cup Finals, (There was no Wembley Stadium at this time) was considered a possibility. Then, only two years after that first Football League game, and after such a large expenditure, the Directors delivered a bombshell. In what must surely be the craziest move ever made by a Football League Club, it was announced that Charlton Athletic F.C. would be moving to 'The Mount' at Catford - the home of non-League Catford Southend F.C.!

THE MOUNT AT CATFORD.

In the vain hope of emulating Arsenal's change of fortune when they moved from the Plumstead area, the Charlton Directors decided to make this disastrous move in a desperate attempt to increase support. The fact that Charlton had only finished 16th and 12th in their first two Football League seasons had hardly encouraged good gates at The Valley. The Catford Club (who had been founded in 1899, and by 1923 were playing in the fairly humble surroundings of the London League) were able to offer little at The Mount. The enclosed Ground lay in the South-west corner of Mountsfield Park (the park still exists), with entrances off Brownhill and Carswell Roads. But there was no potential for big crowds as there were at The Valley, and in addition to more or less flat - unterraced - standing areas, there was only a tiny seated Stand on the East side of the pitch. Therefore another enormous sum of money had to be spent in order to provide the facilities for staging Football League matches.

Work proceeds on the ill-conceived Ground at Ringstead Road, Catford (Summer 1923)

(Catford Journal)

Work commenced in earnest, with a proposed moving-in date during November. Messrs. Humphreys, the Contractors, carried out the work, the principal task consisting of an enormous volume of soil - 44,000 tons - which was cut out of the ground and regraded to form a large embankment on one side of the pitch. Broad, deep, beds of clinker were laid to form a surface cover to the terrace and elsewhere. Opposite the terrace a 2,500 seated and 1,500 standing capacity Stand was to be built, but time (and probably money!) resulted in only a temporary stand being erected. To add to the Club's woes, a workman was killed, just days before the first game, from a clay fall. Clearly the Ground was far from ready or indeed safe for spectators.

After spending more than £17,000 The Mount was finally ready - to a degree - but not until the 22nd of December 1923 when a scoreless draw was played with Northampton Town. This match, and the next versus Q.P.R., produced encouragingly good crowds of around 8,000, but the novelty soon wore off, and aided by frequent bad weather - in a poorly protected Ground - the numbers dropped to around 3,500 early in 1924.

The last match at The Mount was played against Bournemouth and Boscombe on May the 3rd, when the homesters were beaten 1-2. Further expenditure was intended including the removal of the nearly new Grandstand at the Valley at a cost of £5,000. The eventual intention was to build a Stadium that would hold a crowd of 80,000! Even the proposed sale of the old Ground would surely not have balanced the books, in a venture which at the best was risky, and in the light of its final outcome, a disaster!

What was an even greater affront to the Club's true supporters - which probably caused even more indignation than the Club's second move away from The Valley 62 years later - was the original plan to fully amalgamate with Catford Southend, and to adopt not only that name but also play in the non-League Club's colours! It was only the refusal of the F.A. to grant F.A.Cup excemptions in the early rounds, under the Catford name, that prevented this final identity change, although the nickname 'The Kittens' was used. Ironically far and away the best home attendance of the season, was the 20,057 present for the F.A.Cup match with Wolverhampton Wanderers on the 24th of February 1924, a game that due to the lack of seating at Catford had to be played - at The Valley!

The season had dragged on with one disaster after another. A large number of Charlton's fans refused to accept Catford as 'home', problems occurred at The Mount with pitch subsidence, and a poor playing season resulted in ever decreasing crowds. By the season's end, home attendances had dropped to around 1,000, which was less than had watched the old Catford Southend team and was lower even than the numbers watching the Athletic's third team games that were played at The Valley! Although the move was a financial disaster, it was confidently announced on May the 9th, that Charlton would continue playing at Catford.

"Despite the financial difficulties experienced further improvements are planned". These included the re-instatement of the sunken portion of the pitch, and the erection of a permanent Grandstand. But the Directors could only having been kidding themselves! Three weeks later the estimated further costs of upto £12,000 could not be found, and the plans for a continued stay at The Mount were abandoned.

BACK TO THE VALLEY.

With the Supporters Club urging, and Humphrey's Limited promising further financial help, for a return to The Valley, the Directors had little hesitation in taking this course of action. This unhappy year had it's repercussions on the old Catford Southend Club, for with Charlton's move back to The Valley, the Catford Club reformed, but never really recovered from a year of non-existance, and they folded, mid-season, in January 1927.

Always on a financial knife edge, it was the Gliksten brothers who bailed out the Club in 1932, when it was at a particularly low ebb.

The sad sight of The Valley in 1989.
(Dave Twydell)

Although the Club were to enjoy many years in the First Division, and recorded an enormous record attendance of 75,031 - and even then there was room for more - in February 1938 (versus Aston Villa), there were relatively few improvements carried out on the Ground over the years. A covered enclosure was added at the North end in 1934 at a cost of £3,000, but it was to be another 47 years before any further significant addition was made. In 1981, the Jimmy Seed (seated) Stand (named after the Manager who was the principal instigator of the Club's success each side of the Second World War) was opened at the South end. At their peak the Club could attract fifty and sixty thousand attendances, yet these were dwarfed in 1974, when an estimated 100,000 were present - for a Pop Concert by 'The Who'!

The ill conceived move in 1923 caused financial disaster and dissatisfaction amongst the fans, yet there were two more relocations that were later supposedly considered. The little known amateur Club, Slough Centre, played at Belfast Avenue, a Ground that was well developed for a Club of this stature but had potential for much more. Slough (just to the West of London), in 1955, was a rapidly expanding area, and could surely provide sufficient support to host a Football League Club. It was reported in January of that year that Charlton Athletic F.C. were thinking of moving there!

Some seven years later a rumour circulated that Charlton were considering a merger with the Essex based Southern League Club Romford (who, although financially stretched at this time owned their own fine Brooklands Ground); Romford's Secretary firmly denied this suggestion. Both reports were probably no more than rumours, but in view of the Club's earlier and radical move to Catford, these may well have been serious considerations. Slough Centre F.C. folded in 1956, and Romford ceased playing in 1978! Over the years there were to be many milestones achieved at The Valley. On the 3rd of January 1920, the first, and only, F.A.Amateur Cup game was played (the Club lost to Oxford City), and on the 25th of September 1920 the first F.A.Cup game took place, a six goal win over Catford Southend (perhaps the event that led to the two Clubs amalgamating - "if you can't beat them, join them"!). Floodlit football came to The Valley, at a relatively late date, on the 20th of September 1961, when Rotherham United were the visitors, and the Ground had the honour to stage the first ever televised Cup-tie (other than a Final) in 1947. But not only Football (and Pop Concerts) have been seen at this venue. Motor Cycle meets and Horse Gymkhanas appeared during the 1920's, it was a Physical training centre during the Second World War, Midget Car Racing was tried in 1948, and more recently American Football made it's debut. Following War damage at The Den, it was even 'Home' to Millwall during the 1943/44 season.

Despite the Glikstens being credited as the Club's benefactors, over a period of some fifty years, the fact remained that even during their financially successful First Division days, the question of Ground improvements was given a low priority. The vast open terrace on the East side was left to decay, and coupled with poor access and exits, in 1977 the capacity at the Ground was dramatically cut from 66,000 to a mere 20,000. Four year later this allowance was reduced to 13,000. By this time the Club's coffers were far from full, but even so a successful Lottery raised £350,000 over a period of two years, and paid for a new roof to the main Stand (replacing the first of 1922 vintage), seating under the North Stand, and a third covered and seated area that spanned the South end. The capacity had now been raised to 20,000 with half this number in seats, but by 1985, when average gates were down to around 5,000, the Club reached the edge of extinction.

CHARLTON

ATHLETIC

OFFICIAL MATCHDAY MAGAZINE SEASON 1985-86 CANON LEAGUE DIVISION TWO
SATURDAY, 21st SEPTEMBER 1985 KICK-OFF 3.00 p.m.

STOKE CITY

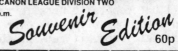

Souvenir Edition
60p

We're with the Woolwich!

The programme for the last match played at The Valley.

SELHURST PARK.

The full story of Charlton's move to Selhurst Park is not relevant here, and in any event has been fully documented elsewhere. But briefly, the Club's troubles multiplied. The Glikstens sold out the Club to Marman Ltd., and after a brief respite, the Club was on the point of folding completely, when Sunley Construction stepped in and became the new owners. But the Ground itself was still owned by Michael Gliksten, who supposedly turned down a generous offer to purchase, and instead the Club had to accept a high priced seven year lease arrangement. A further blow occurred following the Bradford City fire tragedy, when the open East Terrace was closed, the only option being to rebuild at an estimated, and completely impossible, cost of two million pounds. Even with a three sided capacity of around 14,000 it was still possible to continue operating, then the final blow was delivered. Michael Gliksten decided to fence off two acres of the site - which was not part of the leasing agreement - supposedly in preparation for developing the land. But this area represented the main access and car park for the Football Ground; the Club's former lifetime supporter had apparently severed their lifeline for it was now impossible to stage matches.

Charlton moved to Selhurst Park, and at the time of writing this venue constitutes their current Ground, yet those precious two acres at The Valley still lie dormant, and Greenwich Council (the Club's main sponsors at the time of the latest move) who had always pledged their support for the Club's return to The Valley, turned down a planning application in early 1990 for improvements that would ensure a financially viable move back 'home'!

By the late 1980's, The Valley was a sad spectacle. The East terrace had even more weeds and the concrete had crumbled further. The main (West) Stand had been demolished, and the 'new' (1981) North Stand had become all but roofless. Work to returf the pitch was undertaken in 1989, but with the Club in it's present state of virtual limbo, it remains to be seen whether the Charlton Athletic team will ever run out onto this pitch once again.

CHESTER CITY

The exact locations of all of the Club's former Grounds (probably little more than fields) cannot be accurately pinpointed. The Faulkner Street Ground was no doubt the larger of the two fields shown, and the Tomkinson Street enclosure was probably the small field

The formation year of the football club that eventually became the current Chester City has been established as 1884, but some form of football in the town can be traced back at least to the 16th century. The Shrove Tuesday form of the game commenced at the Roodee, the area that contains the current Racecourse. Football in the modern recognised form probably started in 1875 with Chester Garrison fielding a team, also at the Roodee. However, one year later there were no reported Clubs in Chester, and it wasn't until a further year had passed that Chester Wanderers first came upon the scene. Their superiority was challenged with the formation of Chester Rovers in 1879, and they too played at the Roodee. By 1884, the Rovers had changed their home Ground to Faulkner Street in the Bishopfields, now known as the Hoole, district of Chester. During that year the Wanderers and the Rovers combined, and the amalgamated teams became known as plain 'Chester'. By now there were around 20 Clubs in the area, but each fell by the wayside, and Chester F.C. became the sole Senior survivor.

FAULKNER STREET.

It is doubtful if the Ground was anything more than the open field that existed at the, then, end of Faulkner Street, but where Prescot, William and Edna Streets have since been built. It was also not ideal from a playing sense, since the pitch had a lengthways slope. The Club at this time had a membership of 150, but even so often had difficulties in raising a full team for matches played outside of the town, as was the case for the first game of the 1885/86 season at Earlestown on the 5th of September. Such problems did not exist for home matches, and the first match at Faulkner Street that season, versus Northwich Victoria, drew a large crowd.The difficulty in raising a team was not confined to Chester F.C., for earlier, in January 1885, Chester's home tie with Davenham in the Cheshire Senior Cup produced a farcical situation. Everton arrived in the town, mistakingly expecting to play a Friendly match, and when the Davenham team eventually arrived there were only seven players; Everton stepped in and made up the missing numbers for the visitors! The mixed eleven went on to win the match, before a large attendance.

LIGHTFOOT STREET.

Chester were unable to emulate the more successful Clubs within the County, at Crewe and Northwich, and generally struggled for financial survival. In 1887, the Royalty Theatre in Chester organised a Charity Concert in an effort to raise funds for the Football Club, in order for them to carry out Ground improvements. It was not long before a switch was made to the old Show Ground in Lightfoot Street, but this new venue probably had few, if any, facilities for either Spectators or Players, and in reality meant a move to the field immediately adjacent, and to the South of, that previously used in Faulkner Street.

The Club became founder-members of The Combination in 1890, and nine unremarkable seasons followed in this League. The Club effectively folded at the end of the 1897/98 season, being at that time £288 in debt. A new Club was formed and in August 1898, the Committee agreed to form a completely new Club, rather than take on the liabilities of the old, and as a Company issued shares at £5 each. Investigations regarding a suitable Ground had been made, and although they could have continued playing on the Ground of the former 'Chester F.C.', the Landlord wanted to not only increase the rent, but also to move the hoardings closer to the pitch and hence reduce the size of the Ground. The 'new' Club had high hopes, and the possibility of building a purpose designed Athletics Ground - for their own use and other teams and sports - was being considered. Therefore the £50 expenditure that would be necessary to carry out the changes at Lightfoot Street, for what may have been only one year, was not considered worthwhile, and the Committee set out to find an alternative venue for their home games.

The timber Stand at Sealand Road that was demolished in 1979, and replaced by a larger part cantilever structure, that was built behind the original.

BACK TO FAULKNER STREET AND WHIPCORD LANE.

The Club's first match, a scoreless draw with Northwich on the 4th of September, was played on the Ground at Faulkner Street, which was also referred to as Tomkinson Street (the enclosure was at the East end of this thoroughfare) - the former home of their predecessors. But their stay at this venue only lasted until 1903 - the site became a housing estate - and an alternative venue was found in Whipcord Lane. The actual site of this Ground is difficult to pinpoint since it could have been one of several fields to the West of the Lane. But it appears that there were few, if any, facilities for the occupants, although £40 was spent on improvements during their first season of occupancy. The Club played on this unsatisfactory Ground for two years, but with a bar from entry into the F.A.Cup for the 1904/05 competition, due to the undersized pitch, coupled with an upturn in their fortunes on the field, it was obvious that a move would have to be made. On the 14th of April 1906, a probable record attendance at Whipcord Lane of over 4,000 was present when the Club played Whitchurch, as Chester made a challenge for the Championship of the Combination. They finished in the runners-up spot, as they did from 1904 to 1908, and by the end of the season positive moves were made towards a new Ground. The last game was played at Whipcord Lane on the 10th of November, when Birkenhead were beaten by four unopposed goals in front of another large crowd. Of the Whipcord Lane Ground, like its Faulkner Street counterpart, there are no traces, for housing was also soon built on the site.

The seated Stand at Sealand Road. Comfortable and with few obstructions, yet was due to be demolished in 1990, only a few years after being built.

(Dave Twydell)

An overall impression of Sealand Road in 1990, from the visitors end that was closed off during the Club's final season at the Stadium. (Dave Twydell)

SEALAND ROAD.

A move was made just a few hundred yards to a site set within virtual open countryside, in Sealand Road. A ten year lease was obtained from the owner - the Earl of Crewe - and between seven and eight hundred pounds was spent on providing the Club with a worthy Ground. Two covered stands were built, one seated, to hold a total of 3,000 spectators, and although the building work was not complete, the first game was played at this new enclosure on the 15th of December. Bangor were the visitors, £31 was taken at the gate, and a four goal home win ensued.

Even within the terms of the 1990's, the Sealand Road Ground is well situated - away from the town centre, and with ample and easy parking in the area - but on the 28th of April 1990, the last match was played on the eighty-four year old enclosure. A poorly supported Club that has achieved few successes during this long period has been forced to move for financial reasons. The sale of the Ground was necessary to pay the debts, and a neat and very acceptable Ground - a new seated Stand was built in 1979 while the covered enclosures to one end and one side were renovated in the 1980's - has fallen to the Developers lust. The future appears grim for a Club now forced to Groundshare, and with little money to finance a new Stadium. However moves at the present time (late 1990), suggest that a ground may be built, part in Wales and partly in England!

The end of the City at Sealand Road came with this unpretentious (standard format) programme on the 28th of April 1990.
....

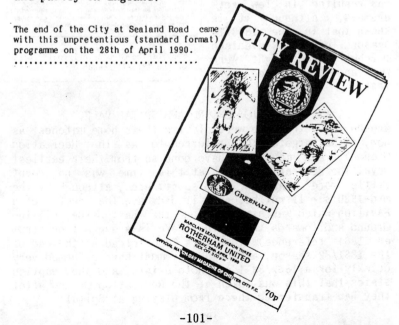

CITY REVIEW

GREENALLS

BARCLAYS LEAGUE DIVISION THREE
ROTHERHAM UNITED
SATURDAY 28th APRIL 1990
KICK OFF 3.00 P.M.

OFFICIAL MATCH-DAY MAGAZINE OF CHESTER CITY F.C. 70p

CHESTERFIELD

There are a number of doubts concerning the early days of Chesterfield F.C. which include the dates when they played at their two Grounds, their possible folding at one time, and the relationship with the Spital Football Club.

The formation of Chesterfield Town F.C. has been recorded as 1866, although a contemporary reference of 1881, refers to 1865, and under the name of plain 'Chesterfield'. At a meeting in 1871, some rudimentary rules were drawn up, when it was also decided that the season would last from October until March. Members subscriptions were set at 10p, and training and practice matches would take place on wednesdays and saturdays. Unfortunately the status of the Club around this time has resulted in few references, although it is known that in the 1873/74 season of the seventeen matches played eight were won and only three were lost.

CHESTERFIELD FOOTBALL CLUB.

President :
J. CUTTS, ESQ.

Committee :
MR. MARRIOTT. MR. STANTON. MR. SYMES. MR. MUGLISTON.
MR. NALL. MR. TOPLIS. MR. THOMPSON, MR. WHOMERSLEY.

Hon. Secretary and Treasurer : MR. C. W. ROLLINSON.

BYE-LAWS, RULES, AND REGULATIONS. SEASON 1871-2.

1. That this Club be called the Chesterfield Football Club.
2. That a Committee of Management be annually appointed, to consist of a President, Eight other Members, and a Secretary, who shall also act as Treasurer ; both President and Secretary to be considered as ex-officio members of the Committee.
3. That an Election of Officers take place at the Annual Meeting of the Club, to be held the second week in September.
4. That the Committee shall meet at least once a month during the season, and that four form a quorum.
5. That the season commence in October, and end in March, and that practice days be Wednesday and Saturday.
6. That the subscription be Two Shillings each year, due at the commencement of each season, but the committee be empowered to make such further call as shall be necessary.
7. That the Secretary have the sole management of the matches and the selection of teams subject to the approval of the Committee.
8. That prior to the commencement of each season the Secretary shall render an account of all moneys received and paid by him on behalf of the Club, which account shall be audited by two members of the Committee and verified by their signatures and then submitted to the Club.
9. That, if it should appear by the accounts that there is a balance in the hands of the Secretary, the amount shall be carried to the club funds of the ensuing year.
10. That any member, feeling himself aggrieved by any other member, or members, may bring his complaint before the Committee for their decision, and that the Committee have the power either to fine or expel such members complained of, and that such fine shall not exceed five shillings.

Copy of the Club's original rules of the 1871/72 season.

THE RECREATION GROUND AND SPITAL VALE.

Around 1880, the Club were playing their home matches, as now, at Saltergate (then referred to as the Recreation Ground), and may well have done so from their earliest days. The Recreation Ground at this time was no doubt little more than an open sports area, although by the mid-1880's - if not before - it did have the benefit of a Pavilion which was situated on the East side of the Ground and towards the South. There is a suggestion (from an 1884 reference) that this Club folded at the end of the 1881/82 season, although they must have reformed very quickly for a 1882/83 team photo exists, and the caption states that this was taken at the Recreation Ground after they had transferred there from playing at Spital.

There was also in the town another Club that vied with support, that of Spital F.C. Once again their formation date is debateable, 1866 being given by one source, whereas the 1881 reference gives the founding year as 1873! There is no doubt that at least during the early 1880's, the two Clubs were completely separate organisations, Chesterfield being Members of the Sheffield Association while Spital opted for the Sheffield New Association. Spital F.C. played at Spital Vale, an area just to the East of the main town centre. At this time the area was very open, with a number of farms and a multitude of fields, one of which would have been this Club's home Ground. The two Clubs were on a par with each other for several years around 1880, but by 1884 it was recorded that they were both playing at the Spital Ground. One year later reference was made to Spital F.C. having Dressing rooms at Horns Inn in Lordsmill Street, a thoroughfare in the centre of town. By 1887, Chesterfield were playing at Saltergate, therefore it would appear that a second return was made to their former Ground. Meanwhile Spital was still going strong and by now had adopted the rather novel shirts which were of a Union Jack design!

There is little doubt that from this time on, Chesterfield remained at Saltergate.

Team Group of 1882/83 season at the Recreation Ground.
(Derbyshire Times)

COVENTRY CITY

In the immediate area, of the village of Stoke (on the outskirts of Coventry) goes the honour of the formation of the first football Club, in 1869. Coventry Association followed one year later, but for many years the sport was overshadowed - at times even ridiculed - by the exponents of the oval shaped ball code. Although a Club of still fairly early 'vintage', Coventry City's origins were somewhat unusual in that they evolved from an original Works team - rather than the more common Church or Cricket Club connections of their contemporaries elsewhere. Cycling had become popular towards the end of the 19th century, and it was the workers of the Singer Company - bicycle manufacturers - that formed a Football Club in October 1883. The Hillfields area of the town was also the centre for the Company, and in the Lord Aylesford Inn several enthusiasts set about creating the Singer's Football Club.

PLAY UP

G. SINGER, ESQ., (PRESIDENT.)

SINGER'S

(FINAL) SINGER'S TEAM :- (1891.)

GOAL :
E. KIRK.

BACKS :

(RIGHT.)
T. CASHMORE.

(LEFT.)
J. GLEW.

W. EDMUNDS,

HALF-BACKS :
T. CANNINGS,

W. HOWELL.

FORWARDS :

H. BANKS,
C. PRETTY,

F. MOBLEY,

W. DORRELL,
T. BIRD, (Captain.)

A Singer's match line-up, probably referring to the 1891 Birmingham Junior Cup Final team.

-104-

DOWELL'S FIELD.

The White Lion at Gosford Green was ideally situated as a headquarters, for not only did the helpful Landlord provide a backroom as a dressing-room, but the Inn was also conveniently situated close to the Club's first Ground, over eight acres of open grassland and known as Dowells Field. The Club's early years were very low key, such that reports of their matches were never recorded, the first mention being a short report in 1885 when Singers shot twelve goals past the Royal Artillery Club - a final 12-1 scoreline. It was to be some years before the Club gained any degree of status, for they were just one of many. So much so that a writer to the local newspaper in December 1887 expressed that as a newcomer to the town, he was surprised that there was not a good Association Football Club there! But Singer's were a Club with ambition, for they joined the Birmingham County F.A. just one year after their formation. But Dowells Field was unsuitable for a progressive team, and so in 1887. a move was made a few hundred metres North to a site off of the Stoke Road.

STOKE ROAD GROUND.

Although only half the size of the former venue, this new field had the distinct advantage of being almost completely enclosed by dense lines of hedges and trees. Two entrances into the Ground were possible, not off the frontage on Stoke Road, but via the opposite end of the field from nearby Catherine Street and an alley located behind the White Lion Inn. It was now possible to make an entrance charge, 2d. (1p) being the fee in the early days. One of the Club's first matches at Stoke Road was the 4-0 victory over Bourneville Villa on the 26th of November 1887. The Club had a successful season, the greatest triumph being their progress through to the semi-final stage of the Birmingham Cup. Support rapidly gained momentum with gates of nearly one thousand being achieved on more than one occasion, and at the Club's A.G.M. in August 1888, a credit balance of nearly £5 was recorded.

The Club continued their rise in the football world, as did the numbers supporting them, and the next season when Unity Gas Works came to Stoke Road for a Birmingham cup-tie, there was a record attendance of 1,400. This was exceeded shortly after, when 2,000 came to see Aston Villa Reserves make an appearance in Coventry. The Ground to this date was still only a naturally enclosed field,

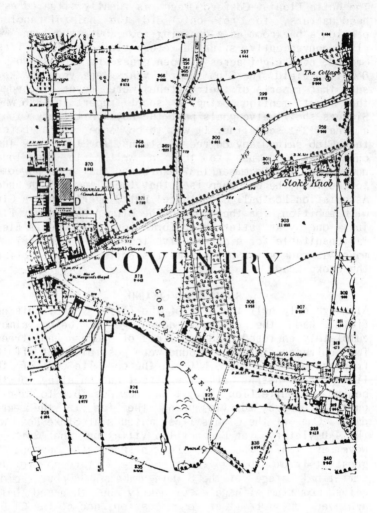

1889 Map. The two former Grounds (outlined) were situated close to the current Highfield Road Ground – which was developed immediately to the North of the Stoke Road enclosure.
(Ordnance Survey)

but with ever increasing crowds it became necessary to
prevent encroachment onto the pitch with the provision of
a stout wire and post barrier, and with the now regular
newspaper reports a Press box was erected within the a
newly formed reserved enclosure. Singer's had risen to
become the premier Club in the town, and the sport was
gaining credibility in this Rugby stronghold. For a few
years their main opposition for supremecy came from
another Bicycle Works team, Rudge. Matches between the
two teams produced fierce partisan support, and often
scenes of violence from both sets of supporters! By now
the Club were of sufficient standing to entertain and
visit the likes of Small Heath, and on such a trip to
Birmingham the team could be accompanied by upto 800
supporters. However, in 1891 these numbers had swelled to
2,500 for the Club's first appearance in the final (and
capture) of the Birmingham Junior Cup, at Perry Barr. The
victory led onto further glories in the 1891/92 season,
and the gate receipts for the year totalled £411, showing
a profit of £19.

After these years of progress the team's fortunes dipped,
not least due to the fact that a slump hit the Company,
and several players were lost to other Clubs. It was
perhaps not an ideal time to turn professional, but the
Club did - in part - when they fielded mixed teams of
Amateurs and Professionals. The 1892/93 season also saw
the Club play their first F.A.Cup match. A 0-3 defeat to
Burton Swifts ensued, a match played at 8.00 a.m. on a
wednesday! The latter half of the season was a nightmare,
and as the Club regularly lost, the supporters stayed
away in ever greater numbers. For the first time the
Club's closest opponents, Rudge, gained the upper hand
and for a short time it appeared that it would be the
rival bicycle Company who would wear the mantle of 'Town
team'. Even Singer's entry into a League competition for
the first time - the Birmingham - for the 1893/94 season
was not looked forward to with much relish.

At this period the idea of changing the name to 'Coventry
City' was first mooted. This was soon quashed by the
Singer's Directors who declared that if this should come
to pass, then the Company would continue football under
their own name, and woe betide any employee who chose to
play for 'the opposition'! The Club's fortunes continued
precariously, but despite their struggles at least some
attempt was made at Ground improvements during the Summer
of 1896.

Duckboards were installed around the Ground, a measure that would at least keep the feet dry of the dwindling number of supporters.

There was a slight improvement on the field during the 1897/98 season, and with the decline of the Rudge team – and their final demise in 1898 – the way was clear for Singer's to become the undisputed premier Club in Coventry. The last match of the season was a Friendly versus Foleshill Great Heath, and this fixture was to become the last under the Singer name. At last a covered Stand was built for the spectators comfort, not at the old Ground but on the adjoining field which was to become the current Highfield Road. Despite this additional expenditure, the Club were able to show a £32 profit, generated principally from increased gates which totalled £445 over the season.

The 1898/99 season became the last at the Stoke Road Ground, where the building Developer was ready to pounce. But it's passing hardly raised a tear, since the facilities were minimal, although by way of contrast far more effort was put into making the new Highfield Road Ground comfortable for fans and players alike. One of the last matches played at the Stoke Road Ground was a Friendly game versus Nottingham Forest, and this highly prestigious meeting attracted such interest that a crowd of between four and five thousand were present. Eleven days later, on the 15th of April 1899, another large gathering (second only to the Forest game) saw the locals watch their team lose their last Birmingham League match to the Reserve eleven of Wolverhampton Wanderers. Two weeks later the curtain came down at Stoke Road for the last match there, when Second Division Club Barnsley St.Peter's won a friendly encounter by 2-1 before a disappointingly small crowd.

THE GROUNDS TODAY.

The first match was played at the new venue with Shrewsbury Town in opposition, and a healthy crowd of 3,000 were present to see the single goal victory. Dowell's Field was already partly built over by the turn of the century, it's location being to the South of Binley Road at the junction with St.George's Road. The site of the Stoke Road Ground was rapidly developed after Coventry's move next door, and the North end of King Richards and Mowbray Streets now covers this former Ground.

CREWE ALEXANDRA

It may perhaps be the evocative title that gives the Club
a certain charisma, but although there are few teams
older than the Alexandra their history has been marked
with a consistancy of near non-achievement! The
'Alexandra' suffix to the Club's name was the name of a
well known house which was patronised by those connected
with the railway works. With several of the Club
Presidents, and support coming from the railwaymen
themselves - the Club formed an inextricable bond.

EARLE STREET CRICKET GROUND.

The Alexandra Athletic Club was formed in September 1866,
with only a dozen members, and although a number of
sporting pursuits were soon taken up by an increasing
membership, cricket was the principal interest. As a
playing area, the Club chose a large field, just South of
Earle Street, and wedged between the Grand Junction and
Crewe and Manchester Lines of the London and
North-Western Railway Company. The large field offered no
facilities, and was probably most notably distinguished
by the two small lakes that lay on the Western boundary!
The Ground's location (as were the later Football
Grounds) is significant for a town whose very existance
was dependant on the railways - wedged as it is between
the lines. A form of football was played by the
Cricketers, as a winter sport, but the style chosen was
more allied to the Rugby form.

It wasn't until 1876 that a definite move was made to
create a football section that operated under Association
Rules. The original intention was to provide football for
the younger members of the Railway Company; however,
after a period of around two years there was insufficient
support and the membership was thrown open to outsiders.
Football soon became one of the principal features of the
Athletic Club, and they continued playing at the Earle
Street Cricket Ground, until 1877 when all of the
sporting activities were moved to the Alexandra
Recreation Ground.

ALEXANDRA RECREATION GROUND AND NANTWICH ROAD.

The new venue covered, in total, around the same area as
the Earle Street headquarters, and was located alongside
Crewe Railway Station and Nantwich Road.

However, the new headquarters offered the luxury of dressing rooms that were located at the Ground. A more definitive football section was created in 1878, and the overall Club was entitled, 'Crewe Alexandra Cricket, Football, Athletic and Bicycle Club'.

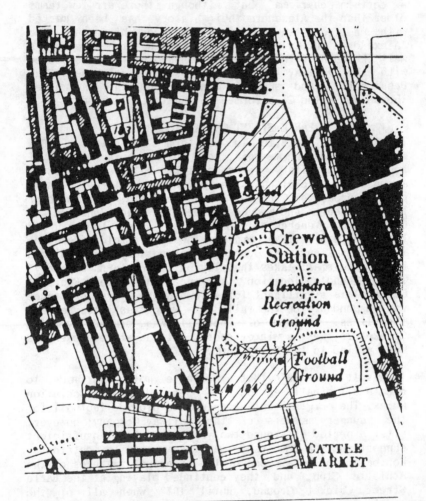

Three of the former Grounds, in 1898, plus the current Gresty Road enclosure (lower hatched area) almost overlap each other. Extensions to the railway resulted in the 'Football Ground' being re-built less than a pitch length to the West. The upper hatched area is the site of the Old Sheds Field Ground. (Ordnance Survey)

The early trend to experiment with a form of floodlight football was undertaken by the Club on Monday the 18th of November 1878, when a crowd of between 1,500 and 2,000 paid for entry into the enclosed Ground; many more chose a free view from Nantwich Road, but were able to see little of the action. Lighting was provided by a portable agricultural engine, which drove two 'Gramme' electrical machines. Two large lamps, one at each end of the pitch, were supported by several poles and guy ropes, and supposedly produced 6,000 candle power each. But the illumination was generally a big disappointment, particularly that located at the West end, and on one occasion during the proceedings, the playing area was plunged into total darkness when both lamps failed! The pitch was 110 yards long, and from the description given it would appear that this ran from West to East (but was probably later relocated from North to South). After pre-match entertainment by the 36th CRV Band, two matches were played. The first was a 'rough and tumble' affair when the football team played Congleton Amalgamated, under Rugby rules, and this was followed by a more entertaining Association Rules game with a team from Nantwich.

The original Nantwich Road venue was principally a Cricket Ground, a large enclosure with Nantwich and Gresty Roads, plus the railway lines (to the East) and the cattle market, forming the four boundaries. Within this area, in the North-west, a cycle racing track formed an approximate oval, and eventually a 30 metres long Grandstand was built on the 'straight' of the cycle track, on the West side. Adjoining the Stand was a large Pavilion, with the main entrance to the Ground in Gresty Road, near to the junction with Nantwich Road. Except on the Grandstand side, raised cinder embankments - between five and metres wide - ran round the perimeter of the cycle track. This whole enclosure only encompassed about one third of the Recreation Ground, leaving large open areas to the South and East. In 1884, the Football Club took over a direct tenancy of the Ground and £650 was spent on improvements.

The Alexandra soon became one of the major Clubs in Cheshire, although it wasn't until 1887 (but captured frequently after that date), that the Cheshire Senior Cup was won, a competition that was first competed for in the 1879/80 season.

In 1886 a home cup-tie with Nantwich drew over 3,000 fans
to the match. For some years the Club used the enclosed
Ground within the Alexandra Recreation Ground, although
an individual Football Ground was built, in the
South-east corner in 1897. The earlier enclosure was used
for the F.A.Cup semi-final in 1887 - Aston Villa versus
Glasgow Rangers (the last season with Scottish entries).
The match was recognised as a great honour for the town,
and the Ground was considered as being one of the best
appointed in the Country. A crowd of around 7,000
(including many from the Birmingham area) were present,
with many sporting their favours.

Strong rails - as opposed to the more usual posts and
ropes - ensured that the crowd did not encroach onto the
pitch. Within the Pavilion, provisions were made for the
Press, with many Clerks and messengers being present,
while the Grandstand, and a temporary one were filled
with paying spectators. A few weeks later there was a
megre crowd of only 500 for the Welsh Cup semi-final
between Davenham and Oswestry.

But Crewe Alexandra F.C. themselves were well supported
at this time, and attendances of 1,500 versus Darwen,
3,000 for the Welsh cup-tie versus Northwich, 2,500 when
the Druids were the visitors and 1,500 for the game
against Chester, were present for games during the
following season. But more notable was the team's own
appearance in the F.A.Cup semi-final in 1888 (they first
entered the Competition in 1885), at which stage they
lost to Preston North End. Earlier, in the 5th round the
home tie with Derby County attracted an attendance of
5,000, but in the fourth round the Alexandra were
involved in an incident which led directly to rule
changes in the Competition. After drawing 2-2 with the
London based Club, the Swifts, they lost the replay which
was played at the Queen's Club. However before the match
an astute Crewe Official measured the height of the
crossbar with a two foot rule, only to find it one inch
lower than that permitted. A protest was made after the
game, and the F.A. had little option, despite their
abhorence of such an unsporting gesture, but to order a
second replay (when the result was reversed in the
Cheshire Club's favour!) From that time on the rules were
ammended requiring that any such protest should be made
known to the Referee before the match started, rather
than after the event; the incident came to be known as
the 'Two foot rule'.

Support at the gate continued and football became a popular spectator pastime in the area. That same season, on the 4th of February, a further honour was bestowed on the town, when the Alexandra Ground hosted the International between England and Wales, when a crowd of 6,000 was present.

The 1889/90 season saw the Club enter the Football Alliance (and the Ground was used for another F.A.Cup semi-final). Although no League honours were won during the Club's three year membership, a good run-in to the last season ensured the Club membership of the newly formed Second Division of the Football League. The Club had reverted to Amateur status, but some excellent results were obtained, including a 11-1 victory over Birmingham St.George. Attendances also remained high, including 2,000 for a friendly visit of Stoke in April, and the last match of the season on the 23rd of that month, when 5,000 were present to see the locals beat Nottingham Forest by 2-0.

On the 10th of September 1892, and in glorious weather, the Club got off to a good home start in the Football League, when 2,000 fans were present to see their favourites win by the only goal of the game. The local derby with Northwich attracted 4,000, but the optimistic start was not sustained and by early November the team were bottom of the League, and only a meagre attendance was present for the match versus Walsall. The Club reverted to Professionalism in 1893, but this could not reverse the trend, attendances rarely exceeded 2,000, and after the Club's third re-election bid - in four seasons - they received only four votes, and were thrown back into non-League football. The last League match on the Recreation Ground was played on the 28th of March - a seven goal defeat to Liverpool - and on the 3rd of April the last 'home' game had to be moved to the Ground of Sandbach St.Mary when a surprisingly good attendance witnessed a 1-2 defeat to Loughborough.

A VARIETY OF GROUNDS.
After several reasonable years, the Club were out of the Football League, and, presumably due to the end of their lease, without a home. An entry was made into the Combination, but the lack of a suitable home venue resulted in the first match on September the 5th being switched to the Ground of their opponents, Middleton.

A Ground sub-Committee had been rapidly formed to try to overcome the problem, but an approach to use the enclosed Ground previously used by Crewe Carriage Works was met by silence from the Railway Company, and the request to return to the Alexandra Recreation Ground was turned down. The home programme finally got underway later in September, but the (unidentified) Ground was soon to cause problems. After the League match versus Macclesfield, Officials from the Combination measured the dimensions of the pitch, only to find that it was ten yards shorter than the minimum allowable, and decreed that all home games that had been undertaken in this competition should be replayed - on a legal sized area! Three games came into this ruling, being those against Macclesfield, Chester and Rock Ferry. Frantic efforts were made to secure a suitable site for future home matches, and eventually the Brittania Recreation Ground was secured. But even this choice did not solve the Club's problems, for following the 3-1 home victory over Buckley in the 4th qualifying round of the F.A.Cup on December the 12th, the visitors lodged a protest, and the pitch was found to be seventeen yards to narrow! The re-match - at Buckley - the following week ended in a single goal victory to the Alexandra.

It is probable that the remainder of the season was
played out at Eddleston Road (no doubt the open field
that was later overlaid by Electricity Street) and the
enclosed Ground opposite - and North of- the Alexandra
Athletic Ground (known as Old Sheds Field and probably
the Carriage Works F.C. home venue). The latter soon
disappeared when the Station was enlarged, and the
Railway track area increased in width; these were later
partly removed, and a Car Park partially covers the area
that was once this Football Ground.

A NEW RECREATION GROUND.

The 1897/98 season was played in more settled
circumstances. After efforts by F.W.Webb, the Railway's
Chief Mechanical Engineer, it was announced that the Club
would have one of the best football Grounds. It is not
clear if this referred to the previously used Cricket
enclosure (at the Recreation Ground) - where at least the
opening home match was played - or at a completely new
enclosure, which was constructed in the South-east corner
(the North-west corner of the Ground almost touching the
boundary of the Cricket enclosure), and hard up against
the railway lines.

The Earle Street Cricket Ground, later known as the Alexandra Athletic Ground,
was used by the Club on two occasions. The Stadium is now used (1989) for motor
sports and has retained it's basic shape, but a more depressing and delapidated
enclosure would be hard to find!   (Dave Twydell)

Turnstiles were included, and the main entrance was situated opposite Catherine Street. A quarter pitch length Stand was built along the South side, with a small adjoining Pavilion, and on the East and North sides embankments were formed. In view of the special arrangements that were made on the 18th of September 1897 for the visit of Chirk, this was probably the first match at this new arena. At 2.00 p.m. the local Brass Band struck up, and marched to the Recreation Ground. By the kick-off there was a crowd of 3,000 present, and the entertaining match that followed produced a three goal victory to the Alexandra.

The Club, now settled on their own Ground, sparked off a revival in its fortunes, and by mid-October they were perched at the top of the Combination. The crowds flocked back to support the team, 3,000 present for Chester's visit, nearly 4,000 when Stoke Reserves and Rock Ferry each came to Crewe, close to 5,000 for Wrexham's F.A.Cup visit; the latter match produced gate receipts of over £60, and a 4-1 victory to the homesters. In the semi-final of the Cheshire Cup, great interest was aroused when the newly formed, and highly acclaimed, New Brighton Tower were the visitors. Even an hour before the kick-off the entrances to the Ground were besieged, and a man was knocked down and killed by a passing vehicle. Close to 8,000 fans (a record for the Competition) were present to see two goals shared, but the Alexandra bowed out of the Competition in the replay.

The runners-up place in the League was achieved at the season's end, and for the 1898/99 season a move was made to the Lancashire League. The support for the Club continued (3,000 for the first League game, over 4,000 for South Liverpool's F.A.Cup match, and 5,000 when Horwich came to the Railway town). Such enthusiasm was not confined to home matches, for the - essentially railway - fans travelled in their hundreds, on 'Specials' (trains) for the Club's away fixtures. But the bubble soon burst, and after winning no honours, a loss of £144 was reported on the 1899/1900 season, this was mostly caused by the poor gates for the Reserve team, which was abandoned for the next season. £912 was taken in match receipts plus £64 in season tickets, but the wages bill came close to £800.

Although the team continued to provide good performances on the field, attendances of 4,000 (versus Aston Villa

Reserves in January 1905), and 5,100 for the Barnsley
F.A.Cup visit), were rare, and half these numbers were
more common.

Continuing lack of success, due to indifferent
performances continued on the field, and a loss on the
1906/07 season of £51 was recorded. However a great deal
of expense was incurred due to another Ground move which
became necessary in 1906. An expansion of the number of
Railway lines, and the enlargement of the Station,
resulted in the considerable reduction in width of the
Recreation Ground. The independant Athletic Club had to
vacate their headquarters - they moved to the former
Earle Street enclosure, considerably improved the Ground,
and renamed it the 'Alexandra Athletic Grounds'. The old
site of the Athletics Club now contains an office block,
which is used by British Rail. There was sufficient space
left for a Football Ground, and the Club moved, to the
West, but less than a pitch length away, and built the
current Gresty Road Ground.

The Alexandra Athletic Ground - later known as the L.M.R.
Sports Ground remains basically as it did in the early
1900's, a near circular arena, and is used principally
for motor sports. But the years have taken their toll,
and a more delapidated sporting venue would be difficult
to find!

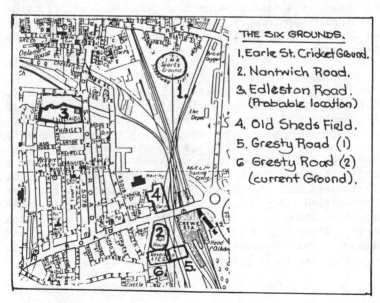

THE SIX GROUNDS.

1. Earle St. Cricket Ground.
2. Nantwich Road.
3. Edleston Road.
   (Probable location)
4. Old Sheds Field.
5. Gresty Road (1)
6. Gresty Road (2)
   (current Ground).

CRYSTAL PALACE

The original Crystal Palace Football Club dates back to 1863, and in 1871, the Club took part in the very first F.A.Cup Competition. However this Club, formed from the workers at the more famous 'Crystal Palace' itself, never rose to prominence, and it was not until 1905 that the current team was created. Initially the Company that owned the Grounds of the same name, decided to form a professional football team and enter the Football League. But following objections from the F.A., a separate Company was formed, and in 1905 the new 'Crystal Palace F.C' came upon the scene, and was immediately accepted into the Southern League.

THE CRYSTAL PALACE.

The choice of home venue was inevitably the Football arena within the Crystal Palace Grounds, the 'home' at that time for F.A.Cup Finals. The team remained there for ten years, but the newcomers career hardly started in confident fashion, for their first match supposedly attracted just twelve spectators - of whom half were alledgedly Officials! But support was not long in coming, and within a short period of time, upto 4,000 were attracted to this vast Football Ground. But in 1915, when the arena was taken over for the War effort, the 'Glaziers' had to seek a new venue. (For full details of the Crystal Palace Ground, see separate section under this heading).

LONDON COUNTY ATHLETIC GROUND, HERNE HILL.

The Glaziers initial years had been fairly successful, with an immediate promotion into the first division of the Southern League, at the end of their first season, and respectable placings - culminating in the runners-up slot in the last (1914/15) pre-war campaign. Although there was a somewhat hostile attitude from the general public towards Clubs who continued to play during the First World War, the Palace elected to carry on, and for this period they made use of the London County Athletic Ground at Herne Hill. This venue was about three miles North of the Club's initial home 'base' at Sydenham, and although a well enclosed Ground, it was somewhat less imposing than their previous headquarters.

(Top): The Palace's home pre-first World War at Herne Hill Cycle Track, little changed in 1989.
(Bottom): The Grandstand at Herne Hill is probably the original structure that was built c.1880.

(Dave Twydell)

The pitch was set within an oval shaped, and slightly banked cycle track - one of the most popular of sporting events that were held at the Ground. By the late 19th Century the Athletic Ground had been laid out on what were formerly open fields. Even before the turn of the Century, Herne Hill could boast of an attractive Grandstand with a seating capacity of around 300, plus open seated stands each side of the Grandstand, which catered for perhaps another 500 spectators. Further seats were provided for in a flat and narrow paddock area, with standing spectators around the rest of the oval track.

The Palace's time at this venue was limited to just four - wartime - years, and is not, perhaps, particularly memorable with respect to the Club's history. However, Herne Hill does provide a big bonus for the Ground seeking Historian, for the Stadium remains intact to this day, and in many respects retains much of what was present before the turn of the Century! The Grandstand was built following the forming of the London County Athletic Ground Limited in 1892, and although superficially changed, this original Structure is still present, being easily identified from old photographs and Ordinance Survey maps as the same building today. The ornate cast iron columns are the most notable feature, and the paddock - now minus seating - still lies adjacent to the cycle track.

Cycling at Herne Hill in 1908, a few years before Palace's move there. (Croydon Public Library)

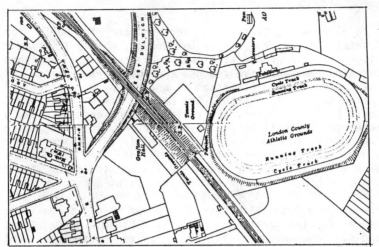

The London County Athletic Ground in 1914, was also the home of Crystal Palace F.C. for a few years.

Even the uncovered seated areas remain, albeit, substantially rebuilt. The standing areas are unlikely to house spectators today, but the now partly overgrown banked slopes remain together with some, presumably original, timber sleepers. From it's earliest days, Herne Hill Stadium (as it is now known), was principally used for Cycle racing, and in 1926 a World Record was set, at a time when meetings would attract upto 20,000 spectators. Substantial refurbishment was undertaken in 1948 when the Cycling events for the Olympic Games were held there, and the Local Council has continued to keep the Stadium in good order. Entry can only be made via Burbage Road, and a visit is most rewarding, to this, one of the best examples of an old, former Football Ground.

THE NEST - CROYDON COMMON ATHLETIC GROUND.
With the cessation of hostilities, Crystal Palace F.C. made another move, this time nearer 'home' territory, at The Nest, near Selhurst Junction Station; the former home of Croydon Common F.C. The 'Robins', as the earlier occupants of this Ground were known, enjoyed a brief existance at a Senior level in Football. This Club entered the Southern League in 1907, and achieved a second promotion to the First Division in 1914. The last pre-war season of 1914/15 saw the Club finish just one place above bottom, but at the War's end, they did not re-appear on the scene.

Even as early as 1919, plans were in hand to build for Crystal Palace F.C. their own Ground, when a lease on a piece of waste ground at Selhurst was considered and soon taken up. But for five seasons the Glaziers resided at the Croydon Common Athletic Ground, having been granted a lease from the owners, the London, Brighton and South Coast Railway Company. Their stay encompassed the team's inaugural Football League days, when they were elected to the newly formed Third Division in 1920. Five figure crowds were the order of the day as the Club swept straight into the Second Division following their Championship win at the end of this first season.

The Croydon Common Athletic Ground was hardly a suitable venue for the spectators despite the team's good support and reasonable success. The playing area was of rectangular shape, with rounded corners, but the facilities consisted of little more than a covered seated stand stretching two thirds along one side, and open banked areas elsewhere. Even the occupants of the stand, despite it being roofed, got wet in the front rows if it rained! The Stand side was enlarged after the war, by encroaching on the previous Athletics track that ran outside of the football pitch.

The only entrances were off of Selhurst Road - conveniently opposite the Station - via one of fifteen turnstiles. The fans paid their one shilling (five pence) or twice this amount for a seat in the Stand (Ground Season tickets cost £2). But despite the poor facilities, large crowds flocked to the Ground: " All around the ropes the crowd was arranged on every conceivable accessory. Lemonade boxes, trestles, lorries, planks were plentiful..." (29th January 1921, versus Hull City. Attendance between 15,000 and 20,000).

The last Football League game was played at this venue when Barnsley were beaten 3-1 on the 3rd of May 1924. The Stadium had been built on part of Selhurst Wood, but soon after the Palace's departure, it was demolished, and became a cleaning shed and additional railway sidings. Nothing remains of the old Ground now, although the current wide entrance to this current British Rail property is located where the entrance to the former Athletic Ground was located.

Train passengers get a brief view of the match versus Manchester United at 'The Nest' in September 1922.

Goalmouth action in the F.A.Cup versus Hull City at 'The Nest' in the 1920/21 season.

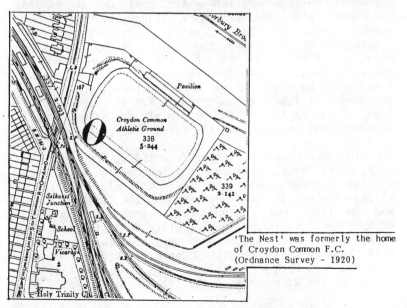

'The Nest' was formerly the home of Croydon Common F.C.
(Ordnance Survey - 1920)

DERBY COUNTY

By the time that William Morley had the idea, in 1884, of forming a football section from within the Derbyshire Cricket Club, the Derby Midland Football Club, was already in existance. Morley, a Clerk at the Midland Railway Company, approached his father, who was on the Cricket Committee, and the suggestion was readily approved. The original intention was that the new football team should be called "Derbyshire County F.C.", but this was instantly turned down, as the Cricketers jealously guarded their own name!

THE RACECOURSE GROUND.

Naturally enough though, the County Cricket Ground - the Southern area within the Racecourse - was chosen as the Club's home ground, although this was not the first time that the winter sport had been played on the hallowed green. A few years earlier a Club by the plain name of "Derby", who were registered with the Birmingham F.A., had used the venue, but this Club soon slipped into obscurity. Also, and more recently, the Derbyshire Senior Cup Final was held at the County Ground.

Having settled on the name of 'Derby County', the first game was played at Great Lever, on the 13th of September, where a humiliating six goal defeat ensued. One week later the newcomers staged their first home match, versus Blackburn Olympic. This was a very prestigious occasion since the former F.A.Cup winners had been the first team to wrest the trophy away from the South, in 1883. the County were far from disgraced when they lost by the narrow margin of 3-4. There was an attendance of 1,500, at an entrance fee of 2½p - ladies free - and Spilsbury, who within six months was to gain International honours, was the first home goalscorer.

The Club soon became a forceful outfit, and only two years after their formation, they reached the third round of the F.A.Cup when they lost to Small Heath (Aston Villa). Two years later they reached the last sixteen, and in 1889, were matched in a local derby game with Derby Junction. A single goal victory took them through to the last sixteen again, when they lost to Aston Villa, this time by a 5-3 scoreline. During this time, the Club were honoured with a semi-final F.A.Cup tie that was played at the Racecourse on the 14th of March 1885.

A painting of the Racecourse. The football pitch would have been located in the foreground to the left of the tents; artistic license shows the Grandstand much nearer than in reality!

One year later, a second semi-final match took place in Derby, when a staggering crowd (the highest ever to that date of any game in the competition) of 15,000 saw Blackburn Rovers overcome the Swifts by 2-1. One year later the first Final to end in a draw was played at the Oval (before a 12,000 attendance). The replay was played at the County's Ground, before another crowd of approximately 12,000.

Mid-19th century picture of the ornate Grandstand at the Racecourse.

Whilst these numbers of spectators may not appear particularly large, it is doubtful if more than a small proportion saw much of the action! Although the Racecourse in it's entirety was a very large arena, the football pitch was tucked away in one corner of the Cricket Ground area. There was admittedly a very ornate Grandstand - with a balconied viewing area for the favoured few - and three banks of open and covered seated stands. However these were provided for the racing fans and for the patrons of cricket, and since they were located about 300 metres from the nearest portion of the football pitch, the view of the match would have been somewhat distant! The only facility that could have been used to real benefit would have been a small pavilion (principally provided for the cricketers), located to the south-east of the football pitch, and this could have only been of benefit to a few of the footballing elite. Apart from a small embankment just to the west of the pitch, the vast majority would have thronged around the level grassed areas.

It would seem to have been a strange, and somewhat unsuitable venue for top class football matches, and one can only surmise that the choice was due to the centralised location of Derby coupled with the rapid rise to fame of the County Football team, plus the prestige of staging such matches at the old established Cricket/Racecourse Ground. It should also be remembered that Football Ground development as such was very much in it's infancy at this time, and therefore there were most likely no other more suitable venues. The Racecourse Ground was used on three more occasions for semi-final ties (in 1890, 1892 and 1895) when geographically the arena provided neutral ground for the competing Clubs.

Attendances for Derby County matches were rarely specified, although estimated crowds of 3,000 for the F.A.Cup game with Long Eaton Rangers and 4,000 later in the 1886/87 season versus Liverpool Ramblers, were said to be present. On the 15th of September 1888, the first Football League match was staged at the Racecourse Ground, when a 2-1 defeat by West Bromwich Albion was watched by 3,000. Two weeks later a new 'composition' football was first used, but after splitting into two parts during the game, the experiment was never repeated! Crowds generally hovered between two and three thousand that season, except for the local match with Derby Junction in the F.A.Cup, when around 4,000 were attracted to the Ground. With similar attendances during the next two seasons, the record attendance for a Club match was realised when the second round Cup game with Sheffield Wednesday drew a crowd of 7,500.

The 1891/92 season saw at last, a regular rise in interest by the locals, with 7,000 viewing the League game with Everton, and a thousand less for Sunderland's visit. The latter game however was played at the Baseball Ground, a venue that was occasionally used by the County until their permanent move to this, their current Ground, in 1894. One year later the crowds flocked to the home games, when attendances were generally between five and eight thousand, and a new record of 10,000 was achieved for Preston's visit on the 10th of September. But this five figure crowd was dwarfed when 15,000 saw (or at least seen by a proportion of those present!) the F.A.Cup match with Sheffield Wednesday. This game, in the first round, was finally brought to a conclusion, after two earlier void encounters, due to protests over the use of ineligible players!

The overall increased figures may well have been influenced by the effective absorption of the Derby Midland Club, and the folding of the Junction Club, leaving the path clear for just one Senior team in the town.

With such large crowds, the County had outgrown their home, and the 1893/94 season was to be the last at the Racecourse Ground. Even so, these last appearances produced contrasting degrees of support. Having fought their way through to the third round (quarter-final) stage of the Cup, an all time record attendance was present to see them lose 1-4 to Blackburn Rovers. Yet on the 2nd of April 1894, and despite a successful season which saw the team finish third in the League, a paltry 2,125 showed up for the final game at the old Ground; this last match produced six goals, shared equally with Burnley.

In contrast the first game at the Baseball Ground drew 10,000 for Sunderland's visit. This venue was not completely new for the Club, since a few games had been staged there, when Race Meetings clashed with the Football fixtures.

THE GROUND TODAY.

The Ground, which was already staging Horse-racing in the early 19th Century, developed from what was known as the 'New Pastures' and consisted of little more than a huge and roughly oval shaped area. In 1849, an impressive new Grandstand was built, and a Hotel, plus two later other Stands (part open seated) were added to, at the South-east corner - located and angled for the spectators of Racing and Cricket rather than for the Football arena. By 1900, the Ground had changed little, although a large pavilion was erected at the North of the cricket boundary. The Grandstand was demolished in 1911, and the other structures are no longer, but today equally impressive spectator facilities are present; but now only for Cricket. The Racecourse as such has disappeared, to be replaced with 'Racecourse Park' at the Northern end of the former enormous enclosure - which was over 800 metres long - and roads around the perimeter approximate to the former lines of the racecourse track. Needless to say nothing remains of the Football area - the small pavilion was removed in the early post-second World War years - but then there was precious little there in the first place!

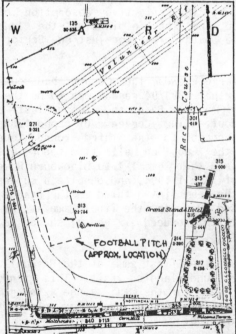

1881 Map. The football pitch is almost lost in this vast enclosure!
(Ordnance Survey)

DONCASTER ROVERS

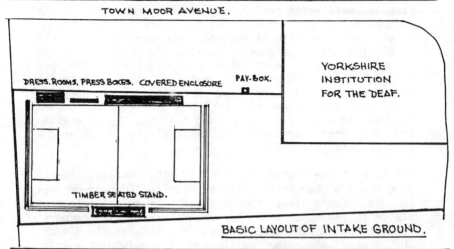

TOWN MOOR AVENUE.

DRESS. ROOMS. PRESS BOXES. COVERED ENCLOSURE   PAY-BOX.

YORKSHIRE
INSTITUTION
FOR THE DEAF.

TIMBER SEATED STAND.

BASIC LAYOUT OF INTAKE GROUND.

The Rovers humble beginnings started in September 1879, when one of the Masters at the Yorkshire Institute for the deaf approached one Albert Jenkins, and suggested that he 'get up a team' to play the deaf school's boys at football. After a four goal lead to the Institute, the match finished as a 4-4 draw. The success of this somewhat insignificant contest led to Mr. Jenkins resolve to form a proper football team.

Within a month, Doncaster Rovers had played their first match, a fixture at Rawmarsh, on the third of October. The initial tie-up with the Deaf School remained for many years for the School's playing field became the Club's 'home' Ground from 1885 to 1916. The early years saw the Club appearing at open areas on Town Moor (where football pitches are still to be seen) and at Belle Vue. The latter location not to be confused with the current Ground, but located at what is now Bennetthorpe.

THE INTAKE GROUND.

On the 26th of April 1885 Elsecar were entertained, and beaten (3-0), in the first game at the Deaf and Dumb School Ground - doubtless at that time an unenclosed field. It was not until November 1886 that the Ground was first referred to as the Intake Ground.

Although, throughout their history, the Rovers have seldom been a well supported Club, they became an early member of the Midland League (in 1891), by which time a Stand had been built at the Intake Ground. No doubt finance restricted the quality of this Stand, for it was to have an unhappy and short life! Only a few months later, on the 10th of December, the roof blew off, but within two days a match was nonetheless played at the Ground. Amazingly only nine days following the roof damage, an enlarged Stand was built and ready in time for the game that day versus Long Eaton Rangers! However, this was not the end of the Club's bad luck, for on the 22nd of December 1894 a new Stand that had been erected for the Press and the teams Officials, also suffered a similar fate in a gale!

The turn of the century seasons in the Midland League produced two Championship titles, and the runners-up spot in the Club's last campaign. But even this elevated status failed to attract the crowds in large numbers. However on the strength of these two Championship titles, the second occurring at the end of the 1900/01 season, the Rovers were elected into the Second Division of the Football League. The Club's application to join the Football League was originally unsuccessful, but following the late resignation by the shortlived New Brighton Tower Club, the Rovers were invited to join the fold. This move was not without its problems since their late departure from the Midland League was not welcomed by the Management of that Organisation.

The 1900/01 season had been a good one, with the Club winning 28, and drawing 5 of the 43 first team matches played; the last game - as a non-League team - ended as a three goal home win over Gainsborough Trinity, in a friendly match on April the 27th. On September the 7th - only four days after their invitation to join - Doncaster played their first Football League match, when they entertained Burslem Port Vale. Six goals were shared before no more than 2,000 fans. The Club made a reasonable start to the season by winning most home matches (and conversely losing most of those on their travels). On November the 23rd, when they entertained Champions-elect West Bromwich, the two goal victory was considered one of the best games ever seen on the Intake Ground.

The Club's Intake Ground was hardly upto the standard of the venues of their opponents. The small Ground, with limited facilities, was within the school grounds, and located on the South-west side of the field behind. The rest of the area (adjacent to Town Moor Avenue) was not part of the School grounds. In January 1902, the Club were granted a license to sell alcohol (beer and spirits), together with tea and coffee, in the 'Refreshment Booth'. But the public were unwilling to support the team in reasonable numbers, and when Newton Heath visited the Intake Ground on February the 22nd, the attendance of around 3,000, was referred to as an 'excellent gate'; a few days later the Reserve match versus Wath (in the Sheffield and Hallamshire League) attracted only 300 spectators - and this was probably a record attendance for a second eleven fixture!

The Intake Ground c.1900. The South-east corner of the Deaf and Dumb School is to the left. Entry to the Ground was across the field from the road and behind the small building; the Stand can just be seen behind this building. The white 'bar' is the pitch perimeter fence behind the far goal.

By the season's end, despite a very creditable seventh final placing in the League, the home average attendance over the season was only between two and three thousand. The crowds did increase slightly over the latter half of the campaign, and there were over 3,000 present for the Easter Monday game with Glossop. The poor support in general had, however, been boosted dramatically on March the 28th, when Championship chasing Middlesbrough attracted what was to be the all time record crowd at the

Intake Ground, of around 6,000. The visitors brought 1,000 supporters with them, and the fixture produced great interest amongst the home fans. A temporary Stand was erected on the 'Town' side of the Ground, and the compact little arena was filled to capacity. Although a scoreless draw resulted, it was generally regarded, once again, as one of the best games played at the Ground. It was also the noisiest, with many spectators creating a cacophony of sound with their tin trumpets! The size of the enclosure and the smallness of the pitch was summed up by a Middlesbrough supporter with the comment that... "It was not much bigger than a ping pong table." (!)

One week later, and in direct contrast to the Football League match crowd, the Reserves game against Roundel (in bad weather), attracted a probable record lowest attendance at the Intake. At the start of the game there were three spectators in the uncovered area, with just a handful in the Stand; after perpetual rain the unprotected trio left at half-time! But the Rovers were not the only Club who could not attract good attendances, for the fixture at Barnsley on April the 5th - which was expected to produce a good gate - saw a gathering of only around 1,000, with barely 100 Doncaster fans making the short trip.

The 1902/03 season became another financial struggle, not helped by a poor start, and in October there was less than 2,000 present when Burton United were the visitors, and only 2,500 for Glossop's appearance. Despite the financial restraints a significant Ground improvement was made on the town side. A new, 1,000 capacity covered seated Stand, complete with glazed ends (for better viewing), was built by Messrs. Mullins and Richardson. This new addition was formally opened for the Stockport County match on November the 8th. But the weather put a damper on the proceedings, and with heavy rain just before the match, only a small number attended. The generally poor run of results continued, although the visit by Aston Villa in December boosted the crowd to around 3,000. The Rovers finished third from bottom, and somewhat unfairly failed in their re-election bid. But they bounced back after just one season's absence. The Club's second appearance lasted for just one year, before a pathetic record (just eight points) saw them cast out once again. It was to be some years before they were to grace the Football League again, and then only after two Ground moves.

This second venture into the Football League became a financial struggle once again, although despite such poor results (just one win and two draws by the start of 1906), the attendances were quite reasonable - by Doncaster's standards. Nearly 2,000 for Liverpool's visit (there were 14,000 at Anfield for the return fixture), and 3,000 when they entertained Bradford City over Easter. The last Football League match at the Intake Ground was played on Easter Monday, when Grimsby were the winners by two goals, before a crowd of 2,000.

The 1905/06 season saw the Rovers back once again in the Midland League, and with a deficit of £60 carried over. Season tickets at this time cost 7/6d. (37p) in the Stand, 25p elsewhere, and half the latter price for Juniors. The next decade was a generally lean period, and by the outbreak of the War, the poor crowds were mostly made up of servicemen. In 1914 the Club were reformed, but the cash problems continued, and in early December 1915, the Club was suspended for three weeks following a dispute over a Player's wages. At the end of the season, and in common with most non-League teams, the Club had little option but to suspend operations until the end of the War. During the war years the Intake Ground was used as a depot for the Army.

By 1912 the Ground had been developed to a fair standard. Along the Town side there stood the main Grandstand, and opposite a narrow covered, and possibly seated, enclosure - which was referred to as the 'chicken coop'. Alongside this enclosure there were two press boxes, and the dressing rooms at the far (North-east) end. Behind both goals there was just flat standing, with wooden duckboards (to protect the feet from the muddy ground) around the ropes to the perimeter of the pitch. The main, and possibly only entrance to the Ground was off Town Moor Avenue. A walk across the adjacent field led to a turnstile enclosure at the South-east corner. The Structures to the Ground were of a temporary nature since they just 'sat' on the ground, without foundations. By the, just, pre-war period the rental charged to the Club was 14 guineas per year (£14-70p).

Team Group before the first match at Bennetthorpe - September 1920.
(Doncaster Gazette)

BENNETTHORPE.

On the 30th of April 1919, a meeting was held at the
Cleveland Cafe, when over 100 enthusiasts vowed to reform
the Club. Old debts of £150 remained, but with the
intended issue of 20,000 shares of 50p each in a new
Limited Company, these debts were soon discharged. It was
hoped to use the old Intake Ground since much of the
'old' Club's assets remained there, but legal problems
relating to the old and new Clubs prevented this course
of action. A number of possible venues were suggested
including Elmfield Park, Fishers Park, York Road and
Belle Vue. Eventually with the support of the Doncaster
Corporation, Belle Vue was chosen, and the Club given a
two year lease. However, this was not the site of the now
well known Ground (the title referred to the general
area), but a simple, large open field on the South side
of Bennetthorpe.

A practice match was played on the 14th of August 1919,
at which more than 3,000 spectators were present
(receipts of £70), and the fans were also entertained by
the Doncaster Subscription Band. But despite the
enthusiasm of the new Club, it was to be another year
before they were able to play competitive games, with
their election into the Midland League. Volunteers set
about preparing the Ground for League matches, and the
Club were given permission to erect enclosure fencing.
During the Club's short occupation it is probable that
the 'new' seated Stand was in reality that from the
Intake Ground. Season ticket prices were set at 25
shillings (£1.25) which included admission to the Stand,
and entrances were formed off Bennetthorpe and the lane
(which later became Wellbeck Road) which ran behind the
other side of the Ground.

All was ready for the first Midland League game on the 28th of August 1920. A 'vast crowd' were present to see the locals go down 1-2 to Rotherham Town. Despite a generally poor season, the crowds held up well, and for the first game of the 1921/22 season an attendance of 7,500 was present. The last Midland League game played at Bennetthorpe was against Nottingham Forest Reserves (a two goal defeat), and on the 11th of May 1922, the Rovers were beaten by Halifax Town by 2-4 in a Friendly game that became the last match at this shortlived Ground.

As the two year tenancy drew to an end, the Corporation offered the Club an undeveloped portion of Low Pasture, a piece of rough ground, but on a more permanent basis. With the Club more financially secure than ever before, over £4,000 was spent on preparing the Ground. The Bennetthorpe Stand was moved to the new venue, a new main Grandstand was built, and banking was created, to form what was considered would be the finest Ground in the new Third Division North. Unfortunately their application for a re-entry into the Football League received insufficient votes! But this disappointment was shortlived, for one year later their second bid was successful. The Club's new (third) Ground was formally opened by Charles Sutcliffe on the 22nd of August 1922, when, before a crowd of well over 8,000, Gainsborough Trinity were beaten by 1-0; the Ground soon became known simply as - Belle Vue.

TEMPORARY GROUNDS.
During two of the Club's periods in the Midland League, temporary venues were used. After the referee was attacked following a home defeat in early March 1893, the Club were ordered to play two matches at least seven miles from Doncaster. Mr Edwards of the Swan Hotel, Askern put a field at the Club's disposal, and the attendances of around three and four thousand represented the two highest crowds of the season! In April 1908 the crowd attacked the opposing Worksop team, after a visiting Player had kicked Jones of the Rovers; "in a most dangerous place"! The opening two matches of the 1908/09 season were ordered to be played outside of Doncaster, and the Park Road Ground of Conisborough St.Peter's was used.

THE GROUNDS TODAY.

The Intake Ground, named after this district of Doncaster, still exists as an open playing field (the division between the two areas behind the School having now gone) but the site of the Bennetthorpe Ground was developed soon after the Club's departure. The William Nuttall Cottages, built for local Spinsters, now cover the second home of the Rovers, with Bennetthorpe, Welbeck, Danum and Sandbeck Roads now forming the boundlaries.

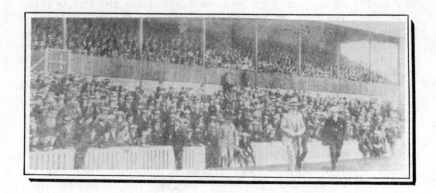

The opening game at Belle Vue – September 1922 – The Stand was moved from the Bennetthorpe Ground.
(Doncaster Gazette)

EVERTON

Like many towns and cities in England, winter sporting pursuits in Liverpool, were split between Rugby and Football. In the late 1870's it was the oval ball which had the greatest support, and the Everton Club was formed with this preference, by members of the St. Domingo Congregational Church, at the Queen's Head Hotel, Village Street in November 1879. Near to the Hotel was 'Ye Anciente Everton Toffee House'; an influence on both the Club's later name and nickname? But at the outset the Club was simply known as St.Domingo Football Club.

STANLEY PARK.

For the first four years the Club home Ground was the South-east corner of Stanley Park (which was first opened in 1870) in the Anfield District of the City; an unfenced expanse of grass with no facilities whatsoever. On matchdays, the Players would have to carry the goalposts from the Park Lodge in Mill Lane to the pitch. On the 23rd of December 1879, St.Peters were soundly beaten by six unopposed goals, in St.Domingo's first match. One year after their formation the Club changed their name to Everton and although the Club's early fixtures were of a minor nature, and attracted no more than a handful of spectators, it was not long before the first of many battles with their main protagonists, Bootle, was fought. The two became the leading Clubs in Liverpool, both vying for the local football support in the rugby-dominated City.

PRIORY ROAD GROUND.

Everton joined the Lancashire F.A. for the 1880/81 season, and one year later their status had risen to such an extent that they entertained Bolton Wanderers in their first game - a 1-13 defeat! A meeting was held at the Sandon Hotel in March 1882, at which a Mr. Cruitt offered a fenced and gated field off of Priory Road for the Club's use as a home Ground. By now crowds of upto 2,000 were common for many of the Club matches in the open Stanley Park. Everton moved to the Priory Road Ground in the Autumn of 1883, with the first fixture being a representative match between the Liverpool and Walsall District teams. Six goals were equally shared, and the match receipts amounted to thirteen shillings (65p).

Facilities at the Ground were very limited with just a shed' as a changing room and a small Stand for Club Officials. A newspaper writer of the day described these facilities as: "There was some sitting area, with a not very Grand Stand, and a not very grand dressing room for the Players"! There is no obvious evidence of the exact location of this Ground, but a very likely field was a 'T' shaped plot on the West side of Priory Road now covered principally by Clovelly and Douglas Roads. Everton won the Liverpool Cup in January 1884, and their increasing popularity led to their early withdrawal from the Priory Road Ground. Mr.Cruitt became increasingly annoyed by the noise and exuberance displayed by the supporters, and the Club were forced to seek pastures new!

ANFIELD.

Mr.Houlding of the Sandon Hotel also held the tenancy on a field off Anfield Road which was owned by Orrell Brothers (Brewers) and was offered to, and gratefully accepted, by the Club. Initially the Hotel was used not only as a headquarters for the Club but changing rooms were provided there for the teams. Hoardings were quickly erected around the field, railings installed around the pitch, and an open seated Stand was built on the Anfield Road side. The first match at Anfield took place on the 28th of September 1884, and a resounding 5-0 victory was achieved over the visiting Earlestown team. By the end of the season the total gate receipts had leapt up to £200 as compared with the Priory Road total of £45.

By now Everton were edging ahead of their keen rivals Bootle, but matches between the two were still a major attraction and a cup-tie at Anfield produced a gate of £39. These figures however, were dwarfed within four years, when the total receipts of the 1888/89 season reached a staggering £5,188. It came as no surprise that as the Club's growth and success continued, so did the rent at Anfield, from £100 in 1888 to £250 two years later. The Club's first F.A.Cup match was played at Anfield in 1886 when an excellent game resulted in a one goal win by the Rangers team from Glasgow. On the 8th of September 1888, the Club, who had been elected as founder-members, staged their first Football League match. Accrington were the visitors for this historic occasion, and the homesters celebrated with a 2-1 victory which was seen by a crowd of 9,000.

The years income of £5,188 had risen by three years later
to £8,624 (including gate takings of £5,748 and programme
sales,a modest £68).

By now Anfield had been developed into one of the best
Football Grounds in the Country. In addition to the deep
elevated and open Stand on the North-east side another
had been added, although narrower, at the other end. On
the South-east side a slim but full length 'pavilion'
(probably a covered and seated Stand) had been built with
a similar structure - but only half pitch length - on the
other side.

The team ended as runners-up in the League during the
1889/90 season, and one year later topped this with the
Championship. The support for the Club continued to grow,
leaving the hapless Bootle Club out in the cold. Even so
there was still an incredible interest taken when the two
Clubs met - on Boxing Day 1889, the Hawthorn Road Ground
of Bootle was jammed solid with a record crowd of 20,000
for a Friendly match visit from their near neighbours.

During the 1891/92 season, niggling disagreements over
the previous few years between Everton and the Club
President, Houlding came to the boil. For some time
arguments had continued between the two over the ever
increasing rent that was charged for the Anfield Ground.
Houlding was also the owner of the Sandon Hotel - the
headquarters of the Club - and had the concession rights
for refreshments at the Ground. He had also - at a high
interest rate - loaned the Club money. A large majority
of the Club members considered that Houlding's interests
were channeled more towards himself rather than the Club!
An irreversible spilt in the Club formed, with Everton
F.C. moving to pastures new, whilst Houlding - virtually
alone - formed Liverpool F.C. who were to occupy the now
empty Anfield Ground.

As early as 1889, the Club Committee were considering
moving from Anfield to a new site, although they were
also reluctant to leave all of the fixtures and fittings
that had been installed under the Everton name. The
continual bickering over the rent led to the Club
offering £180 for the 1890/91 season, to which they
received no reply, as Houlding distanced himself further
from them. The Club Committee eventually decided upon a
barren plot of land on the other side of Stanley Park,
and after forming the Club into a Limited Company, they

purchased the site for the not inconsiderable sum of £8,090. This Ground, Goodison Park, was soon transformed into arguably the best Football enclosure in the Country.

1893 Map. Showing the Everton Ground at Anfield, with the possible location within plot '359' of the Priory Road Ground. The Stanley Park pitch was probably within '353'. Note the Standon Hotel on the corner of Houlding Street, (Ordnance Survey)

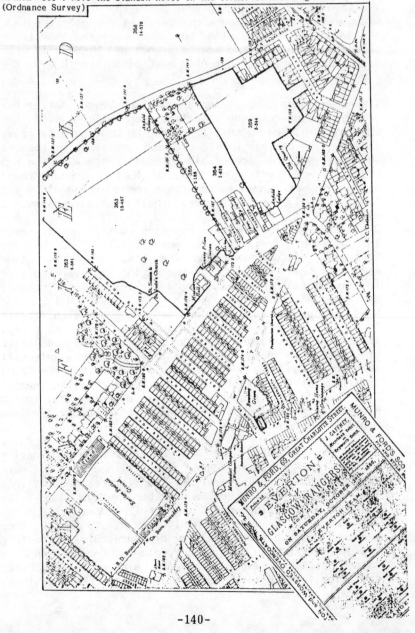

FULHAM

Although one of the earlier of Southern Clubs that eventually aspired to Football League status, Fulham, were around for fifteen years and just one of the many London teams that played at a minor level on a succession of undeveloped Grounds. For this reason the accurate tracing of their Grounds becomes particularly difficult!

STAR ROAD AND THE RANELAGH CLUB.

The Club were founded as St.Andrews Fulham in 1879, and as suggested by their title were strongly influenced by Church connections. In this case it was St.Andrews, but in West Kensington rather than Fulham itself. They started playing on a patch of land in Star Road near, Earls Court, and close to the Queen's Club which was later to become an International Football venue. At this time the area abounded in fields, but by the late 19th century had been developed and built on. Some idea of the quality of the playing surface can be judged by it's nickname. the 'Mud Pond'! The playing area was small measuring only 85 by 65 yards. Within a short time a move was made to the Ranelagh Club off Fulham High Street, a mile or so South of Star Road. For changing, the players used a room at the nearby Eight Bells Public House. Once again the stay was for a limited period, during which time they dropped the 'Fulham' from their Club name, and when the Ranelagh Club moved, the Football team had to seek a new venue. This Ground was close to the Hurlingham Club Grounds (now Hurlingham Park) and quite probably on the site which now contains Ranelagh Gardens and Avenue.

LILLIE ROAD AND OTHERS.

A short trek up North was made to Lillie Road, Fulham Cross, close to the earlier venue in Star Road. Once again it is doubtful if the exact location of this 'Ground' can be confirmed, but it may well have been the site of the current Lillie School (at the Dawes Road junction); the whole area is now submerged into suburbia. In any event for around two years, until 1884, the team became wanderers. Eel Brook Common was also used, a large, flat and grassed area which has probably changed little over the intervening century. Putney Lower Common and Pursers Cross off of Parsons Green Lane, were also known to be used during this brief interval.

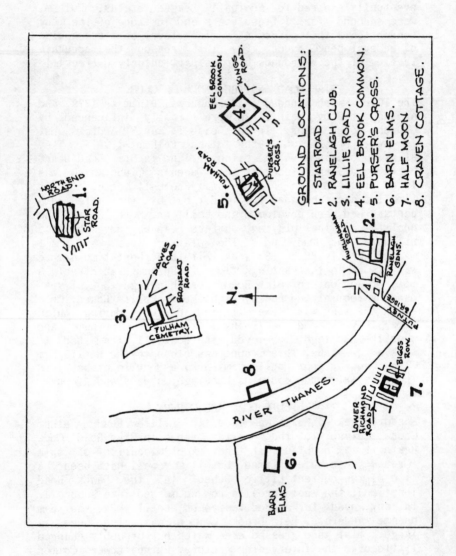

GROUND LOCATIONS:

1. STAR ROAD.
2. RANELAGH CLUB.
3. LILLIE ROAD.
4. EEL BROOK COMMON.
5. PURSER'S CROSS.
6. BARN ELMS.
7. HALF MOON.
8. CRAVEN COTTAGE.

Poskell's and Standfeld's Field were referred to a well,
but these may well have been alternative names for two of
the aforementioned Grounds. Needless to say they were all
unenclosed, but Pursers Cross was imortalised with a
road, which still exists, of the same name.

BARN ELMS.

The move this time took the Club to South of the River,
where they met up with the Ranelagh Club once again, who
were by now occupying the large open sports area of Barn
Elms. It is probable that the Club's matches were played
on the oval shaped sports pitch which existed to the East
of the Golf Course and the Pond. The services of the Red
Lion Public House were used for Dressing rooms. This
Ground was close to the River and coincidentally opposite
the later Craven Cottage Ground. Barn Elms remains as an
open and undeveloped area, with the Ranelagh Club still
maintaining a presence there.

THE HALF MOON GROUND.

After yet another brief stay, the penultimate change was
made for the 1889/90 season. On this occasion it was to
an established Ground, and although enclosed it was
probably still lacking in facilities. The Club remained
South of the Thames, and near to Putney Bridge, at the
Half Moon Cricket Ground which was shared with the Wasps
Rugby Club. This Ground was located adjacent to Biggs Row
and off of Lower Richmond Road, and was large enough to
contain two pitches. By now the Club had risen
sufficiently in stature and had an enclosure where it was
possible to receive paying customers (at threepence per
head). Support could often be counted in the hundreds. So
called 'Top hat and bonnet' matches were played on Easter
Mondays, which were Charity games. In 1890 the Club
became plain 'Fulham F.C.', and their name change was
celebrated with their winning of the West London Observer
Football Challenge Cup.

The Club played at this venue for four years, but when
the Ground was closed in 1894 - for development - Fulham
F.C. were forced into yet another move. But by now they
had become an established Senior Club, and moved to
Craven Cottage, which was named after the original house
that had stood on the site until it was destroyed by fire
in 1888. The former Wasps Rugby Ground has since been
redeveloped and a four storey block of Flats now occupies
the site.

GRIMSBY TOWN

Team group of the first (1878/79) season, for one year known as 'Grimsby Pelham'

Although the Club has always been 'Grimsby', they started, and currently play, within the adjacent town of Cleethorpes! The Club were formed from within the Worsley Cricket Club, following a meeting that was held at the Wellington Arms in Freeman Street, on the 20th of September 1878. The name of 'Grimsby Pelham' was initially adopted, but the suffix was changed to 'Town' just one year later.

THE FIRST CLEE PARK.

Local opponents at this time were few and far between, the only other teams in the town were the Wanderers and White Star, and coupled with a severe Winter, the 1878/79 season consisted of just two matches! Both were against Brigg Brittania, which resulted in two defeats - by the only two goals of the game in the first (away) fixture, and by 1-4 at home. Home, was at Clee Park, within a large field that lay between the sea and Grimsby Road. The football pitch was in the South-east corner, and this site is now crossed by Daubney and Barcroft Streets. Initially facilities were non-existant, but the Ground was presumably at least enclosed, for gate money was taken during the first season, when 6/9d (34p) was taken - for just the single match! Whilst this form of income was almost negligible, after one year of existance the Club had a capital of nearly £4; no doubt the near total inactivity meant few outgoings, whilst the members subscriptions formed the bulk of these assets!

THE SECOND CLEE PARK.

For the 1878/79 season the Club moved, but only to the smaller and adjacent field, which is now crossed by Lovett Street. Since this was also referred to as Clee Park, one can assume that this name referred to the general local area. But the new venue was only shortlived, for in 1880 the Town moved back to their former field - which became known as Clee Park Gardens - after they secured a lease on it at an initial annual rental of ten shillings (50p). Facilities were still non-existant, and it was not until the 1882/83 season that dressing rooms for the teams were provided, which consisted of two bathing vans borrowed from the nearby beach! This facility for the Players was later improved when a nearby 'Dancing Saloon' was utilised. But it was not long before the Club provided suitable accommodation for spectators, and after an advance from Henry Smethurst, a Stand was built which held around 500 spectators. As the Club progressed, so were the facilities at Clee Park improved, and by the mid 1880's a second Stand was erected at the Ground. The 1883/84 season produced gate receipts of £154, and a profit on the year of £16. At this time a season ticket to the Ground cost five shillings (25p) and half as much again for the Stand. Within a few years the gate receipts had risen to over £600 in a season, but attendances approaching the 6,000 for Lincoln's F.A.Cup visit during the 1884/85 season - which realised record receipts of £180 - were rare. Attendances at Clee Park Gardens varied quite dramatically, dependant on the quality of the opposition, but were generally around 1,000.

Along with a number of other Clubs of the period, the Town experimented with Floodlit matches, and two such games were played in April 1889. 'Wells Lights' were used, from eight pylons spaced around the Ground. At the foot of each pylon, tar was pumped from a barrel and under pressure converted into a gas light. On the 9th of April, Rotherham were beaten by eight unopposed goals, and one week later Boston succombed to a 5-1 defeat.

In the pre-League days, the Club depended on Friendly matches, but the 1882/83 season saw their first entry into the F.A.Cup. Their initial match would have been a daunting prospect since they were drawn at home to the redoubtable Queens Park, but the Scots refused to travel to Lincolnshire, and so the Town received a bye.

In the 2nd round they were thrashed by Phoenix Bessemer
(a Rotherham Works side) with a 1-9 scoreline. Two years
later they reached the 4th round, but on this occasion
were beaten by Old Carthusians, by three unopposed goals.
Most of the Clubs opponents consisted of local Clubs, and
on the 13th of March 1886, they reached the semi-final of
the Lincolnshire Cup. The opponents on the day were
Lincoln City, and a record attendance of over 5,000 was
attracted to the game at Clee Park. After 90 minutes the
score stood at 1-1, and after the visitors refused to
play extra time, the match was abandoned by the Referee.
Grimsby were not willing to replay the match, and since
they were judged to be blameless, the game was awarded to
them; they went on to win the Cup, for the first time in
their history. The Club entered the Combination in the
1888/89 season, a League in which many fixtures were not
completed. Attendances during the season generally varied
between 800 and 1,500, with the top League crowd of 4,000
for a match versus Gainsborough. The visit of Preston
North End in the F.A.Cup that season provided the Clee
Park enclosure with it's record crowd of 8,000. The
cancelled League matches took their toll for a loss of
£240 on the season was realised.

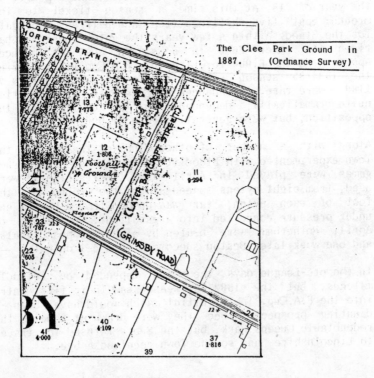

The Clee Park Ground in
1887.   (Ordnance Survey)

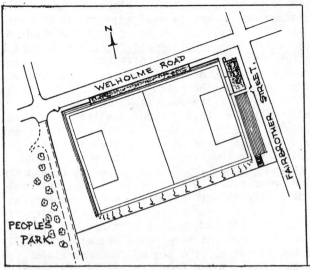

Probable layout of the Abbey Park Ground (based on written information). The East end had covered and uncovered Stands, a covered Stand on the North side banking on the South, and the Dressing rooms in the South-east corner. (Dave Twydell)

ABBEY PARK.

The end of the 1888/89 season saw the expiration of the Clee Park lease, and after a detailed search for a suitable venue, a move was made to a more centralised Ground that became known as Abbey Park. The Right Honorable E.Heneage M.P. offered the site which was readily accepted by the Club. The cost of moving the Stands and preparing the new Ground amounted to around £300, and on the 30th of August 1889, the first match was played there when West Bromwich Albion were surprisingly, and easily, beaten by 6-1 in a Friendly encounter. The Railway Servants Brass Band provided the pre-match entertainment for the 3,000 crowd that was present. The Town joined the Football Alliance as founder-members, and in their first match beat Newton Heath by 3-1, at Abbey Park. Attendances varied quite dramatically during these pre-Football League days, from around 500 for Bootle's visit during the 1890/91 season to a few of 4,000; generally the crowds numbered around 2,000, and gate receipts were normally around £60 per match.

The Ground, so named due to its situation near the site of a former Abbey, was located adjacent to People's Park (which still exists), and South of Welholme Road; now in Grimsby rather than Cleethorpes! The original surface for the pitch was reasonable, although one half had to be relaid. Simons the Contractors undertook the removal and building work plus the pitch drainage which consisted of land drains at 10 metre centres across the pitch - quite an innovation for this period! The 114 by 74 yard pitch was somewhat bigger than the Clee Park enclosure and was enclosed with a wire rope supported by timber posts at three yards from the touchlines. The main, seated Stand, was erected along the Welholme Road side, and the main entrance, complete with folding doors, was at the East end (off Fairbrother Street), where entry cost 5p. A second entry point was off Welholme Road, which provided access to the Park end, and at a charge of 2½p. To the left of the main entrance there was a 800 capacity open Stand, and to the right a seated, covered Stand for 300 (that had been moved from Clee Park). This was divided into two (reserved and unreserved sections). Season tickets (for the Reserved section), cost one guinea (£1-05). Opposite the Main Stand (on the South side), a large embankment was created. The Reporter from the 'Eastern Daily Telegraph' was well catered for, since a Press Box was built in the North-east corner of the Ground.

There were two 14 foot square dressing rooms in the South-east corner, and wood gratings ('duckboards') were laid all round the flat areas adjacent to the pitch. The capacity of Abbey Park was only approximately 10,000, but it was recognised as one of the neatest and well developed Grounds of the period.

By now the Club could field a powerful team, and they became members of the Football League Division Two in its first season of 1892/93. To generate capital the Town became a Limited Company since large crowds had always been a rare sight (for additional revenue, Baseball matches were considered in 1889). Although the Town immediately became one of the leading Clubs in the Division, promotion eluded them for a number of years, but a notable run of home matches saw them undefeated for over two years. At last bigger crowds became more frequent, generally between two and three thousand, in the inaugural Football League season.

By the 1894/95 season the average had risen to nearer
4,000 (the Leicester Fosse visit attracted 5,000) and
similar figures were repeated in the next campaign, with
the best League assembly on the 28th of April of 6,000
for Woolwich Arsenal's visit; the visit of West Bromwich
Albion on the 15th of February 1896 in the second round
of the F.A.Cup produced a new Ground record of 7,500. The
Club's strong challenge for promotion was repeated during
the 1896/97 season (when they again finished in third
place), and Arsenal (again) and Newcastle attracted
record gates of 10,000 at each game - the average
attendance was around 5,000. A similar five figure
attendance was present for the F.A.Cup game against
Bolton Wanderers.

(Top and Bottom): c.1898 action at Abbey Park.
(Grimsby Central Library)

The 1897/98 season produced only a final mid-table placing, and the fickle fans ensured that the average gate dropped drastically to no more than 3,000, with a pitiful low of 700 for Loughborough's visit, and a high of 5,000 for the local derby with Lincoln City. A slight boost in performances the following year raised the average to around the 4,000 mark.

In 1896, the seven year lease on Abbey Park ran out, and although the Landlord - Edward Heneage - consented to a three year extension, when this expired it became necessary for the Club to move again. Mr Heneage complained of the bad behaviour of some of the Players, although since the site was very soon to be developed for housing, this may well have just been a convenient excuse for not allowing the Club further time on the site! The last Football League match at Abbey Park was a memorable encounter, for Darwen were thrashed 9-2, and this became the Town's all-time record League victory, but was seen by only 2,500 fans.

The former Ground is now covered by the houses of Welholme Road (South side), Legsby Avenue, and the West side of Fairbrother Street.

Once again all the fixtures and fittings had to moved, and after dismantling the Stands, they were moved and re-erected back in Cleethorpes, just a few hundred yards East of the Club's original Clee Park Ground. The two Stands were rebuilt on the South side and behind the East end goal. On the 2nd of September 1899, Blundell Park was opened when six goals were shared with Luton Town, before an attendance of 4,000.

The Stand taken from Abbey Park, and re-erected at the Cleethorpes end of the Blundell Park Ground.

HALIFAX TOWN

The first 'serious' Association Football Club was formed in the town in September 1894, following a meeting at the Black Swan Hotel. A Field was first used as a Ground at the end of Pickles Lane (now Gibraltar Road), but after one year the Pheasant Ground at Pellon was considered more suitable. However, following talks with the Rugby Club, an amalgamation took place between the two ball sports, and apart from a few games at the Pheasant, other games were played at Thrum Hall. Within a short period of time, and with another occasional alternative Ground at Newstead, the Rugby men increasingly opposed their 'round ball' enthusiasts until the latter game was dropped altogether. After this short but serious attempt at popularising Football in the town, it was not until 1910 that another, and more successful attempt was made.

SANDHALL GROUND.

On the 26th of February 1910, the Halifax Football Association took out a lease on a field at the Sandhall side (West) of the town where Official and representative matches were played. But after the formation of Halifax Town F.C. in May 1911 (following a meeting at the Saddle Hotel) the field was leased to this new town Club. With a healthy capital of £1,250, and as a Limited Company with professional players, they were elected into the Yorkshire Combination and finished the first (1911/12) season in a modest 7th position out of 14 teams. Their first match was played at Bradford's Valley Parade, against the Reserve X1 of the City team, which was lost, but this did not deter 2,000 fans turning up for the first home match, versus Scarborough. It was no dream start for this contest ended as a one goal defeat.

Already the Club were ambitious enough to enter for the F.A.Cup for the next season, and met with reasonable success. After beating South Kirby Colliery in their first match (at home) on the 16th of November - at one stage they were 1-3 down but fought back to triumph by 6-3, they then overcame Nelson after a drawn match. Queens Park Rangers were the next opponents, but despite being drawn at home, the Club agreed to reverse the tie for £200, but put up a creditable performance in London, going down by 2-4 in front of a 10,000 crowd; the match receipts amounted to only £263!

By now the Club was playing in the Midland League, and this better class of football was found to be a strong challenge for in the three seasons leading up to the war, a mid-table placing was the best that they could achieve.

Although it was only used for a few years, the Sandhall Ground was turned into quite a reasonable venue. It was located off of Sandhall Lane (quite close to Thrum Hall), and bounded by the current Bob Lane. It took just one week for the venue to be 'put in order', which included the enlarging of the pitch. On the Sandhall Lane side there was a narrow Stand at one end that stretched for about half the pitch length, and a small open Stand alongside.

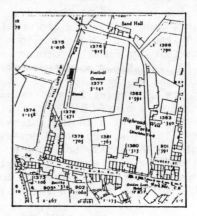

Map of 1919. By then the Ground had in fact been demolished. (Ordnance Survey)

c.1913 Photograph taken at the corner of Bob Lane and Gibbet Street. The Sandhall Ground was to the left of the lane at the top of the picture. Note the remains of a match poster advertising a match versus Gainsborough Trinity.

This latter Stand was the first to be built, and was erected by H. Bancroft & Sons (Joiners), and after gaining permission from the Halifax Corporation it was erected in two weeks and within a month of the Club's initial occupation. Constructed of timber, it contained 13 tiers of seats with a total capacity of 500.

The centre portion was sectioned off for the Directors, but there was no cover - and it remained so. The other three sides were variable width, flat standing, areas and the entrance was probably only off the Sandhall Lane side, where there was a single turnstile. Almost as soon as the Ground was vacated by the Club the site became built upon and formed the Asquith's Munitions Factory, and nothing now remains of this shortlived enclosure.

EXLEY GROUND.

After the hostilities had ended, the Club was reformed in June 1919, following another meeting at the Saddle Hotel. Notable at this meeting were several pre-war Players. The Directors managed to secure a lease at the Exley Ground, the former home of Salterhebble Rugby Club. Due it's lack of facilities, and it being somewhat remote from the town centre, this was considered as only a temporary measure. They would have preferred to have used the Cricket Ground at Thrum Hall on a more permanent basis, but the suggestion brought predictable objections from the nearby Rugby Club members! Two other possible sites were Spring Hall, which did not materialise, and part of the Shay Estate, which was soon to become the Club's permanent home. The Exley Ground which was located to the South of the junction of Exley Gardens and Park Lane - and nearly opposite the now departed Zoological Gardens - probably had very few facilities, although there were some shallow embankments. Although being in such an undeveloped area, these comforts may very well have followed in the course of time should the Club's stay have been longer. As well as being some distance from the town, it was also high up on a hill which no doubt caused problems with transport to the Ground. £500 was spent on the minimum of requirements for the Club to stage Midland League matches.

The 'new' Club got off to an unfortunate start when a Player had his leg broken in the pre-season trial game! Back in the Midland League once more, the Town's first match was lost by three unopposed goals at Mexboro' before a 3,000 crowd.

One week later, on the 13th of September 1919, Scunthorpe United were the first visitors to Exley and they were beaten by 4-1. Despite two largely uneventful seasons, the Club were somewhat fortunately elected to the new Third Division North, as founder-members in 1921. The only real notable events were a loss of £300 on the first season, which led to a Public meeting in July 1920, and the use of 56 Players during that campaign! The last Midland League match at the Ground was versus Sheffield Wednesday Reserves on the 23rd of April 1921. The last match at Exley was a prestigious West Riding Cup semi-final versus Bradford F.C. on the 9th of May. Not only was this game won (by the only goal), but the record attendance was also set at this venue when approximately 4,000 fans paid £139.

With the original objections removed regarding the erection of hoardings on the Shay Estate, the Club were able to move to this more conveniently located, but largely undeveloped Ground for their first Football League match. The Exley Ground remains as an open field.

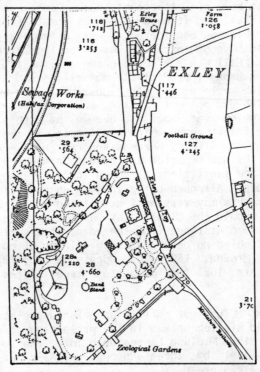

The Exley Ground in 1919.
(Ordnance Survey)

-154-

HULL CITY

Hull City belong to a very small band of Clubs that have moved to a new Ground since the second World War. Their previous venue was reasonably well developed, but previous to this they mingled closely with the teams of two other sports.

Although founded a year or so earlier, it wasn't until 1904 that the Club first took part in matches. There had been another 'Hull City', an amateur Club, that attempted to make it's Association mark in this Rugby stronghold, and until 1903 played at Dairycotes, a venue that was occasionally used by the later - but non-related 'City'.

The 'Threepenny' Stand at the Boulevard Ground, little changed from the turn of the century days. Still the permanent home of Hull R.F.C.   (Dave Twydell)

BOULEVARD GROUND.

The Club first took to the field during the 1904/05 season, when Friendly matches were played. An arrangement was made whereby the Club made use of the Hull F.C. (Rugby) Boulevard Ground, at a rental of £100 per annum. The Boulevard Ground, located to the West of the town centre - off Division Road - was originally (from the late 19th Century) known as the Hull Athletic Ground, and in keeping with this title consisted of an elongated oval shape.

On the North-east side, a covered Grandstand of about 50 metres long provided spectators with seating, with the only other facilities consisting of a refreshment room and dressing rooms - at the northern end. By the early 20th Century, a cycle track had been added as well as open seated stands - alongside the Grandstand and around the Northern curved end. Further cover was also built along the South-west side. After the short stay at the Boulevard by Hull City, the Ground was drastically reshaped to form a rectangular enclosure, and although over the years the Grandstand side has been improved, the opposite accommodation still retains the quaint 'threepenny stand'. This remnant of a byegone era consists of a narrow and steep wooden terrace of seating with a corrugated iron roof.

The football Club's first game on the 1st of September, resulted in four goals shared with Notts. County, followed nine days later when Everton Reserves were beaten in another home fixture. The only really competitive matches in this inaugural season were in the F.A.Cup, but it was a shortlived experience. With the Rugby Club having preference for their fixtures, the venue for the preliminary round game had to be 'reversed' and was played at the opposition, Stockton's Ground. A 1-1 draw resulted, followed by a 1-4 defeat in the replay - which was also at Stockton.

For the 18th of March fixture with Scarborough (a resounding six goal win) alternative accommodation had to be sought as the host Club had been drawn to play at home in the Rugby League Cup. On this occasion the undeveloped Dairycoates ground (now built over) was used. One week later the venue had to be changed also, for following crowd trouble during the Hull R.F.C. and Hunslet cup-tie, the use of the Boulevard was suspended! On this occasion, the Anlaby Road Cricket Ground was used, when a scoreless draw with Manchester City was played.

Despite only Friendly matches, 29 home games were played, and the season was considered successful, so much so that the Club turned professional and applied for entry into the Football League. After just a year of playing, the Club hardly had a 'pedigree', but sporting politics took a hand, which provided the Club with a rapid rise in status. Hull was very much a Rugby dominated town (with two senior Clubs), and the Football League ever anxious to spread the Soccer gospel, ensured that the City's application was successful. An extension of the Football

League admittedly ensured that all the Clubs applying for election were accepted, although the hapless Doncaster Rovers (Second Division tail-enders) were voted out. While Hull City could have been considered fortunate, Chelsea were no less so, since they only had a Ground, but no team or previous match experience!

CIRCLE CRICKET GROUND.

The intention was to continue the shared arrangement with Hull R.F.C., then a bombshell was dropped when the Rugby authorities, jealously guarding their own interests, ordered that no paid admission could be taken at the Boulevard for the City games. Such a situation was clearly impossible for the now professional Football League Club, and alternative arrangements had to be rapidly made. Fortunately a reasonable alternative was found, and less than a half a mile away, at the Circle Cricket Ground that was located just off of Anlaby Road. As Cricket Grounds go, this was a relatively modern one, and had only been developed around the turn of the Century. It was aptly named, for the playing area was literally circular - ideal perhaps for cricket, but somewhat remote for many football spectators on the boundaries. The Club had already experienced playing at the Ground, but now as a fully fledged Football League team, there was a woeful lack of spectator facilities. Before the 1905/06 season had started, the City Club made it known of their intentions to find a more permanent home venue, but in the interim steps were taken to improve the Cricket Ground. A new covered Stand was erected adjacent to the Pavilion, together with a portable Stand - to accommodate 1,000.

On the 2nd of September all was ready for the Club's opening game in Hull. The fixture attracted between seven and eight thousand spectators, who were kept waiting due to the late arrival of the visiting Barnsley team. In perfect weather, and after entertainment from the Band of Newland Orphanage, the match kicked off 15 minutes late. Early in the first half, the City took the lead through Spence, and to the continued delight of the locals, the homesters went on to record a 4-1 victory. The day was a resounding success from start to finish. One week later the City won by the only goal at fellow newcomers Clapton Orient - the Londoners first League match at the large, but very basic, Millfields Road Ground (attendance of 3,000), followed two days later when the Yorkshire team were the first Football League visitors to the Stamford

Bridge home of Chelsea. A unique trio of games - three new teams to the League, and three inaugural matches at each Ground. Between times, the Reserves appeared at Goole Town - and in doing so became the first visitors to that Ground!

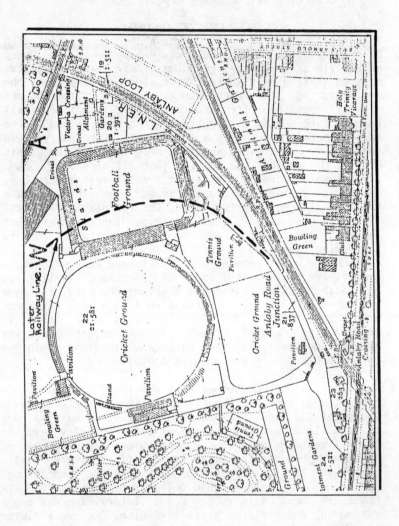

The map of 1911 shows the two principal former Grounds of the City, that lay side by side.
(Ordnance Survey)

Despite the promising start, the City came down to earth at Chelsea, when they were thrashed by 5-1 before a crowd of 5,000. This setback did not deter the fans, for the second match at Anlaby Road (two goals shared with Burnley) attracted another gate of over 7,000. However two weeks later there were barely 3,000 present for Burton United's visit, the poor weather no doubt discouraging many spectators.

On October the 7th Grimethorpe United were easily demolished by 8-1 in the first F.A.Cup round, but on another dismal day, the pouring rain attracted no more than 2,000 to Anlaby Road. Unable to postpone their home Football League with Manchester United on the 28th of October, it was left to the Reserves to travel to Denaby in the 2nd qualifying round match, were they won by 2-0. At this time the Manchester Club were the League leaders, and sensing a record gate - plus an apparent relaxation on the part of the Rugby Authorities - the game was played at the far more suitable Boulevard Ground. By half-time a crowd of some 10,000 paying gate receipts of £250 were present, both figures being records for the fledgeling Club. A one goal defeat somewhat quelled the enthusiasm of the locals.

On the 18th of November, and back at Anlaby Road, Leeds City were the next opponents in the F.A.Cup. An estimated crowd of 3,000 were present, however since the game was abandoned - scoreless - after 50 minutes, the thick fog made an accurate assessment of numbers somewhat impossible! The next Wednesday, the re-match finished 1-1 (attendance of 3,000), followed by a 2-1 success in the replay. As Christmas approached, Oldham Athletic came to Hull and were beaten 2-1 before a somewhat poor crowd of 4,000. By now the City had reached the 1st round proper - the Club received excemption to this round in subsequent years - but the end came on the 13th of January when they were beaten 1-0 at home by Reading, in front of 9,000. During the previous months, a permanent site had been settled on; an open area immediately adjoining the Cricket Ground, when a lease was agreed with the owners, North-Eastern Railway Company.

By mid-November work on the new Ground was moving at a great pace, and with turf laying finished in early December, it was confidently predicted that the opening game could be played at the new venue in the coming March. The last game played before the first at the new venue occurred on March the 10th when the City lost at home to Glossop. Surprisingly this match was staged once again at the Boulevard. In view of the local Press statement that... "Association Football is making big inroads into the Rugby stronghold...", it was indeed strange that the Rugby hierarchy allowed the game to be played there! On March the 24th, Blackpool shared four goals with Hull at the new Anlaby Road Ground, although the grass had hardly had time to bed itself down!

ANLABY ROAD.

The Anlaby Road Ground was immediately adjacent to the Circle, and most of the site had been - previous to the establishment of the Cricket Club - a separate fenced of, five acre field. It was an incredibly cramped enclosure, with two railway lines virtually enclosing the two ends of the Ground; one in fact almost clipped off the South easy corner of the pitch! To the West, at one point, the boundary of the Cricket field lay within ten metres of the rear of the main Stand. The only access to the Ground was from Anlaby Road, and along a narrow roadway which ran alongside one of the railway lines. At the time of the building of the Football Ground, the more or less triangular whole site contained also (in addition to the main Cricket Circle), two further small cricket fields, and a Bowling Green - all within little more than 21 acres.

July 1945, demolition of the main Stand at Anlaby Road.
(Hull and Yorkshire Times)

Within a few years the compact headquarters of Hull City F.C. was able to boast of a seated, half pitch length, Grandstand, and covered areas to the North extending around half of the East side. By the 1920's the soil embankments were concreted and the main Stand was replaced by a longer and wider structure. This new Stand seated approximately 4,000, and was a replacement for the original that was lost in a fire in 1911.

Over the years support for the Club remained at a fairly high level, with the team maintaining a generally mid-table placing in the Second Division. But relegation in 1930 produced a not surprising drop in gates - at least for three years - until they regained their lost higher status, only to descend once more in 1936. But it was to the F.A.Cup that the Club could look to for some exciting and well attended clashes. In the first full season at the new Ground, 21,795 saw only ten minutes of action in a replayed cup-tie versus Tottenham Hotspur - abandoned due to fog. One year later, 16,000 attended the Woolwich Arsenal game and in 1909 Chelsea drew an 18,000 crowd to Hull. Before the First World War, F.A.Cup ties produced attendances of between eleven and eighteen thousand.A run through to the fourth round in the 1920/21 season produced new record attendances; 26,000 (£2,700 receipts) to see the three goal defeat of Burnley and 27,000 for the scoreless draw with Preston North End. For the latter game, a huge crowd had already assembled by 1.00 p.m., who, at the final count paid £3,600 at the gate. Average (League) attendances at this period were around 8,000. The 1920's were the heyday for the Club, at least as far as the Premier Cup Competition was concerned, with crowds varying between thirteen and a new record of 28,603. This large crowd attended the Bolton Cup-tie on the 12th of January 1924.

The best run of all came ironically in the relegation season of 1929/30, when the team reached the Semi-final stage. The all time record attendance came at the sixth round stage on the 6th of March, when 32,930 fans packed into the enclosure - in midweek - to see their favourites score the only goal in this replayed game. With the general drop in the Club's abilities, which led to infrequent Cup successes, attendances were lower during the 1930's. Only 6,000 were present for the visit of non-League Scunthorpe in 1937, and a high during this era was reached with the earlier visit of Manchester City in 1933.

As early as 1930, with a view to a move, land was purchased one kilometre to the West of the Anlaby Road Ground. Such a move was to become necessary due to the proposed Railway Developments, by the owners – the Railway Company. Probably constricted due to lack of money (most of the years leading upto the Second World War were to be spent in the Second Division), coupled with the absence of the expected Railway improvements, progress was slow to say the least. By the time of the war hostilities in 1939, the Club were still playing at Anlaby Road! The Club closed down at the end of a poor 1940/41 season, and formally vacated the Anlaby Road Ground in August 1943. However play re-commenced for the 1944/45 season – back at the Boulevard (Rugby) Ground! The coming back into the fold was far from successful, and attendances were generally poor, only 4,000 for the Leeds United game as an example. The final Boulevard match resulted in a humiliating 2-8 defeat to Rotherham United on the 22nd of April.

There then followed a period when the Club's very existance was in doubt. The Directors were informed that the Rugby Ground would not be available to them again, and in the summer of 1945 permission to develop Boothferry Park, as it was to become known was refused. Although the War was coming to an end, there were still severe restrictions, and creating a new Football Ground was hardly likely to be given priority! The Club had no alternative to once again close down for the 1945/46 season, just when a near full compliment of League Clubs were able to play a near normal League programme. However, this enforced lay-off lasted just one year, and the Club were able to take their place once more in the Third Division North, but now operating from a brand new Ground.

The War took it's toll on the Anlaby Road Ground, and by
1947, much of the structures there had gone. Even so
post-War matches were played by the Third and Junior
teams of Hull City at the old Ground, and continued on
into the early 1960's. At this time the planned Railway
improvements were undertaken, some twenty years after
they had been proposed! These Developments were not as
comprehensive as might have been supposed, and although
little now remains of this former Football League Ground,
there is enough to make a visit well worthwhile. The
'Anlaby Loop' railway line (the one that nearly 'clipped'
off the corner), was re-routed to roughly bisect the
pitch, North to South. However, although the concrete
terracing has long since disappeared, distinct
embankments remain on three sides, and much of the wall
(plus traces of others) that retained the South terrace
is still intact. The side that contained the main Stand
has been levelled, and replaced with a bungalow and
garden for the Cricket Club Groundsman.

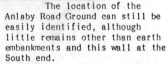

The location of the
Anlaby Road Ground can still be
easily identified, although
little remains other than earth
embankments and this wall at the
South end.

1989, from the nearby road
bridge. The Circle Cricket
Ground - behind the trees - and
on the extreme right the south
embankment of the former Anlaby
Road Ground.   (Dave Twydell)

IPSWICH TOWN

Football, of a sort, had been played in and around the
town for a number of years, notably by the pupils of
Ipswich School who, after their own version of the game,
adopted Association Football rules in 1874. Ipswich Town
F.C. were founded following a meeting at the Town Hall,
on the 16th of October 1878. But the Club did not start
their life under this name, for there was already an
'Ipswich F.C.' - the local Rugby Club - who came into
existance four years earlier. Therefore for clarity, the
new Club adopted the title of 'Ipswich Association F.C.'.

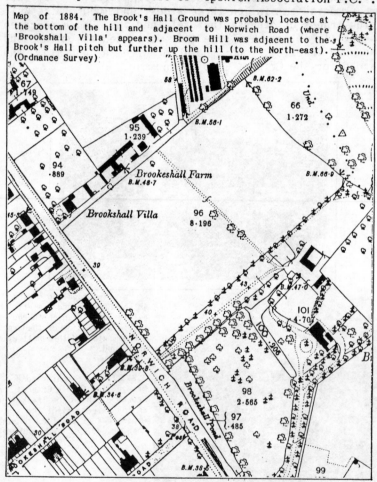

Map of 1884. The Brook's Hall Ground was probably located at
the bottom of the hill and adjacent to Norwich Road (where
'Brookshall Villa' appears). Broom Hill was adjacent to the
Brook's Hall pitch but further up the hill (to the North-east).
(Ordnance Survey)

BROOM HILL AND BROOKES HALL.

Founder-members of this 'town' team included a number of ex-Ipswich schoolboys, and it is apparent that there was a close association between the two bodies. As a home Ground, Broom Hill was chosen, and in view of the reference of it being 'the Club Ground', and the notable absence of any difficulty in finding a suitable pitch, this leads to the reasonable assumption that Broom Hill had already been used for football. Broom Hill is an area to the North of the town centre, and the Ground used by the Club was a large field, bounded by Norwich Road, and sandwiched between Brookes Hall and Brookeshall Farm. Early references to the Club's home matches refer to the Norwich Road side, and the various references in these formative years to 'Brook Hill' and 'Brookes Hall' Grounds, suggest that the two were adjacent to each other, one close to Norwich Road and the second, further up the hill. There is no doubt that these Grounds were not enclosed, and facilties were limited to a crude shed for Dressing Rooms.

The Club's first match consisted of an encounter between 'The Secretary's Team' and 'The Club', when four goals were shared. On the 2nd of November the Club staged their first competitive fixture when Stoke Wanderers were easily beaten by six goals to one. One month later Floodlit football came to the town when Ipswich F.C. challenged United Suffolk, and beat them 5-3 in a mixed rules game. Several Association Players took part in this 13-a-side game. The two prominent Football Clubs in the town, one playing to Rugby rules and the other keeping to the Association code, maintained a careful harmonious relationship but in 1888, their paths were to merge with Portman Road as the focal point.

Floodlight Football comes to Ipswich - in 1878! (East Anglian Daily Times)

Programme from 1887, one of the earliest matches played at Portman Road.

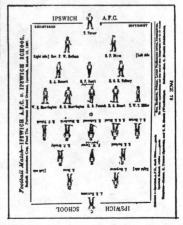

-165-

The 1878/79 season finished with twelve games played and only three were lost. One year later the record was even better for in seventeen games there was only one defeat. At the A.G.M. in September 1881, it was agreed that new dressing Rooms were required at Broom Hill, to replace the basic hut that had sufficed up to that time. These arrangements - an outhouse with water provided from an outside pump - were transferred to the nearby Inkerman Public House (which was and still is located at the junction of Chevallier Street and Norwich Road). Although according to a Football Book of 1881, The Crown and Anchor also provided Dressing-room facilities for an unstated period.

The Club's expenditure was covered by five shilling (25p) subscriptions from the members, for as true amateurs, the taking of gate money at this time was unheard of! However this attitude changed in the 1883/84 season when a match versus The Pilgrims (from London), was played at Portman Road. Entrance charges raised over £10, and the match produced a healthy profit. Although the Broom Hill Ground was still the Club's home, and was also the venue for most Suffolk County matches, it was recognised that the Portman Road enclosure - the joint home of Ipswich F.C. and the East Suffolk Cricket Club - offered not only better facilities, but also a superior pitch; it was flat, whereas at Broom Hill there was a pronounced slope.

As interest in Rugby declined in the town, and Football came to more prominence, the use of Portman Road by the Association Club increased. On the 20th of March 1886, the Ground was used as a venue for the final of the Suffolk Challenge Cup, when the largest football crowd ever in the County, assembled to watch a 2-2 draw between Ipswich Association and Woodbridge. The town side eventually lost the second replayed game. One year later there was an attendance of over 1,000 at Portman Road for the Final tie in the same Competition, and on this occasion the Association Club recorded a 3-1 victory over their old foes, Ipswich School.

The 1887/88 season became the last at Broom Hill, and on the 18th of February 1888 the last game was played there, and won, when Framlingham College were overwhelmed with a 7-0 scoreline. During the Summer serious talks were held with the Rugby Club regarding an amalgamation of the two bodies, and on the 1st of October this suggestion became a reality. At last the superior and more centrally located Portman Road Ground was to become the home venue for the newly named 'Ipswich Town F.C.' However, the football pitch at this time was located behind the current Ground, the site of the current training area. The Broom Hill and Brookeshall pitches were built on, and became residential areas early in the Twentieth century.

The flat area behind the modern West Stand was the playing field of the original Portman Road Ground.   (Dave Twydell)

LEICESTER CITY

In Leicester, as in many other towns, Rugby dominated the
Winter sporting scene during the late 19th century. But
Football was not without it's followers, and there were
several minor teams in the town, including Clubs formed
from pupils at Wyggeston and Mill House Schools.
Leicester City were formed in 1884, principally by a
number of old Wyggestonians. The first meeting was held
in a garden shed behind the current Fosse Road South, and
a Club membership fee of 9d. (4p) was agreed upon.

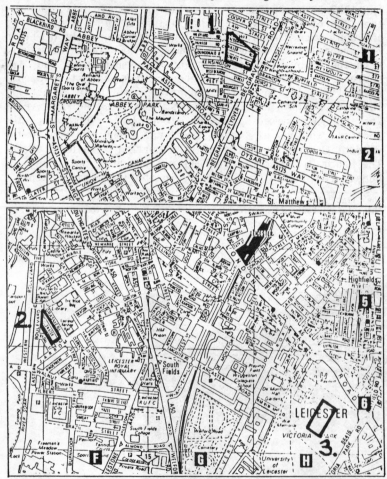

1. Mill Lane.   2. Belgrave Cycle Track.   3. Victoria Park.

FOSSE ROAD SOUTH AND VICTORIA PARK.

The Club name of Leicester Fosse ('Fosse' colloquially meaning moat or ditch) was a predictable choice since the new team were able to rent a field that lay off of the modern named Fosse Road South. After just one game (the team's performance bode well for the future for that match resulted in a thrashing of Syston Fosse by five unopposed goals), the Club moved away and continued with their home matches at Victoria Park, plus four encounters at the Racecourse. The first game at the Park was played on the 3rd of October when Trinity Band of Hope were easily overcome with a 6-0 scoreline. By the season's end there was plenty to be pleased about; of the fifteen matches played, only three were lost and there was a balance left in the Club funds of one shilling and tenpence (9p).

By moving to Victoria Park on a more permanent basis for the next season, the Club were based in a more central position, and no doubt benefited from a better playing surface. The Club's pitch was probably within the Cricket Ground that existed towards the Northern part of the park at this time. However Club membership fees rose to three shillings, which proved to be a wise move, for by the end of the season they had accrued a deficit of two shillings (10p)! It was difficult to attract support at the team's matches, for although there were often upto 3,000 spectators present in Victoria Park, these were virtually all intent on following the progress of the Rugby Club who played on an adjacent pitch to the Fosse! The Club continued in their generally winning ways, and by the end of the 1886/87 season they had turned the earlier deficit into a credit balance of over £1-50. The Club soon became noticed and with a rising membership (65 members by the end of 1887), a Reserve team was formed for the forthcoming campaign.

BELGRAVE CYCLE TRACK.

It was decided that gate money should be taken at matches, for which an enclosed Ground was necessary, and a move was made to the Belgrave Cycle Track which was located to the North of the town. This Ground was off Belgrave Road, and is now the site of Buller and Roberts Roads. The football pitch was within the oval shaped cycle track and on the South side had an open seated Grandstand (about 20 metres long). On the Belgrave Road end there was a large Refreshment Room, but there were no Dressing Rooms at the Ground, and for this facility, the

Players used the White Hart Hotel - approximately one mile away! On the 29th of October 1887, the Fosse played their first cup match, when St.Saviours were visited. The Club was winning 4-2 when the match was abandoned due to bad light, but the home replay on November the 26th was comfortably won by 5-0. Three weeks earlier the first match at Belgrave, and the first at which gate money was taken, was played. By the end of the season the Club had accrued over £8 in entrance monies, and were able to show a credit on the year of £2-67. But the Club's standing was insufficient to outbid the Rugby Club for the usage of the Cycle Track Ground, and a move had to be made back to Victoria Park, after just one year. Despite this blow, the Club effectively turned professional with their signing on of Harry Webb from Stafford Rangers.

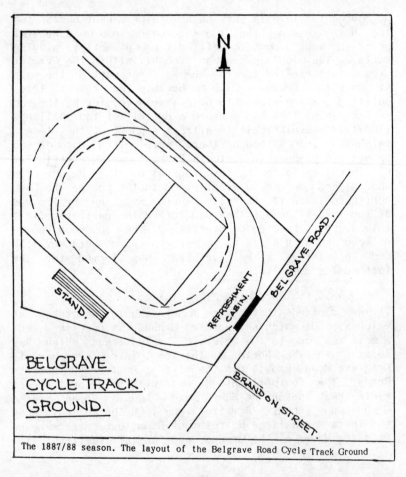

The 1887/88 season. The layout of the Belgrave Road Cycle Track Ground

BACK TO VICTORIA PARK AND ON TO MILL LANE.

The Club's stay at the Park lasted for less than a full season.(no doubt there were difficulties in taking gate money), and early in 1889 they moved on to Mill Lane. This Ground although probably enclosed had no facilities either for players or spectators. The first match at this new venue, on the 5th of October, was ceremoniously kicked-off by the Club President, Sir Thomas Wright. But with poor weather - and no protection - the match receipts came to a meagre 19p; Mill Hill House were beaten by 3-1.

But interest in the Club was increasing and by the end of the season the receipts from home games totalled £85, although there was an overall loss of £6. The morale of the Fosse was boosted further by their winning of the Leicestershire Senior Cup. Coalville were beaten by 4-0 in a replay (attendance of 700) after a draw, which produced a crowd of 1,500; both games were played at the Athletic Ground, Loughborough.

The 1890/91 season was one of great encouragement for support had never been higher. The match receipts trebled over those of a year earlier and a profit of £15 was made. Loughborough (who also later attained Football League status) became the Club's chief protagonists, and their first meeting that season, at Mill Lane, produced a record attendance of 2,500 and receipts of £23. The second game was played at Belgrave Road when £27 was raised for Charity, and when the Fosse played at Loughborough they took 1,500 fans with them. A Friendly game with Notts. County (four goals were shared) attracted record receipts of £30. The Club also entered for the F.A.Cup for the first time, but they lost at home by 4-0 to Burton Wanderers. However the end of the season ended in trauma when the Club were informed that they must vacate the Ground as it was required by the Leicester Corporation for building purposes.

AYLESTONE ROAD CRICKET GROUND AND FILBERT STREET.

By a stroke of good fortune a Miss Westland who was walking one day with her uncle noticed a patch of land off Walnut Street and remarked that it would make a good Ground for the Fosse. The idea was taken up, and after securing the site, work was put in hand to enclose and develop it. But the work was not finished by the start of the 1891/92 season, and a temporary home at Aylestone Road Cricket Ground had to be used.

The Club had been voted into the Midland League, and their first two home matches in this competition were played at this shortlived venue. On the 12th of September Derby Junction were beaten by the only goal of the game, and four weeks later Grantham Rovers were overcome with a 3-1 scoreline.

Loughborough were also entertained when an attendance of 3,000 was present, and an F.A.Cup match was lost to Small Heath. The last match at the Cricket Ground was won by 6-1, when Nottingham Olympic were the visitors. By late October the new Ground, which was to become known as Filbert Street, was ready, and on the 7th of November Nottingham Forest provided the opposition in a Friendly match.

THE GROUNDS TODAY.

The shortlived Fosse Road South venue was one of many fields located to the West of the town. Victoria Park is still a large open area on the other side, and South of, the City centre. The use of the Belgrave Cycling Track entailed a three kilometres move to the North, and the site is now occupied by shops (on the main road) and small terrace houses behind. The former Mill Lane Ground is now occupied by a tall factory and warehouse building plus terrace houses. Aylestone Road Cricket Ground is well South of the town centre, and is now the well known Grace Road County Cricket Ground.

LEYTON ORIENT

The Orient are regarded as a somewhat 'Cinderella' Club within London, being in close proximity to the likes of Tottenham, Arsenal and West Ham, yet their two earlier Grounds, at which Football League matches were played, had the potential for large attendances.

CONFLICTING ORIGINS OF THE CLUB.

The Club, according to one historical version, are considered to be older than their somewhat more illustrious neighbours. In 1881, Star F.C. changed their name to Trafalgar. Seven years later this Club semi-amalgamated with the Saracens Club and, as one Historian relates, adopted the more familiar name of the Orient. This name was proposed by a member, Jack Dearing, an employee of the Orient Shipping Line. The link up is obvious, Clapton - the area (this suffix coming several years later), and Orient - part of the Company name; but there was no official influence from the Shipping Line itself. The Trafalgar Club, until the amalgamation, had the use of two rooms above Gregory's sweetshop in Millfields Road, one of which was used for training purposes (the Club had several other sporting sections), whilst the other room was used as a Clubroom. The Shop virtually faced the Hackney Marshes (to the East) and opposite was South Mill Field, which by the 1890's was used as a large Recreation Ground. At the end of Millfields Road, and adjacent to the Hackney Cut (a Canal), on the North side of the road, the Trafalgar Club played their home matches.

A more recent version of the Club's formation claims that in the summer of 1881, and in common with several other football teams they were founded by a group of workers who were members of the Clapton Park Cricket Club. These men were Clerks of the Orient Shipping Line, and hence was derived the unique prefix to the Club's name. In the Club's early years they occupied two unenclosed Grounds, the first adjacent to Clapton Cricket Club, and the second at the Clapton Rugby and Cricket Grounds, where two railway carriages were used as Dressing rooms. They moved to the Pond Lane Bridge Ground in 1892, and from this point on, these first two versions of the Club's formulative years coincide.

A third version tracing the Club's roots, the most recent and therefore probably the most accurate, states that the Football Club were not formed until 1891. From a group of cricketers at Homerton College (from 1881), twelve keen members created the Glynn Cricket Club on the 3rd of March 1888. There was a tie-up with the Eagle Cricket Club in 1890, and one year later at a meeting, Mr. Dearing (again!) suggested that the name of 'Orient' should be adopted. Later that year a football section was created, with matches being played at Glyn Road. The road still exists - it runs off Millfields Road - and the former field is now built over with houses.

Whichever of these three differing versions is correct, all agree that the Club played at the Pond Lane Bridge Ground in the early 1890's, at which point the main relevance of this chapter commences!

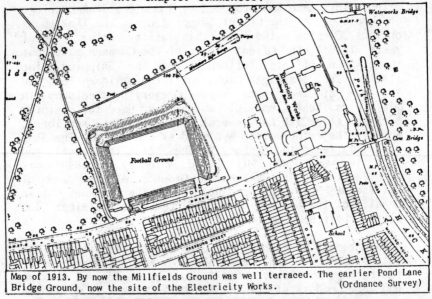

Map of 1913. By now the Millfields Ground was well terraced. The earlier Pond Lane Bridge Ground, now the site of the Electricity Works. (Ordnance Survey)

POND LAND BRIDGE AND MILLFIELDS ROAD GROUNDS.

The Club's use of this open Ground continued until 1896, when an Electricity Sub-station was built on the site. A move to the adjacent field was made, the site of the former Whittles (or Baileys) Fireworks Company. Whippet Racing had already become popular on the site, and as the Football Club became more popular, collections were taken at matches. Such donations augmented the members' fees, but it was not long before steps were taken to ensure their future as a Senior Club.

Admission to the Ground was first charged at 3d. (1p), and the initial game was an exhibition contest versus a Ladies team! A lease had been obtained on the field, and with a new enclosure fence, it became known as Whittles Athletic Ground. Facilities at the Ground were almost non-existant for some time, although two railway carriages (from the Clapton Ground?) or tram-cars were placed within the enclosure, and used as Dressing rooms for a number of years. Large but rudimentary terraces were soon created from the slag that was deposited at the adjoining Power Station.

After a spell in the Clapton and District League the Club became founder-members of the London League in 1896, and by 1902 the Ground had been renamed the Millfields Road Ground. The Club turned professional in November 1903, and started their career in this capacity by demolishing Shepherds Bush by eleven unopposed goals, before a home crowd that numbered 1,300. During the 1904/05 season an initial entry was made into the F.A.Cup, when the first match was won over Enfield. By now the Ground had an expected capacity for 12,000, but after they became a Limited Company in 1905, ambitious plans were made to increase this number to 40,000.

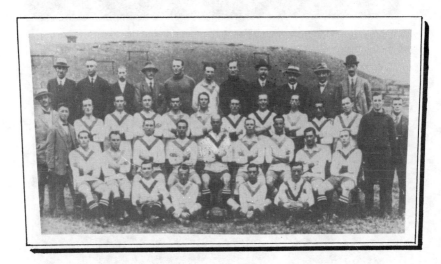

Team Group of the 1921/22 season. Note the still undeveloped banks at Millfields.

The Club's fairly rapid rise was rewarded when they were elected into the Second Division of the Football League, and played their first home match in this company on the 9th of September 1905. Hull City were the visitors, but a crowd of only 3,000 was present to see the homesters lose by the only goal of the game.

(Top): The Stand at Millfields, which was later purchased by Wimbledon F.C.
(Bottom): The new 3,000 seater Stand at Millfields, September 1923.   (Sports Pictur

A report in a Hull newspaper was not very complimentary about the Millfield Ground: "The Ground may be all right when it gets properly trimmed up, but at present it is in a raw, unfinished state. On Saturday it presented a thoroughly washed out appearance in the pelting rain." The reporter went on to say that there was only a small and clumsily erected shanty for the Press, and no other covered accommodation on the Ground! This was nine years after the Club first took over the Ground, and the proposed Grandstand, to hold 2,000, was far from completion at this time.

The Orient were poorly supported, although there were 4,000 present for the F.A.Cup match against Clapton, and it soon became apparent that their grandiose scheme was going to flounder. By January 1906, the Grandstand was still only partly completed, when a Creditor filed for the Club to be wound down. To keep going £200 was needed urgently, whereupon one generous supporter donated £50. This allowed the Club to complete their fixtures, and the first home match after the crisis produced an encouraging crowd of 5,000 for the match versus Burnley. A new Company was soon formed with five shilling shares that produced £3,000 capital. The Grandstand was at last completed, and consisted of a narrow near full pitch length covered and seated enclosure set back from the pitch and alongside Millfields Road.

Over the next few years some of the slag terraces were concreted, and substantial standing areas were possible at both ends and in front of the Stand. On the North side a narrow strip of concrete terracing was backed with a further slope that was formed from the original slag waste. The Club's fortunes gradually changed for the better, and attendances rose as, at last, the Club started paying their way. A new record crowd of 13,846 was present for the 1911/12 season opening match versus Derby County on the 2nd of September, and the F.A.Cup match versus Everton produced gate receipts of £556 from an 11,000 attendance. One year later the first home League game shattered the earlier record when a crowd of 21,000 was present for the visit of the much respected Burnley team.

The First World War halted the Club's progress, and with a notable show of patriotism ten Club players - a record number from those teams in the Football League - joined the Footballers Battalion.

Casualties during hostilities resulted in losses to the team when peacetime allowed a return to League football. But the team played on, and during the 1923/24 season £30,000 was spent on a new Stand of steel and concrete. Other proposals included coverings to both ends, which never materialised.

Two crowd scenes at Millfields in the match versus Leicester Fosse, 1910/11 season. (Lotinga's Weekly)

During the 1925/26 F.A.Cup sortie an excellent run through to the quarter finals finished at Millfields versus Manchester City, but in the 5th round, a staggering all time record crowd of 63,000 reputedly packed into the Ground to see the homesters beat Newcastle United. The official attendance of 38,219, and probably more reliably the record, were present when Tottenham came in the 1928/29 season.

But financial matters soon turned bad again, and it was only the intervention of the Clapton Stadium Syndicate who introduced Greyhound Racing to Millfields that saved the Club. This joint tenant spent £80,000 in 1927 on sorely needed Ground improvements, and before long the tail began to wag the dog! By now the Ground had been developed into a large Stadium, with the familiar oval shaped inner area - for greyhound racing - around the perimeter, and substantial concrete terracing banks on three sides. The Grandstand on the Millfield Road side was wider than its predecessor, while opposite the huge terrace was covered over much of its length.

The structures over both the seated Stand and the standing terrace consisted of multi-span roofs rather than monopitch coverings. Access into the Ground was only possible via the Stand (South) side. But such a well developed Ground was of little consequence for the Football Club, who, with low gates could hardly take full advantage of the facilities on offer. In a near bankrupt state the Football Club had to hand over the Stadium to the Greyhound Authority, and during the summer of 1930 made plans for a move to another Ground. Brighton were the last Football League visitors on the 3rd of May 1930.

LEA BRIDGE ROAD.

The new Ground was only about half a mile to the North of Millfields and lay conveniently next to the Station of the same name. It was already an established Speedway Stadium, located within a generally undeveloped area, but in a somewhat bleak setting. The Ground was fairly well developed, and coupled with improvements during the Orient's seven year occupation resulted in a somewhat disjointed enclosure! The overall site was more or less triangular in shape with access only from the road side with the other main boundary being provided by the railway line. The pitch was surrounded with an elongated oval shaped cinder track for the speedway riders. The central area was little more than a 'rough weedy field', and one of the first tasks was to returf the future playing pitch. Initially shallow, but fairly wide, unconcreted embankments were present all round, and a covered and seated Stand was located on the West side.

Although quite wide, this Stand was at one end of the Ground (with a view to later extension?) and being only about 50 metres long it gave the Stadium a somewhat lopsided appearance. Eventually some areas of the embankments became concrete terraces, but only as odd shapes and in random locations! Much of the railway (East) side was treated this way and with a narrow covered enclosure erected diametrically opposite the Stand. Around the circular shaped North end, and also alongside the Stand there were reasonably wide concrete terraces. The South end was left as a fairly flat standing area. There was cover (seated and standing) for 4,000 spectators and an overall capacity for around 20,000, with plenty of room for further expansion - which was never required or undertaken.

The Club's seven year stay at Lea Bridge was a generally unsuccessful one, and was, as ever, accompanied by a number of traumas. The pre-season trial matches produced encouraging crowds of 6,381 and 4,772 at Lea Bridge Road. The first home League match was versus Newport County (the Orient had been relegated to the Third Division South two years earlier) on the 3rd of September 1930. A Supporters Club was formed, and it was hoped that the new Ground would herald a new successful era for the Club; at the end of the season the team finished in a lowly 19th League position! But within two months of their move to Lea Bridge, the Club found themselves banned from using it!

Programme covers: The last at Millfields, one at Wembley Stadium, and the first at Lea Bridge Road.

A BRIEF STAY AT WEMBLEY STADIUM.

A poor start resulted in early League match attendances of only five to six thousand. But this problem was dwarfed when the Club Officials were informed by the Football League that the narrow pitch must be extended by a metre on both sides in order to provide a reasonable space between bylines and the perimeter fence to the speedway track. Although admittedly only a very narrow strip was present, the Club had received no complaints from either opposition teams or Officials.

But the League nonetheless ordered that this work should be undertaken in seven days. This left the Club in an impossible position for as Tenants, they could hardly dictate to the Speedway Authorities and in any event the cost of radically changing the speedway track was economically - and within the time scale - quite beyond the Club.

An amazing interim measure was taken whereby the Club arranged to temporarily move to Wembley Stadium! Two matches were played there, when high-flying Brentford were beaten in the first ever Football League match played at the Cup Final Venue on the 22nd of November. The attendance of 10,300 reflected the novelty value of such an event, but two weeks later when Southend were entertained at Wembley the attendance dropped dramatically, although the Orient achieved another - rare - win. Somehow the cash was found, an agreement was made with the Speedway Authorities, and Lea Bridge Road was adapted for the football team to return to their proper home after these two journeys to such a unique venue.

BACK TO LEA BRIDGE ROAD.

The following few years produced only slightly improved placings, as the Club struggled for success in the shadows of their more illustrious neighbours. The Club soon got into debt again, and at one time nearly folded. During the meteoric and shortlived rise of nearby Thames Association F.C. there was talk of the two Clubs merging, but this did not come to pass, and while the Thames F.C. sunk, the Orient struggled on alone. Attendances during the 1930's rarely rose above 7,000, but on the 13th of March 1937 (only a few weeks before vacating the Ground), the local derby game with Millwall produced a record attendance of 20,400 at Lea Bridge Road. The option of extending the Ground's capacity had not been taken up, for the crowd was described as being unmanageable and were frequently forced into invading the pitch. Another Club's misfortunes became beneficial to the Orient. The Orient, in debt, were anxious to move from their somewhat unsatisfactory home at Lea Bridge Road, and the financial problems of the amateur team Leyton F.C. who were playing at the Osborne Road (later known as Brisbane Road) Ground provided an answer. Initially the Local Council, who owned the Osborne Road enclosure, refused permission for the Orient to take over at Osborne Road.

Leyton F.C. owed money to their Landlords, and no doubt the Council were very wary of another Club whose past, and current, record was hardly one of affluence! But eventually a suitable agreement was made, and it only remained for the Orient to complete their 1936/37 season fixtures at Lea Bridge. On April the 29th, Southend United were beaten 3-0 in the last game at the old Ground.

The Osborne Road Ground, which had been used for football for many years, had already been moderately well developed. It was also situated in a better catchment area, being about one mile South-east of Lea Bridge, and within Leyton. The first game at the new home was played on the 28th of August 1937, when a very large crowd of 14,598, which included the Football League President C.E.Sutcliffe, saw the Orient share two goals with Cardiff City.

THE GROUNDS TODAY.

The Millfields Road Ground continued to be used for many years for Greyhound racing, under the name of Clapton Stadium. The Ground was demolished in the 1970's, and the 'Millfield Estate' of three and four storey housing now occupies the site. When Speedway Racing came to an end at Lea Bridge Road in the post-war years, a small Industrial Estate was built there, with two roads and factories now on the site.

The Lea Bridge Road Ground in 1933.
(Aerofilms)

LINCOLN CITY

Lincoln City were founded in 1884, with the main intention of capturing the Lincolnshire Senior Trophy from Spilsby - who were founded in 1870 - and who had a hat-trick of successes from the inaugural year of the competition in 1882; in the event it was not until 1887 that this ambition was finally realised. Football in the town, at this time, was not a new sport for it first became popular in the early 1860's, and by 1884, there was a host of Clubs in the district including, Lincoln Lindum, Ramblers (who played at Sincil Banks - a location that was to become the later Ground of the City), Rangers, Albion and Rovers. The formation of Lincoln City was an amalgamation of three of these Clubs.

JOHN'O GAUNTS GROUND.

As a home Ground, the new Club chose a field behind St.Mary's Guildhall which was, and still is, located in the High Street. St.Peter's Church was adjacent to the Guildhall, and opposite the Church was John'O Gaunts house, which was demolished in the late 18th century. Behind the Guildhall were several small structures, which at varying times have been Craft Workshops, a Chimney Sweep's store, a Brewery and - around the year of the formation of the Club - Stables. Erroneously these became known as John'O Gaunts Stables (in reality not having any connection with the earlier house), and hence the Football Ground became known as 'John'O Gaunts'.

The Club had several fields to choose from, including a pitch in South Park (a large area to the South of the town centre, the former home of Lincoln Rovers, and used by the second eleven of the new Club), the somewhat suspect sounding Cowpaddle (a few hundred metres to the East) and the aforementioned fields adjacent to the Sincil. John'O Gaunts was probably chosen not only for it's closeness to the town centre, but also provided the option of enclosing the field and hence charging entrance money. It is doubtful if there were any facilities for the players (other than the provision of a dressing-tent) or the spectators, and the pitch was far from perfect since it had a pronounced slope. The main, and perhaps only, entrance was via the doors within the large arched opening of the Guildhall.

The first match was played at
John'O' Gaunts on the 4th of
October 1884, when Sleaford Town
were the visitors, and after the
3.20 p.m. kick-off were
resoundedly beaten by 9-1.
Despite being a new Club, they
were fortunate in being able to
entice the renowned Nottingham
Forest team to Lincoln one week
later. The visitors arrived late,
the kick-off was delayed until
4.00 p.m., and before a good
attendance the homesters were
beaten 2-4.

Poster advertising Lincoln
City Swifts (Reserves)
versus Nottingham Forest
reserves. 12th Sept. 1891.

The Club had been immediately accepted into the F.A.Cup
Competition, and the first match, on November the 1st,
resulted in a 5-1 victory at Hull Town. Although they
eventually lost to Grimsby in the third round, the
Players and Officials of the newcomers must have been
highly encouraged by the Club's start. In the F.A.Cup the
following season, Grimsby Town again beat the Lincoln
City team, but in the 1886/87 season, the Club progressed
through to the final 16 , at which stage they bowed out
to Glasgow Rangers. The Club had quickly established
themselves as a formidable combination, and they were
also able to attract sizeable crowds to the home Friendly
and Cup matches. By now were also selling season tickets.
Over Christmas 1886 there were 2,000 present for the
match versus Long Eaton Rangers and 4,000 (at an entrance
charge of 6d.- 2½p) when nearby Gainsborough Trinity were
the visitors. During the early years the matches versus
their fellow Lincolnshire neighbours were usually
surrounded with controversy. The games were often
accompanied with a degree of ill-feeling and
confrontations between spectators and players. The match
in January 1887 was no exception, although on this
occasion the dispute was over the share of the, not
inconsiderable, money taken at the gate. Walsall Swifts
attracted a good attendance of 2,000, and another visit
by Gainsborough drew no fewer than 5,000, possibly a
record to that time. the illustrious Preston team were
the next visitors to John O'Gaunts, but a somewhat low
crowd of only 1,500 came to the game. The Club fulfilled
their ambition by winning the Lincolnshire Cup that year,
and the next match at home drew an attendance of around
2,000 for the encounter with Derby Midland.

Encounters with Gainsborough Trinity continued to be one of the best crowd-pullers, even though these were only Friendlies (in theory if not in spirit!). But for the 1888/89 the City became founder-members of the ill-fated Combination - a competition that set out to rival the Football League (also in it's first season), but floundered due to many unplayed matches. That season also saw the John O'Gaunts Ground host its first floodlight match, in November. This match versus Notts. County attracted over 2,000 curiosity seekers, and the illumination was provided by flares that burned from closely spaced scaffold poles. The experiment was repeated soon afterwards, but on this occasion by way of Wellesleys electric lighting. The game versus Sheffield United had its drawbacks since the Players suffered temporary blindness when looking into the glare of the lights!

In 1889, the City became founder-members of the Midland League, and their first match was won at The Northolme, Gainsborough, before 2,500 enthusiastic spectators. By the end of the season the Lincoln team became the first League Champions, and the Players were awarded medals for their efforts. In 1891 the team joined The Alliance, and one year later were elected as founder-members of the Second Division of the Football League. Although the 1893/94 season was only a mediocre one on the field, it was financially successful, even though attendances were down on a few years earlier; the last match on the 28th of April only drew 1,500 to John O'Gaunts for a non-competitive encounter with Gainsborough.

The 1894/95 season was to become the last at the Ground, which had been rented from Mr.R.Dawber, a great supporter of the Club who was to die soon after the Club departed from his enclosure. With the impending development of the Ground, for housing, by January an alternative location was being eagerly sought. Meanwhile, there were other more urgent problems - on the field! The second half of the season saw some bad results, including a humiliating 3-11 defeat at Manchester City, a two goal reverse at home to Burton Wanderers (before barely 1,000 spectators), and another home defeat, this time to Notts. County. There was a large crowd at the latter, but only due to the travelling supporters, who swelled the numbers considerably.

(Top): The Guildhall in 1891, the main entrance to the John 'O Gaunts Ground
(Lincoln Library)
(Bottom): Little changed in 1989. The road on the right runs through part of the site
(Dave Twydell)

On April the 13th the last League match was played at John O'Gaunts, a 5-2 defeat of table-tailenders Crewe. Despite the poor run towards the end of the season, the Club finished four from the bottom, but financially lost £181 over the year.

The enclosure at Sincil Bank was eventually chosen for the Club's new home, a Ground that had been most recently used by Lincoln Casuals. Lincoln City was virtually reformed, with a new Management, new team (only four from the 1894/95 season remained), and a new Ground. The Ground, even before any development work, was considered far superior to the former venue, although much smaller overall. The first game was played against Gainsborough, a Friendly match on September the 2nd, and Woolwich Arsenal were the first League opponents at Sincil Bank.

THE GROUND TODAY.

Although all remains of the John O'Gaunts Ground have long since disappeared (Sibthorp Road, between the Guildhall and the Church, running lengthwise over the site of the earlier pitch), the Guildhall frontage, including the gate below the entrance arch, have changed little from the time when it was once the main access point to the Football Ground.

LUTON TOWN

The Club was created at a Public Meeting in the Council Chambers on the 11th of April 1885. This was not a completely new organisation, but an amalgamation of the leading teams in the town, the Wanderers (not the Club of earlier F.A.Cup fame) and Excelsior. Excelsior were in essence a work's team who were fortunate to have their own Ground - not surprisingly named 'The Excelsior Ground', which was located in Dallow Lane, and was also known as the Town Field. The Wanderers, as the same named famous predecessors, were essentially a Club that catered for the upper class player. The initial formation meeting was somewhat acrimonious since the Wanderers only a few months earlier had already tried to establish themselves as the town's main Club. In the early matches of the new Luton Town F.C. team selection had to be made with great diplomacy, one week the eleven contained five former Excelsior players plus six ex-Wanderers men, and the following week, vice versa! To add to the confusion, for some time the Wanderers continued to operate as a separate Club.

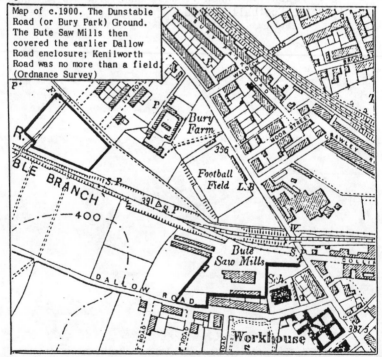

Map of c.1900. The Dunstable Road (or Bury Park) Ground. The Bute Saw Mills then covered the earlier Dallow Road enclosure; Kenilworth Road was no more than a field. (Ordnance Survey)

DALLOW LANE.

The first practice match was held at Dallow Lane on September the 12th, and an immediate entry was made into the F.A.Cup Competition, in which the team lost by three unopposed goals before a crowd of 500 at Marlow. The early years attracted only mediocre support for the 1886/87 season only produced £41 in total gate money, and around £50 one year later. However, local derby matches were popular with the fans, and games with St.Albans normally produced attendances of around 2,000. Four figure gates were also attracted to F.A.Cup games; in 1888, 1,000 were present for the four goal win over Reading and 1,500 for the 10-2 replay slaughter over Chesham. But the Dallow Lane Ground (or Town Meadow as it was also later called) left a lot to be desired. It lay close to the Luton to Dunstable Railway line, adjacent to Dunstable Road School, and the pitch had a pronounced slope. If the wind blew in an unfavourable direction the fans, most of whom had only wooden duckboards to stand on, would be engulfed with smoke from the frequent trains. On one occasion an open goal was missed by a normally reliable marksmen, due, he claimed to a smut of soot that blew into his eye at the crucial moment!

On the 15th of December 1890, five shillings (25p) per week was offered to three players, and when Frank Whitby signed on, he was allegedly the first professional player in the South of England. Support by now had increased, and for the 1890/91 season the total income was over £200. The following season the Club reached the first round proper of the F.A.Cup, and the match - a three goal defeat by Middlesbrough - attracted a record attendance of 4,000. With the continuing increase in interest, the Club built a modest seated and covered Stand measuring 120 feet by 13 feet and 18 feet high. The Stand contained five rows of seats, therefore holding about 500 spectators, and was officially opened on Boxing Day 1893. But the wealthier occupants of the Stand had their critics, and there were repeated accusations of them using bad language and making foul remarks! On the 23rd of December 1893 there was an attendance of 2,000 for Sherwood Foresters visit, and the next April, a crowd of over 2,000 were privileged to witness what many considered as the best game ever at the Ground, when the homesters lost by 2-5 to Third Lanark, from Scotland.

Regular competitive football at last came to the South, with the formation of the Southern League for the 1894/95 season, of which the Town were founder-members. But Friendly games had to supplement the relatively few League games. Over Christmas a crowd of 3,000 saw Wrexham beaten 7-2, the next day Formby were humiliated to the tune of 16-0, and on Boxing Day, Darwen shared six goals with the local team before a crowd of over 4,000. On Good Friday, Third Lanark were visitors again, and another 4,000 plus attendance was present. But the highlight of the season was the incredible ten goal victory over the Derby County Reserve team. By the season's end, 33 games had been won, 7 drawn and only 16 lost. Other notable visitors, in the 1895/96 season were Preston North End who attracted an attendance of 4,000, despite the freezing cold weather, and Accrington who were humiliated with a nine goal defeat before a crowd numbering 1,500. With the visit of West Bromwich Albion on the 30th of January 1897 for the first round of the F.A. Cup match, a record for the Ground attendance of 6,898 were present. Match receipts totalled over £184, which exceeded the previous record by more than £50. An unsuccessful application to join the Football League was made at the end of the season.

An impression, from the North-east, of what the Dallow Road Ground may have looked like.
(Dave Twydell)

DUNSTABLE ROAD.

By now the old Ground was unsuitable in relation to the Club's popularity, and by raising £800 by April 1897, the Club were able to play their first match at the new headquarters on the 3rd of that month. The Duke of Bedford, who made a personal donation of £50, officially opened the new Dunstable Road Ground, on a dull but rain free day. The match, in the United League versus Loughborough was won, and a carnival spirit prevailed, with coloured bunting festooned around, and on, the enclosure. The season ended in high fashion with an eleven goal home thrashing of Rushden on the 16th of April. Following their successful election into the Football League, at the Club's A.G.M. the Club became a Limited Company.

After their League debut, a scoreless draw at Leicester, the first home match on the 11th of September resulted in a resounding 4-0 victory over Gainsborough. The future looked bright for the Club, with the season's gate takings totalling £2,286 (the main expenditure being wages and bonuses of nearly £1,600), and a final mid-table placing. Although losing to Bolton Wanderers in the 1st round of the F.A.Cup, the home match attracted a crowd of 4,500. The next season was a poor one, with only the F.A.Cup victories over Watford and Queens Park Rangers as any real consolation. In the final qualifying round, the Town finally lost to Tottenham Hotspur, after a 1-1 away draw (attendance 10,000), and the same scoreline in the midweek first replay before a crowd of 3,500.

The gloom continued when the Club finished the 1899/1900 season in the second from bottom final League table, and chose not to seek re-election. Financially the year was a disaster, and the gates dropped to less than 1,000 for home matches. But the Club pulled round by appealing for extra support, and this was evident when the new season kicked off with an attendance of over 4,000 for the first Southern League match, at home to Southampton. For a few years the future appeared to be secured, and attendances once again rose to a reasonable level – at the end of the 1903/04 season with gate receipts of £2,500, a profit of £132 was realised; the top gate being the 6,000 who attended the 4th qualifying round F.A.Cup match with Watford. But within the year near disasters struck, both on the playing and financial fronts.

The team were producing poor results, and inevitably attendances were down (even so these were normally between three and four thousand), then it was announced that the Club would have to quit the Dunstable Road Ground as the land was wanted for building purposes.

A fine view of the Dunstable Road Ground c.1905.

The Dunstable Road Ground, or Bury Park, as it was also known, (Bury Farm was adjacent to the Ground) was hardly an improvement over its predecessor in Dallow Lane. It was situated almost directly opposite, on the other side of the railway lines, and just as close since the South corner virtually merged into the embankment. On the North-east side a narrow half pitch long covered, seated Stand was built, and small embankments were raised on all sides. A small covered enclosure provided dry standing opposite the Stand, and although the South-east end formed a large triangular area, most of this was flat, and therefore of little practical use. An entrance off of Dunstable Road was built at this end, whilst opposite the narrow standing area contained the main access points to the Ground, and probably also a refreshment bar. By April 1905 work got underway to construct a new Stadium, barely a pitch length further along, and once again close to, the railway line.

The last match was played at the old Ground on the 25th of April, when in poor weather, a small crowd saw Reading beaten by two goals to nil. But it was a worrying time for the Club since a lowly final position held the risk of relegation, but the Directors were assured that the team would hold it's place for the next season. The pitch was of a similar size to its predecessor, and although the overall area of the Ground was smaller it was of a more practical shape. The old Stand was moved to the new enclosure, but just before the start of the season rumours, subsequently proved to be unfounded, said that it had been condemned! At an overall cost of £2,000, the Kenilworth Road ground was ready for its baptism on the 4th of September 1905.

THE GROUNDS TODAY.

The Dallow Lane (later Road) Ground became the Bute (later Brown's) Saw Mills, and upto c.1960 the old covered Stand remained (albeit later extended) in it's final role as a Shed. The building of a new road that runs along parallel with the railway now embraces part of the former Ground, whilst the rest of the area is now the Dallow Road Junior and Infant School. Hazelbury Crescent and Avondale Road swallowed up much of the second Ground, with a Cinema - later a Bingo Hall - on the Dunstable Road overlying the North-east boundary of the former enclosure. The present Luton Town F.C. Centenary Club Car Park, at one point, just clips the Southern corner of the former Ground.

The photograph, taken in 1990, shows the site of the Dallow Road Ground now part covered (the remainder is the field on the left).

The houses to the right are on the Dunstable Road enclosure, and Kenilworth Road is in the far background, to the right

(Dave Twydell).

MAIDSTONE UNITED

It is somewhat ironic that after 90 years of playing at one Stadium, that one year later the United at their finest hour - promotion to the Football League - should be left having to Groundshare with a non-League team!

THE ATHLETIC GROUND.

From 1894, as Church Institute, and later as Maidstone Invicta, the Club used the unenclosed Postley Field as a home Ground. But within four years of their formation, they were able to move into the far more impressive Athletic Ground off London Road. The Athletic Ground had formerly been an orchard and hop garden, but as a large open area the Bath and West Show - a geographical incongruity - was held there in the 1880's. However, in 1893, a band of progressive sporting men realised the potential of this thirteen acre site, and local business men supporters provided the enormous reported sum of £6,500 to level the site (it varied by thirteen metres from one side to the other), in order for its planned use for sporting events.

The Athletic Ground as it looked in 1897. The playing area was later reduced to include only the southern portion. (Ordnance Survey)

With the intention of holding a variety of sports meetings at the Ground, a large grassed area - principally for Cricket and Football - was surrounded with a cinder cycling track, plus a 130 yard running track on the West side. The Ground was enclosed with a timber fence, and along the West side and part of the South, a narrow band of wooden, open, seating provided a vantage point for 500 spectators. An obligatory Pavilion was built behind the seating midway down the South side, which included dressing rooms, showers and plunge bath. On top of the Pavilion an excellent view of the proceedings was provided for the privileged, and with additional facilities elsewhere, such as a committee room, refreshment bar and adjacent tennis courts, the Athletic Ground provided all the means for the most discerning sportsman.

Within this near natural amphitheatre, the first sporting event was the Church Institute Athletics meeting, held on the 24th of April 1895. One year later, Mr. J.C. Welch became the Ground Secretary, a post he held for fifty years. The entry to the Ground was from London Road, and the spectators that day were entertained by a large variety of sports, including Football, Cricket, Cycle Racing and Gymnastics, with additional entertainment provided by local Military Bands. The only thing to mar such an auspicious opening was the rain that fell during the events. One month later, on the 22nd of May the Ground was officially opened with Cricket match between two Representative teams. It soon became a popular venue with attendances of upto 4,000 for Athletics meetings whilst Rugby was also played there. In February 1896, Mid-Kent Football team used the venue for their home games, but after a highly unsuccessful and short history the team disbanded. After a brief period of good support, the Ground was in danger of being closed, but with a new Committee taking over the lease at £165 per annum, it was saved - for another ninety years!

Maidstone United F.C. made their debut at London Road, when they lost 1-4 to Chatham Town (of the Southern League) in April 1898. The Club saw the potential of a properly enclosed Ground, and on the 10th of September they played the first of 2,062 official first team fixtures at the venue, when Swanscombe were the visitors for a Kent League match. 700 spectators were present, at an entrance cost of 6d. (2½p), and saw the homesters romp home with a 4-0 victory.

The rent paid by the Club for the 1898/99 season was £25 (they were not the exclusive users), and the teams repaid their support with the capture of both the Kent and the East Kent Leagues plus the County Cup.

Four turnstiles were installed in 1906 (and renewed with covered enclosures in 1922). A covered seated Stand was erected in front of the main Pavilion on the South side, with an adjacent narrow one added later, and in 1921 improvements to the terracing running round to the West side enabled standing viewing for 750. In the 1930's the Athletics Ground was still a large rectangular arena, with curved corners, but eventually it was halved in size when the North portion was formed into a separate Sports Ground. A small Pavilion in the North-east corner remained into the post Second World War period, and another large one was added to the independant Ground. Along the 'new' North side, a half pitch length covered and later part seated Stand was built in 1950, (at a cost of £1,500) but the hurricane of 1987 virtually destroyed it. The Stadium continued to be used for a multitude of Sports including many National events, and for many years was 'the' sporting venue of the town.

The first match under Floodlights was played in 1954 versus Finchley, with an attendance of 6,000. But such crowds were a rare sight, and the Ground went into a sad decline. By now the narrow Stand adjacent to the main one had disappeared, but an extension to this principal seated area was added on the other, West, side of it.

A panoramamic view of the Ground (looking East), taken just before 'the end'. (Dave Twydell)

Additional revenue was received with the introduction of Greyhound Racing in 1976, but after three years this stopped, only to start again two years later. The Ground was upgraded with the addition of a Restaurant, further terracing, new Floodlights and the creation of a reserve team pitch on part of what had become the adjacent Sports Ground. The final major change was the enclosure of the Railway end as a visiting supporters area. The Ground had became something of a 'lopsided' Stadium, for on the South side (and including the impressive and spacious entrance from Leafy Lane that led off of London Road) was quite substantial with the fairly large Stand and a high bank of concrete terracing in the South-west corner. But the terracing dropped away drastically at each end providing little more than a walkway around to the fairly narrow North side.

Over a period of ninety years, the Stadium, as a football venue, endured many triumphs and disasters for it's main occupants. A 3-10 defeat was experienced versus Maidenhead United in February 1951 (during the Club's amateur days), and the next season only one victory was recorded at the Ground. But eighteen home victories were enjoyed in the 1982/83 season, and one unbeaten run at Maidstone extended through to September 1954. The Club attracted a record Club attendance of 12,900 on the 31st of March 1923 versus Margate, and the F.A.Cup game with Charlton Athletic in January 1979 produced an official gate of 10,591. The Ground record crowd was present for one of the many Kent Senior Cup Finals, in 1939

-197-

(Tunbridge Wells versus Gillingham), and numbered 13,500.
During the 1953/54 season, the post War heyday for
football, the Club's top average gate for a season was
realised of 2,720.

THE GROUND TODAY.

The sad end of the Athletics Ground came on the 23rd of
April 1988 when Stafford Rangers were the visitors. The
last football match was held there on the 1st of May when
the Maidstone and District Boys Primary League held their
Challenge Cup Finals; Maidstone United F.C. were not
involved in the first event at the Athletics Stadium, nor
the last, yet were very much a part of it in the
intervening ninety years! Within days of the last ball
being kicked on the pitch, some fixtures and the fittings
were removed, the Ground levelled, and a brand new
Furniture Superstore made it's appearance before the
start of the next football season.

Programme cover for the last
match at The Athletic Ground.

MANCHESTER CITY

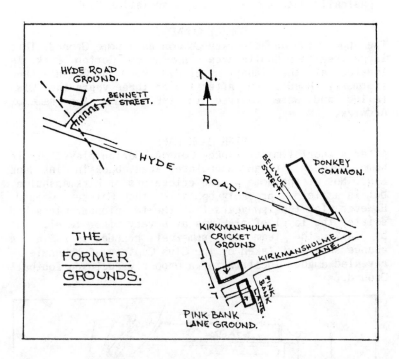

HYDE ROAD GROUND.

BENNETT STREET.

N.

HYDE ROAD.

BELLVUE STREET.

DONKEY COMMON.

THE FORMER GROUNDS.

KIRKMANSHULME CRICKET GROUND

KIRKMANSHULME LANE.

PINK BANK LANE.

PINK BANK LANE GROUND.

In an area which was predominantly Rugby orientated, the City were founded in 1880 as West Gorton. The first 'Ground' chosen by the Club was nothing more than an area of waste land, which was also used for Cricket. This venue was located just off of what became Clowes Street, and needless to say is now within a built-up area.

KIRKMANSHULME CRICKET CLUB.
One year later the Club moved to a Ground that was at least a recognised enclosure, although the facilities were no doubt limited, probably to just a pavilion. The Cricket Club Ground was a five acre plot, and located at the corner of Kirkmanshulme Lane and Pink Bank Lane. Both of these roads still exist, and after being renamed the Paddock Sports Ground, this former sporting venue is now a modern housing development.

However, the footballers were not popular with the
cricketers and were soon banned from the Ground due to
the pitch getting ploughed up after matches. West Gorton
faded away at this time, only to be replaced in 1884, by
a basically new team - Gorton Association Club.

DONKEY COMMON.

The new Club chose Donkey Common as a home Ground. This
large treelined public area - now named Gorton Park is
located at the junction of Hyde Road and Queen's Lane
(formerly 'Road'). But after two or three years the Club
failed and were revived in 1887 under the name of
Ardwick.

PINK BANK LANE.

After a short time at Donkey Common, Gorton played their
home matches at an unenclosed area, back in Pink Bank
Lane. Not at the home of the cricketers of Kirkmanshulme,
but in a field - probably opposite the Cricket Ground.
However for the few years that the two pioneer Clubs had
existed the level of play was at a very minor level. But
by 1887, the team had somewhat grander ideas, and a
chance short cut taken by the Club Captain - McKenzie -
revealed a good location for a properly enclosed football
Ground.

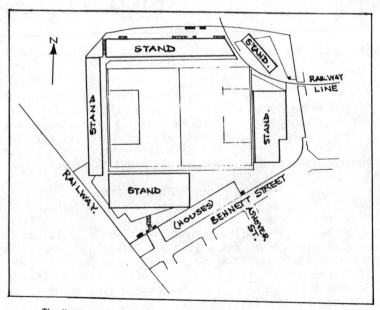

The Hyde Road Ground in 1922, just before the Club departed.
A unique situation with five Stands (seating and standing).

HYDE ROAD.

The area of wasteland was back in the West Gorton district, sandwiched between the lines of the Manchester, Sheffield & Lincolnshire Railway Company, and Bennett Street. The land was was owned by the Railway Company who initially let it to the Football Club for £10, for seven months commencing from August 1887. The change of headquarters also brought about a change of name, to Ardwick F.C. The name change came about after a meeting at the Hyde Road Hotel, convened by Mr Chew (one of the founders of the original West Gorton Club), and Mr. Furniss the former Gorton Captain, the latter subsequently becoming the Secretary of the newly named Club. Within two years the Club turned professional, although for some time the only paid Player on the Club's books was J.Hodgetts, who received five shillings (25p) per week.

The Club's first real success was their progress through to the final of the Lancashire Junior Cup in 1891, when they lost to Blackpool, but that same year they won the Manchester Cup, beating Newton Heath at the last stage. The Club's progress was rapid, since they were elected into the Football Alliance for the 1891/92 season, and one year later became founder-members of the Football League Second Division. Perhaps the Club's rise was too fast, for the end of the 1893/94 season saw them finish second from bottom in the League, and aided by bad management they found themselves in a hopeless financial situation. Some Players were subjected to an auction for their services that was held at a local Public House! The Club, as such folded, but were resurrected as a Limited Company, and under the name of Manchester City.

The new Club made a poor start to their career, losing at Bury on the 1st of September 1894. But the Club slowly rose again, helped in no small way by the aquisition of the legendary Billy Meredith who made his debut for the Club that season, on the 27th of October. Three near misses followed, before the Club were promoted to the First Division at the end of the 1898/99 season. After a short period in the top flight, they were relegated, only to be promoted once again, one year later. This same fate, and same outcome fell upon them a few years later, but from the 1910/11 season through to 1923 they more than held their own in the First Division.

The Club occupied the Hyde Road Ground for thirty-seven years, during which time it was developed into a large capacity Stadium, although in the early years, the Players had to change in a nearby Public House and walk to the Ground. Despite the Ground covering a fairly extensive area it was not of an ideal shape, and the development of the Ground over the years was very 'bitty'.

(Top): The new West Stand at Hyde Road in September 1910. (Athletic News)
(Bottom): November 1920. The Grandstand after it was burnt to the Ground. Within one week a temporary replacement was erected. (Sports Pictures Magazine)

The area behind the West end goal was generally fairly narrow, and in the early days two small embankments were formed, but later this was rationalised when a moderately wide covered enclosure was built over the full pitch width. On the North side of the Ground a full length covered and seated Stand with a capacity for 4,000 became the first development of note and remained until November 1920, when a carelessly dropped cigarette resulted in the whole timber structure being burnt to the Ground.

There was a curious arrangement in the North-east corner, where the close proximity of a railway line resulted in it literally clipping off the corner of the otherwise rectangular fenced off pitch area! A small terrace, which later became covered, was built in the wedge shaped corner - on the other side of the railway line. This same railway line limited the width of the terrace (also later covered) behind the East end goal, and although very wide behind the goal the widths at each corner tapered to virtually nothing. The entry points to the Ground were from the Bennett Street side, and this road coupled with the other railway lines resulted in a large triangular area which once again reduced the standing width at the South-east corner to virtually nothing, but generally produced a very wide area elsewhere.

The final claimed capacity of the Ground was 40,000, but it was a complicated network of standing and seated areas (eventually mostly covered), coupled with arches and railway lines plus limited access points. In a notorious cup-tie at Hyde Road in February 1913, the match with Sunderland had to be abandoned due to the overcrowding in the Ground. The fire in 1920 led to a determined effort to find a more suitable, and larger Ground, although earlier that year, the Club was singularly honoured when King George V put in an appearance at Hyde Road, as a spectator, for the match versus Liverpool.

A move to Belle Vue was given serious consideration at one time. A Football Stadium within this recreation area, which consisted principally of a Zoological Gardens, could have been created from the existing Athletic Ground. But with a potential capacity for no more than 40,000, this would have scarcely been an improvement over the old Hyde Road venue. Belle Vue was abandoned, but the Athletics arena was further developed and later became a Speedway Stadium. The site has now been built over and landscaped.

A site at Moss Side, about two miles from the Gorton area, was chosen for a new Ground, and by the summer of 1923 it was ready for occupation. The last League game at Hyde Road resulted in a scoreless draw with Newcastle United on the 28th of April 1923, apart from the trial matches that were played there at the start of the next season. The new Maine Road Ground, with it's 90,000 capacity, had been designed and built over a three year period, and was opened with a League match against Sheffield United on the 25th of August 1923, when a huge crowd of 60,000 was present.

The Hyde Road Ground has completely vanished, and now contains the Offices and Training Ground of the Greater Manchester Bus Company. The entrance to this depot - with traces remaining of old tram lines - is located at the South-east point of the former football pitch, where it virtually touched Bennett Street. But one large item from Hyde Road can still be seen, for the Stand was purchased by Halifax Town F.C., and to this day forms part of the main enclosure at The Shay.

King George V, a Royal visitor to Hyde Road in March 1920.
(History of the Lancashire F.A.)

MANCHESTER UNITED

The modern day glamour of Manchester United is a far cry from the Club's roots, their previous two Grounds and their financial affairs of yesteryear!

The Club were founded in 1878 by the railwaymen who worked in the carriage and waggon department of the Lancashire and Yorkshire Railway Company's engine shed at Newton Heath. This would have been something of a statement rather than a Club name, and therefore they opted for 'Newton Heath L & Y'. In their early days they were known as the 'Coachbuilders', but it was not long before the 'Heathens' became a more popular nickname.

NORTH ROAD, MONSALL.

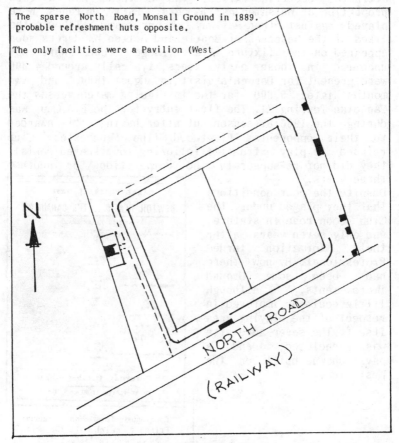

The sparse North Road, Monsall Ground in 1889.
probable refreshment huts opposite.

The only facilities were a Pavilion (West

NORTH ROAD

(RAILWAY)

An unenclosed area of waste land in North Road (now Northampton Road) in Newton Heath, and near to the members workplace was chosen as a home Ground. The Ground was located on the edge of a clay pit, and the playing surface reflected this origin in no uncertain way! Even some years later when the Club had been accepted into the Football League the pitch was considered as being one of the worst in the League, with one end frequently consisting of thick mud, and elsewhere a rock hard surface. As if this wasn't enough to contend with, the Players would find themselves submerged in smoke from the nearby railway works. Bruised from the rock hard surface, covered in mud from elsewhere, coughing and nearly blinded from smoke, the Players then had to face a half a mile walk to the changing rooms that were situated in Oldham Road at the Three Crowns Public House! They later moved to the Shears Hotel. Unlike many Clubs who attracted Scottish exiles, the Heathens had a good proportion of Welshmen as members. Early matches were played against other Railway Company teams, although the likes of the Reserves of Bootle and Bolton Wanderers soon appeared on the fixture list. Large crowds were not uncommon in those early years, typically around 4,000 were present for Darwen's visit in August 1880, and two months later 5,000 for the intriguing match versus the Canadian Touring X1. The first entry for the F.A.Cup was during the 1886/87 season but after having a tie awarded to their opponents, Fleetwood (the Manchester Club refused to play extra time following four shared goals), they did not re-appear in the competition for another three years.

Despite the poor conditions that they played under, the Club soon rose in stature, and only seven years after their formation turned Professional. By now there had been some Ground improvements, although little could be improved in respect of the playing area itself. The seven acre site was enclosed, and a pavilion was built on the West side.

Programme from an unusual Friendly match at the North Road Ground in 1888.

Entrances were along North Road and along the East boundary, with (probably) refreshment huts on the latter side. There was almost certainly no Stands or other protection from the elements for the spectators. However, within this sparse setting the Club became founder-members of the Football Alliance, and before an attendance of 3,000 they beat Sunderland Albion in their first League match on the 21st of September.

Crowd figures were quite good - usually between three and five thousand - despite only a mediocre season. But two contrasting gates were the penultimate home encounter with Walsall Town Swifts which attracted only 1,000 and the last game when around 8,000 were present for Sheffield Wednesday's visit. For the next two years the support was similar, although once again there were wide discrepancies between the best and the worst; Walsall were once again shunned in the 1890/91 season when the season's lowest attendance of 1,500 was present. That season, the Heathens played their first F.A.Cup match at home (one year earlier they lost at Preston), and there was a crowd of 3,000 for the match versus Higher Walton on October the 4th. The 1891/92 season saw the Club finish as runners-up, and support at a high, with no gate less than 3,000, and a probable record at the time of 16,000 for the visit of Nottingham Forest on New Years Day. It is difficult to imagine how so many spectators could pack into the flat North Road Ground, and doubtless many had little sight of the play as they stood ankle deep in mud! Under this cheerless setting the Club were elected into the Football League Division 1 for the 1892/93 season.

A change in status also brought about a change of name for the Club became plain 'Newton Heath', and 10,000 spectators were present for the first Football League match. Two goals were shared with Burnley on the 10th of September, and although throughout the season the gates were high with an average of around 7,000 which reached a peak 15,000 for Sunderland's visit, on the pitch it was a disaster. With only six victories in thirty matches, the Heathens finished bottom of the table, but amazingly two of those wins included a 10-1 thrashing of Wolverhampton Wanderers and 7-1 versus Derby County! By virtue of winning the test match play-offs, the Club retained their First Division status, but for the 1893/94 a move was made to another home venue.

The last match at the old Ground was versus Accrington on the 8th of April when six goals were shared before a lowly attendance of only 3,000.

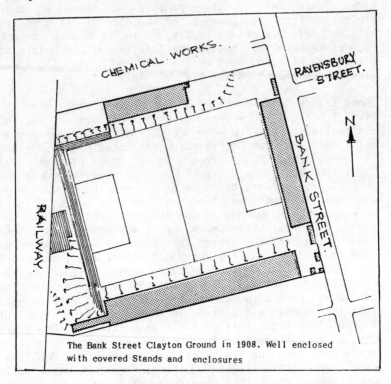

The Bank Street Clayton Ground in 1908. Well enclosed with covered Stands and enclosures

BANK STREET, CLAYTON.

Although any move was bound to be one for the better, it was unusual circumstances that prompted the decision. The North Road Ground was the property of the Deans and Canons of Manchester and they demanded that for the Heathens to continue playing there, there could be no admission charge. This was plainly impossible, and another venue therefore had to be sought.

For some years the alternative, three miles to the South at Clayton, was hardly an improvement for it was at one time described as a muddy waste! The environs of the new Ground were also grim, for it was set amongst an industrial backdrop, with obnoxious fumes from the Albion Chemical works to the North being a constant and unpleasant reminder to those present.

It was hoped that this new Ground, that was more or less forced upon the Club, would attract better gates; this sentiment would seem somewhat strange since the home gates at North Road compared very favourably withthose of the Club's contemporaries.

When the 1892/93 season commenced at this new home there was little to attract support, either with respect to facilities or on the field - the team were relegated at the end of the season! Attendances did not rise, but remained at around the same level as a year earlier, and the best was only 10,000 for the first League match on the 2nd of September when Burnley were beaten 3-2. The Club remained in the Second Division for twelve seasons, and although some of these produced quite respectable final placings in the table, it was generally one long financial struggle. In an effort to attract bigger crowds, by producing better football, the players wages were - for a time - based on the size of the home gates. But rather than encourage the team it tended to make them somewhat selective, for it was said that on some occasions players would establish the number of spectators present, and if there were few, then they would declare that they were unfit to play due to injury!

There is no doubt that over the latter years of the century, attendances were often very poor, sometimes barely reaching four figures, and the very rewarding crowds of around 20,000 were exceptional and only occurred with the likes of the local derbys versus Manchester City. During the 1901/02 season the average crowd was approximately 4,000, but for Burton United's visit on April the 21st, an estimated gathering of only 500 was sprinkled around the enclosure.

By now the Club had reached their lowest financial ebb and were on the point of bankruptcy. The Bailiffs were called in but when they searched the school-room in Silver Street that served as the Clubhouse, the cupboard was all but bare. Just when it looked as if the Heathens would die, a meeting at Islington Town Hall produced five saviours (including former player Harry Stafford), who each put up £200 and ensured the Club's survival. But this action was vastly improved upon when a local wealthy brewer, John Davies, was pursuaded to take an interest. His farsighted plans soon turned the Club into one of the foremost in the Country. The outstanding debts of £2,000 were paid up, and the new benefactor also provided another £1,000 for the Club to buy suitable Players.

There was an immediate and dramatic change around in the Club's fortunes under the new Chairmanship of Mr. Davies, and a new name of Manchester United. After beating Gainsborough Trinity in the first home game of the 1902/03 season, they followed this up with a victory over Burton United, but significantly in front of a crowd of 15,000. The local derby versus the City (who became Champions), attracted a massive 45,000 gate, and the lowest of the campaign was a quite respectable 4,000. Although it was to be another three years before the team were promoted, a new era had begun, and the crowds flocked into the Clayton enclosure. The 1903/04 season saw the average gate at home matches rise to 17,000, and two years later (the promotion season), even the lowest attendance was a healthy 16,000. The team's first game back in the First Division ensured a bumper turnout of 30,000 for the visit of Notts. County, and on the 8th of February 1908, it was estimated that 50,000 had packed into the Clayton enclosure to see the game versus Newcastle United. That season the average home attendance rose to 23,000, which proved to be the best at Clayton. During the next two seasons, when the Club's League performances were not so successful, the crowd numbers were down.

March 1906, the F.A.Cup match versus Woolwich Arsenal at Clayton.

But the United's success did not stop with success on the
pitch, for aided by Mr. Davies, the Ground was at last
developed into a worthy setting for the new found
support. A 1,000 seat Stand costing £500 was initially
provided by Mr. Davies, and the later transformation of
the Ground and described by a local scribe who referred
to the 'Palatial Stands', and 'the 20th century
appointments everywhere'.

Over the years little money had been available, although
£1,000 was spent on basic Ground improvements in 1901,
when a Bazaar was held over four days to raise the money
required. But with their new Saviour at the helm,
substantial alterations were soon undertaken at the
Ground. By 1908, on opposite sides of the Ground, covered
Stands had been built, the southern one a full pitch
length, whilst at the Bank Street end there was a covered
enclosure, of near full pitch width, that ensured
protection from the weather. Topping the main Stand was
an unusual Pavilion which gave a high and exclusive view
from this unique vantage point. For the Players there
were separate changing rooms and baths. Some concrete
terracing was provided at the railway end, and elsewhere
substantial embankments had been formed. 8,000 spectators
could now be accommodated under cover, and with a
capacity of 50,000 the Ground had been transformed into
one of the best in the League. Some improvements were
made to the playing surface, and the Club were honoured
with the Football League versus Scottish League match
which was played at Clayton in April 1904.

The change in the Club's fortunes was dramatic for they
were Football League Champions in 1908, and F.A. Cup
winners the next year. With the Club now attracting
tremendous support, it was announced during the 1907/08
season (during which time the Club had become a Public
Limited Company), that a new Ground was to be built in
the Old Trafford area - some distance to the West - that
would be able to house 100,000 spectators! The last game
at the enclosure attracted only 7,000 for Tottenham
Hotspurs visit on the 22nd of January 1910 - a 5-0
victory. By way of contrast, one month later on the 19th
of February, the first game at Old Trafford pulled in an
enormous gathering of 45,000 for Liverpool's visit. In
January 1909 the Clayton Ground was sold to the
Manchester Corporation for £5,500 - one week before the
plans were approved for the proposed Old Trafford
Development!

But with Mr. Davies putting up the very substantial sum of £60,000, construction of the new Stadium was soon started, and was ready for occupation one year later.

The North Road Ground is now the site of a school, and there is also nothing left of the Bank Street Ground in Clayton. The latter, which was sandwiched between the Railway lines and Bank Street (and opposite Ravensbury and John Heywood Streets) became a coal storage area for the nearby Power Station, but the site is now occupied by a precast concrete fencing company, and there are no reminders left of this very large former Ground.

Manchester United at Practice: "Goal."

(Top): 1907/08 Pre-season trial match at Clayton.
(Bottom): Cartoons relating to the match versus Manchester City, on the 23rd of December 1907.
(Athletic News)

MANSFIELD TOWN

THE EARLY USAGE OF FIELD MILL:

Football goes way back well into the 19th century in Mansfield. In that era Mansfield Greenhalgh became the most popular team and played their home matches at Mill Field (which was also referred to as the Greenhalgh Ground), the same location as the currently renamed Field Mill Ground. The area had been used for recreational purposes even before the earliest reported appearances of this football team. The Duke of Portland owned the Field and Matlock Mills, and rented both out to the Greenhalgh family (who lived at Carr Bank between 1836 and 1907) for their cotton related business. There were four Greenhalgh sons, all of whom were reputed to have played for Notts. County (and one appeared in the first International match with Scotland). But despite the obvious popularity of football in the town, the Works team (nicknamed the 'brown paper parcellers' - for they carried their playing kits in brown paper!) were soon to be challenged by other more formidable Clubs. An early 'Mansfield Town', possibly the same as that which was first referred to in 1871, merged with the Greenhalgh eleven in 1894, to become 'Mansfield F.C.', but the combined Club disappeared around 1900. At one time the 'Town' played at Parr's Cricket Field in Newgate Lane, as did the Mansfield and District Football Club from their formation in 1870.

FOOTBALL AT NEARBY WOODHOUSE:
Nearby lies Mansfield Woodhouse, which despite having a similar name and being immediately adjacent to Mansfield, was until recently very much a separate town. Amongst several Clubs that existed there, and at least from 1874, was the 'Mansfield Woodhouse' team. They were probably the most formidable, since their fixtures included the likes of the Nottingham Club - a match was played with them at Rawson's Ground in 1875. Also in opposition that year was a local derby with 'Mansfield F.C.' The Woodhouse team also made home appearances at the Lords Ground plus the Leeming Lane Recreation Ground, an open area which is still used by amateur teams today.

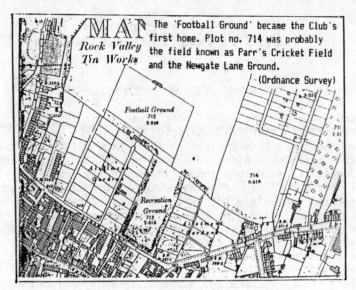

The 'Football Ground' became the Club's first home. Plot no. 714 was probably the field known as Parr's Cricket Field and the Newgate Lane Ground.

(Ordnance Survey)

ENTER THE MECHANICS:

Mansfield Mechanics F.C. was founded in 1901, and played on the Stanhope Street Ground, an area which is now built over, but even before the Mechanic's formation, had been developed into an enclosed football Ground by one of the earlier Mansfield teams. The Ground was approached from North of Pelham Street (between several allotment gardens), and contained probable dressing rooms on the South side plus a small Stand opposite. The Mechanics time at Stanhope Street lasted until 1911, when they moved to Westfield Lane. This venue became known as the Chesterfield Road Recreation Ground, and is still used for minor football today. After one season they moved to Field Mill where they remained until the First World War. The Club never reformed after the Great War, for they lost the use of Field Mill Ground, as it was snatched from 'behind their backs', by the current Mansfield Town F.C.!

THE WESLEYS COME UPON THE SCENE:

It will probably comes as no surprise that many errors and wrongly accredited allegiances with other local teams have been given in the past with regard to the progress of Mansfield Town F.C. Recent detailed research and the recent publication of the Mansfield Town F.C. History has rectified the situation. Mansfield Wesleyans Boys Brigade was founded - as a completely independent Club from any other - in 1910.

PELHAM STREET:

The Wesleyans team first played at Pelham Street, probably the same Ground as that used by the Mechanics team referred to above. The Club's name was derived from their headquarters which were located in Bridge Street Chapel (which was also adjacent to Stanhope Street). The Club name soon changed to Mansfield Wesleyans, and after moving their headquarters to the Carpenter's Arms they became simply Mansfield Wesleys. The Churchmen objected to the 'Wesleyans' in the title since the Club were by now relating to a Public House!

NEWGATE LANE:

By now the home Ground was situated off Newgate Lane since the Stanhope Street Ground had been redeveloped for housing. Recreation Street now cuts through the middle of what was once the football pitch. The Newgate Lane venue was probably one and the same as the Ground that had been used for many years by earlier football and cricket teams. It was probably the three acre field that lay just to the North of Newgate Lane (opposite Bowling Street), and adjacent to the current School. This Ground appears to have remained undeveloped with no facilities for either Players or spectators, and indeed may never have even been enclosed.

THE PRAIRIE:

But the Wesley's stay was only for a very limited time as just prior to the 1914-18 War, the Club moved to a large open area (South of Ratcliffe Gate), which - probably due to this wide open space - glorified in the name of 'The Prairie'! The only entrance to the Ground, which was owned by a Mr. Coupe, was probably via a lane off Ratcliffe Gate, which led to the North-west corner of the Ground. The Club changed their name to 'Town' at this time, but had hardly taken possession of the new Ground before War broke out and football activities ceased for several years. This Ground, although no doubt enclosed, was never developed further, but support for what had become one of the two leading teams (the other was the Mechanics), was very enthusiastic. It is said that even the householders in Broxtowe Drive became season ticket holders, despite the free view of matches that could be obtained from the rear of their houses! The land has now been built over by an Industrial Development.

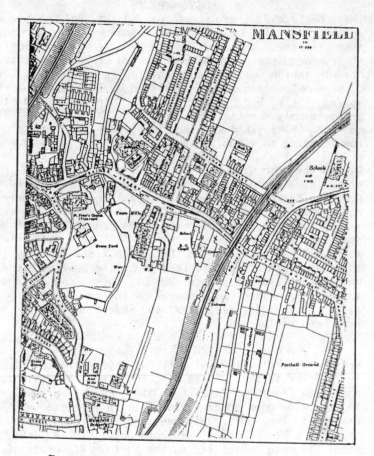

The sparse, and unusual named, 'Prairie ground', that still existed in 1917 Note by then the development of the earlier Stanhope Street Ground. (Ordnance Survey)

THE TOWN MOVE INTO FIELD MILL:

The Mansfield Mechanics team had used Field Mill prior to the War, and despite the subsequent use by the Town team immediately after, the two Clubs remained, separate entities. It is conceivable that the Mechanics members joined up with the Town team, but there is no record of any formal amalgamation.

Whilst the Town flourished, their main rivals folded, since a piracy act by the former left the latter homeless! The Town's move to Field Mill in 1919 would seem to have been an end to their frequent wanderering, but after just one season their future at this venue lay in the balance. After one year's use of Field Mill, Mansfield Town F.C. was the innocent party that was drawn into a dispute over the use of the Ground. But fortunately for the Club, their desire to bring first class football to the town, and the improvements they made to the Ground resulted in them becoming the sole tenants, and eventually new owners.

A most unusual match at Field Mill
- under Floodlights in 1930!

MIDDLESBROUGH

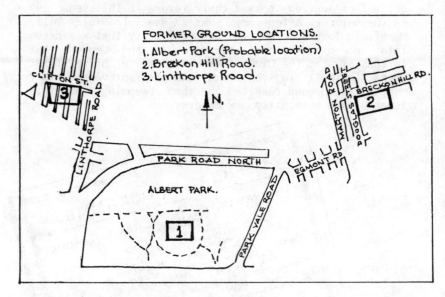

FORMER GROUND LOCATIONS.
1. Albert Park (Probable location)
2. Brecon Hill Road.
3. Linthorpe Road.

N.

CLIFTON ST.

LINTHORPE ROAD

PARK ROAD NORTH

ALBERT PARK.

PARK VALE ROAD

BRECON HILL RD.

MARTON ROAD

EGMONT RD

With their formation in 1876, Middlesbrough F.C. hold the distinction of being the oldest Club in the football fanatical North-east of England. At a tripe supper on the 18th of February 1876, a group of footballers decided to organise themselves into a proper Club; kickabouts on the Archery Ground in Albert Park having sufficed until then. Finding members for the new Club was no problem, but finding suitable opposition was!

ARCHERY GROUND, ALBERT PARK:

The first game of the Club was in fact played against Tee Wanderers, a local Rugby Club, and the contest which only lasted for forty minutes - and under rudimentary rules - was drawn 1-1. The next match against an opposition Club was not undertaken until the 22nd of December 1877 when the team lost at Barnard Castle. On the 26th of January 1878, the well established Tyne Association visited Albert Park in the first home match, and a draw was seen by 150 spectators. The 'Ground' was nothing more than an open pitch, but such was the Club's rapid popularity - attendances were generally around 200 - that their own success was rewarded by them having to seek pastures new!

The local Parks Committee were concerned regarding damage done to the turf from such large crowds, and Middlesbrough had to find alternative accommodation. The expansive Albert Park still exists, to the East of the current Ayresome Park, but the exact location of Middlesbrough's football pitch is, of course, impossible to identify. Although referred to as the Archery Ground, this may well have also have been the Cricket Ground that was located in the South part of the Park.

BRECKTON HILL ROAD:
A field was rented from a Mr.Kemp for a small fee, and since gate money was taken, it can be assumed that the Ground was enclosed. At 3d (1p) a head, 1d for boys and free to women, average gates were around 200 since match receipts were normally not above £3 per match. But this enclosure, that was only a stop-gap, was vacated after just one season, in preference to a better enclosed and more prestigious venue for the ambitious Club. This Ground, just to the North-east of Albert Park, became part of the current Longlands College.

LINTHORPE ROAD:
The Linthorpe Road Ground was an old Cricket Ground located on the West side of this road, and just to the North of Albert Park. In the second season at this venue the Club played their first competitive game when a Sheffield Cup match was contested with Sheffield Exchange, and a crowd of 1,000 was present. In the same competition one year later, more local opponents Redcar were entertained before a 2,000 plus gate. The Club soon established themselves as top-dogs of the North-east and completely dominated the Cleveland Association Cup in it's early years from its inception in 1881.

In 1883 the Club first entered for the F.A.Cup, and although losing the initial game (at Staveley), one year later they progressed through to the last sixteen, when they met the doyens of the Competition, Old Etonians; the game was lost, but by now Middlesbrough were a match for any team. By the 1887/88 season there were plenty of worthy opponents in the North-east, and Sunderland were encountered for the first time. In an F.A.Cup match at Linthorpe Road, a 2-2 draw was fought out before a packed attendance of 8,000 who paid total gate receipts of £69.

Probably the only photograph of the Linthorpe Road Ground (inside the entrance).
Party of Dignitaries in 1887. (Middlesbrough Library)

1889 was notable as the first year of the Football
League, and it also gave rise to a serious rift within
the Club. There was a faction who felt that the time had
come for the team to turn professional, and a breakaway
team was formed, after such an idea was turned down by
the majority. Middlesbrough Ironopolis was created and
for five years the two Clubs vied for support, with
Middlesbrough F.C. finally winning through.

Ironically the reality of professionalism was recognised
by the original Club soon after the breakaway, and it was
they that played the first such match in the town! Two
goals were shared with Gainsborough Trinity on the 7th of
December before a 5,000 crowd. In the following April a
record attendance was recorded at Linthorpe Road when
11,000 spectators paid £280 to see their favourites play
Stockton.

The record was revised a few weeks later with the meeting of the two rival Middlesbrough Clubs for the first time. It was seen by a crowd of 12,000 (£300 receipts). After one year in the Northern League the rift between the two rival Clubs was temporarily healed when they jointly applied, but were unsuccessful, for membership of the Football League. Going it alone once again the Ironopolis achieved this honour in the 1893/94 season, but resigned and folded at the end of the campaign.

Despite the Club's long stay at Linthorpe Road relatively little was provided in the way of facilities. By 1896, it could boast of just one enclosure, the Grandstand on the northern side. This was about half pitch length and reasonably wide, but elsewhere there was no cover. On the other side, and behind the goals there were only narrow, open seated areas, and with flat standing behind, it is difficult to visualise how the five figure crowds were accommodated; many would certainly have seen little of the action! It is possible that a smaller Stand was erected in the later days, but in any event the Stand that was later to grace Ayresome Park was unusually roofed with slates. On the East side, and just off Linthorpe Road, were the Dressing Rooms, Refreshment facilities, and the only entrances to the enclosure. As an earlier Cricket ground the enclosure was much larger, but for football purposes the Ground was contained within the northern portion of this eight acre plot. The site of the Ground is now built over with houses.

Middlesbrough, still at Linthorpe Road, reverted to amateurism in 1892, and proceeded to dominate not only the Northern League, but won the F.A.Amateur Cup on two occasions. In February 1899 the team became professional once again, and were elected into the Football League for the next season. Although their performances in the Second Division were disappointing, the Club made a profit over the year of nearly £180. One year later the Club finished much higher in the table, and home gates receipts nearly doubled to a record £8,347. Promotion was won in the 1901/02 season, and was also destined to be the penultimate one at Linthorpe Road. On the 8th of September, Everton were the visitors in the inaugural First Division match at Linthorpe Road. Such was the enthusiasm that over 17,000 fans managed to cram into the Ground. On the 25th of April 1903 Stoke City and Middlesbrough shared two goals in the last fixture at the Ground, before a crowd of over 8,000.

At a cost of over £10,000, Ayresome Park was ready for occupation at the start of the 1903/04 season. One lasting momento from Linthorpe Road was the Stand which was re-erected on the South side of Ayresome Park where it remained until May 1937. No doubt many of the Club's supporters were ignorant of the fact that their brand new enclosure partly overlaid that of the hapless Ironopolis from a decade earlier!

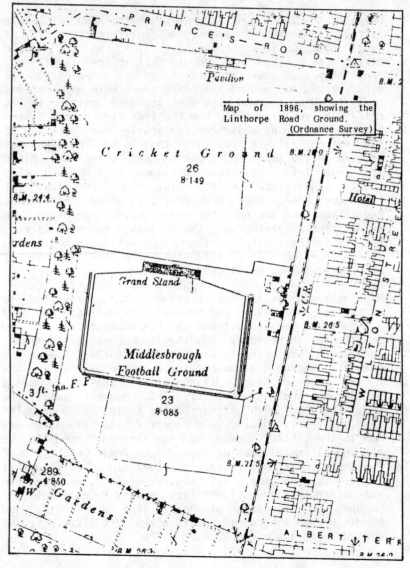

Map of 1896, showing the Linthorpe Road Ground. (Ordnance Survey)

MILLWALL

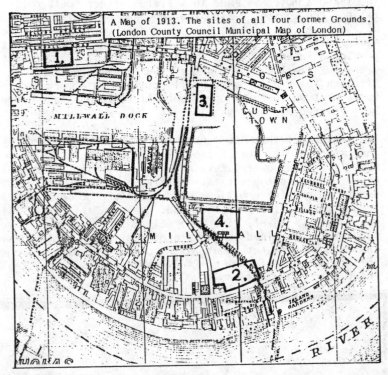

A Map of 1913. The sites of all four former Grounds.
(London County Council Municipal Map of London)

Millwall F.C. is one of a small band of Football League
Clubs that do not play (now) in the town or locality of
their title! Millwall is on The Isle of Dogs, in East
London, and North of the Thames but the Club are now
based South of the river.

GLENGALL ROAD

The Club started life in a humble way and in similar
surroundings. As Millwall Rovers, the Club was formed in
1885, and their first Ground was no more than a
reasonably flat piece of waste ground. This venue was at
the West end, and South of, Glengall Road - now Tiller
Road - opposite Alpha Road. The Club used this Ground for
only one year, and their status at this time dictated
that there were no facilities or an enclosure fence. By
early in the Twentieth Century the site had become a
school, and more recently, in an area that has
drastically changed both physically and in character,
modern housing has been built there.

EAST FERRY ROAD - TWO GROUNDS.

In 1886 a move was made to a field further South on the Island, and located behind the Lord Nelson Public House, at the junctions of East Ferry and Manchester Roads. Once again it is highly unlikely that this Ground was developed in any way, and, still in their formulative years, Millwall moved after four years of occupation. Although the Public House still remains, in a more modern form, what was once an open football field has long since been covered by housing.

The reason for the Club's need to move on was caused by the owners of the Lord Nelson field who were intending to build a switchback railway and create a public recreation area. Such plans never materialised, but the Club in any event had greater ambitions, and their second move was to become their first proper Ground. However, intitially it was hardly ideal, for the 27 acre site was more accurately described as swampland! But with enthusiasm the Club members set about making drastic changes and the not inconsiderable sum of £400 was spent on the new East Ferry Road headquarters.

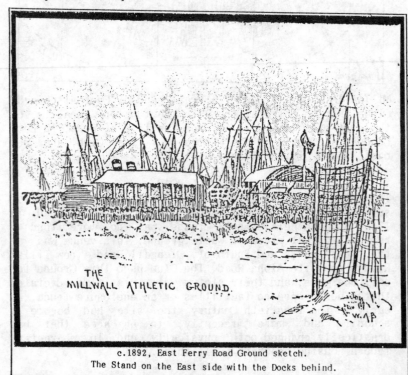

THE MILLWALL ATHLETIC GROUND.

c.1892, East Ferry Road Ground sketch.
The Stand on the East side with the Docks behind.

-224-

Millwall Athletic team group of 1891. The seated Stand
on the East side of the East Ferry Road Ground.

Now known as Millwall Athletic, draining the ground and
levelling became the first priority for the Club - which
was started and completed in just the one month that   led
up to the start of the 1890/91 season. On the West side
(adjacent to East ferry Road), a 500 seated capacity
Grandstand (later enlarged to hold another 100) was
built, and dressing rooms were provided. A large football
pitch which measured 120 by 80 yards was formed, outside
of which a 5 yards width running track was laid to form
an overall near square arena, but rounded at the corners.
There was slight banking to the perimeter,   and a main
entrance on the East Ferry Road side.

By   the   early 1890's, they had become one of the premier
Clubs in the South of England, and were able   to   attract
not   only   good support but managed to entice some of the
top professional teams to South London. A crowd of   3,000
were present for the match versus the 71st Highland Light
Infrantry in September 1891, 2,000 for the third round of
the Middlesex Senior Cup (against Westminster Criterion),
and   ten days later on a dull and very cold day (the 29th
of March 1892), Everton were beaten 2-1 at East Ferry
Road. Although the 'Millwall Athletic Ground' became over
the years, one of the best Football Grounds in London, it
was   some   years   before the Club could finally eradicate
the smell of the former swamp!

Talks of forming the Southern League were first held in 1892, and Millwall became one of the first teams in the South to become professional, one year later. On the 19th of November 1892, the other progressive London team - Woolwich Arsenal - came to Millwall, and attracted not only a record attendance at the Ground, but possibly the biggest ever to have attended a match in London. 14,000 packed into the enclosure, with the gate money totalling £342. In 1894, the Club were the main instigators that at last set the formation of the Southern League in motion.

The Athletic took the League by storm, and after beating Swindon Town by 9-0 in their opening fixture they became the first Club to become League Champions without losing a match. The Club declined an invitation to join the Football League - due to travelling expenses (a decision that they would regret a few years later when their application for membership

Newspaper advertisement of 1894. (East End News)

received only one vote) - and completed the 1895/96 season in much the same fashion as a year earlier. The Club just missed out on a hat-trick of successes, and were then unable to claim a final position in the top three until many years later.

The unimpressive years were considerably enhanced with some outstanding performances in the F.A.Cup, including two semi-finals appearances in 1900 and 1903. Jarrow were beaten in the 1st round of the 1899/1900 competition, followed by a victory at Queens Park Rangers. The quarter final tie brought Aston Villa to Millwall, and the visitors created unparalleled interest. The attendance was expected to reach 30,000, and it was mooted that the spectacle should be held at the Crystal Palace. Although the capacity of the East Ferry Road Ground was only estimated to be 23,000, the game took place in the Docklands. Prices ranged from 2½p to 12½p (the latter for the Reserved Stand and the covered and numbered seats elsewhere). Additional seating was provided for by the hire of chairs from the Essex County Ground. With 5,000 visiting supporters there, a new Ground record attendance was easily established, although this 'only' numbered approximately 20,000. After sharing two goals, the replay ended goalless, but Millwall went through to the semi-final stage by eventually winning by 2-1.

But such moments of success were very rare, and were insufficient to lift the financial gloom from the Club. When they received notice to quit the East Ferry Road Ground in 1901, the Athletic were near to extinction; a Club that so recently had reached the heights in the premier Cup competition - and were soon to do so again. The last Southern L ague match at East Ferry Road on the 6th of April was played versus Luton, and three weeks later Bristol City were entertained in a Western League match. With no new Ground decided upon, it was a sad crowd present, who wondered if this could be the final game for the team.

The land on which the Ground had been built was owned by the Millwall Docks Company and was wanted for a timber yard; after many years the yard was subsequently replaced by an ASDA Superstore, and although the boundaries of this Retail outlet still broadly follow those of the former football Ground, nothing remains of this once large Stadium.

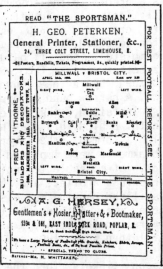

(Upper): Programme from the penultimate season at East Ferry Road.
(Lower): Millwall beat Preston in the 1902/03 season F.A.Cup match. The North bank of the North Greenwich Ground.

NORTH GREENWICH GROUND.

The Club had little time, or money, to find a suitable site and create a new Ground, if they were to continue. However a field was found, about midway between the earlier Lord Nelson site and their just vacated venue. Although still situated close to East Ferry Road, the Ground was to become known, confusingly, as the North Greenwich Ground. But in the Summer of 1902 with cows grazing and potatoes being grown there, it looked a far cry from a future Football Stadium for a professional team! With only an initial seven year lease granted to the Club, they wanted minimum expenditure, even so it was calculated that £2,000 would be required for conversion. A 'Save Millwall Fund' raised sufficient money to turn the plan into a reality, and in only two months, which was a credit to the community who were prepared to save their football Club. With little time available, terraces were created, a 500 capacity Stand was built, and the pitch levelled. It was really a case of 'speculate to accumulate', and it paid off, influenced greatly by the far better access from South of the River that was provided by a new tunnel link from Woolwich to Cubbit Town. A narrow band of open seating opposite the Stand was installed, that stretched for nearly the full pitch length. Behind this seating was the Globe Rope Works, which formed the Northern boundary. Part of the embankments were improved by the acquisition from Poplar Park, of moveable terracing that had been used for Queen Victoria's Jubilee, and behind the railway end, some stabilized banking was also later added. But the dressing Rooms were nothing better than old sheds, and it was several months before a piped water supply was laid on, until then water tubs had to be used!

Season tickets for the Ground and Stand cost fifteen shillings (75p), 50p for the terraces only, and bicycles could be stored during the matches for 1p! On the 18th of September 1902 a friendly match with Aston Villa - who were beaten by 2-0 - was arranged to give the new Ground a prestigious opening. Portsmouth became the first league visitors three days later. Despite the rain there was a large crowd present, but the locals lost by the odd goal in five.

The second excellent F.A.Cup run sealed the Club's success and ensured their continued survival. The run included a home defeat of Luton (before a 10,000 crowd), and a visit from Preston North End.

Many fans were no doubt concerned by the prediction of crowd trouble that was expected with this highly attractive match, and the attendance of 10,000 was well below that which had been hoped for.

But in the latter years at North Woolwich, the Club were never able to reclaim their earlier glories, and for much of the period leading upto their automatic election into the new Third Division they struggled on the field. In all the circumstances it was perhaps something of a surprise that their financial fortunes conversely took a turn for the better. By the end of the 1909/10 season the average gate had risen to around 6,000, although the better and worst attendances were extreme; 2,000 for Coventry's visit in April 1910 and 15,000 for the local derby with West Ham several months earlier, being good examples. Even so it was still something of a financial struggle, and rumours started circulating that the Club were planning to move Grounds. Sites at Bow Railway Works and Deptford Waterworks were considered, along with a venue South of the Thames where it was thought bigger crowds could be enticed. Such thoughts did not please the supporters, although it had to be realised that along with only mediocre support, the North Greenwich Ground left a lot to be desired. A final decision was made to move South to New Cross. Such intentions supposedly brought about the expression - "Keep it on the Island" - referring in general to ensuring that the ball remained in play, but colloquially meaning that Millwall Football Club should remain on the Isle of Dogs!

It was intended to start the 1910/11 season at the new Ground which was located at The Den at Cold Blow Lane in New Cross, but was delayed due to unfinished work at the new venue. One of the last games at North Woolwich on the 24th of September 1910 attracted an attendance of 12,000, and it was admitted that if such figures could be maintained regularly there would have been no need to move. However, the match was versus West Ham, and therefore could not be regarded as the norm. On the 29th of October the Club made their debut at New Cross when Brighton were the visitors, and the attendance totalled 25,000! How strange that in 1910 Millwall found it necessary to make a permanent move to South of the Thames in order to find additional support, whereas three years later, and a few miles up the river, Arsenal also crossed the river - for the same reason - but in the reverse direction!

Although virtually all traces of the North Greenwich
Ground have long since disappeared, the park - which is
still used for football (and cricket) - still retains on
it's Eastern boundary an elevated section of railway;
once the Millwall Extension Railway, it has recently been
re-opened as the Docklands Light Railway. The actual site
of the former ground can easily be imagined, and in the
East corner - where several buildings from the former
Rope Works Company are still standing, an embankment
complete with some timber railway sleepers remains, which
was once the standing area at the railway end.

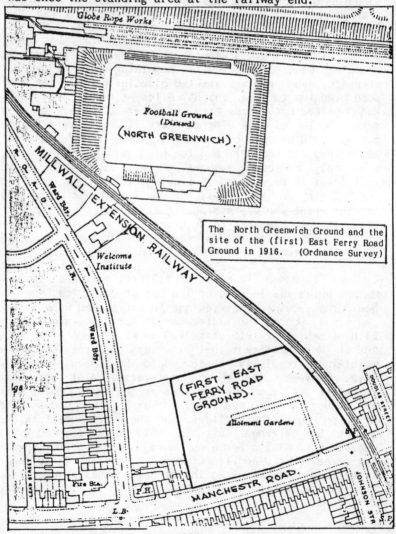

The North Greenwich Ground and the
site of the (first) East Ferry Road
Ground in 1916.   (Ordnance Survey)

The Isle of Dogs has naturally undergone much change over the intervening years, but in the last few the transformation has been most dramatic. From a decayed and rundown area, there now exist Tower Blocks, middle class housing and modern Industrial developments notably near the waterside areas. Change is inevitable, but there are many that would argue that modern buildings cannot replace the character of the Docklands and it's community, that has now been lost forever.

(Top): An (uncredited) artist's impression of the North Greenwich Ground South-east corner (The Christ Church spire on the extreme left)
(Bottom): The view in 1989.   (Dave Twydell)

NEWCASTLE UNITED

It was quite common in the late 19th Century for two
different Clubs to merge and form one strong outfit; but,
as in the case of Newcastle United, it was most unusual
that the two original Clubs should have first seen the
light of day during the same year!

THE WEST END: THE LEAZES.

First on the scene, by two months, was Newcastle West End
who were created from a Cricket team. From the football
Club's inception in 1882, and for three years afterwards,
the Club played at the Ground of the cricketers on Town
Moor. This was little more than a rough patch of land
with nothing to offer spectators or players, except for a
Clubhouse. The Ground was also known as The Leazes, and
has now been for many years the site of the Royal
Infirmary.

ESKDALE TERRACE.

In 1885, the West End were forced to move, when the
playing of ball games was forbidden on the Leazes. For a
year the Club moved to Jesmond, an already established
and enclosed Ground adjacent to Eskdale Terrace.

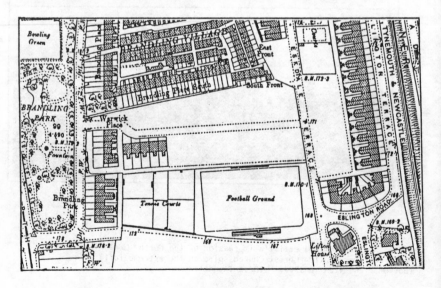

The Eskdale Terrace Ground in 1898. Home of one of the Club's
forerunners - the West End.   (Ordnance Survey)

EAST END WERE BASED ORIGINALLY IN BYKER THEN AT CHILLINGHAM ROAD IN HEATON.

THEY BOASTED A GROWING BAND OF ENTHUSIASTS AIMING TO MAKE THE CLUB TYNESIDE'S BEST.

(Top): An 1889 team group outside the Pavilion at Chillingham Road.
(Bottom): An Artist's impression of the East End Club leaving the
Pavilion at the Chillingham Road Ground.   (T. Canning)

The venue had been the home of the, by now Defunct,
Jesmond F.C., and was at that time occupied by Newcastle
F.C., another Club that was soon to disappear. The two
Clubs shared what was, by the standards of the day, a
well developed enclosure.

The late 19th century Ordinance Survey map (issued after the West End had departed) shows a narrow, and about half pitch length Stand down each side of the pitch. The South Stand, which was slightly wider than its opposite number, was open seated, and behind this was a small building which was presumably the Dressing Rooms - a rare luxury in those days!

The game was already making great strides in popularity in the North-east of England - influenced no doubt by the enthusiasm shown from a short distance North, across the Border. Tyne Association were the acknowledged pioneers, and they were one of the few Clubs available to join the Northumberland and Durham F.A. in 1879. Newcastle Rangers were the first winners of the Association's Cup Competition in 1881, when the final was played at Newcastle's Bath Road Cricket Club. By 1883, and following the appearance of several more Clubs, the two Counties split to form two separate Associations. At the inaugural meeting of the Northumberland F.A., representatives from over forty teams were present, including both the West End and East End Clubs from Newcastle.

ST. JAMES' PARK.

William Neasham, one of the leading instigators of the formation of the West End, had a fourteen year lease on a few acres of land - which had been used for sheep grazing - and in 1886, the Club moved there from their short occupation of the Eskdale Terrace venue. The new Ground, which was known as St.James Park, had previously been used by the, soon to be defunct, Newcastle Rangers Club, since their formation in 1880 until 1882, thereby making it the oldest Football Ground in the North-east. St.James Park was separated from the adjacent Leazes Park by an eight foot high fence and contained a playing pitch which measured 120 yards by 60 yards - long but narrow. This venue was a far cry from the later developed Stadium, since it had a notorious eighteen foot slope from the Gallowgate (South) end, and precious few facilities for either Players or spectators. The first game at St.James Park was a prestigious match with close rivals East End. The Ground was formally opened by the Sheriff of Newcastle, and a crowd of 2,000 - the biggest Newcastle football assembly to that date - at a cost of 3d by ticket or 6d. (2½p) at the gate. On the day, only 7/11d (just under forty pence), was realised, therefore it can be assumed that the vast majority of fans chose to purchase their tickets in advance. The West End won the game by 3-2. In November 1886, the Club played their first F.A.Cup game, when they defeated Sunderland, at home, by a single goal.

THE EAST END: CHILLINGHAM ROAD.

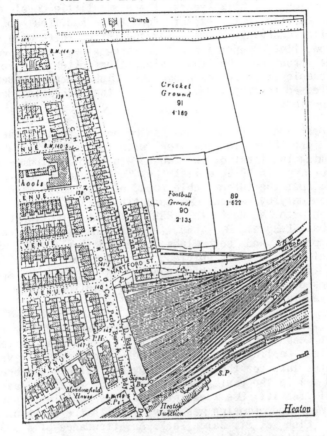

The East End Club's Ground in 1898 at Chillingham Road.
(Ordnance Survey)

Newcastle East End was created in October 1882 from the Stanley Club (in the South Byker District) and were joined soon afterwards by Rosewood F.C., to complete the amalgamation of a team that could challenge for supremacy in the area. The Club's initial Ground was nothing more than an open area of land at St.Peter's in Byker (near Dalton Street), and in 1886 they moved about half a mile North-east to Chillingham Road in the Heaton district.

The new Ground had been used by the Heaton Athletic Club, and initially consisted of no more than a partly enclosed field with a roped off pitch. The Ground was located to the East of Chillingham Road, and ran alongside Spencer Street, with the Southern boundary abutting the Heaton Junction railway sidings. Despite the East End's occupation for six years, there was little development work carried out, except for the addition of a Pavilion/Changing Rooms. For spectators there were only narrow, flat, standing areas on three sides, and a much wider area on the East side. The pitch was of a reasonable standard, although the Club were frequently criticised for the muddy conditions that prevailed during wet periods.

The West and East End Clubs had by now emerged as the two most prominent in the area, with the East Organisation becoming the first of the two to win the Northumberland Senior Cup, in 1885, whilst the 'Wests' had to wait until 1888. But the interminable round of 'Friendly' matches - broken only by various Cup Competitions - was at last brought to a halt in 1888 with the formation of the Football League. By 1889, Professionalism had become widespread, and both Clubs turned to this status, which coincided with their entries into the Northern League competition. Until this change in the Football scene, crowds of above 1,000 at home games of either team were few and far between.

The 7th of September 1889, saw the East End play their first League match. Around 1,500 spectators patiently awaited Darlington's appearance - Darlington arrived 45 minutes late for the kick-off. By half-time the scoreline read 2-1 in the Easts favour, and this remained as the final result. One week later, a fine curtain-raiser for the West End campaign was provided with the visit of the East Club at St. James Park. An attendance of 4,000 saw the homesters win by two unopposed goals. The playing of regular competitive matches provided the right results at the gate, with generally better attendances than before (the East End attracted 3,000 to Chillingham Road for Middlesbrough's visit). By the season's end both Newcastle Clubs were reasonably satisfied, the West End finishing in the runners-up position, and their rivals, in fourth. One year later things were not so good, with both Club ending with lowly placings.

By now it was becoming apparent that there was insufficient support for two top class teams in Newcastle. At this time the North-east did not enjoy the support that other large towns were receiving, and similar fates were shortly to become the lot of the weaker teams in Sunderland and Middlesbrough as well. During the close season the West End became defunct, as did Sunderland Albion, and although they were initially the stronger of the two Middlesbrough Clubs, it was not long before the Ironopolis called it a day. The passing away of Newcastle West End at least occurred in an amicable way.

UNITED AT ST. JAMES' PARK.

Ironically the West End had developed the marginally better Ground. With new Directors and thirty men subscribing £5 each for improvements to St. James Park, it was possible to provide wooden 'duckboards' for the spectators comfort, and tiny enclosures were built on each side of the Ground for the benefit of the Press. But there were still no dressing rooms on the ground, the home Players having the luxury of changing at the Lord Hill Public House (opposite the Ground), while the visiting team had to make their own arrangements in the town, and walk or be transported by charabanc to St. James Park!

The East End chose to become a Limited Company in March 1890, and 50p shares were sold to the public which realised £800 of the 2,000 issued. With a more secure financial base (and nothing spent on the Ground), they soon became the more successful of the two Clubs. The more progressive East End outfit paid the players, in addition to 15 shillings (75p) for a win and ten for a draw, a one shilling bonus for every goal scored, and their more innovative methods paid off. There was never a formal merging of the two former Clubs. West End invited the Easts to take over the St. James Park Ground, the future lease at Chillingham Road was in any event uncertain, and several of the Directors (and three Players) from the now defunct Club joined East End. The Club, no longer in the East end of the town finally decided upon the title of Newcastle United, in December 1892, although this name was not legally changed until 1895. The first game at St.James Park was played on the 3rd of September 1892, against Glasgow Celtic, and 7,000 were present (receipts of £147) to see the start of the new era of football in Newcastle.

THE GROUNDS TODAY.

Of the former Grounds of the two Clubs, the sites of the Chillingham Road, and the Eskdale Terrace Grounds are the most readily identifiable. The Heaton Junction sidings that lay to the South of the former East End's venue have all but disappeared, and this area has reverted to virtual waste ground. Houses on the East side of Spencer Street have been built along what was the West side of the Football Ground, the rest of the enclosure having been largely built upon.

There was a Cricket Ground immediately North of the Football Ground - where Cleghorn and Richardson Streets now lie. The earlier division line between the two sporting enclosures coincides with a break in the Spencer Street houses and continues on to form Marleen Avenue.

Eskdale Terrace still exists, and the Ground of the West End was located on the present Royal Grammar School and adjoining playing field site.

Spencer Street in 1989. The Chillingham Road Ground was to the right of the road.   (Bill Gibbs)

NORWICH CITY

Although Norwich City were not founded until 1902 - the
first meeting took place on the 17th of June at the
Criterion Cafe - football had been played in the town
many years earlier. As far back as 1868 a Norwich Club
played at the Newmarket Road Ground, the venue chosen by
the later City Club.

NEWMARKET ROAD.

The Newmarket Road Ground was the obvious choice for the
ambitious newly formed Norwich City F.C. since of several
sports grounds, this was the only one that could offer a
Grandstand. The Ground, which at this time was owned by
Town Close Estates, was leased out to the Norfolk County
F.A. for various County Cup Competitions and also for
occasional County football matches. In addition the
Norfolk County Cricket Club made occasional use of the
venue in the late 19th century. But with such under usage
the County F.A. were more than willing to sub-let it to
the new football club at an annual rental of £25-00.

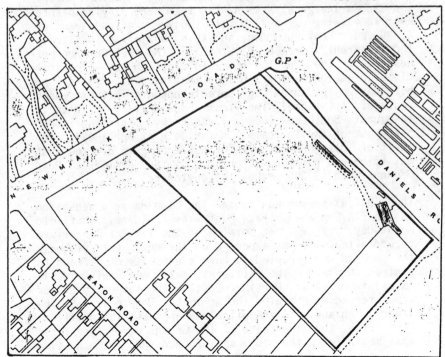

Map of 1938. Newmarket Road retained most of it's earlier Football Ground features.

There was little expenditure for the Football Club, since the Ground was already enclosed and the narrow forty metres long Grandstand had a capacity for around 600, seated on timber benches. In the early days, another seated or standing covered enclosure, was added on the opposite, South-west, side of the pitch. The pavilion, which was used as changing rooms was (and still is!) located in the South-east corner of the 170 or so metre long field. Additional open seating - which consisted of several tiered timber benches - was provided around the perimeter of the playing field, and which allowed further standing behind. Compared with many Clubs that were founded in an earlier era, the Newmarket Road Ground offered a quite substantial and well equipped enclosure.

The Club gained immediate entry into the Norfolk and Suffolk League, which had been formed in 1897, and the City kicked off their first campaign with an away match at Harwich & Parkeston on the 6th of September 1902. Before a crowd of around 2,000, two goals were shared. A few days later the Newmarket Road Ground staged it's first League game, when, in front of 1,700, Ipswich Town were entertained. Although no honours were claimed during the Club's inaugural season, the team were playing before ever increasing numbers. Within two years attendances of 6,000 were not uncommon, and this popularity inevitably led to a rent increase, to £102, for the 1905/06 season. Respect for the Club led to rapid election into the first division of the Southern League that season, despite them not having captured any notable honours in their three years of existance. The team had a very creditable inaugural Southern League season by finishing in 8th place out of twenty teams. On the 14th of April 1906, the visit of Tottenham Hotspur for a League game created what was to become a record attendance at the Newmarket Road Ground, when 11,500 packed the enclosure.

The 1907/08 season was to see the Club cause a sensation in the F.A.Cup when they beat the holders, Sheffield Wednesday, by 2-1 at Norwich on the 11th of January. A record attendance was expected on the day, yet although the Ground was expected to have a capacity of fifteen to sixteen thousand, the official gate was only 10,336 (Receipts of £670). For the occasion two temporary Stands were erected, one behind the Newmarket Road goal with the other at an angle to the pitch and opposite the pavilion. New terms for the lease of the Ground were given later that month, when the Club was informed that the Education

Committee were to have the use of the enclosure on all days except Saturdays, and furthermore the Football Club were to be reponsible for the staff and equipment necessary for its upkeep. Such conditions were unacceptable to the Club, and prompted a move. The new Chairman - Mr. John Samuel Pyke - since February 1907 (who had been elected following a broadroom rift) was able to help with a site he had purchased on the other side of town. The last match was played at Newmarket Road when Chelsea were entertained in in the Hospital Cup. Six goals were shared in front of 6,150 spectators on the 30th of April.

(Top): Team Group at Newmarket Road in 1906. The seated Stand was on the North-east side.
(Bottom): One of the last matches at Newmarket Road in March 1908. (Versus New Brompton)
(Norwich Mercury)

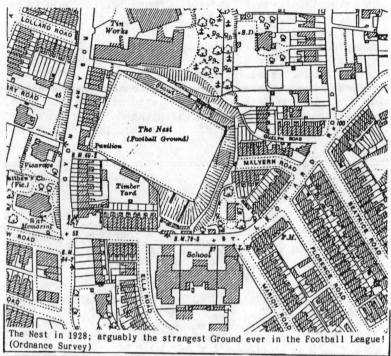

The Nest in 1928; arguably the strangest Ground ever in the Football League! (Ordnance Survey)

The Chairman had purchased a disused chalk pit that lay just off Rosary Road, that was known as Rump's Hole, and work started in earnest to transform it into a Football Ground. To perceive such an undertaking must have taken a great deal of imagination, for 'The Nest', as it was to become known (derived from the Club's by now popular nickname of 'The Canaries') was surely the strangest site imaginable! Although the Rosary Road end was moderately flat, the East end of the site contained steep chalk faces with a veritable shear cliff at the far end. The initial work involved the removal of the lime kilns and ancillary buildings plus the huge quantities of earth in order to provide a level pitch area. This left the amazing site, immediately at the end of the pitch, of a near vertical face at the Malvern Road end, upon which a series of walkways and small flat platforms at different levels providing good, albeit somewhat precarious, viewing!

Difficult work constructing the Rosary Road ('The Nest') Ground in August 1908. (Norwich Mercury)

The design of the Ground was under the direction of the ubiquitous Archibald Leitch, an Architect who had already undertaken the design of several Football Stadiums, notably Fulham, Chelsea and Manchester United. Leitch was to continue such football work, and until the Second World War was, more than any other individual, to leave his mark on the creation of Football Stadiums throughout the United Kingdom. The Nest however, could not honestly be considered as one of his best. The site was severely limited in size, and hardly provided the ingredients for an innovative design. The use of the 'cliff' end could hardly have been altered, whereas behind the Rosary Road goal there was only room for a small triangular section of terracing with barely room for a single line of spectators along the rest of the goal line. The Stands from Newmarket Road were dismantled and laboriously transferred by horse and cart, to be re-erected at the new enclosure. The large Stand (which was enlarged at a later date) stretched along much of the North touchline before it virtually merged into the chalk wall. Opposite, the smaller of the Stands was built hard up to the touchline, for once again there was little room on this side for any standing spectators - except at the East end, where effectively a large terraced area was created from the hillside. The final additions to this strangest of Grounds was a roof that was placed over the only reasonably sized flat area at the cliff end, and a small pavilion that was wedged in to the South-west corner. There were however a variety of entrances. Two off Rosary Road - giving access to the main Stand and the end terrace; one halfway up St Leonards Road, and the third at the end of Malvern Road which gave direct access to the top of the cliff. Initially the capacity was stated as 12,000, but in view of the intended figures of 25 to 30,000 later, it is probable that some of the aforementioned facilities were not installed immediately.

Despite the cramped and unusual quarters, the Club succeeded in providing the town with one of the best enclosures in the Southern League, and a fast construction period that allowed them to kick-off the 1908/09 season at this new home. Trial matches were held at Newmarket Road before crowds of around 2,000, followed by the inaugural match at Rosary Road on the 1st of September, a Friendly versus Fulham. the Band of Watts Naval Training School provided the pre-match entertainment, followed by the Chairman, Mr. Pyke, formally kicking-off. The occasion was not matched by the weather for incessant rain kept the attendance down to less than 4,000, but those present went home happy following the Canaries 2-1 victory. Four days later a Reserve game versus the second eleven of Swindon attracted an attendance of 4,000. The first team were thrashed at Swindon by 2-10 that day, but an excellent attendance (in good weather) of 12,000 was present for the first home Southern League match versus Portsmouth, which finished scoreless.

The first professional match at The Nest (versus Portsmouth 1908), the near vertical East end not completed.

A poor playing start was made to the season - which continued to the end - but the fans were generally faithful and attendances included 6,000 in the rain when Plymouth were the visitors, and 7,100 for top of the table Southampton's visit. But a problem occurred when the Club were drawn at home in the F.A.Cup. Their opponents, Reading, complained of an undersized pitch, and with this being upheld, the match had to played on a neutral Ground. Poor to indifferent playing seasons that led upto the First World War did not normally discourage the supporters, and on the 19th of September 1910, a Club and Ground record attendance of 13,473 was present for the Hospital Cup match versus Newcastle United.

After the war a new pitch was laid and a number of improvements were made. Dressing rooms and Bathrooms were upgraded, and a new Recreation room for the Players, plus new accommodation for the Directors were added. The Canaries were elected into the new Third Division for the 1920/21 season, and the first game at this level produced a crowd of 12,000 for Plymouth's visit. But the precarious nature of the Ground was emphasised when a packed crowd of over 14,000 resulted in a wall collapse at the concrete reinforced cliff face end, with sixty - none serious - injuries! the Clubs fortunes on the field continued in a low vein until a dramatic improvement to a final third place in 1933, that was followed by the Championship one year later. But the Club knew that drastic improvements had to be made to the Ground, or a move made, as the Football Authorities became more critical of Clubs' venues. In the Summer of 1933 soil was added to the Rosary Road end, which at least improved the playing service, although at this time a move to Boundary Park was mooted but never acted upon. During the Club's best season to that date, an attendance record for a League game of 22,363 was present for Newport's visit on the 2nd of April 1934.

The Canaries promotion to Division Two created great interest and although the League results were indifferent there was only one gate that failed to reach five figures. But the real excitement was saved for the F.A.Cup when the Club reached the 5th Round. This biggest game in the Club's history brought Sheffield Wednesday to Norfolk once again, and the Rosary Road Ground was packed, with the gates having been shut well before the kick-off. The team narrowly failed by the only goal of the game, but the attendance of 25,007 which produced receipts of £2,387, represented a record. It was now apparent that if the Club were to progress, then drastic improvements had to be made to the Ground, with the re-building of the main Stand being the first priority. Mr. Pyke, who had by now relinquished the Chairmanship, but was still a keen supporter, considered that less than £6,000 would be necessary for the work, which to the successful Club was well within their capabilities - when they moved to Rosary Road they were virtually penniless. No doubt Mr. Pyke was also keen for the Club to stay at the Ground, since there were still seven years on the lease remaining! However, the Football Association informed the Club that the enclosure was unsuitable for large attendances, and the Club's plans for improvements were considered insufficient. A move had to be made, and suggestions which included Boundary Park (again), St.James Hollow and Barrack Street were all dismissed.

On the 6th of May 1935, the last Club match was played at Rosary Road, when Arsenal were the Canary's opponents in the Hospital Cup, and the novelty of using two referees as an experiment was used.

The City loose to the Corinthians in the F.A.Cup, January 1929.
(Sports Pictures and Football Mirror)

A marvellous crowd of 14,600 (a record for the annual match and over 1,000 more than any previous games) bade the Ground farewell. Five days later the use of the Ground came to an end when an attendance of 1,985 was recorded. The 'A' team thrashed Sherringham in the Norfolk Senior Cup Final - the first time the Cup was won by the Club. By June the 1st a decision had been taken, and the Club announced of their immediate move to Carrow Road. Archibald Leitch was again involved, and a Stadium to hold 35,000 was planned. The first match at the new, rapidly built venue, on the 31st of August was watched by 32,000, a figure well in excess of any crowd that had previously attended a fixture in Norwich.

THE GROUNDS TODAY.

Despite the long passage of time, features of both previous Grounds of Norwich City remain. At Newmarket Road, on the South-eastern outskirts of the town, the field which was once the Football ground remains intact, but is now used as a School Sports Ground. But most surprising of all, the pavilion - little changed from nearly a century ago - remains, albeit in a delapidated state; the day is not too far distant when this poignant reminder of the Club's beginnings will no doubt be removed! The Rosary Road Ground has long since disappeared, to be replaced with several Workshops and Builder's Merchants. But the 'cliff' face is clearly visible, and it's usage as a terrace may still be apparent, but access is now prevented. But at least this memorial to perhaps the most unusual Ground to grace the Football League is likely to remain as a permanent one.

The site of 'The Nest', from the West, in 1989 - now a small Industrial Estate.
(Dave Twydell)

THE NOTTINGHAMS

The two Nottingham Clubs, Forest and County, would hardly wish to be grouped together to form one! But due to several inter-related Grounds that each have used, it is logical to follow their moves concurrently. With the County being the oldest Football League Club and founder-members of same, and the Forest having the honour of being the third most ancient, delving into the locations and histories of each Clubs' several Grounds is something of a nightmare (from a Research point of view!).

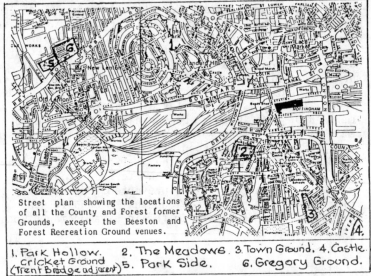

Street plan showing the locations of all the County and Forest former Grounds, except the Beeston and Forest Recreation Ground venues.

1. Park Hollow. 2. The Meadows. 3. Town Ground. 4. Castle. Cricket Ground (Trent Bridge adjacent) 5. Park Side. 6. Gregory Ground.

PARK HOLLOW.

In the mid-19th Century, the town of Nottingham was clustered around the Castle, and it was here that Notts. County first put down their roots. To call their first venue, at Park Hollow, a 'Ground', is something of an exaggeration, for this Ground was nothing more than a reasonably flat, irregular shaped depression in the generally sloping surrounds of the Castle, known collectively as 'The Park Estate'. Some half a mile to the West of the Castle lay the Barracks of the town, and even in the early 1800's smart individual houses started appearing with the disappearance of the Barracks themselves in the earlier part of this Century.

However it was some years before the Hollow was built upon, and for two years – from the Club's formation in 1862 – this became the playing area of the 'Notts Football Club', as they were originally known. In these formulative years, any resemblance to 'football' as we know it today was purely coincidental, (the Club's formation preceded the Football Association itself) for the sport was almost entirely devoid of rules and the game was played by any number of Players. The antiquity of the Club ensured that other competition was non-existant, and these early days were spent with the Club playing games, with teams drawn from its own membership!

On the 7th of December 1864, at the George IV Hotel, the Club formally came into being, although rather grandly they declared that the Club was formed "for the County", and hence their title Notts. (viz. Nottinghamshire) Football Club. Perhaps not unreasonably in view of their seniority, they later tended to become somewhat aloof from the 'other' major team in the area, the 'town' Club, Nottingham Forest. The day after the Notts. Club inaugural meeting they played their first proper game, against the Trent Valley Club, a twenty a-side match – at The Meadows.

FOREST RECREATION GROUND.
Further North in the town, another challenger was created, (at the Clinton Arms Hotel, Sherwood Street in 1865), The Forest Football Club. This team's 'Ground' was little better than the County's so far as enclosure was concerned, and since their appearances were made at the Forest Recreation Ground (which previously had been covered with trees and formed part of Sherwood Forest) their chosen name was synonymous with the location. This venue had been used previously by the Forest's founders, for Shinney – a form of Hockey. Whilst the Ground may have lacked enclosure, it was far from cramped for there was room at the Eastern end, for at least three football pitches on this vast expanse that was surrounded by a Racecourse. At the West end there was even a Grandstand (which was built in the 18th century and only finally demolished in 1912), although somewhat removed from the football area it is doubtful whether it would have been used for football spectators. However, there were dressing rooms, within a thatched Pavilion, that was probably located about mid-length on the South side of the Recreation-cum-Racecourse.

The now demolished thatched roof pavilion at the Forest Recreation Ground, probably on the South side. No doubt once used by the Forest Club (1865 - 1879).
(Notts. Local Studies Library)

Forest Recreation Ground in 1881. The Forest probably played on the area immediately to the right of the Grandstand. Note the the pavilion, bottom of map.
(Ordnance Survey)

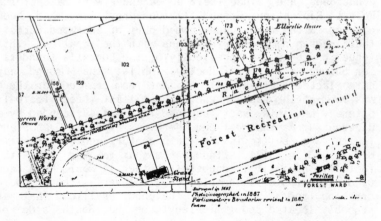

The first proper match was a local derby for the two Nottingham Clubs on the 22nd of March 1866 at the Forest Recreation Ground. With a mixture of both Football and Rugby rules, 11 Notts. Players lined up against 17 from the Forest, and the result ended as either a scoreless draw, or a one goal victory to the Forest - a newspaper report of the time conflicts with the result given from the memory of a contestant some years later! The fixture was well supported from both sexes.

The game was played at the West end of the recreation area, adjacent to the Grandstand. Whilst at the Recreation Ground, the Forest were able to claim a trio of 'firsts': In 1870, at an Athletics Festival there was supposedly the first bicycle ('velocipede') race, they were the first team to use shinguards (in 1874), and for a home match versus Sheffield Norfolk in 1878, a whistle was first used as an aid to controlling the game.

THE COUNTY AT THE MEADOWS.

The Notts. Club's permanent move to The Meadows, in 1864, was probably with a view to playing on a defined arena, and more in keeping with their serious approach towards the game. The Meadows lies a short distance South of the Castle, and the actual football pitch was probably situated on the site of the, later named, Meadows Cricket Ground; a contemporary painting of around this time clearly shows the Castle in the background, and a modern photograph - taken from the location of this Cricket Ground - produces a similar view.

There were no facilities for either spectators or players at the Ground, although a natural enclosure was formed by the surrounding trees. For this reason important games were played at the Trent Bridge Cricket Ground, which was later to become the permanent home of the team. The oldest Club in the World (Sheffield F.C.) was played at The Meadows on the 2nd of January 1865, before 'a large crowd', but it was not for another twelve years that the Notts. team entered for the F.A.Cup, when they met and were beaten by this same Club.

Notts. soon adopted Football Association rules (in 1867) by which time their Headquarters were located at the Lion Hotel, and in March 1873 a scoreless draw was played (at Trent Bridge Cricket Ground) with a London F.A. XI, the first team from afar to visit the town.

(Above): A 'football' match c.1820 at The Meadows.
(Below): 1989, and The Meadows is still an open recreation area. (Dave Twydell)

In March 1875, Queens Park were entertained and a 1-1 draw resulted - earlier that year the Notts. Club had lost in Scotland by six unopposed goals! Although there were by now a number of other teams in the town, notably Nottinghams - Law, Castle, Manufacturing Co and Lace - but the two oldest (The Forest and County) rose above the others, and were both soon supplying Players for International matches.

NOTTINGHAMSHIRE CRICKET GROUND, BEESTON.

It was more than just friendly rivalry that separated the two Senior Clubs in the town, and in 1877 the Notts. Club, ever mindful of their more genteel background moved on, to the more suitable (in their eyes) Ground of the 'Gentlemen of Nottinghamshire Cricket Club', at Beeston. Fate declared however that the two teams should meet in the F.A.Cup, on the 16th of November 1878 - the first for the Forest - and 500 spectators were drawn to the match at Beeston (a record crowd for a football game in the town), which was lost by the homesters. This venue was marginally better than the previous one, for it could boast of a small pavilion in the Southern corner of the Ground, and was enclosed.

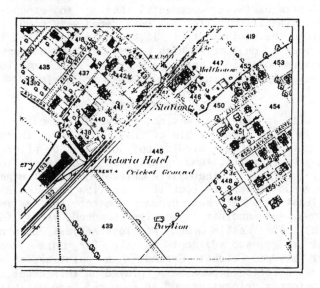

Nottinghamshire Cricket Ground, Beeston, 1883. A few years earlier the home
Ground of the County.   (Ordnance Survey)

THE FOREST AT MEADOW CRICKET GROUND.

The Forest had unparallelled success in the Cup Competition, for they fought on to the semi-final stage, only to lose to the renowned Old Etonians. After fourteen years at the Recreation Ground, the Forest moved on (although like their arch-rivals they too made use of Trent Bridge for important games), and moved in to the Meadows Cricket Ground in 1879, that had only just been vacated by the Notts. Club. Around this time the Castle Club folded, and most of the members joined the Forest.

The Notts. Club's move to Beeston was a strange one - although it was generally thought for snobbish reasons - as the Ground was some distance outside of the town boundary, although for a short while this removal appeared to be satisfactory. On the 30th of November 1878, a massive crowd of some 4,000 attended one of the earliest of floodlight matches when Derbyshire were entertained and beaten by the only goal of the game, however the meeting was held not at Beeston, but at the Trent Bridge Cricket Ground! The game was a great financial success, with spectators paying 6d. for entry, double this for members enclosure on the pavilion side, and Carriages (with occupants) having to expend 2/6d (10p). The illumination was considered very good, for it provided the equivalent of 12,000 candles. The lights were mounted on 5 metre high poles, but were extinguished on several occasions, and the weather - which was foggy - did not help the situation!

CASTLE CRICKET GROUND.

Football in Beeston was not an overall success, and at one time with a membership of less than 40, there was talk of the Club winding-up. So, in 1880, after three uneasy years out of town, a move was made back to the central area, to the Castle Cricket Ground. The name of this venue did not reflect it's location for there were at least two cricket grounds nearer the Castle (The Meadows and another some few hundred yards further South). The Castle Ground was located just South of the Trent Bridge, and adjacent to the far more developed Trent Bridge Cricket Ground - a painting of c.1860 depicts a football game being played on this exact site, but before a cricket ground as such had been established.

The Castle Cricket Ground (c.1902), County's unpretentious Ground from 1880 - 1883. The view is looking towards Loughborough Road, with the pavilion almost out of the picture on the right. County Hall now covers the site. (Notts. Local Studies Library)

Once again facilities left a lot to be desired for within its near six acres, there was only a pavilion (in the South-east corner), although the Ground was reasonably enclosed with the Trent forming a natural boundary to the West, and the playing area on the East side was set-in some distance from the Road. But for the Forest Club, things were looking much rosier, when they moved, also in 1880, to the Trent Bridge Cricket Ground next door! But the County's move was not an immediate success, for yet again there was talk about the Club disbanding.

THE FOREST AT TRENT BRIDGE.

Although the younger of the two Clubs, the Forest's success in the F.A.Cup through to the semi-finals during the 1878/79 season was repeated one year later. During this latter run, two significant results proved their superiority over the Notts. Club, for they comfortably disposed of the renowned Turton and Blackburn Rovers Clubs, with a 6-0 scorelines! But this new found fame decreed that The Meadows was not suitable as a permanent base - an ever increasing number of games were of sufficient importance for them to make use of the Trent Bridge Cricket Ground - and so in 1880 they took up residence at this far better equipped venue. This venue of over 10 acres had been developed, due to the principal enterprise of William Clarke - cricketer and bricklayer - to include a number of facilities for spectators, including some covered standing and seated areas plus a large refreshment room. But despite their successes, their stay was for only two years, and it must have been more than just coincidence that their removal was followed soon after by the, more 'gentlemanly', Notts. Club's tenancy in 1883. Such an assertion is reinforced by the fact that the Cricket Club's Secretary took over the same role with the Notts. Football Club during their occupancy of the Cricket Ground!

The Forest Club's brief glory days in the late 1870's were supplemented by the Notts. Club's rise in the early '80's, by which time they probably took over the mantle of the top town team. In 1881, the Club attracted a record crowd of 4,000 (to - at this time - their temporary home at Trent Bridge), for an F.A.Cup 3rd round match with Aston Villa (which was lost 1-3). And in 1883, they reached the semi-finals (when they lost to the Old Etonians at the Oval). This run was repeated one year later when they fell at the penultimate hurdle to Blackburn Rovers.

At last the Club had found a suitable and more permanent home, for their stay at Trent Bridge lasted for nearly thirty years.

PARK SIDE AND GREGORY GROUNDS.

The Forest Club's move in 1882 resulted in a journey across town, and nearer to their roots, when they took residence in the Lenton area for a few years. Although the stay was short, during this period two different Grounds were used. Due to such abbreviated occupations, the exact locations of these venues are difficult to determine with certainty. The first, named Park Side, cost the Club £300 to develop, but it is unlikely that it offered anything more than the most basic of facilities. Park Side was located on the North side of Derby Road, and almost certainly between the railway line and the present Cottesmore School. It would seem that the field – for it is likely that it was little more than that – was the area opposite the then, as now, Lenton Recreation Ground. This venue consisted of nearly six acres and is now a Sports Ground that runs alongside the present Johnson Road.

The stay at Park Side lasted only three years, before the Forest were on the move again. The distance was but a short one, and almost certainly to the field adjacent to the smaller Park Side Ground, the Gregory Ground. A further £500 was spent in providing basic facilities (which included some provision for spectators) and Ground enclosures.

There were around 2,000 spectators present for the Ground opening, but the much maligned Local Press - as they considered themselves - were most critical that there were no provisions for themselves (a common criticism of the period). The old Park Side Ground appears to have been taken over by the Lenton United Cricket Club after Forest's short 'hop over the fence'. Although their tenure was once again for just a short spell, they did play their first Floodlit match there, against Nottingham Rangers, in March 1889. A number of Wells Lamps were used, and the novelty attracted a crowd of 4,000.

By this time, the Club were playing second fiddle to the County, for the latter gained entry to the first Football League in the World in 1888, whereas the Forest, although represented at the League's inaugural meeting were barred entry due to their continued Amateur status. However they did become founder-members of the closely allied Football Alliance one year later, and their fortunes were about to take an upward step.

THE TOWN GROUND.

The move to a new Ground coincided with the Club turning professional, and in the 1891/92 season, only their second at this level, they once again fought through to the semi-finals of the F.A.Cup, a feat accomplished by their more Senior neighbours one year earlier. But the Forest were thrashed 6-2 by West Bromwich Albion after two one-all draws. This season ended with the Club not only becoming the Alliance Champions, but they were accepted into the enlarged Football League.

The Racecourse, looking North-west, c.1870, at which time the Forest Club were in occupation. The Club probably played just to the right of the Grandstand; could the small group of figures (right side near bottom) be some of the spectators at a match?

Nottingham Forest at The Town Ground, the North side. c.1895.

This wise move to the Town Ground lasted for eight years, until 1898. Once again the precise location of this venue is difficult to pinpoint. It was sited either at the, then, end of Bathley Street, or such that this thoroughfare formed the northern boundary to their enclosure (the probable only surviving photograph that shows part of this Ground does not help to clarify the location). However there is no doubt that the Town Ground was far superior to all of the previous headquarters of the Club.

The cost to the Club to initially develop the Town Ground amounted to £1,000 on the site that was formerly known as Woodwards Field. The Ground occupied 15,000 square yards, and had to be first levelled considerably due to a considerable slope towards the River. Comfortable standing room was provided on one side with a 120 yard banking of six tiers for 2,000, with a flat area at the top for more. Opposite, a covered and seated Reserved Stand (plus the important facilities for the Press!) ran for 50 yards and contained eight rows for 1,000 spectators, with standing room in front. At the Wilford end a bank was built with, at each end, several rows of open seats (with timber gratings for comfort in inclement weather).

The first match on the new Ground was played on the 3rd of October 1890, and the announcement of the fixture immediately caused controversy. Originally Wolverhampton Wanderers (Football League members) were to provide the opposition at the Ground opening. However, the County were scheduled to play a League match that day, just a few hundred yards away at Trent Bridge. The Forest were informed that if their fixture was not altered, then all League Clubs would be barred from arranging fixtures with the Club. The Forest wisely backed down, and played a game against the Queens Park team from Scotland instead. The area was a mass of supporters travelling in opposite directions, with the County enticing 6,000 to their fixture and between three and four thousand to the Town Ground. The Mayor of Nottingham performed the traditional honours, and 'kicked off' at the Forest match, which the homesters won 4-1.

The Town Ground had the honour of being the first at which crossbars and goal-nets were used (replacing the primitive tape and posts only), at a North versus South game in 1891. The Forest stayed at the Town Ground until

1898, when they made their next, and final move, to the City Ground (at an initial cost of £3,000 - eased no doubt by their F.A.Cup win that year) which was not much further than the other side of the Radcliffe Road from Notts. County's Trent Bridge home!

THE COUNTY AT TRENT BRIDGE.

During the Forest's expensive and frequent moves, the County settled into the Trent Bridge Cricket Ground for twenty-seven years (until 1910). During this prolonged period, the venue was developed quite extensively from a venue with little spectator accommodation, to one with seating or standing covered enclosures to most of the perimeter. The main benefit to the Football team were the Pavilion and Stands on the East side, for it was on this portion of the large and approximately square pitch that the football area was marked out during the Winter months.

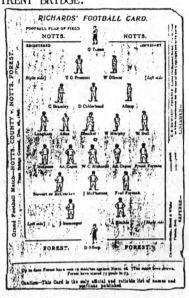

Match Card of Notts County at Trent Bridge, 1896/97 season.

By 1910, a continuous line of banked covered seats and standing areas ran down the East side, with slight banking at each end. On the West side the football pitch was just roped railed off, where just a thin line of spectators, on raised platforms, were allowed. Although midway along the West side a small and moveable seated Stand (which was frequently re-located to prevent undue wear on the Cricketing area) provided a comfortable additional viewing area.

The first game at the Ground was versus Walsall Swifts in September 1883. That same season, 12,000 were present for an F.A.Cup win over their local rivals, and this was increased by a further 3,000 when Bolton were the later visitors. Their inaugural period at this new setting led to an undefeated run at home during the season.

The County's dominance on the football scene in the early Trent Bridge days eventually had to make way to their rivals. Although between seven and eight thousand were present for the County's first home game in the 1894/95 season, just a few months earlier on the 17th of February, a record Football League low attendance for a scheduled saturday match, of only 300, were present for the Crewe fixture; despite the Club's onward march to the F.A.Cup Final! After a prolonged period in the Second Division, even a First Division fixture on the 27th of March 1901 versus Preston only attracted 1,500. The Club's own Ground it was hoped would increase more support, and of great concern was the Club's necessity to use alternative venues (The Meadows and Castle Cricket Grounds in the 1880's and the Forest Ground subsequently) during the overlap of the Cricket season each April and September! Some opponents complained of their 'away' fixture being at Trent Bridge with others at the current Forest Ground, and the Football League were also unhappy with these variable arrangements.

But the County played on until October 1908, when the Trustees of the Cricket Ground refused to renew the lease to the Football Club, that finished at the end of the 1909/10 season, making a move a necessity. In January 1909 the site that was to become the Meadow Lane Ground was examined, and accepted by the Club the next month, at a cost of £6,000. The final game at the Cricket Ground was played against Aston Villa on the 16th of April. The Trent Bridge Ground was honoured by it's staging of F.A.Cup semi-finals in 1893, 1896, 1899, 1901, 1902, 1905 and 1908. Whilst in their first season at the Ground, the Club remained unbeaten in the Football league and went onto the semi-finals of the F.A. Cup itself; ten years later they stayed the full distance, and as a Second Division team won the trophy.

THE GROUNDS TODAY.

Despite the number of different venues that the two Clubs have had over the past, near 130 years, there is little left to identify the sites as former football fields; although in most cases there was little to show when the Clubs were in occupation themselves! The final irony of the Clubs frequent changes has resulted in the 'Town' team (Forest) being situated outside of the town boundary, whilst the 'County' team are domiciled within!

The Hollow has long since been re-contoured and built over with houses. The Meadows Cricket Ground however has been retained as the 'Queens Drive Recreation Ground', an open play area including facilities for bowls. The Beeston Cricket Ground was located immediately South of the railway line, and to the West of the now named Station Road. This site is now occupied by Car Parks and buildings of the Plessey Company. The Castle Cricket Ground, which became the Athletic Ground (but was still used for Cricket around the turn of the Century), is now the home of County Hall. The only Ground that has been retained, albeit vastly developed from those late 19th Century days, is of course the Trent Bridge Cricket Ground.

Despite it's antiquity, the Forest Recreation Ground has not only retained the name, but still covers the same area, and is used very much as it was over 100 years ago. At the West end, where the Grandstand was located, is now a large Car Park, but a modern Pavilion midway down the South side of the Ground is approximately in the same location as the earlier Thatched model. The (probable) location of the Park Side Ground in the Lenton area is now a Sports Ground, whilst the adjacent, and the former Gregory Ground, has been built over with several roads occupying the former field. The Town Ground site has been redeveloped several times, and now contains new modern housing.

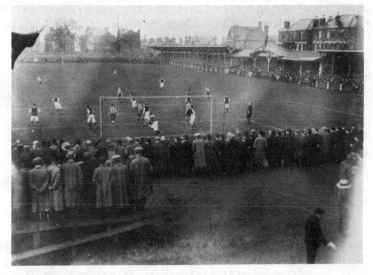

Action from the last match for the County at Trent Bridge, versus Aston Villa.
16th of April 1910.   (Notts. Local Studies Library)

OLDHAM ATHLETIC

In the late 19th century, and particularly in the North-east of the Country, there were countless 'Pub' teams. Down amongst the Cotton Mills in Lancashire, one such team was formed in 1897 with the name of Pine Villa. The Club was created principally by the Licensee and his son of the Feather-stall and Junction Hotel.

PINE MILL:

The new Club's first Ground was located just to the West of Oldham town centre at Berry's Field which was situated to the rear of the Methodist Chapel in Garforth Street, Chadderton. As dressing-rooms, a Smithy close to the Featherstall and Junction Hotel was used. The 'Ground', was no more than one of two unenclosed pitches, and it was not long before an alternative venue was obtained. By the side of the stark, Pine Cotton Mill, a suitable piece of land was found and rented. The Club had started their life somewhat later than their contemporaries in the area, and there were by this time many local Leagues already in operation. Pine Villa chose the Oldham Junior League Division Two for their first season in 1897/98. Two successful years followed, during which time they were promoted, and then finished as runners-up in the First Division; the Champions being local rivals Greenacres.

Elsewhere in the town a Professional team had existed by the name of Oldham County. In the County's short history as a professional Club they had hardly flourished. One season in the Combination, was followed by two in the Lancashire League, in the last of the these campaigns they failed to complete their fixtures, and by 1899 had gone into liquidation. Football had a hard task to compete with the more popular Rugby game in the town, but Pine Villa made a bold move when they decided to take over the old County enclosure, the Athletic Ground, in Sheepfoot Lane.

ATHLETIC GROUND AND HUDSON FOLD:

The Club's status was raised with their election to the Manchester Alliance League whereupon they changed their name to 'Oldham Athletic'. In the first game at the new

Ground, Berry's Reserves were beaten on the 2nd of September 1899. But within a few months the Club were in dispute with the Landlord, which resulted in them transferring to a Ground at Hudson Fold, the same - to all intents and purposes - as the former venue at Pine Mill. The move proved to be costly, but the team performed well and finished the season as runners-up in the Alliance. The next season saw a further elevation with the Club's entry into the Manchester League. Although no honours were won within this company, they made steady progress on the field for the next few years, but were still stretched in terms of finance.

OLDHAM ATHLETIC
Association Football Club.

SEASON 1899-1900

President: Geo. T. Elliot, Esq.
Vice-Presidents:
F. Aldred, Esq.   Dr. Heslop.
H. Calley, Esq.   Dr. Clegg.
H. Rowley, Esq.   Dr. Hearne.
A. Howarth, Esq.   A. Raynor, Esq.
T. Jacques, Esq.   J. Winterbottom, Esq.
Committee:
Mr. G. Worsley.   Mr. J. Bell.
  „ F. Brooks.   „ H. Lees.
  „ W. Taylor.   „ F. Steninson.
  „ F. Marsland.   „ J. Schofield.
         Mr. H. Garland.
Secretary:
Mr. W. Platt, 5, Cambridge Street, Werneth
Fin. Secretary:
Mr. H. Lees, 45, Cottam Street, Oldham.
Treasurer:
Mr. G. Linsey, 395, Buroley Lane.
Headquarters:
Willow Bank Hotel, Featherstall Road.
Club Colours:
Red and White Shirts, Dark Blue Knickers.
This Card admits to all Football Matches during Season except Cup Ties.

NOT TRANSFERABLE.

NOTE.— Should any person use this card but

Mr. R. NUTTALL.
same to be forfeited without question.

Members Card for the first season as 'Oldham Athletic', and The Pine Mill as it was when the Athletic played nearby.

Determined to succeed, the Club developed the Hudson Fold Ground to a good standard for a Club at their level. In 1905, the enclosure was enlarged and embankments were formed. In addition to two dressing rooms, a pavilion (a small members stand) had also been built. Eventually in 1906 they became a Limited Company, which provided the Club with the means to rise higher in status. The 1906/07 season saw a move back to the Athletic Stadium, a venue which eventually became known as Boundary Park.

At this time the Athletic Ground was little more than a fenced enclosure, but was seen as having greater potential than Hudson Fold. The former Hudson Fold Ground, long since disappeared, was located adjacent to the current Westhulme Hospital, approximately where Westhulme Avenue now runs.

OXFORD UNITED

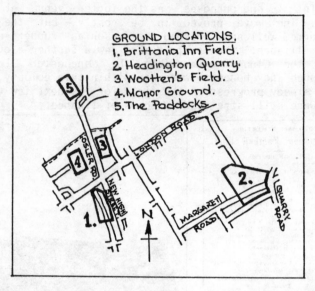

GROUND LOCATIONS.
1. Brittania Inn Field.
2. Headington Quarry.
3. Wootten's Field.
4. Manor Ground.
5. The Paddocks.

Although the United are one of the most recent of Clubs to adopt professionalism and gain election to the Football League, they have a long history that stretches back to the late 19th century.

The Club were founded as plain 'Headington' by a 50 year old football playing Vicar and the younger Doctor Hitchings, on the 27th of October 1893 at the Brittania Inn. By coincidence, the more Senior Club in the City for the greater part of the last 100 years, was reformed just four days later. But Oxford City, who were first created in 1882 never aspired to the Football League, and are currently making a bold attempt to regain Senior level football, after folding following the loss of their White House Ground in 1988.

BRITTANIA INN FIELD.
Headington, who added 'United' just three months after their formation, first played on a field at the rear of their first headquarters, the same Brittania Inn. This basic field, unfenced and with no facilities whatsoever, was very narrow - barely 50 metres wide - and the Club stayed at this somewhat unsatisfactory venue for only one season.

Probably the first match was played on the 25th of November 1893, when Cowley Barracks were entertained and won the game by 2-1. Reports of the early games of the United, who had entered the football World at a most minor level, were infrequent, but when Victoria were entertained at the Brittania Inn Ground, the founding Vicar played in his last match.

HEADINGTON QUARRY AND WOOTTEN'S FIELD.
For more than 25 years the Club moved between several venues, most of which were at the time no more than unfenced fields. The 1893/94 season saw the Club playing at Headington Quarry, doubtless at the adjacent, and later named Recreation Ground, which at this time was just a large expanse of open ground. The next season the Club were elected to play in the Oxford City Junior League, and home games were played on Wootten's Field which was located off of Sandy Lane (now Osler Road); this field was probably opposite the current Manor Ground. The Club did not make a very auspicious start to their League career, losing the first two games, and not recording their first win until the 8th of December, versus Wanderers Reserves.

MANOR GROUND.
In 1898, the Club moved to a new field on the other side of Sandy Lane, being three and a half acres in area. This 'Ground' was unfenced and had no facilities whatsoever, and no doubt the use of Brittania Inn was continued, as it was for the first match on the 1st of October. Clarendon Press were defeated by four goals to nil, and the teams retired to the Inn for tea after the match. By early 1899, the field was referred to as the 'Manor Ground', and was doubtless the same site of the Club's current Ground.

During the 1902/03 season, the Club lost their lease on the Manor Ground, possibly provoked by an unsavoury incident on the 28th of February. In the Oxford City League match versus Victoria, the visitors gained a win following some dubious decisions by the Referee. The incensed home supporters encroached onto the field and together with the players remonstrated with the Referee, who than had to be safely excorted off the field by a policemen! The Club were then ordered not to play a match within three miles of their home Ground for a month, whereupon the United scratched from the rest of that season's fixtures!

BACK TO THE BRITTANIA INN AND HEADINGTON QUARRY.

This rejection meant another move, and the Club choose to go back to the, far from ideal, field at the rear of the Brittania Inn, where they stayed until 1909. Although the size of the pitch was far from satisfactory it sufficed for a team that were still playing at non-Senior level. For a short while a move was then made back to the Quarry Recreation Ground - where their first match (before a crowd of 500) was 'away' at 'home'; the opposition being Headington Quarry.

The narrow Brittania Inn Ground in 1899.   (Ordnance Survey)

BACK TO THE MANOR GROUND.

But a return to Sandy Lane was soon made. Overall this venue proved to be the most popular since it had a good pitch, and being very well drained was of particular benefit to the spectators for it ensured that their feet kept dry! After the First World War, Sandy Lane became Manor Road and the Club had risen in status and played in the Oxfordshire Senior League. But the Ground at this time - although well roped off - offered nothing for fans or spectators alike, and another move was made next season. By this time the Club could command good support with frequent four figures attendances. The last match before another move was against Cowley, and a two goal defeat of the homesters ensued.

THE PADDOCKS.

This latest Ground was just a matter of a few hundred metres down the road to a different part of the large (at that time) Manor Park, and which was known as the Paddocks. It was enclosed, with the (later) benefit of dressing rooms, and with an entrance off of Manor Road. The first game at the Paddocks, as it was known, saw the Reserves entertain the Cowley second eleven on the 16th of September 1922, in an Oxford District League Division 2 match (a 1-3 defeat), and the first, first team match was in the F.A. Amateur Cup when St. Frideswides were beaten. By coincidence – for the second time – Cowley were the visitors again, this time for the last game at the Paddocks, and at last the United beat these opponents, by 5-1.

BACK TO THE MANOR GROUND - TO STAY!

At last the Club's wandererings finished in 1925, when they moved back yet again to the Manor Field – which had by now become the Manor Ground. The venue had been brought for the local community for Football, Cricket, Tennis and Bowls usage by the Headington Sports Ground Company. The Club had completed their circular tour, and were now to settle down in one place, at last! On the 26th of September, Deddington were the first visitors, but this auspicious occasion was dampened when a vehicle breakdown caused a late arrival of the opposition, and the game did not start until 4.10 p.m.!

THE GROUNDS TODAY.

The Quarry (now Quarry Fields) Recreation Ground is smaller than previously, since Margaret Road runs through what was formerly the Southern portion. In this 'lost' area there had been a Pavilion during the Club's later occupation of the Ground. Lime Walk and Latimer Road off of London Road, now border what was once the Brittania Inn Field. The Paddock Ground was situated off the North of the currently named Osler Road, as it makes a sharp turn, and is now the site of the Hostel to Radcliffe Hospital.

1990. Part of the former Quarry Recreation Ground venue is still used for football (behind the building). Taken at junction of Margaret and Quarry Roads. (Dave Twydell)

PORT VALE

The Club started its life in 1879 with the name of 'Burslem Port Vale', a name that identified their location, as opposed to their successor, which dropped the town prefix. In fact the question of location was the factor that brought into being the Burslem Club. The late 1870's saw the Potteries district already as a thriving football area, albeit the teams at that time were very low key - apart from Stoke who were already established as the area's leading Club. The founding year of the Burslem Club has been claimed as 1876, although a contemporary football handbook of 1889 gives the formation of the Club as 1879.

In 1879, the principal Club in the immediate locality was a team associated with Porthill (but in the newspaper, not named as such), who played their matches at Wolstanton - both places to the West of Burslem. A meeting that year took place at Lime Kiln Lane, Longport (an address that has been recorded as a former Ground as opposed to a meeting place), when a number of members of the Porthill Club complained of the difficulties of having to travel to Wollaston for matches from their homes in Burslem - a mile or so away. On this basis a breakaway group formed Burslem Port Vale F.C. It has been said that the 'Port Vale' suffix was derived from the "Port" in Longport, and the "Vale", a house in nearby Middleport - possibly where later meetings were held.

THE MEADOWS, LONGPORT.
The first Ground - certainly nothing other than a flat piece of land - was at The Meadows, Longport. It was not long before the Club had established itself above the rest, and in 1881 were honoured by a visit from Preston North End F.C. the Club soon became a success in the area, and the large support for the team demanded something better in respect of a home Ground.

MOORLAND ROAD ATHLETIC GROUND.
In 1884 a move was made to a site in Moorland Road, and although only initially another patch of waste Ground, nonetheless the Burslem Club managed to attract Everton as the first visitors to their new surroundings. Moorland Road Athletic Ground, as it was formerly named, although no doubt lacking in facilities, was enclosed, and the playing area was surrounded with a cycle track.

By 1885, the Club had turned to professionalism - upto two shillings and sixpence per match paid per player - and they started to make their mark in the F.A.Cup competition, with some good runs. The 1885/86 season saw the Club through to the last sixteen (the 5th round), although this wasn't really indicative of their abilities. Chirk and the Druids from Wales were easily beaten, followed by a walkover when Leek scratched in the third round and a bye in the fourth! After holding Brentwood to two drawn matches, the Burslem eleven scratched from the competition since they considered that there was little point in travelling all the way to Essex again, to play on an open Ground with no paying spectators! This season also saw the very first meeting of the two top Potteries teams, the Burslem Port Vale and the eleven from Stoke. The match attracted great interest locally and a crowd - at Stoke - of between eight and nine thousand were present to see the visitors somewhat unluckily lose by 1-3.

COBRIDGE ATHLETIC GROUNDS.

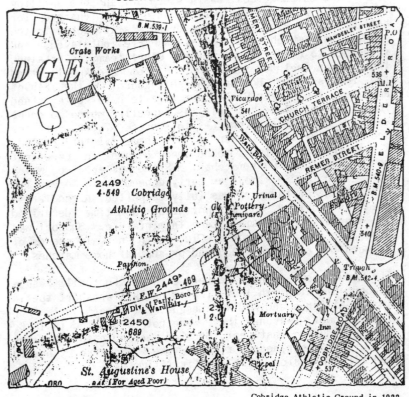

Cobridge Athletic Ground in 1922.
(Ordnance Survey)

The Club's home in Moorland Road was shortlived, for in 1886 the local Corporation purchased the land, and the Burslem team had to seek pastures new for the commencement of the 1886/87 season. The Moorland Road continued to be used by the Burslem Athletic Club, eventually being renamed as Burslem Park, and is situated opposite Port Vale's current Vale Park Ground. The new venue in 1886 was at the Cobridge Athletic Grounds, and was, and still is, situated South of Burslem (just to the North of Hanley) in Waterloo Road. A cycle track encircled the central field area, and there were Tennis Courts at one end of the roughly oval shaped enclosure.

This Ground was created from waste land, and was officially opened on the 4th of September 1886, when an Athletics Meeting was held with over £100 on offer as prizes. Two days later the Football Club kicked off with a highly attractive fixture, when Preston North End were the visitors. Season Tickets were available at four shillings (20p) and six shillings, but for the inaugural match the entrance cost was a steep 6d. and one shilling (double the prices that were subsequently charged for home matches). Even so a large crowd was attracted to the game, in which the homesters were outplayed, and succombed to a seven goal defeat. Other teams entertained that season included South Shore (from Blackpool), and the Rovers from Bolton and Blackburn. On the 15th of November, the nearby Stoke team were to have entertained the Preston Club, but this was cancelled which no doubt swelled Burslem's crowd - to over 7,000 - for Accrington's visit, when a 3-2 home victory ensued. Within two years the Ground had become an excellent centre for the Club's matches. A Stand was erected, which cost £200, and - almost an early conception of executive boxes - the seated area was fully carpetted! A good Press area was provided, and a reporter of the time described the Ground as a " Bramall Lane in miniature." Support was good for this ascending Club with normal crowds of between two and three thousand present at home matches.

The Club became founder-members of the Football League Second Division, in 1892, following earlier short spells in the Alliance and Midland League. But after just four fairly poor seasons they were not re-elected in 1896. Although during that year, Burslem were able to lower the colours of their nearby rivals Stoke - who were by now in the First Division - for the first time.

This year also coincided with a new Managing body for the Club, after several years when support had declined. Attendances then began to rise, despite the Club's reduced status, although still insufficient to properly run a professional team, but their prowess on the field was such that they were elected once again into the Football League Division 2 for the 1898/99 season, when it was hoped that the better quality opposition would encourage larger gates.

On the 3rd of September the Club made their renewed entrance in the Second Division, and they got off to an encouraging start with a two goal home win over Barnsley. Even more encouraging for the newcomers were the five straight victories that followed. But the Club could not maintain the momentum, and a mid-table placing was the final position at the end of the season. Despite the better quality of opposition that were played, there was little of encouragement in respect of attendances at home matches, and a year later the Club came close to folding. Mediocre years were to follow, during which the Club were never able to finish higher than halfway up the table. The final straw came at the end of the 1906/07 season when a mid-table placing at mid-season, was followed by a bad run that saw the team reach rock bottom. A final position of 13th (of 20 teams) ensured that a re-election application was not necessary, but the impoverished Club – home gates rarely exceeded 1,000 – were forced to resign from the League before the start of the following season. In June 1907, the Club finally gave up the unequal struggle and disbanded.

A new Club was created, shortly after the floundering of the Burslem team, initially under the unassuming title of Cobridge Church. With the influence from several of the old Club's members, the new team was renamed 'Port Vale', and were ambitious enough to play in the North Staffordshire League for the 1908/09 season, where they stayed for three years; this same season also saw the reformation of the Stoke Club. The Cobridge Athletic Ground was used once again, but with football becoming more selective and critical, it was not long before the Club decided on a move to a more suitable venue. The Club had risen up the football 'ladder' and became founder-members of the Central League, but despite some good performances they were unable to attract spectators in sufficient numbers. Their second season in the Central (1912/13) was noted for its 'highs' and its 'lows'.

On the credit side the Club finished in a very respectable fourth place and captured the Birmingham Senior Cup, but conversely financial problems were looming again. The Cobridge Ground was suffering from subsidence, hardly condusive to a good pitch, and its open position - coupled with little cover - made the venue far from attractive for spectators.

In 1989 the Stadium is much changed, but the dressing rooms and enclosure are located where the original Pavilion was.
(Dave Twydell)

On the 28th of April 1913, Blackpool Reserves were the visitors for Port Vale's last game at Cobridge. Despite the homesters high place in the table, the heavy rain, helped to attract a lamentably low attendance - the lowest ever for the Club in the Central League - and a two goal defeat was the sorry outcome. But already moves were well underway to move the Club just South to Hanley, where it was felt that a better Ground in a more central location would bring the fans in. However a somewhat unsympathetic Council did not finally approve the plans until February, which resulted in little time to transfer an open area - known as Kent Recreation Ground or, earlier, Kent Field - into a properly equipped Football Ground.

THE RECREATION GROUND, HANLEY.

The proposals for the Ground were somewhat ambitious; a 30 metre Grandstand (the central portion with 500 tip-up seats) including dressing rooms etc. under - on the West side - and opposite, a full length covered terrace (holding 10,000) with a 5 metre wide paddock in front. The central area of the East side was also to be seated, while at each end embankments would be formed. The total capacity was expected to be 42,000, and the pitch was to measure 116 by 76 yards, wider and longer than the Cobridge playing area by four yards. Work commenced on the 1st of March.

A new 24,000 share issue was planned, and with the Club £1,672 in debt, public support was vital. But the gamble paid off, for on Monday the 1st of September, despite earlier bad weather, an enormous crowd of 18,000 (the official figure) was present for the Central League visit of Blackburn Rovers. Not only was this a record attendance for both the league and the Club, it was one of the biggest ever seen in the Potteries area. At entrance charges of sixpence, one shilling and one shilling and sixpence, the Directors faith paid off and attendances continued at a level far higher than previously; 12,000 for the visit of Liverpool Reserves, 6,000 versus Southport, and 11,000 (receipts of £286) for a home F.A.Cup match. However, the Ground was barely ready, and the grandoise plans had to be delayed for some time; and initially the Players had to change in some nearby stables and then enter the venue from outside! Eventually the Grandstand was completed, at a cost of £12,000.

The Ground was of an irregular shape, being the space left behind various shops, houses and St.John's Church, and was enclosed between Bryan, Chapel and Hanover Streets. The main entrance was beside a school, off Bryan Street, which led to the main Stand, with other points of entry from a walkway - curiously named 'The Slabs' - which ran North to South, opposite and parallel to Bryan Street, plus access to the South terrace off Kent Street. There had been two slight natural embankments in the Ground's former days, which ran in line with the later length of the football pitch, and a slight re-alignment of these probably aided the forming of new embankments. The covered enclosure was later provided opposite the main seated Stand which ran near full pitch length.

The Club were hastily voted back into the Second Division after the hapless Leeds City were expelled after the start of the 1919/20 season; Stoke had also rejoined, although somewhat more conventionally at the start of the season. Although both teams had a poor playing season, the local derby in Hanley on the 6th of March produced a massive new record attendance of 22,993. By the late 1920's the Club managed to improve on several poor seasons, and in 1927 raised sufficient capital to purchase the Ground from the local Corporation. The Club remained at the Old Recreation Ground until, and against good advice, it was sold back to the Corporation for £13,000 in 1943. The team continued playing at the Hanley venue, on a seven year lease, although in 1944 they purchased a site for development which was located back in Burslem.

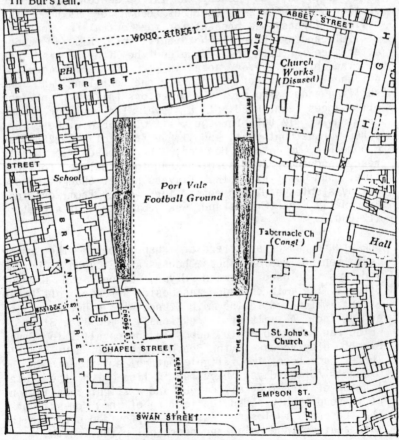

Plan of The Recreation Ground in 1938.
(Ordnance Survey)

At the end of the 1949/50 season the Club played their last match at the Old Recreation Ground, before moving to the newly named, but - similar to their move in 1913 - hardly completed Vale Park. On the 22nd of April 1950, Aldershot were the last visitors to the old Ground, when they won by the only goal of the game, before an attendance of 9,000.

Despite the long passage of time that has elapsed, the Cobridge Athletic Ground still remains, although now renamed Cobridge Stadium. The overall area of this arena remains the same as it did in the early years of the Century, as does the central playing area. A single storey structure is located on the South side, in the same position as the original pavilion. But this former sparse enclosure now contains several small covered enclosures for the benefit of Greyhound and American Football fans whose organisations are now the principle occupants. Until the mid-1980's, part of one embankment remained at the Old Recreation Ground, but even that has gone now, regraded and built over to form a multi-storey Car Park. In the South-east corner the large St.Johns Church still stands, one of the few remaining buildings that still exist that used to surrounded the former Football Ground. But a physical memory of the Hanley Ground moved to Burslem, for the enclosure at the North end had previously graced the Old Recreation Ground. Port Vale had a training Ground opposite the Cobridge Stadium, but this partly fenced off centre - complete with a small seated Stand - was erased in 1989.

A fine Aerial View of The Recreation Ground in 1937.   (Aerofilms)

QUEEN'S PARK RANGERS

By changing Grounds a total number of seventeen times –
thirteen different venues (not counting a few 'home'
matches played at Highbury and Stamford Bridge) – the
Club hold the record in the Football League. It would
probably be possible to produce a complete book relating
to these feats alone!

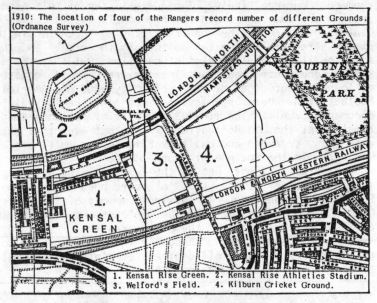

1910: The location of four of the Rangers record number of different Grounds.
(Ordnance Survey)

1. Kensal Rise Green.   2. Kensal Rise Athletics Stadium.
3. Welford's Field.   4. Kilburn Cricket Ground.

WASTELAND NEAR HARVIST ROAD.

Queens Park Rangers are one of a rare band of teams in
the Football League whose name does not obviously define
their location. They were formed in 1885 at Droop Street
in the Queens Park district of West London. However, with
the co-operation of the Reverend Gordon Young, St.Judes
Church was chosen as the Club's first Headquarters, and
hence their first name was evolved, that of 'St. Jude's
Institute'. For around one year, the team's first
'matches' were played on a patch of wasteland near
Harvist Road and adjacent to the site that was later
destined to become the Kensal Rise Athletic Ground. But
such contests were probably of a very minor nature, and
it was not until 1886, when the Institute team
amalgamated with Christchurch Rangers, that the Club were

to rise above the very minor status of their contemporaries in the area. Several of the Institute's players lived in the Queens Park area, and with the addition of 'Rangers' (from the Christchurch Club), the final nomenclature becomes obvious. Some of the Christchurch players decided to carry on as a separate Club - Paddington F.C. - a Club that only finally disappeared during the 1950's.

WELFORD'S FIELD.
Income was generated from the Players subscriptions of 7/6d. (37p) each, and a venue was rented - at a cost of £8 per annum - at Welford's Field. This Ground was located behind 'The Case Has Altered', a Public House which was demolished due to enemy action during the Second World War. There were a number of open areas in the Kensal Green district at this period of time, but Welford's Field was probably an unenclosed Ground on the West side of Chamberlayne Wood Road, and South of Kensal Rise Station. Facilities were non-existant, although there was a small natural embankment on the East side. The site has long since been built over by houses.

LONDON SCOTTISH GROUND.
Within two years, by 1888, the team were on the move again, this time to nearby Brondesbury, and the 'London Scottish Ground'. Despite it's somewhat impressive title, the exact location has not been traced, suffice to say that this Ground was probably only in existance for a short period, before it too was swallowed up by the expansion of London. But the location was certainly an improvement on Welford's Field since it was enclosed. For the privilege of playing there, the Club paid £20 per year, and managed to carry on despite gate money of only 8p at some games! But it soon became apparent that this Ground was far from ideal due to a badly draining pitch, so much so that football matches became impossible towards the end of the 1889/90 season, when all remaining home games had to be played at the Club's opponents.

HOME PARK, KENSAL RISE GREEN AND THE GUN CLUB.
A move was made back to Kensal Green, this time to Home Park. Once again this was probably little more than a field and is therefore difficult to accurately locate. But the Club's stay was a very short one, probably for less than a full season, and by 1892 two more venues had been used! After Home Park came Kensal Rise Green, which if taken literally would have been the land bounded by

Ashburnham Road, Langler Road and the London and North Western Railway line; just to the West of Welford's Field. The sixth new 'Ground' required a move out of the immediate locality, to the Gun Club at Wormwood Scrubs. The Scrubs is better known for it's prison (the Gun Club was almost directly behind the H.M. Establishment), and the vast area of open playing fields that still exist today. At last the Club could boast of a readily identifiable Ground, for the Gun Club was enclosed, and offered a dressing room block on the North side of the pitch and a probable railed or taped off pitch with a footpath surrounding the playing area. The entrance was in the South-east corner of the site, with a paybox, and the Club's playing area was part of a larger field which also contained a rifle range. The Ground lay behind the currently named Hammersmith Hospital and a sports ground, both of which still exist today. After the brief occupation by the Rangers, the large field became an Airship Garage, and this area which was used by the Rangers is now an all weather football pitch which is adjacent to the current West London Stadium.

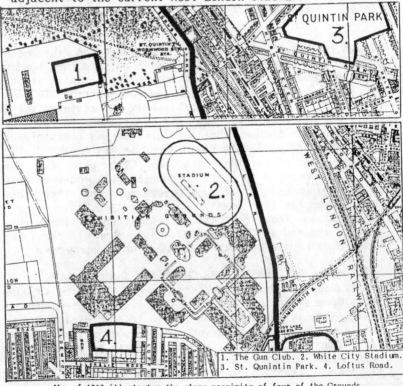

1. The Gun Club. 2. White City Stadium. 3. St. Qunintin Park. 4. Loftus Road.

Map of 1910 illustrates the close proximity of four of the Grounds. (Ordnance Survey)

KILBURN CRICKET CLUB.

The rapid changing of Grounds continued, when a return to
Kensal Green was made. This time it was to the home of
the Kilburn Cricket Club which was located by the side of
Harvist Road, probably one of two fields which lay
immediately to the East of Chamberlayne Wood Road, and
once again close to the Welford' Field headquarters of a
few years earlier. This venue offered little more than a
Cricket Pavilion with separate dressing rooms for two
teams. The breakaway group that had formed the Paddington
Club were encountered in the West London League during
1892, and there was obviously a great deal of animosity
between the two teams, for the match was riddled with
rough play. Many Players were injured, such that several
were unable to play again for several weeks, and the
Rangers refused to undertake the return fixture! By now
the public were responding to this up and coming team,
for there was an attendance of over 1,000 at the
Paddngton game. This crowd was overshadowed during the
1894/95 season when the Club entertained Old St.Stephens
in their first F.A.Cup match. The 'largest crowd ever'
was present at Harvist Road, but after holding the
visitors to a draw, the Rangers lost the replay. Later
that season West Bromwich Albion were pursuaded to visit
Kensal Green, and a crowd that paid £140 saw the locals
lose 1-4 in this friendly fixture.

KENSAL RISE ATHLETIC STADIUM.

By now the Club had become a much respected organisation
and the large crowds that were following them, could not
be accommodated at the Kilburn Cricket Ground. Therefore
yet another home venue had to be sought. In 1896, a ten
year lease, at an initial rental of £100 per year (rising
to £150) was agreed upon at the nearby Kensal Rise
Athletic Stadium - initially known as the National
Athletics Ground - an enclosure where the Club had
occasionally played before in local Cup Finals. The
Stadium was without doubt far superior to any of the
Club's previous seven Grounds. It was located within a
large enclosed site and just North of the railway line.
One entrance was located immediately adjacent to Kensal
Rise Station, and the other - with a pathway that led
direct to the large Pavilion/Grandstand - off of College
Road. Narrow, uncovered embankments surrounded most of
the oval shaped arena, which had been built to
accommodate a variety of Sports. A new record attendance
was present when spectators paid a total of £150 to see a
match with Brentford F.C. But the Club also gained an

unsavoury reputation when an incident during a match at Richmond resulted in the team having a Player sent off. They were fined £4 and the Athletic Ground was closed for two weeks. Five figure crowds were present for to matches in early 1900, when Wolverhampton Wanderers (in the F.A.Cup) and Millwall, were the visitors.

ST. QUINTIN'S AVENUE.

The Rangers turned professional in 1898, and this was followed with their formation into a Limited Company with the issue of £5,000 in shares. But running a professional team became a financial struggle, and when in 1901 the Landlord of the Athletic Ground won his case in the Appeal Court to terminate the Club's lease, yet another home venue had to be sought. A suitable site, but with less facilities, was found to the South, at the rear of St.Quintin's Avenue in North Kensington. The Ground was barely suitable for a professional Football Club since it was lacking in facilities for spectators, and the Players had to use the Latimer Arms Public House, in nearby Latimer Road, as dressing rooms. In any event their stay was a short one, for the local residents took the Club to Court - they were unhappy with a professional Football Club on their doorstep - and the 'wanderers' were forced to make another move in 1902. This latest Ground was almost certainly the current West Kensington Recreation area (then known as St. Quintin's Park), now an unenclosed park, and probably not too dissimilar to those turn of the Century days.

Action from a Rangers match versus Southampton, c.1905.
The background suggests that this was taken at the St. Quentins Avenue Ground.
Map of 1914 showing the location of the Park Royal Ground.
(Ordnance Survey)

BACK TO THE ATHLETIC STADIUM.

The Club's ninth move was made, this time back to
familiar surroundings at the Kensal Rise Athletic
Stadium, but by now the rent had been raised to £240 per
annum. The first season, 1902/03 proved to be financially
successful for total gate receipts of £4500 (an increase
on the previous year of over 30%) resulted in a profit of
£600. One year later things were even rosier with a
further 30% increase at the gate. But with only an
initial two year lease, the owners - All Saints College -
although offering a further six year option on the
Ground, also wanted a large increase on the rent! By
March there was already talk of another move, and for the
1904/05 season the Rangers moved to their tenth new
Ground - after less than twenty years in existance. One
of the last games at Kensal Rise was a visit by Everton,
which attracted a gate of 7,000, and one week later, on
April the 30th the final match took place. In a Southern
League game, Millwall were beaten by 2-1.

AGRICULTURAL SHOWGROUND, PARK ROYAL.

The latest move was made West once again, this time to
the Agricultural Society Showground Enclosure. The vast
100 plus acre site was purchased by the Royal
Agricultural Society for £26,146 in 1902, after a 50 year
lease had been taken out on it one year earlier. An even
greater sum of money was required to fully develop the
Showground - in a few months £42,000 was spent before any
permanent structures were erected!

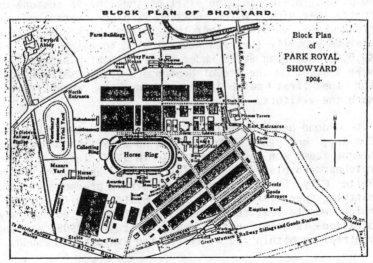

The Club's 'Football Ground' between 1904 and 1907, was the Horse Ring enclosure at the
Agricultural Showground, Park Royal.   (Royal Agricultural Society of England)

A Private Company, Park Royal Limited, was formed, and one of the fund-raising ventures was to sub-let parts of the area. Queens Park Rangers became one of the principal tenants, with their use of the Horse Ring oval shaped enclosure. There were two levels of banking all round, with a seated Grandstand on the North side and a smaller Reserved Grandstand opposite. The large arena had a claimed capacity for 40,000 capacity. Financially the move was not successful (the three years spent at the Showground produced reduced attendances), not only for the Club, but also for the Agricultural Society who were forced to first vacate, and later sell the site. These factors prompted yet another move.

PARK ROYAL STADIUM.

This latest choice proved to be of a more permanent nature, and was to be the first true 'Football Ground' for the Club. The site was sandwiched between Coronation Road and the railway line (a few hundred metres South-east of the Agricultural enclosure), and in a comparitive location to the Athletic Ground at Kensal Rise, being adjacent to a Station. Meanwhile back at Kensal Green, a new professional Club had been formed - 'Kensal Green United' who were to play at the Athletic Ground.

The two and a half acre Park Royal site was soon developed into a fine arena, with a large seated and standing covered enclosure (although this was not completed in time for the start of the 1904/05 season) on the railway side, with shallow sloping terracing and crush bars on the other three sides. Park Royal had a claimed capacity (but was never tested to this limit) of 40,000, including 9,000 under cover, of which nearly half were seated. On the 3rd of September, 12,000 were present for the first match in new surroundings, when Plymouth were the visitors.

The Ground had been built by the Great Western Railway Company, and the Club, by now an established Southern League team, won the Championship in 1908. In 1912, a few matches were played at the fairly new and very large White City Stadium, when a coal strike prevented trains carrying spectators to Park Royal Station. White City - which was to feature as the Rangers home on two separate occasions in later years - was built in 1908 as the centrepiece within the newly created Exhibition Ground.

PARK ROYAL: New Ground of Queen's Park Rangers.

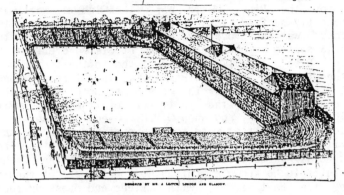

(Above): The Park Royal Ground as it was envisaged in September 1907. (Athletic News)

(Below): The Spacious Park Royal Ground was also used for other purposes! (Grange Museum)

Queen's Park Rangers' Football Ground, Park Royal, Willesden. SITE OF JOLLY JUMBO'S BOXING AND WRESTLING CARNIVAL, Saturdays, June 27th, and July 4th, 1908, at 2 p.m.

LOFTUS ROAD.

But for the First World War, the Club may well have permanently settled at the Park Royal Ground. However the enclosure was taken over by the Army, and the end of the 1914/15 season matches were played at Stamford Bridge and Kensal Rise. In 1917, the Club moved to the former home of the disbanded Shepherds Bush F.C., in Ellerslie Road. Just a few years earlier the Ground was nothing more than an open field on the perimeter of the White City Exhibition Grounds, and when Q.P.R. moved in, the venue could offer little more than an enclosed Ground with a Pavilion located along it's Southern side. The Stand from Park Royal was re-erected at Ellerslie Road (the Ground was later to be known as Loftus Road - the street running along the East side), with Offices and dressing rooms underneath, but little more was added for a number of years.

WHITE CITY STADIUM.

By the dawn of the 1930's, the Club had become a well supported Third Division South Club, and after fourteen years at Loftus Road - when it would have been reasonable to assume that the team at last had reached their final home - the Board of Directors decided on yet another move! This time it was just a few hundred yards East to the spacious White City Stadium (likened by many to a slightly scaled down Wembley Stadium), with it's capacity for 60,000 spectators, which included 6,000 under cover. Ignoring the few games that were played at this venue in 1912, the move provided the Club with their 13th new Ground, and to that date their fourteenth move! This latest upheaval, in 1931, appeared to be well chosen, for the opening match produced an attendance of 18,000 on the 5th of September (a three goal defeat to Bournemouth), and despite a mediocre season the average attendance for the season was a healthy 17,000. In January 1932, the Club's all time record crowd, of 41,097, was present for the visit of Leeds United in the F.A.Cup, and one year later the White City was used for a rare Football Association sanctioned Floodlight match when two Representative teams were in opposition.

BACK TO LOFTUS ROAD.

But the bubble soon burst, and after managing only sixteenth in the League at the end of the 1932/33 season - when gates of under 10,000 were 'lost' in the vast arena - a move back to Loftus Road was made before the start of the next campaign.

With losses totalling £7,000 over two seasons, and an overall deficit of over £34,000, it was clearly necessary for the Rangers to limit their outgoings. The Club's use of the White City was to prove to be their last - thirteenth - Ground, but not the last move, for during the 1962/63 season the same Stadium was tried again for a few months. The White City was certainly a more prestigious venue, but with relatively small crowds the Arena lacked atmosphere, and so at the end of this season, the Club's seventeenth - and final - move was made, back to Loftus Road.

THE GROUNDS TODAY.

The various former Grounds of the Club that were located in the Kensal Green area, including the Athletics Stadium, have all long since disappeared. Before the turn of the Century, the urban sprawl from London had begun, and all of these former venues are completely obliterated by a variety of housing (Industrial buildings on the Athletics Ground) that has been built on the sites. Park Royal became a vast Industrial site, including the predominant Guinness factory, but where it is a surprise to see in one area cows grazing, and cricket being played on another. Of the Agricultural Grounds the specific site has not been traced, if it was in fact separate from the Park Royal Ground. Park Royal was used upto the Second World War by Park Royal F.C., and although left as an overgrown building site for many years, inevitable Industrial Units now cover the former arena. The mid 1980's saw the sad disappearance of the White City Stadium.

The demolition of the White City Stadium. This landmark (at the West end of the A40 Westway) has now been replaced by an Office Block and a Sports Ground. (Dave Twydell)

READING

A public meeting at the Bridge Street Rooms, called by Mr. J.E.Sydenham and a group of friends led to the creation of the Club in February 1871. Therefore the Club is not only one of the oldest in the Country, but the longest lived of Football League Clubs in the South. Subscriptions to members of 25p per annum were agreed, and the new Club were well supported from the start since many of the members were prominent men in the town.

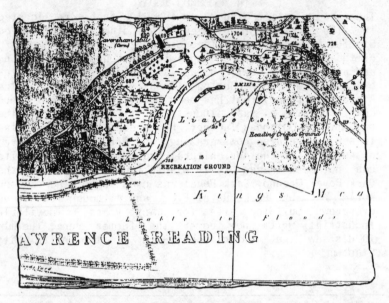

Map c.1890 showing two of the former Grounds (The Recreation Ground and Reading Cricket Ground). (Ordnance Survey)

READING RECREATION GROUND:

The first match was played during the 1871/72 season, a thirteen-a-side contest with the Grammar School. Although matches were probably few in number, the campaign ended with the Club undefeated during that period. Opposition was limited at this time, but included the likes of Henley, Marlow, Wycombe and Swifts - names that were early contenders in the F.A.Cup and some still exist today. The Recreation Ground without doubt was nothing more than an unenclosed area with no facilities.

The Ground was just to the North-east of the town centre
and immediately adjacent to the River Thames. It was
formerly known as King's Meadow (a name that was later
adopted again), and was formally opened as the
'Recreation Ground' by the donor George Palmer in 1875.
Football and other sports are still played on this large
open area. The Club continued on in their generally
winning ways, and one of the twelve matches played during
the 1874/75 season included that against Reading Hornets,
a Club that was to amalgamate with Reading F.C. in 1877.

READING CRICKET GROUND.

The Club's first entry into the F.A.Cup Competition took
place during the 1877/78 Season, when South Norwood were
entertained and beaten, on the 7th of November. The game
was played at the Dolphin Stadium in Slough, no doubt a
more suitable venue for such a prestigious game since it
was enclosed. The Club lost their next match in the
competition to Upton Park. Although the Recreation Ground
was still the official home venue, for which an annual
rent of £3 was paid, matches were increasingly being
played at The Reading Cricket Ground. The Final of the
Berks. and Bucks. Cup (the first year of the competition)
took place at this venue, and Reading were victorious
over Marlow thanks to a last gasp goal in the final
minute of extra time. For the occasion the pitch was
roped off and a marquee was erected. The Ground was
situated immediately adjacent to the Recreation Ground,
and was also pleasantly located next to the Thames – it
was often referred to as the 'Riverside Ground'. It was
probably at least partially enclosed and had a small
Pavilion in the North-West corner. Very much the same
site still exists to this day, with trees providing an
enclosure barrier from the adjacent Kings Meadow; the
enclosure is now a general Sports Ground, with a modern
Pavilion.

Another notable game during the same season was that
against the Old Etonians in the F.A.Cup. A measure of the
Club's capabilities was their performance against this
famous Club who were in their heyday. The contest was
lost, but only by a single disputed goal; the Old Boys
went on to win the Cup! A large crowd was present at the
Cricket Ground, and a gate of nearly £2 was taken. The
Cricket Ground became the normal home venue for matches,
but in 1882, a move was made to the other side of town.

COLEY PARK:

Although this area of Reading, just South of the main A4, did contain a park, since this was the first enclosed Ground for the Club (for which £5 per annum was paid), it is most likely that the site was one of the many fields in the area that have since been built over. The first home match on October the 3rd, brought Marlow to Reading for which a gate of £1-40 was taken. It was not a happy start for the homesters as they crashed by four unopposed goals! The Club's stay at Coley Park lasted for seven years, but within that time it is unlikely that there were any facilities of note provided there. During these years little of merit was achieved, and by the end of the 1888/89 season it was decided that another move was to be made. Before the commencement of the following season, the Club amalgamated with Earley F.C.

CAVERSHAM CRICKET GROUND:

Once again the Club removed to the other side of the town, this time to Caversham, just North of the Thames. The precise location of this Ground is not obvious, but the very rural nature of the locality at this time could have meant that the team played on any one field of many!

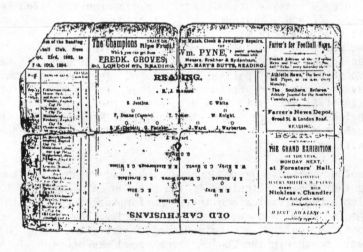

The oldest known Reading programme.
1893/94 season, an Amateur Cup match at Caversham.

Over Christmas of 1892, Burslem Port Vale were defeated at the Cricket Ground, their presence being the first from a professional team. Although the Club had become a respected combination, at least in the South, they were humiliated in the 1st round F.A.Cup game at Preston North End during the 1893/94 season. Heavy rain kept the crowd down to 2,500 at Deepdale, but this did little to dampen the homesters spirits as they romped away with an 18-0 victory (seven up at half-time)! In 1894 the Club became founder-members of the Southern League. The team at this time was still amateur, but finished in a mid-table position, and eventually turned professional on the 27th of May 1895 at the Club's A.G.M. This was not approved by some of the Players who broke away to form their own Club, Reading Amateurs. During the 1893/94 season, the team entered for the F.A.Amateur Cup in its inaugural season. The home game against the Old Carthusians attracted 1,000 spectators, but the homesters were defeated by the eventual winners, with a 1-4 scoreline.

The Cricket Ground was found to be far from ideal since it was liable to flooding (suggesting that it was located close to the River, and perhaps nearly opposite the former Reading Cricket Ground venue), and was unsuitable for the large crowds that were now being attracted to watch the team. In addition access was difficult, since the bulk of support came from the more populated town (Reading), for which an awkward Ferry trip had to be made to cross the Thames. Therefore, in 1896, it was decided that another move was desirable, and initially it was intended to go to the Estate of Palmer Park on the Eastern outskirts of town. But Councillor Jesse offered the better prospect of a lease of four acres at a former gravel pit at Elm Park. The Club moved there for the start of the 1895/96 season, and Holloway College were the first visitors on the 5th of September when an attendance of 2,500 was present.

ROTHERHAM UNITED

It was not until 1925, that the current Rotherham United
F.C. came into being, but the ball was literally first
kicked in organised fashion in the town, back in 1870.

On the front page of the Rotherham and Marsborough
Advertiser, the following small advertisement appeared on
the 24th of December 1870:

> " Rotherham Football Club.
> The opening game will be played in the field
> opposite Eastwood House, Doncaster Road on Monday
> next, December 26th, kick off at 10.30 a.m.
> A second game will be played on Tuesday the 27th
> inst. at the same time and place.
> Intending members will be allowed to play.
> Proposed subscription: Two shillings and sixpence.
>
> J.J. Christie, President.
> Henry Hart, Secretary."

EARLY DAYS AND SEVERAL GROUND CHANGES.

No match reports followed, and it was not until 1872,
that it was first noted in the Press, that a team by the
name of Rotherham Wanderers, were playing on Jarvis's
Field in Clifton Lane. The Field belonged to a tenant of
the Red Lion Hotel, and this venue was later to become
the Clifton Lane Cricket Ground.

The name of Thornhill Football Club first put in an
appearance in 1877 (the first game of the season, and
possibly of the Club, was on the 4th of October), with
their home venue off the Greasborough Road at nearby
Northfield. One year later the unlikely named Lunar
Rovers were founded, and they kicked-off their career in
the Clifton Grove area of Middle Lane, later moving to
the Doncaster Road end of this Lane and finally to the
Cricket Club's Ground that had by now been established in
Clifton Lane. The strange name of this team was derived
from their many matches that were played by moonlight,
but in 1882, they changed to the more acceptable and all
embracing 'Rotherham', presumably the first Club of this
name had passed away, and the Wanderers were in a decline
that was never halted.

Around this time Thornhill made a Ground move, this time with a degree of permanence, when they settled down at the smaller Red House Ground, around half a mile away from their roots.

THE RED HOUSE GROUND OF THORNHILL.

Despite the Thornhill (later United, in name) Club eventually becoming the true forerunners of 'Rotherham United', they played second fiddle for many years to the Rotherham (later with 'Town' added) team.

1923 Maps show two of the former Grounds: (Above) The Red House Ground now completely built over, but (below) Clifton Lane is still essentially the same. (Ordnance Survey)

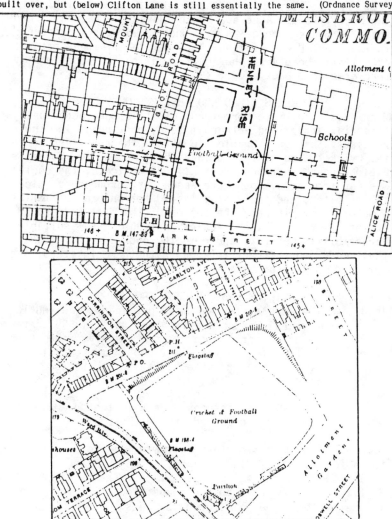

Until their final move to Millmoor in 1907, the Red House Ground could offer little for spectators. It was located near the junction of Henley Grove Road and Park Street, and for dressing rooms the Red House Inn was used, at the intersection of these roads.

This very cramped Ground provided only narrow flat standing areas down the sides and at the Park Street end of the pitch, plus a deeper, non-seated, viewing area at the other end. Eventually small Club Offices were provided - and Toilets! There were scant mentions of the team until they entered the Midland League in 1903 (via the Sheffield Alliance and South Yorkshire Leagues), and the Red House Ground was well summed up with a reference in the local Press of 1895: "... devoid of either natural or artistic beauty... the ball had to be continually recovered from backyards." (!)

COCKER'S FIELD AND WEST END GROUND.

Meanwhile the more prominent, but almost perpetually financial struggling Rotherham Town, continued in their restless fashion. Unable to afford the rent payable to the Cricket Club of £5, in 1886 they moved to Cocker's Field (near Sherwood Crescent) off Wellgate. The choice was far from good, for there was a very pronounced slope to the pitch, and their stay lasted for only a few months - before they finished the season at the West End Ground, Ickles. While the Ickles pitch was suitable, accessibility was not, and come the end of the season, they made up their differences with the Cricketers, and returned to Clifton Lane.

CLIFTON LANE CRICKET GROUND.

This time the Town's stay was more permanent, and during their four years' Ground-sharing they built a 500 seated Stand. For a brief period in their history, the Club found success both on the field and in monetary terms, with the probable record attendance to that time, to watch a game in Rotherham, of 4,000, during the 1888/89 season. The opponents were the highly renowned Preston North End, and the interest was such that despite the rain, this large crowd packed around the ropes.

Of particular note in the following season, was the formation of the Midland League, of which Rotherham Town were founder-members. On September the 14th, the Sheffield Club provided the opposition at Clifton Lane, in the first League game for both teams.

A good attendance paid their 4d. (1½p) entrance money and the home supporters were rewarded with a 3-1 victory. Bizarre circumstances led to the Club playing a F.A.Cup tie at Clifton Lane of just 6 minutes duration! A local derby match with Rotherham Swifts (shortlived local opponents who folded in 1891) was played in the competition, but was abandoned in extra time due to poor light. The following Monday saw the two teams in battle, this time at Clifton Road, but with six minutes remaining, and the homesters leading by 2-1, this too had to abandoned, once again due to the gathering darkness. The Swifts refused to concede defeat, and so the final minutes were played out at the same venue a few days later, when the Town added one goal to their tally. But the local rivalry was far from friendly. At the initial match at the Cricket Ground, the Town goalkeeper ended up in Hospital after being kicked, the Swifts team were pelted with mud after the premature but final whistle, and a visiting player was struck over the head with an umbrella!

The Town Club finished as League runners-up in the first two seasons, and their status was such that a visit of Royal Arsenal was arranged during the 1890/91 season. But the Londoners decided at the last minute to not bother to attend which resulted in the Town receiving a paltry £5 in compensation despite an outlay of three times that sum. 'No shows' for League games by Kidderminster and Warwick County plus £12 wasted on a journey to Staveley helped to sorely test the Bank balance; and by January 1891, the Club's deficit stood at £247. However, by the season's end, this sum had been reduced to £64. Gate takings for the season amounted to £270 (including £56 from the Stand patrons), from which £152 accounted for Players wages and only £7-10. in Rent.

What in effect was the last game played at the Cricket Ground, was fought out with Burnley on April the 18th (a single goal victory), before around 1,000 spectators. The danger to the Club of folding completely was averted, but problems arose regarding their continued use of the Clifton Lane Cricket Ground, which had by now been taken over by the local Racing Company. It was intended to enlarge the Ground, in order that the Football pitch did not encroach upon the Cricket square, but difficulties over a new tenancy agreement dragged on throughout the Summer. But eventually Rotherham Town F.C. announced of the move to a new venue at nearby Clifton Grove.

CLIFTON GROVE.

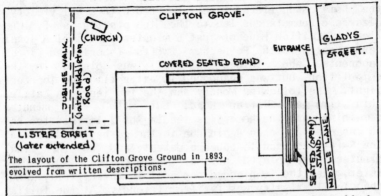

The layout of the Clifton Grove Ground in 1893,
evolved from written descriptions.

This was the first arena that could be truly called a
'Football Ground', and although the stay was short - only
five years (until the Club's demise) - the Town's short
Football League career was played at this venue.

Initially there was some disquiet from the locals, for
the Ground was situated off Middle Lane, just South of
Clifton Grove and opposite Gladys Street, in a
residential area. Eventually the fears of the residents
of having a Football Club in their midst was allayed,
except for the occupants of six houses in Clifton Grove,
who had their view to the South blocked out by the
covered (corrugated iron) and seated Grandstand that had
been rapidly moved from the Cricket Ground! An open
Stand, threequarters pitch width long, was erected at the
Middle Road end, where the entrance to the Ground was
located. The site had been a flat piece of land, formerly
tenanted by one Silas Garner, but was distinguished by
the furrowed - 115 by 75 yards - pitch! However, with
nine foot high hoardings erected, the Club could feel
proud that Clifton Grove was ready for action by the 5th
of September, for the Reserve team (known as 'Rotherham
United'). Despite it's low status the game attracted one
of the biggest crowds ever in Rotherham, with both Stands
being well patronised.

The opening, competitive, first team match at home was
not until the 26th of September since the fixtures had
been arranged with the expectancy of the Club playing at
the Cricket Ground, and hence the avoidance of a clash of
sporting fixtures. Grantham Rovers were the visitors for
a Midland League fixture, and an excellent attendance of
3,000 witnessed an entertaining 2-2 draw. There were only

1,000 present two weeks later, but the poor weather accounted for this drastic reduction. A memorable benefit match was played in December, when 1,500 paying customers - at 1d. entrance to Ground cost - received full value when the locals thrashed Staveley by twelve unopposed goals. The League Championship was won following a last match victory over Wednesbury Old Athletic, which was cheered on by 4,000 fans. At last things were looking up, and by now the Club had become a Limited Company.

For a short period the Club enjoyed a rare successful period, which led them into the Football League for the 1893/94 season. But the perennial problem of attendances were to lead to the downfall of the Club. The end of the season balance sheet showed the total attendances produced £482, but this was only half of the previous campaign's total when the team rode high in the Midland League. But the £100 losses on the year, despite the halving of Players wages costs, were principally put down to labour problems in the coal trade - on which Rotherham depended. Just three seasons were enjoyed, or endured, before the end of this status, and of the Club, came about. Attendances at Clifton Grove had dropped to pitiful levels - a mere 'handful' for Reserve games, and even the all conquering Liverpool team only encouraged a few hundred to the Football League game. In September 1892, the Town had the honour of being the first visiting Club to a Liverpool F.C., at Anfield. The last home game in the Football League, on the 16th of March 1896, was watched by only 300, and of those it was estimated that 100 came from the visitors Lincoln City!

At the season's end it was announced that only £550 had been taken at the gate for first team matches (and a paltry £40 for the Reserves), and with the Players wages alone amounting to £470, £77 was lost on the season. Even the A.G.M. in August was poorly attended. The Directors had had enough of digging into their own pockets for funds, and the Club didn't even bother to apply for re-election to the Football League. Rotherham Town just quietly died, and it was not long before the Clifton Grove Ground was turned into a housing site, which it remains to this day.

This left Thornhill United to take over the role as the top 'Town' team, albeit in a low keyed fashion, as they only played in the Sheffield Alliance and South Yorkshire Leagues.

CLIFTON LANE CRICKET GROUND YET AGAIN!

Yet within nine years, there was to be another 'Rotherham Town' on the Football Map. Two minor Clubs in the Town, Rotherham Casuals and Rotherham Grammar School, combined in 1899, to become, 'Rotherham Club'. The Clifton Lane Ground became the new Club's home Ground, but misfortune (or mis-management?) was soon to strike them. With the closure of the Racecourse, the Grandstand was purchased from the Racing Company, which was later found to be rotten, but the poorly funded football team had little option but to make the best of a poor buy!

The early years of the twentieth century saw the Cricket and Football Clubs at Clifton Grove affect Ground improvements, and the latter - after some years in the Sheffield Association League - were finally elected to the Midland League in 1903, together with the Thornhill Club. Once again the town was presented with two teams on a par, yet both competing for limited support. But despite this adversity neither team were disgraced in such senior Company.

Both Clubs, however, continued to struggle financially. Thornhill United were unable to play cup-ties on their small pitch, but could not afford to seek new pastures. Meanwhile in 1904, over at Clifton Lane, another concerted effort was made to capture the limited support of the locals. A Limited Company was formed, under the name of Rotherham Athletic, when 3,200 shares of `1 each were issued, and a 21 year lease - at `80 per annum - was taken out on the Ground. In the following April, the team's name was formally changed to 'Rotherham Town'. Not to be outdone, and seeing themselves as the more senior of the two (and certainly the elder), the Thornhill Club became 'Rotherham County'!

MILLMOOR FOR THE COUNTY.

With the continuing rivalry, which was not always friendly, between the two Clubs, the new 'County' took a positive step to prove their seniority when they at last changed their home venue in 1907. A plot of land, described as, " a grass plot of not much practical utility...", was leased from the Midland Railway Company. The two old stands that had eventually been built at the Red House Ground were moved across town and made into one, voluntary labour levelled the playing pitch, and so the Millmoor Ground was created.

Team Group c.1905, presumably taken at the Red House Ground.

It was only a good run in the 1907/08 season F.A.Cup
competition (to the first round proper), that prevented
the Town Club from being eclipsed by their neighbours,
but fame brought it's penalty. Several players left to
join Football League Clubs, and the Club's fortunes
dipped in the years prior to the First World War. By the
start of the 1913/14 season the Club were `247 in debt,
and the Directors sent out a plea for funds, to prevent
the closing down of this latest Rotherham Town Football
Club. Sufficient funds were raised to clear the debts
(including an additional `214 by the end of the season),
but despite agreeing at the A.G.M. to continue playing
during the War period, a few days later the decision was
rescinded, and the Town withdrew from all Competitions.

But by now there was no doubt that the premier team in
the town was that of the County. With a brand new Ground
and a claimed capacity for 15,000 spectators (a pre 1914
record crowd of 11,000 were present in 1911 when the two
local rivals met), it was the Millmoor Club that
gradually edged ahead. In recognition of their Midland
League Championship wins in four consecutive years to
1915, and after the cessation of hostilities, the Club
were elected to the Second Division of the Football
League.

Although overshadowed by their local rivals, Rotherham
Town struggled on for a few more years, and despite their
hoped for inclusion into the new Third Division of the

Football League, their ambitions exceeded the true realities of the situation. Although a planned new Stand (including dressing rooms and offices etc.), plus concrete terracing was planned for, the vision was never fulfilled. By 1922, the Club were seriously faced with the prospect of extinction, as were the hapless earlier occupiers of Clifton Lane. There was serious talk at last of an amalgamation of the two Clubs, and the Town struggled to the end of their 1922/23 season Midland League fixtures, whereupon they tendered their resignation from the competition. But the County were also struggling financially, and with the bitterness that had formed over the years between the two organisations, the amalgamation plans were abandoned.

AMALGAMATION AT LAST.

The Town's re-admission was secured into the Midland League and with expenditure cut to an absolute minimum, another two seasons passed by before, at last, the long overdue pooling of resources came to fruition. Two County shares were issued for every three of Rotherham Town, and at last a single Club of Senior standing was formed in the town. The new 'Rotherham United' Club was inaugurated, and to prevent yet another 'Town' Club being created, the lease of the Clifton Road Ground was taken up - which by now was also used by Rotherham Amateurs - and used by the new Club's third team for home matches.

The Clifton Road Ground remains today, but with no traces of the former occupancy of the senior Football Club, but the unloved Red House Ground, together with the adjacent Public House have been completely removed from the scenery. In their place, new roads and an Industrial Development have been created. On more or less the centre spot of the former narrow football pitch, there is now a roundabout where Henley Rise meets the dual carriageway Ring Road of the town.

-298-

SCARBOROUGH

Although Scarborough did not finally make it into the
Football League until 1987, the long path took 108 years,
therefore making them one of the older of Football Clubs.

The cricket team outside the Pavilion in 1874. The football team (originally known as
'Scarborough Cricketers Football Club') played here for one season, 1886/87. The pavilion
was located in the North-east corner of the Marine Parade Cricket Ground.

NORTH MARINE GROUND.

The first Cricket Club in the town was reputedly founded
in 1849 and played at Castle Hill. In 1863, the 'modern'
Club first saw the light of day, and for a number of
years they rented the North Marine Ground, this was
probably one and the same site as the current well
developed enclosure. As the Club rose in stature, so did
their wealth, and in 1869 they were able to purchase the
freehold of the Ground, at a not inconsiderate sum of
£3,800. The venue was enclosed - complete with a Pavilion
and (open) seating for 4,000 - with a well drained level
playing area. As was so common with Cricket Clubs in the
North of England, the summer sportsmen wanted a winter
outlet, and so, in 1879, came the birth of a footballing
section. This new sporting section played under the title
of 'Scarborough Cricketers F.C.', and inevitably made the
North Marine Ground the venue for their own matches.
Within months of their formation, the Cricketers played
an evening Football match with the aid of Electric
lighting, but for many years football was very much a
minor pursuit in the town. Cricket was the major sport,
along with Tennis (which was also played at North Marine)
and Hockey.

But as football became more popular, the footballing
Cricketers cast off this dual role, finally dropping
'Cricketers' from their title in 1887 - which coincided
with a move to another Ground. the 1886/87 had been a
very successful one in respect of matches, for of the 22
played, 16 were won and only four ended in defeat. One
year earlier the Football Club had captured their first
trophy, when they beat Hull Town in the Scarborough and
East Riding Cup Final. Their financial dealings were,
however, very moderate with only £16.50 being realised in
subscriptions and under £35 being taken at the gate,
which resulted in a positive balance of £15, from the
previous year's activities. The name change was effected
before the end of the season, and to celebrate their
independance a prestigious end of season friendly was to
have been played with Preston North End, but this fixture
never materialised.

RECREATION GROUND.

A well appointed Recreation Ground was opened in 1887,
that lay immediately adjacent to the Cricket Ground, and
it was to here that 'Scarborough F.C.' moved for the
1887/88 season. This Ground was enclosed, and had a
Grandstand that measured 30 by 6 metres wide with several
rows of open seating each side. An earth embankment
stretched along the opposite - North-west - side. Several
entrances were located along the North Marine end.
Although the facilities for spectators were ample, the
elongated oval shape of the central grass area (which was
surrounded by a 8 metre wide track) restricted good
viewing from the two sides only, as the playing area
measured over 200 metres in length.

The first game played at the new Ground, was a pre-season
trial in which the proposed first eleven played 'the next
fourteen'! The numerically fewer team won the contest by
8-3. The first match against an opposition team occurred
on October the 8th, when Ebor were equally overcome with
a 7-0 scoreline. Despite the importance of the occasion,
there was only a small attendance, due mainly to the rain
that continued before and during the game. One week later
Scarborough entertained Shankhouse in what was the
homesters F.A.Cup debut. Although tiring of friendly
contests, the public turned out in force for this
competitive encounter, and saw the locals take a three
goal interval lead. But the seaside team were no match
for their prominent opponents, for they collapsed in the
second half and finally lost 3-5.

Over Christmas a football tournament was held in which 20
teams took part. After the final, Scarborough played
Leeds in a match which was won 2-1 before a crowd of over
2,000. Scarborough remained at the Recreation Ground for
eleven largely unremarkable years, representing a town
that was not really interested in football. In 1898, the
Recreation Ground was sold to a Development Company, and
by the turn of the century, there was nothing left of
this well appointed, but shortlived Ground.

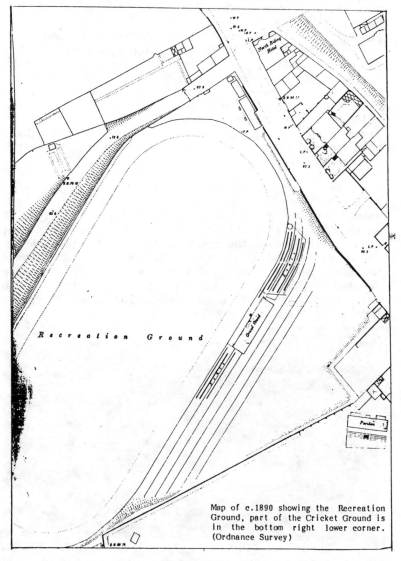

Map of c.1890 showing the Recreation
Ground, part of the Cricket Ground is
in the bottom right lower corner.
(Ordnance Survey)

Then, as now, the site was covered with the houses to Woodall Avenue. The subsequent enforced move coincided with the Club's more ambitious outlook, for after twenty years in the football 'wilderness', during which period they only played Friendly and Cup matches, they were elected into the Northern League Second Division for the 1898/99 season. Two previous attempts at joining had been turned down, and now at last, they were able to play regular competitive matches. Fortunately the Scarborough Corporation stepped in and leased the Club a field off Seamer Road, on the southern outskirts of the town. The Football Club formed itself into an Athletic Company and issued 1000 shares at £1 each which were quickly taken up. With this financial fillip the Directors were able to set up at the new Ground, and a 250 seat Grandstand was built plus wooden fencing to enclose the venue. The opening match on the 'New Recreation Ground' - which later became known as the 'Athletic Ground' (and finally Seamer Stadium) - was played on the 22nd of October 1898, when two goals were shared with Loftus, in a Cleveland Senior Cup match.

THE GROUNDS TODAY.

Although the old Recreation Ground may have been shortlived, the North Marine Cricket Ground still remains in this Cricketting stronghold. This fine enclosure has been built up over the years, and provides ample seating (both covered and open) and is often used for County matches. Various modernised enclosures and seats are located on the East and South sides, as they were in the days when the Scarborough footballers took over the Ground for the Winter months.

The Marine Parade Cricket Ground in 1989, looking West. Many fatures are the same or similar to those when the football team played there. The Recreation Ground was adjacent, to the extreme right of the picture.   (Dave Twydell)

SCUNTHORPE UNITED

The original Scunthorpe United were founded in 1899, but
for the first decade or so operated at a minor level
playing only in the local football league. A few years
earlier the main contestants for representing the area
had been Brumby Hall and Scunthorpe Town. Brumby Hall
affected a merger but the new team rapidly vanished from
the scene, while Scunthorpe Town had become defunct by
the end of the 1898/99 season. But the newly created
United team were not without competition, since from 1902
they had close rivals in the North Lindsey team. The
United made an unsuccessful attempt to join the Midland
League in 1907, and this was followed two years later
with their first entry into the F.A.Cup Competition. Both
moves were made in order to try to establish the Club as
the principal Football team in the town.

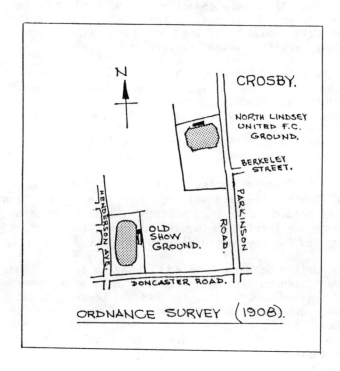

THE OLD SHOW GROUND:

North Lindsey played their home games at Crosby (just a few hundred yards from the Show Ground), one of five villages which at that time included both Brumby and Scunthorpe itself. The United had the Show Ground (which in later years had 'Old' added as a prefix), at their disposal. By 1910, although with few facilities, it did have Dressing Rooms, This factor pleased the local puritans, who abhorred the thought of the possible corruption if the Players had to change in a Public House! The two rival Clubs played in the Lindsey League, and the last scheduled match between the two, in February 1910 was cancelled as the Goalkeeper was the only team member from North Lindsey who bothered to turn up! Although playing at only a local level, the two Clubs were both in debt, and sensibly a meeting was held on the 9th of April, with a view to an amalgamation. The idea, although adopted, met with disinterest, since only a few enthusiasts were present for this important gathering. The apt title of 'Scunthorpe and Lindsey United' was adopted, and it was decided that the home Ground for the new Club would be at the Show Ground since this offered better, albeit limited, facilities.

On the 10th of September the first home match was played (against Grimsby Rovers), and the new Pavilion, which cost £50 was formally opened. The local Vicar made a sporting gesture by sending a half sovereign to the Club, but only on the understanding that the Club remain Amateur and that the Dressing Rooms were kept well away from Licensed Premises!

When Scunthorpe United (the 'Lindsey' was dropped from the Club's title in 1956), moved to their new Glanford Park Stadium for the start of the 1988/89 season they became the first Club to move to new, and independent, premises for over three decades.

The United became a Limited Company in 1912 (whether the vicar demanded his money back has not been recorded!), and gained entry into the Midland League. In 1921, the Ground was purchased for £2,900, in preference to the modest £10 per annum rent. But at the same time the Club's first attempt to join the Football League was denied them.

The premature end of the Club nearly came in 1925 when a series of problems tested the Directors resilience. With the depression being felt badly by the Club, attendances were down to barely four figures and the finances were at a low ebb. After the West Stand was destroyed in a fire, the Club came very close to folding, but were saved at the eleventh hour. The replacement structure lasted until the Club's departure from the Ground. Two years after the Club's lowest ebb, they won the Midland League, and in the 1927/28 season they reached the second round of the F.A.Cup. In the first round Rochdale were beaten before a new record attendance at the Old Shgow Ground of 5,305, but the next cup game saw Rotherham held to a draw before a crowd of 8,030. Eleven years later this record assembly was easily broken when Watford were the visitors (in a second round F.A.Cup match) and the Ground was packed with 11,800 fans.

Although the Club ceased activities during the Second World War, it was used occasionally by Grimsby Town for some of their War League matches. A new record attendance was established at the Old Show Ground in 1942, when two 'foreign' teams appeared in Scunthorpe; Grimsby and Sunderland fighting out a F.A.Wartime Cup semi-final before 11,896. With the upsurge in interest in the game following the period of hostilities, crowds flocked to the Old Show Ground to see the highflying United. In 1948, two crowds of 12,736 and 13,775 were recorded within a few days for an F.A.Cup replay and another second round appearance. One year later the average Midland League gate at home reached 8,000 (the top crowd totalled 11,573) and this emphasised the Club's claim to be admitted to the Football League.

At last, in 1950, their perseverance was rewarded, and the first League match - versus fellow newcomers Shrewsbury Town - drew a crowd of 11,847. Another new record was established for the next home match when the local derby game with Lincoln City resulted in an attendance of 14,840. But this gathering was dwarfed in 1954, when the United played Portsmouth in the 4th round of the F.A.Cup, and an all-time highest crowd was established when 23,935 enthusiasts packed into the Ground. Probably funded by the profits from this Cup run, Ground improvements included the covering of the Doncaster Road end, and in 1957 the floodlights were first switched on.

The East Stand: The first in England with a substantial cantilevered roof.

1958 became the Club's most successful year. They reached the fifth round of the F.A.Cup (after beating Newcastle United at St.James' Park), and were promoted to the Second Division of the Football League. But during the close season the Ground suffered when a fire destroyed the timber East Stand. The replacement structure was hoped to become something of a showpiece since it was the first cantilever Stand ever erected at a British Football Stadium. But it did not receive this deserved status for the more impressive Stand at Sheffield Wednesday which was completed four years later took the subsequent glory! Ten years later the Club reached a low ebb when they dropped down to the Fourth Division for the first time, but four years later they bounced back up again. The United's elevation to the Third Division was followed one year later with the replacing of the Fox Street cover; its forerunner had survived from pre-war days.

In 1985, talks commenced with regard to a Ground move that was primarily prompted by the new safety of Grounds requirements that followed the Bradford City disaster. Within two years work had started on the new Stadium, and the end of the 1987/88 season saw the United just lose out on promotion back into the Third Division. The last match at the Old Show Ground became a sad event. Not only was it the final game at this old Stadium, but a victory was necessary for the last possible promotion place.

On the 18th of May 1988, Torquay United were entertained in a play-off game, but the crowd of 6,483 (double the home average for the campaign) went home disappointed as their favourites could only draw, this result following the first leg defeat in Devon.

No true supporter wishes to see their team move to a new ground, preferring the old with all its warts and memories. At the end, the Old Show Ground was able to offer covered seating or standing accommodation on all four sides, quite r narkable for a Stadium that was to be demolished. But with the Safety of Grounds Act reducing the Old Show Ground's capacity at one time to 5,000, it was clearly not viable to spend a six figure sum in order to raise this limit. Within weeks of vacating the premises, demolition on the Old Show Ground commenced, and the site is now a Safeways Supermarket.

Aerial view of the Old Show Ground - the cantilever Stand is to the right.

SHEFFIELD WEDNESDAY

In some repects the City of Sheffield can be considered
as the birthplace of Association Football, with the
formation of Sheffield F.C. in 1857, the oldest Football
Club in the World. Yet the formation of the Wednesday did
not occur for another ten years, making them almost a
late developer in the area!

LONDON ROAD.

On the 4th of September 1867, the Wednesday Football Club
was created out of the Sheffield Wednesday Cricket Club
who, at this time, were already forty-two years old. A
meeting at the Adelphi Hotel decided to create the Club
in order to give a winter sporting interest to their
members. The Football Club started with a membership of
over sixty, and the first match was played and won, on
the 31st of December at Dronfield. As a home Ground, a
field off London Road, which is now the site of the
Highfield Library, was chosen and used until 1870. On the
15th of February the Club played, and won, their first
Cup final when the Garrick Club were beaten in the
Cromwell Cup.

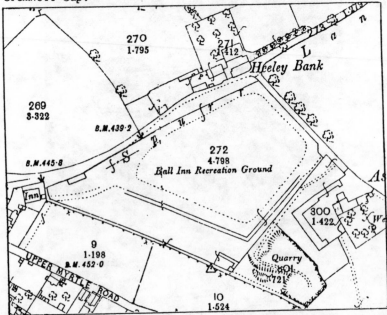

Ball Inn Recreation Ground (off of Myrtle Road) - currently an enclosed football ground.
(Ordnance Survey 1895)

MYRTLE ROAD, HEELEY.

From the 1870/71 season the Wednesday played their home games in Myrtle Road, Heeley. This may well have been at the Ball Inn Recreation Ground, which still exists, located just off the junction with the current Thornborough Road. There were no facilities whatsoever here, and with the Club already commanding good support, important matches were played at the Bramall Lane Cricket Ground, and continued until 1895. The Recreation Ground as it is currently named, is now a well developed enclosure, complete with floodlights plus a two storey Clubhouse, and commands an expansive view over the City.

BRAMALL LANE - ON OCCASIONS.

The Wednesday soon became a powerful team in the locality, and in November 1872 they moved further afield when a game was played against Derby County - a 14-a-side match! Football was still very much played under rudimentary rules, but during the 1871/72 season the first Sheffield versus London match took place, at Bramall Lane, with the Wednesday supplying seven of the home team players. The Sheffield Association instigated a Challenge Cup Competition, and the Wednesday fought through to the first final when they played Heeley on the 10th of March 1877 at Bramall Lane. The biggest football crowd of some 8,000, was the biggest ever seen at this Cricket enclosure, and they witnessed an exciting game with Heeley taking a three goal half-time lead. In the second period the Wednesday drew level at 3-3, and scored the winner in extra time. The Club became frequent winners of this Trophy, and first entered for the F.A. Cup Competition in the 1878/79 season.

SHEAF HOUSE GROUND.

Although important games continued to be played at the Bramall Lane enclosure, a home Ground, from 1877, for other games was chosen at the adjacent Sheaf House Ground. Whilst being considerably smaller than the Cricket Ground, it was at least enclosed and had a narrow open seated Stand at the North end. The Bramall Lane Ground was far better equipped for spectators with substantial seating areas on three sides, albeit uncovered, and a large Pavilion on the South side. The 1881/82 season saw the Wednesday reach the semi-finals of the F.A.Cup when they lost in a replay to Blackburn Rovers; the two matches were played at Huddersfield Rugby Club and at Whalley Range, Manchester.

Earlier they had beaten their main rivals Heeley at Bramall Lane, before a crowd of 4,000. The Sheaf House Ground continued as the normal home venue for nearly ten years, during which time the Club became embroiled in the controversy with regard to professionalism.

In 1887 after the birth, and virtual instant death, of Sheffield Rovers - the team was composed of self-confessed professional players - the Wednesday openly turned to paying Players. This move was made during a fall from grace for the Wednesday and during these declining years, the role of the top Club in the City was taken by Lockwood Brothers, a firm's team.

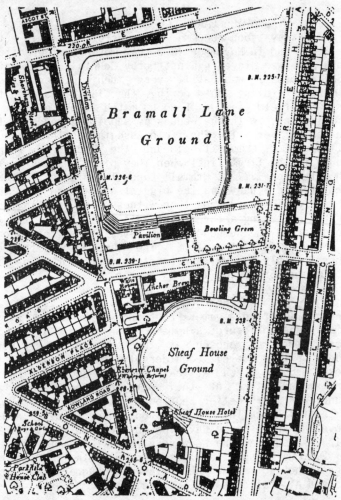

Sheaf House and Brammall Lane (the latter, then just a Cricket Ground) were used for important matches.   (Ordnance Survey 1895)

ENDCLIFFE.

For a short period a new home Ground was chosen at Endcliffe, to the West of the City centre. The Ground, according to the O.S. Map of 1894, was located off the Eccleshall Road between the current Bruce and Hickmott Roads. It was little more than an enclosed field, with narrow standing areas. However, it was the first home of the Wednesday that could be truly called a 'Football Ground', since the previous three venues were not exclusively for this sport. The downturn in the Club's fortunes almost led to their extinction, but the winning of the Sheffield Cup in 1887 restored their prestige.

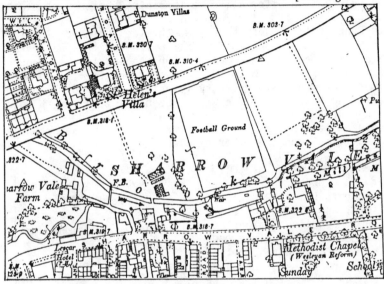

The Hunter's Bar ground. (Ordnance Survey 1895)

OLIVE GROVE.

With a renewed burst of confidence, it was announced at the Club's A.G.M. on the 6th of June 1887, that the Wednesday were to move to a Ground that would not only be worthy of a powerful Club, but also one that would be for their exclusive use. The Ground became known as Olive Grove, but at this time was little more than three and a half acres of flat swamp land! The site was located immediately adjacent to the Midland Railway line, North of the present Olive Grove Road, and approximately midway between Heeley Bank and Myrtle Roads. Coincidentally it was virtually halfway between, and in line with, the former Myrtle Road and Bramall Lane venues.

The land was leased from the Duke of Norfolk, and work commenced immediately to drain it - this included diverting a stream - and construct facilities for spectators, all at a cost of £5,000. By the start of the 1887/88 season, a great deal of effort had produced the basis of a good enclosure, although there were initially no changing rooms, and this had to take place in a nearby Pub! The 110 by 70 yard pitch was surrounded with a strong iron railing. On three sides, and outside of the railing, a six foot (two metre) wide flat cinder surface was laid (an improvement over the discomforture of grass or soil and an alternative to the later choice - at other Grounds - of the ubiquitous timber pallets or duckboards). The very narrow North side (hard up to the railway lines) contained a full pitch length open seated Stand that could accommodate 1,000. Access to the Ground was at each end. Within a few years the facilities were improved upon, with covering to half of the North Stand (at the East end) and a wider but half pitch length open Stand at the Heeley Bank Road end, being added. Short covered enclosures were built (one of which was probably a Pavilion), on the other side and end.

The first match at Olive Grove brought the renowned Blackburn Rovers to Sheffield, and a creditable 4-4 draw resulted before an attendance of nearly 2,000. The Wednesday were invited to discussions with regard to the formation of the Football League, but declined the invitation, and it was not for another five years that they finally entered the fray, alongside their much younger neighbours, Sheffield United; Wednesday in the First and United in the Second Division. Meanwhile support for the Wednesday at Olive Grove was good, and attendances numbering 2,000 were not uncommon.

OPENING MATCH at Olive Grove.

MONDAY, SEPTEMBER 12th, 1887.

THE WEDNESDAY v. BLACKBURN ROVERS

BLACKBURN TEAM.

Right Wing.   Goal   Left Wing.

H. Arthur.

Jos. Beverley.   A. Chadwick.

Jas. Heyes.   John Barton.   Jas. H. Forrest.

R. Douglas. H. Walton. R. Birchton. L. H. Heyes. J. Barisford.

WEDNESDAY TEAM.

J. Smith.

F. Thompson.   J. Hudson.

K. Brayshaw.   W. Betts.   A. Beckett.

H. Winterbottom. G. Waller. T. E. H. Wilson. T. Cawley. W. Mosforth.

Umpires: T. B. Mitchell; H. Ellis   Referee: J. C. Clegg.

But the F.A.Cup was always the main attraction, and a replay against Notts. County in 1889, attracted 6,000 with a further thousand for the second replay. Missing, and probably later regretting, their chance to join the Football League, the Club became founder-members of the Football Alliance, and duly won the Championship. The Club nearly reached the pinnacle that season, for they fought their way through to the F.A.Cup Final at the Oval, but were unceremoniously defeated by Blackburn Rovers with a 1-6 scoreline. Further good runs in the Premier competition eventually led to their winning it in 1896.

The Club were honoured with a representative match at Olive Grove in April 1891, when the Football League met the Football Alliance, and the ensuing draw tended to confirm the feeling of many that the two Leagues were virtually on a parity with each other. The Club's election into the First Division of the Football League ensured even greater support for the team, and on the 29th of October a new record attendance (well in excess of the previous best) of 20,000 came for the match versus Sunderland. On the 21st of January 1893 another large crowd, this time totalling 17,000, was present to see the locals beat Derby County by 3-2 in the F.A.Cup. True to the attitude of the period, Derby lodged a protest (regarding illegibility of players), the replay was then won by the County, which was countered by the Wednesday lodging their own protest! Once again this was upheld, and in the second replay at Olive Grove, and before a 10,000 gate, the Sheffield eleven finally won through. The games had generated takings of £900. With a series of good Cup runs, despite only moderate performances in the League, the Wednesday were a well supported Club, and at the end of the 1893/94 season a credit balance of £311 was realised on the year. The coffers were swelled by a share of the receipts of £741 that was taken at the F.A.Cup match versus Aston Villa, when a new record crowd of 22,100 was present. The following season this number was dwarfed when an all time record attendance of 28,000 crammed into Olive Grove to see their favourites beat Everton in the quarter finals of the same competition.

The 1895/96 F.A.Cup Campaign saw the Club become the winners for the first time, and on their route to the final, they beat Sunderland, before another enormous gate (at 22,000 the best of the day) and receipts of £729.

The next three seasons were poor ones by the Wednesday's high standards, for not only did they progress no further than the second round of the F.A.Cup, but at the end of this period, their 18th place in the League table warranted relegation to the Second Division. Their woe was not eased by the success of neighbours United, who, after winning the Championship in 1898, went onto to win the F.A. Cup the following year.

To add to the Wednesday's problems, their occupation of Olive Grove was about to finish. The lease for the Ground had expired on the 29th of September 1898, and although a renewal was expected to be a formality, this was not to be. The Club was given a few months leeway, and to add to their demotion problems, a new Ground had to be found for the following season. There was a crowd disorder at the Everton match on the 4th of March (a 1-2 defeat), but nine days later a bizarre 'game' took place. Back in November, the home match with Aston Villa was abandoned, due to bad light, with ten and a half minutes of play left. The Football League ordered that the remainder of this match should be undertaken, and so, after leading by 3-1, the Wednesday added another goal in the continuation game! This farce was followed by a Friendly game, and the homesters again triumphed, by two unopposed goals. Only 3,000 spectators bothered to turn up, but this had swelled to over 5,000 for Burnley's visit on the 1st of April. Although the Wednesday won both points, they were still deep in relegation trouble.

On the 15th of April the last match at Olive Grove was played, but as the team slumped to a 1-3 defeat - which booked the Club for Division 2 - only 4,000 loyal supporters were in attendance. At the end of the month the Club officially wound up, but immediately re-appeared as a Limited Company, and with the £7,000 that was quickly raised, they were rich by the standards of the day.

The Club's chosen new home was something of a gamble, for rather than keeping to the town area, a long trek North, to a venue outside the border of Sheffield was made, to Owlerton. The Club's fears of reduced support due to the move and relegation were alleviated, for with the advantage of an expanding catchment area, 12,000 were present for the opening match.

Overall the move was for the better, since the surroundings were more open, and with the main Stand that was moved from Olive Grove, the team immediately felt at home! Of the old Olive Grove Ground there is now no trace, for the site is now a depot for the City of Sheffield Transport Department.

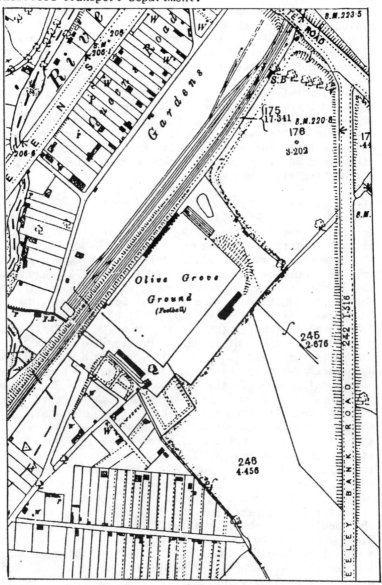

The Olive Grove Ground. (Ordnance Survey 1895)

SHREWSBURY TOWN

The game of football in the Shrewsbury area arrived long
before the modern version of the mid-1800's. Since at
least the 16th century a form of the game had been
played, although such activities were generally frowned
upon, and in 1562 two persons were sentenced to prison
for playing football on All Saints Day! As in many other
areas, football became popular in the town from its
importation by the sons of middle class men, following
their initial introduction during their Public School
days. In Shrewsbury's case the game was already, to a
degree, on their doorstep, for it had became popular by
the early 1870's (with at least twelve teams in the town)
due largely to the 'day boys' of Shrewsbury School. This
enthusiasm was to gradually spread within a few years, to
the working class men and boys.

The first town Club, Shrewsbury Football Club, was
founded in November 1874, but played no proper fixtures
before, probably, floudering one year later. A second
attempt to form a Club was made in 1875, and this time
the attempt was successful. Most Home matches were played
on the Monkmoor Racecourse, and the 1875/76 season saw
the team playing a number of games, albeit all within the
County. This Club won the Shropshire Senior Cup in its
inaugural season of 1877/78, and also played at the
Armoury Field (where the first County Cup Final was
played) and the Cotton Hill Playing Fields. But they
gradually drifted into oblivion, as did Shropshire
Wanderers who were based in the area and who reached the
semi-final stage of the F.A.Cup in 1875. Shrewsbury
Engineers, later winners of the Shropshire Senior Cup,
experimented with Floodlit football in December 1878. But
the match versus Newport and played at the Racecourse, as
a spectacle, was a failure since of the four lights - one
at each corner of the field - only two worked properly!
In 1879, the first Club named Shrewsbury Town were
founded, and played their matches at the 'Monkmoor
Ground', which was equipped with, at least, dressing
rooms for the players. But the Club made little impact on
the local scene, and it was left to Shrewsbury Castle
Blues who came to the fore in the early 1880's. However,
a defeat by Oswestry Town in 1882, led to rioting amongst
the two sets of supporters, and this Club disbanded soon
after that unsavoury incident.

MONKMOOR RACECOURSE.

On the 20th of May 1886, the modern day 'Shrewsbury Town F.C.' were formed, following a meeting at the Turf Hotel, Claremont Hill. The initiative came from former members of the Castle Blues Club and others from the earlier Town team. As an amateur organisation, the new Club took over the Ground at Monkmoor Racecourse. The first match by this new team was played in a 6-a-side tournament, that was held at the Ditherington Flower Show. They won - and lost - in the final, when they were defeated 4-5 by their own Reserve eleven! In September 1886 a few hundred spectators saw the initial first team match, at Wellington, when two goals were shared; Alty Davies being the Town's first goalscorer. The first competitive match was played on October the 1st, which resulted in a most encouraging 6-1 defeat of Stafford Rangers in the Birmingham Cup. But there was no cause for celebration a few weeks later when a scratch team lost at Crewe Alexandra by 1-17! However, by winning the Shropshire Cup that season, and the next two, it was obvious that this Club intended to remain for a longer period than their predecessors.

A match at the Racecourse (One of the Town's former homes). The pitch markings and lack of goal nets suggest that this was taken pre-1882, and therefore before the current Club had been formed.

(Shrewsbury. Castle Gates Library)   -317-

The F.A.Cup was first entered in 1887, and after beating Macclesfield by 3-1, they lost by ten goals to two at Chirk. On Christmas Eve 1888, before a home crowd of 1,200 (at twice the normal entrance charge), the Club lost by ten unopposed goals to Wolverhampton Wanderers in the Birmingham Cup. One year later, Aberdare were humiliated by fifteen goals to nil in the Welsh Cup, and this was followed in the 1890's with a 21-0 victory over Mold Alyn Stars. High scoring matches were to become a feature of the Town Club! Until 1889, the Club continued to play on the Ground which was situated within the enclosed area of the Racecourse at Monkmoor, to the East of the town centre. The Ground offered little for spectators since the Grandstand on the North-west side was too remote from the football pitch, and the fans could only watch from flat standing areas. But it was possible to levy an entrance charge since the Racecourse itself was enclosed.

AMBLER'S FIELD.

With a desire to reduce expenses, a move was made the short distance to the other side of Monkmoor Road, at a lower rental charge. This second Ground, known as Ambler's Field was probably little more than an enclosed field, for which the normal entry fee was 3d. (just over 1p), and double this amount if the luxury of the Reserved enclosure was preferred where timber boards protected the feet! Refreshments were available within the Ground. The Monkmoor Racecourse, after later use for Agricultural Shows, disappeared in the 1920's, and is now the area containing a recreation ground, Schools and housing, to the South of Monkmoor Road. Ambler's Field was located opposite the Racecourse Grandstand, and the site is now bounded by Monkmoor and Underdale Roads, between Ashley Street and Underdale Avenue. Following the initiative taken by the Town's Secretary, the Shropshire League was founded in 1890, and in the Club's first League match they lost at Wellington before a crowd of 400. But throughout the first season only three defeats were sustained, and in April 1894 they recorded a 11-1 victory over Hereford. By now the Club had moved again, this time to Sutton Lane, at a further reduced rental charge. But this Ground, which was well South of and somewhat remote from the town, attracted generally small attendances (gates realising upto £15 were rarely taken), apart from a record to that date, when 2,000 were present for the match versus Old St.Stephens in the F.A. Amateur Cup.

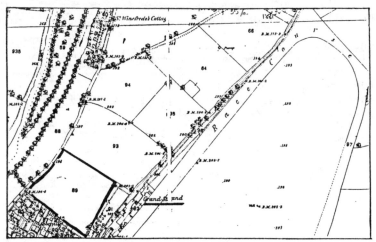

The locations of the Racecourse and Amblers Field Grounds in 1881 (the latter, ref. '89')
(Ordnance Survey)

THE BARRACKS GROUND.

After two years (in 1895), another move was made, this
time to the Barracks Ground at Copthorne. This new venue,
on high Ground to the West of the town centre, is now
bounded by Copthorne Road and Drive, and to the East of
Porthill Drive. Initially the Ground was very basic, and
it was some years before a Grandstand was built. The main
entrance was almost opposite Granville Street, and it was
probably on the far West side of the Ground that a
building for refreshments was built. The facilities on the
Reserved side consisted of school desks and chairs, but
no cover!

The Club entered the Birmingham League for the 1895/96
season, and the hopes of improved Gates was realised,
although the first home match was lost by 14-0 to the
Wolves. A new record attendance was achieved on Boxing
Day, when 3,500 watched the 3-1 victory over Wellington.
But it was realised that the only route to success was to
turn professional, and this was undertaken at the end of
that season. The Club re-entered for the F.A.Cup in 1898
(following a trio of entries in earlier seasons), but
there was little in the way of success, and into the
early 20th century it was a bleak time on the playing
front. As the years advanced, the Club gradually became
more of a force on the field, and in 1908, a new record
attendance was set, when a 1-1 draw was fought out with
old local rivals Wellington, in front of a 5,000 plus
gate.

In 1910, The Shrewsbury Council purchased the Gay Meadow Fields, and after the Town Football Club played their last match at Copthorne - a 2-0 victory over Walsall in April - they moved into, and rented part of that area, that became known as the Gay Meadow Football Ground.

(Right): Match Poster of 1895.

FOOTBALL MATCH.

ENGLISH CUP TIE.

SATURDAY, OCTOBER 5th, 1889.

Nantwich v. Shrewsbury Town,

ON

AMBLER'S FIELD,
ENTRANCE OPPOSITE RACECOURSE GRAND-STAND.

NANTWICH.

W. Rassall.

GOAL.

S. Davies.   K. Shenton.

T. Critchley.   W. Buckley.   K. Crawford.

W. Cartwright.   K. Buckley.   E. Hind.   R. Ball.   K. Prince.

G. Rowlands.   A. Davies.   P. Murphy.   A. Ellis.   K. Pearson.
(Captain.)

W. Harris.   L. Edwards.   J. C. Davies.

W. Steedman.   J. Jones.

(GOAL.)

J. Kaibrook.

SHREWSBURY TOWN.

KICK-OFF AT 3·30 P.M.

ADMISSION 3d.; Reserved Enclosure (Boarded Floor) 6d.
REFRESHMENTS ON THE GROUND.

W. B. WALKER (Late Drury & Dovey) PRINTER, Shrewsbury.

(Below): The basic Barracks Ground, in 1902, in the Copthorne District.
(Ordnance Survey)

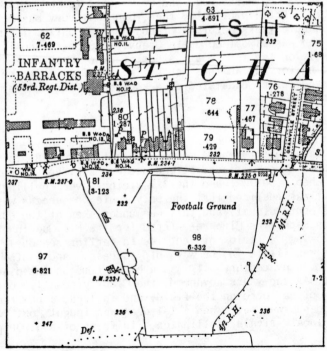

-320-

SOUTHAMPTON

In 1885 Southampton were founded, as St. Mary's Young
mens Association, and made their inconspicuous start on
the 28th of November of that year. Their opponents that
day were Freemantle, another new Club who were destined
to become the Club's main competitors for some years. But
the Saints won this first encounter with a 5-1 victory.

NORTHLANDS ROAD.

The 'Ground' on this occasion, such as it was, was
nothing more than an unfenced strip of land in Northlands
Road. By coincidence this venue was located opposite the
County Cricket Ground - that was to later to become the
Football Club's Ground for several years - and by the
turn of the century became a Bowling Green and Tennis
Courts complex; it is currently the home of the Bannister
Bowling Club.

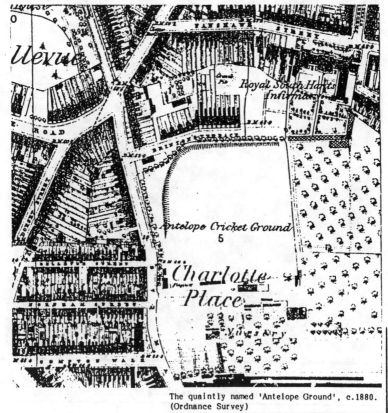

The quaintly named 'Antelope Ground', c.1880.
(Ordnance Survey)

-321-

ANTELOPE GROUND.

A move was soon made to the more suitable Antelope Ground nearer the town centre. This Ground was located at the junction of Brinton's Terrace and St.Mary's Road, and until 1885 had been used by the County Cricket Club. This strange name was taken from The Antelope Inn, where the Cricket Club was founded in September 1863. For such a novice Football team the Ground offered facilities far in excess of most of their contemporaries. There was a small Stand under which the visiting teams changed (this was probably on the South side of the Ground). The homesters made use of the 'All England Eleven' Public House as a dressing room, that was situated at the North-west corner of the Antelope which conveniently had a rear access onto the Ground. There was also a roofed enclosure, that was little more than a large shed, which embarrassingly collapsed during a match with Sheffield Wednesday! The main, and possibly only, entrance - complete with turnstiles - was at the corner of Brinton's Terrace and St. Mary's Road. The North and West sides had small grassed embankments. To complete this very acceptable Ground, there was a flagstaff in the South-west corner where a red and white flag was proudly flown when a match was due to be played!

c.1890. Dressing Rooms at the Antelope, probably in the North-east corner of the Ground. A poster advertises a St.Mary's versus Freemantle match.

After a low key start, the Club were soon able to attract good numbers of spectators, and the Hampshire Junior Cup was first won in 1887, and further successes followed in the next three years. But the greatest interest was reserved for matches versus Freemantle who were based on the other side of the town. The Club's first Hampshire Junior Cup tie in November was played at Freemantle's Ground (a field at the rear of the Anchor Hotel in Redbridge), when a crowd of around three thousand saw the Saints win by the only goal of the game. Such was the interest that later rounds were staged at the new County Ground where the facilities were better than those at The Antelope. The 1888/89 Junior Cup semi-final match versus Cowes was replayed at the County Ground when for the first time cheap railway tickets were issued for supporters from outlying districts. The crowd of over 3,000 was a record for a football match in Hampshire and included around 1,000 Ladies.

On the 24th of October 1891, the Saints played their first F.A.Cup game, when Reading attracted a record crowd of 4,000 to the Antelope. The visitors were thrashed by seven unopposed goals but their Secretary made an immediate telegraphed protest to the F.A. due to the claim of Southampton fielding two unregistered Players. In order to pay for the message, the Secretary borrowed some money from the gate takings! Support continued to increase, and by the early 1890's the Club could boast of a membership of 600. Such interest provoked them into becoming a professional Club, and when Freemantle were entertained (at the County Ground) for a Hampshire Senior Cup match during the 1892/93 season the attendance record was broken with a 6,000 gate which produced receipts of £122; on this occasion however, the homesters lost the encounter by 1-2. The 1893/94 season was the last before the Club became founder-members of the Southern League, but only after their original application had been refused. However the decision was subsequently reversed when the 2nd Scots Guards withdrew. The season had seen the Saints realise a profit of £86, after deductions which included Players wages of £221 and £41 Ground rental. Income was generated from £157 members subscriptions (at 17p per head - Ladies were free!) and £612 gate money.

The first League game was played at the Antelope Ground on the 6th of October when Chatham were beaten by 3-1. The F.A.Cup entry that season produced the Club's all time record score - 14-0 versus Newbury before a 4,000 gate. Later home victories were achieved over Reading (5-2), and Marlow (7-3) both before 5,000 attendances. In the final qualifying round Warmley were easily brushed aside with a 5-1 scoreline but before a lower gate of only 3,000. This took the Club through to the 1st round proper when they met Nottingham Forest, once again at home. The game created great interest and a new record crowd of 7,000 was present to see the non-League team lose by 1-4. A final third place in the Southern League ensured continued support, and the next season another good F.A.Cup run produced attendances of between four and five thousand in the early rounds. On the 1st of February 1896, the eventual winners - Sheffield Wednesday - were entertained at the Antelope Ground in the 1st round proper, and before an all time record attendance of 12,000, the homesters only narrowly lost by the odd goal in five. A packed Antelope Ground had by now become almost commonplace, but the site was only rented, and the Club were forced to vacate it as building work was soon to commence. A move was made over to the County Cricket Ground which was already familiar to the Club in view of the many cup-ties that had been played at the venue. It was fitting that the last game at The Antelope should have been against their old and close rivals, Freemantle. In a friendly encounter, on the 29th of April 1896, the visitors won by the only goal of the game.

COUNTY GROUND.

On the 2nd of September the first opponents at the County Ground - now as a regular home Ground - was Kettering in a pre-season Friendly match watched by only around 1,000; the novelty of this venue was lost since in view of the Club's past usage, it was hardly a 'new' Ground! 1897 became a significant year in the Club's history for they won the Southern League Championship, and in July became a Limited Company with a share capital of £5,000; at this juncture they also dropped the 'St.Mary's' from their title to become plain 'Southampton F.C.' The season had seen yet another good run in the major Cup Competition with two home games attracting crowds of 5,000 and 8,500, before finally losing to Newton Heath in a second round replay.

During the 1897/98 season a magnificent F.A.Cup run took the Club through to the semi-finals, the first time that a non-League team (since the pre-League days before 1888) had achieved such a distinction.

Home victories included, Bristol City (11,000 gate), Eastville Rovers (8,000), Leicester Fosse (10,000) and Newcastle United (12,000). After a scoreless draw with Bolton - before a 15,000 new Club record crowd - the replay was comfortably, and somewhat incredibly, won by 4-0. The end came at the hands of Nottingham Forest, but only after another replay. For the second year running, the Southern League Championship was won to cap a memorable season.

(Above): Football at the County Ground in 1898 (versus Newcastle).
(Below): A similar view at the County Ground in 1989. (Dave Twydell)

Whereas the Antelope Ground, which is now principally
Graham and Clovelly Roads, was centrally located and
could probably have been built into a good Stadium, the
County Ground had it's limitations. Once again the Saints
were only tenants, this time of the Hampshire Cricket
Club, but also the lack of banking and Stands would limit
them in their ambitious plans. Having become by now
probably the most successful Club in the South, they were
confident enough to secure a former duckpond and for
around £10,000 (an enormous sum of money at this time)
convert it into one of the Country's foremost Football
Grounds.

On the 3rd of September 1898, the first game was played
at the Dell. Meanwhile just up the road, the Cricket
authorities were able to pursue their sole interests, as
they still do to this day. This Ground still retains a
number of features that date back a century or so.

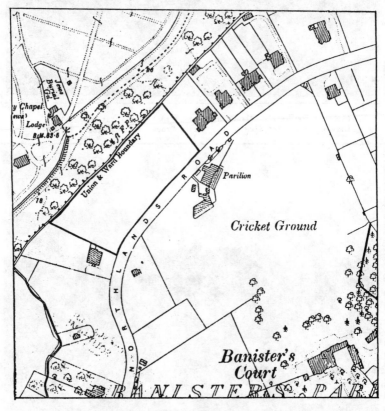

The County Ground in 1897, and the former Northlands Road Ground
on the other side of the road.   (Ordnance Survey)

SOUTHEND UNITED

Although Southend United F.C. were not formed until 1905,
by this time the town already had senior representation -
albeit at an Amateur level - in Southend Athletic. This
Club had been playing from towards the end of the 19th
Century, probably initially under the name of
'Southend-on-Sea' and based at The Marine Park, which was
almost on the seafront. By 1900, they had changed the
suffix in their name to 'Athletic'. Marine Park was later
to become the venue for the United's home games (for
fifteen years), but a vastly changed Ground and under a
different title. Southend United are the only Club in the
Football League to have started their life at, and are
currently using, in effect, the same Ground, despite
alternatives in the interim period!

The formation of Southend United in the Summer of 1906
led immediately to their acceptance into the Southern
League for the forthcoming season. The Athletic meanwhile
realised, too late, that their prowess within the town
was in danger, for they also sought an entry into the
same League, but their application arrived too late for
consideration. The United obtained the most votes of all
the aspirants. The United chose for their home matches,
the Roots Hall Field in West Street, Prittlewell (around
one mile North of Southend centre), a Ground that
ironically the Athletic had also used at one time.

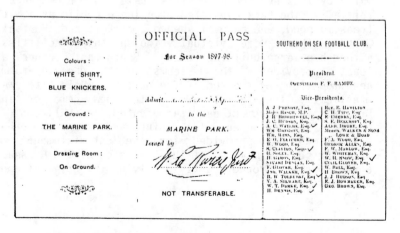

A forerunner of the United who occupied Marine Park.
This later became known as The Kursaal Ground. (Southend-on-Sea Museum)

ROOT'S HALL:

This first Ground was adjacent to a large property of the same name but had limited facilities, consisting of little more than a pitch (with a pronounced longitudinal slope) surrounded with flat standing areas, and a seated Grandstand. The new Club's practice game attracted 850 spectators, enough to no doubt give Southend Athletic cause for concern, and despite their earlier amalgamation with Southend Victoria, they were never able to make a serious challenge to their professional neighbours.

On the 2nd of September 1906, the United played their first League game (in the Second Division) against Swindon Town Reserves - which was unluckily lost by the only goal of the game. For the next home game, 2,000 spectators were fortunate enough to be present to see their locals demolish the Royal Engineers (Aldershot), by twelve goals to nil!

Initially the Club were successful, gaining promotion to the First Division, but returning to the lower fold four years later. They were promoted once again in the Summer of 1913, but after only two seasons, the First World War meant a curtailment of activities for the Southern League. The last game at Roots Hall (at least for forty years) was played on May Day in 1915, when the United secured a 3-1 victory and thereby avoided another relegation.

Meanwhile things were happening over at Marine Park, which by 1912 had changed it's name to 'Luna Park'. Initially the Park consisted of a large public area with trees, a pond, and an oval shaped Cricket and Football Ground. There were virtually no spectator facilities, although a large building in the South-east corner at least provided the teams with dressing-rooms accommodation. By the end of the War, the whole site was drastically transformed. Under the new name of 'The Kursaal', an amusement park was created. A Ballroom, a Scenic Railway, an Ice Rink and numerous other attractions were provided for the entertainment of visiting Holidaymakers. At the East side of 'the Kursaal, a new Football Ground (partly overlying the original one) was incorporated.

Southend United
Football Club, Limited.

Registered Offices.
ROOTS HALL. WEST STREET.
SOUTHEND-ON-SEA.
Ground-ROOTS HALL.

GROUND
SEASON TICKET.
£1 1s. 'NOT TRANSFERABLE'.
all Matches with the
Ties and Benefit
hes over which
control.

SOUTHEND UNITED FOOTBALL CLUB Ltd.

Season Ticket, 1909-10

STAND, UNRESERVED.

NOT TRANSFERABLE

THE KURSAAL:

The new Ground was laid out with 5,700 grass turves
(which came close to disaster following a long dry spell
during the summer of 1919) and resulted in one of the
best pitches in the Southern League. The 115 by 75 yard
playing area was surrounded by a fence, three yards from
the touchline. Initially facilities were limited,
although diagonally opposite the dressing-rooms (that
were situated in the pavilion, which had remained from
the 'Marine Park' days, in the South-east corner), was a
'covered terrace' for the Directors; apparently a most
important factor! A start was also made at this time on
terracing around the Ground. Wide entrance approaches
were created from both Woodgrange Road and from Beresford
Road.

It was not long before a Grandstand was built on the East
side (half pitch length), and narrow bands of concrete
terracing were completed to all four sides (including an
open paddock in front of the Grandstand, and an enclosed
one to the small 'Director's' Stand).

Within the main Pavilion a Gymnasium was included, and for the spectators a refreshment pavilion was provided. The Ground, located most unusually within an amusement park (a notable parallel in the Football League was that at the Tower Ground of New Brighton F.C.) had a claimed capacity of 36,000 - which was never even half reached.

On the 30th of August 1919, Portsmouth were the first visitors to The Kursaal Ground - accompanied by Mr. Meek's Hippodrome Band (to 'brighten the event'). A very satisfactory crowd of 5,400 (paying gate receipts of £270) was present, but those spectators went home unhappy after seeing their team lose by two goals to nil. The Club's stay at the Kursaal lasted until the end of the 1933/34 season, and in view of their generally mediocre placings in the League (including one re-election application), the attendances which generally hovered between six and eight thousand (with the occasional five figures) could be considered quite good.
The later addition to the amusements of a scenic railway, which overlooked the North end of the Ground, may well have been considered a more exciting experience than those generally seen on the football pitch! The last Football League game at the Ground on the 28th of April, attracted only 4,000 spectators, when Norwich were the visitors, and a scoreless draw resulted. One week later the last match at The Kursaal was played between the Reserves of the United and Aldershot, which was attended by only a few hundred enthusiasts.

original Roots Hall Ground in 1906 was little more than an enclosure with a perimeter fence und the pitch. The far left of the picture shows the changing rooms with 'Southend United tball Club' painted on the roof.
(Southend Standard)

The first team gate receipts at home totalled £7,702 , resulting in an overall loss on the season of £263. Even at this stage there was some doubt as to where the team would be playing for the forthcoming season.

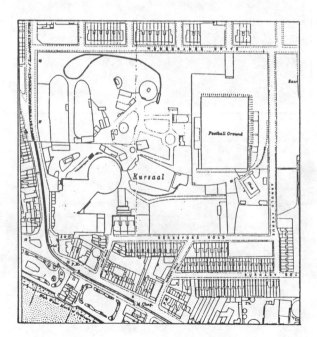

1921. The Kursaal Ground within a large amusement centre of the same name. (Ordnance Survey)

THE STADIUM, GRAINGER ROAD:

This Stadium - the site of a former brickworks - was not constructed solely for the Football Club. However a Grandstand was included, and there were plans for the erection of Dressing Rooms, Stores and Offices at the North end... "suitable for use by a Football Club"... therefore it must have come as no surprise to find Southend United F.C. deciding to move there! Soon after the end of the 1933/34 season, work got underway to remove stones from the playing area, and grass sown for a playing pitch.

The first game on the 25th of August 1934, at the Stadium, created unprecedented interest, for although only a reserve fixture (albeit versus the attractive Tottenham team), a record second team crowd of over 8,000 were present. True to form, the game was lost (2-6) by the homesters - as were the Club's previous debuts at their new homes. The initial first team match, four days later, however, produced a 2-1 victory over Aldershot. On the first day of September, Exeter City provided the opposition in the second Football League fixture. This latter match was lost (1-2), but a very healthy attendance of 11,500, paid £680 at the gate. Entrances were located off Grainger, Maldon and Sutton Roads, at a standing cost of one shilling (5p), and just over half price for boys.

(Above left): An aerial view of The Kursaal Ground in 1928. (Aerofilms)

(Left): A packed Kursaal Ground watches a Schoolboy match in January 1934. (Southend Standard)

Action in August 1919, the first game (a Practise Match) at the new Kursaal Ground. (Southend Standard)

The venue became a 'typical' dual purpose Stadium, with Greyhounds providing the other attraction. Another Stand was later erected opposite the main structure, and a thin band of concrete terracing was provided elsewhere, to form a familiar oval shaped Ground.

This inaugural season at the new Ground, was a near disaster, for the team finished second from bottom in the Third Division South, and had to make - a successful - re-election application. The only really bright spot in a dismal season, was the annihilation of the amateurs Golders Green (later to become Hendon), by 10-1 in the first round of the F.A.Cup; the Seasiders joint record score for a competitive match. A somewhat mundane existance followed in the years to come, and although there was never a repeat of the awful 1934/35 season, above a mid-table position was rarely achieved, save for 1950, when a serious challenge for promotion finished with a final third in the division.

Attendances rarely reached five figures, but in 1936, an F.A.Cup match with Tottenham Hotspur drew an all-time record crowd to the Grainger Stadium of 22,862 and receipts of £2,913.

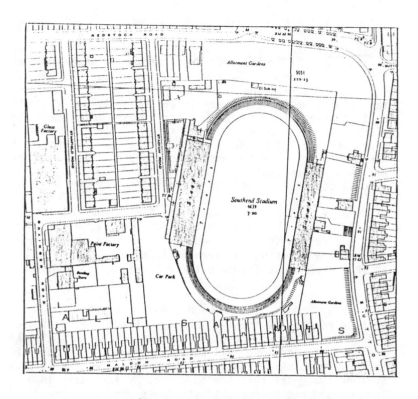

(Above): The Athletics Stadium c.1970.
(Ordnance Survey).

(Below): The Stadium at Grainger Road, pictured in 1985 shortly before it was demolished.
(Chris Ambler)

After 20 years as a tenant, the Club were finally able to move to a venue of their own. On April the 30th 1955, the locals beat Brentford by 3-2 (the winner coming from Roy Hollis in the dying minutes) before an attendance of 8,000. Meanwhile, up the road, the Company of Boulton and Paul were erecting the steelwork for the first Stand at the Club's new home. It was in Prittlewell, and at Roots Hall, to where the Club made it's final move, and in effect a move back to where they had first started 35 years earlier. Although the site of the 'new' Roots Hall was more or less the same as before, the pitch was now set in a hollow that had been created by the gravel removal over the preceeding decades.

It was a coincidence that the first home game of the 1955/56 season should be against Norwich City - the Club who had helped to bring down the curtain at the Kursaal, but on this occasion a record (League) attendance of 17,700 were present to see the 3-1 defeat of the Norfolk team.

THE GROUNDS TODAY:

Nothing remains of the two former Grounds in Southend. Within two years of the Club's move from the Kursaal, the Football ground had all but disappeared, with just the East Stand being the only remaining relic, and within a further two years this too had gone. By the early 1950's, the Ground had become the site for a scenic railway, but it was not long before this was built over to provide housing by way of several blocks of flats. Even the Kursaal complex itself has now been almost completely erased, with little left other than the impressive entrance at the East end of the former large amusement centre.

Just a half mile to the North-west, the Greyhound Stadium remained until the 1980's, being now overlain by a Superstore. But at least a memory lingers on with a new entrance road that in effect bisects the former sporting venue, by the name of "Greyhound Way".

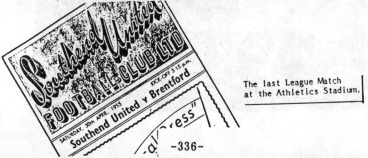

The last League Match
at the Athletics Stadium.

-336-

STOCKPORT COUNTY

By living in the shadows of their bigger Manchester
neighbours, the Club has seldom hit the headlines, but
its formation goes back to the early 1880's.

HEATON NORRIS RECREATION GROUND:
The idea of forming a football Club was conceived in a
cafe on Wellington Road South in 1883 by several young
men of the Wycliffe Congregational Chapel. From this
meeting, Heaton Norris Rovers F.C. was created. The
formation of a football Club was somewhat unusual, since
the area was ruled, in the sporting sense, by the Rugby
game. No records appear to have survived from the Club's
first season, suffice to say that the team was playing at
only a very minor level. Without doubt the Ground was
nothing more than an open field, probably one of those
that then existed at the the end of Church Road.

HEATON NORRIS WANDERERS CRICKET GROUND:
Before the end of the first season a move was made to
another open field, but also with no facilities, that was
located at the Brinksway, a road which still exists, and
is located just South of Heaton Norris centre.

One of the first recorded games of the Club was versus
Stalybridge reserves on the 11th of October 1884, a match
which ended in a 0-3 defeat. The following week a game
was played at the Ground of Christ Church (Heaton
Norris), at which a lot of ill-feeling was shown. With at
least two Association football teams in the area, a shift
in interest was beginning to move away from the oval ball
sport.

The football Club soon formed a close bond with the
cricket team, and they eventually combined. During the
summer of 1885, Heaton Norris F.C. was formed, but this
team only lived for one year, when they also threw their
lot in with the Rovers. However, the Rovers were in fact
to drop the suffix in their name three years later.

CHORLTON'S FARM:
The 1885/86 season saw the Club playing their home
matches on a different field, this time located in
Chorlton's Lane, which lay off of the Didsbury Road.

c.1885. The rural setting of the approach to the Chorlton's Farm Ground.

The Club were still struggling, often against superior opposition, and the first game of the season ended in a six goal thrashing at Whaley Bridge. However the team was soon to emerge as a powerful force, but once again their stay at a new home venue only lasted for one year.

ASH INN GROUND:
The move to this, their fourth Ground (which was located on Manchester Road), was also no more than a temporary stay, this time lasting for just over one year. The Ground was shared with the 'Heaton Norris Cricket Club', a confusing title, but once again was unfenced, and therefore gate money was not possible.

WILKES FIELD, BELMONT STREET.
After the start of the 1887/88 a move was made to this Ground which was back in the centre of Heaton Norris, and located off Wellington Road North. Although no doubt this venue was still very basic, for the first time gates were taken. The hold of Rugby in the area was definitely on the wane, for the Football Club were frequently able to attract four figure attendances, with a high of 2,000 during the season. Wilkes Field presumably suited the Club, for their stay lasted for two seasons! A measure of the Club's credibility can be judged from their first fixture of the 1889/90 season when they were hosts to the Newton Heath (later Manchester United) Club. By now the the team were known as plain 'Heaton Norris F.C.' and during the summer of 1889, they were ready to move to a more permanent Ground.

By the turn of the century, the fields in Belmont Street had been given over to housing.

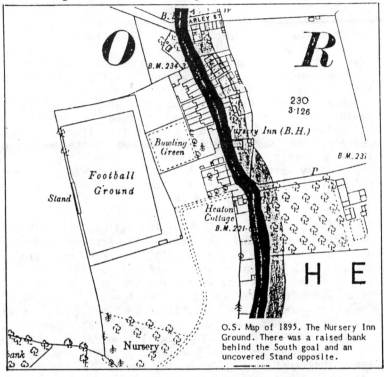

O.S. Map of 1895. The Nursery Inn Ground. There was a raised bank behind the South goal and an uncovered Stand opposite.

NURSERY INN, GREEN LANE:

Initially the Nursery Inn Ground was nothing more than an open field, but within a year extensive work had been carried out to make the venue into an enclosed and compact arena.

A small wooden Stand was installed by the Players themselves along the far side from Green Lane. At the North (Heaton Moor) end, a large uncovered Stand was built which was credited with a capacity of 4,000, and at the opposite end a large embankment was formed. The Ground was located behind the Nursery Inn and dressing rooms were provided in a barn which was located in Green Lane. Spectators entered the Ground in an opening between the barn and the Inn, and passed a bowling green before reaching the football field.

During the season a memorable game was won when the 2nd Cheshire regiment were beaten by thirteen unopposed goals.

Senior status came rapidly to the Club following their change of name to Stockport County during the 1890/91 season (the town became a County Borough in 1889), which followed their adopting professionalism. The 1890/91 season saw the team reach the semi-finals of the Manchester Senior Cup, at which point they lost by 1-3 to Newton Heath before a crowd of 5,000 at Ardwick. The following season started badly with five straight defeats, but much could be put down to the quality of their opponents, for the team were by now competing in the highly rated Combination. When Bolton Wanderers were entertained at Green Lane, the County only narrowly lost by 1-2, before a crowd of 4,000.

The Club's stay in the Combination lasted until 1894, by which time they found themselves in serious financial difficulties. In order to compete, they were compelled to expend £345 in players wages over the 1893/94 season, an increase from £185 over a year earlier. A move was made into the Lancashire League for the following season, and the first game in this competition resulted in four goals shared, at home to Chorley. The County first entered the F.A.Cup in 1895, when a single goal home defeat to Burton Wanderers was suffered. The 1896/97 season saw the team reach the final of the Manchester Senior Cup, when a four goal defeat was suffered at the hands of Manchester City. But the match, which was played before a 15,000 attendance at Fallowfield, had to be replayed due to the earlier appearance of an ineligible Manchester City player.

Despite several unremarkable years in non-League football, the Club were elected to the Second Division of the Football League for the 1900/01 season. On September the 1st, a creditable 2-2 draw was obtained at Leicester Fosse, but in their first home match, one week later, the County lost to New Brighton Tower by 0-5. The Club's first two seasons in such high company were something of a struggle, but the announcement of a move to a new Ground was greeted by the supporters with optimism. The last Football League game at Green Lane, resulted in a 3-2 victory over Burnley, on the 20th of April 1902.

The Nursery Inn c.1900. The opening in the wall led to the Ground, and the building to the left, housed the Dressing Rooms.

The Nursery Inn Ground, despite the Club's change of name, was located in the area of their birth - Heaton Norris - but the move to Edgeley Park required a move, to the South and, to the West of Stockport. It was somewhat ironic that the Club who struggled in their early days for support with the Rugby Clubs, should now choose the home of Stockport Rugby Club! Edgeley Park had been used by the oval ball Club since 1891, and although the venue was initially shared, it was the County who finally made the Ground their permanent home.

The Green Lane Ground was still used for a while for some Reserve team games, but around the turn of the century it became a housing site. The Nursery Inn itself however still exists, albeit in a rebuilt form.

SUNDERLAND

When Sunderland F.C. were founded in October 1879, they were one of the earliest of teams in the North-east of England; of Clubs of any note, there were only three in the area that were older, and in respect of current teams, only Middlesbrough - formed in 1877 - have lasted longer. But this factor in itself presented problems, for the Club had difficulty in finding opponents!

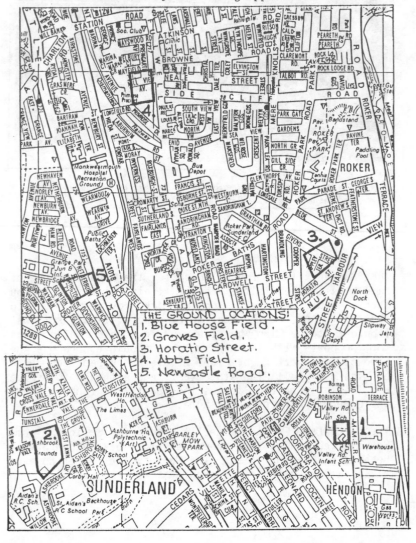

THE GROUND LOCATIONS!
1. Blue House Field.
2. Groves Field.
3. Horatio Street.
4. Abbs Field.
5. Newcastle Road.

The principal founders of the Club were the teachers John
Graystone and James Allan, who both taught at Hendon
Board School. They created the 'Sunderland and District
Teachers Association (Football Club), following a meeting
that had been called for at the British Day School in
Norfolk Street. The first football season passed with few
games played and no real home Ground, and in October 1880
the Club became open to outsiders when they were renamed
'Sunderland Association F.C.', in the hope that more
members would join, and more matches could be undertaken.
A pitch was rented, for an annual fee of £10, in the
Hendon district, which was known as Blue House Field.

BLUE HOUSE FIELD.

The first home game at this venue was played on the 13th
of November 1880, when they suffered a single goal defeat
to Ferryhill. The Club's occupation lasted for only two
seasons, and no gates were taken, since the venue was
nothing more than an unenclosed field. However, despite
its humble start, the Blue House Field was taken over by
the newly formed Sunderland Albion in 1886, six years
after the older Club departed. During their brief four
years of existence, the Albion developed the Ground by
enclosing it and providing a Grandstand plus a cycle
track. The area has, over the years, seen many changes,
and it is now only partly developed, with housing. What
was once a Cricket Ground - adjacent and to the North of
the football area - is now a playing field, next to
Valley Road Junior School. The former Football Ground
itself is mostly covered by the current Valley Road
Infant School, and the Blue House Public House that once
stood just South of the Ground has long since gone.
Commercial Road was once just a footpath that ran down
the Eastern border of the Ground, and where this road
meets Corporation Road, is the modern Blue House Pub.

During Sunderland Association's two year stay at the Blue
House Field, their major achievement was to reach the
semi-final of the Northumberland and Durham Cup in 1882,
their first entry into the competition. The last match at
the Hendon Ground was played on the 21st of January 1882,
when Derwent Rovers were beaten by the only goal of the
game.

GROVES FIELD, ASHBROOKE.

The Club's second home was occupied for just one season,
during which time only four matches were played there.
Groves Field, Ashbrooke, was again undoubtably another

open field, although near to the turn of the century, and under the name of Ashbrooke Athletic Grounds, the site was transformed into a respectable enclosure with open seated Stands and a Pavilion included. This Ground is now the Ashbrooke Sports Club, a well developed arena lying deep down in a natural bowl, with a pavilion and a covered Stand, the latter's origin dating back to the turn of the century. Sunderland's quartet of matches all ended as victories - possibly the only Senior Club ever to have won every match throughout the period at a single home venue! On the 4th of November, North Eastern were beaten 2-1 at the inaugural match, and in the farewell game, Bishop Middleham suffered a 3-4 defeat on the 10th of March 1883.

HORATIO STREET.

Sunderland also stayed at their third Ground for only one season. The field above Horatio Street and at the bottom of Roker Street was referred to as a 'Clay Dolly Field'. Castle Eden were beaten by 8-1 in the first home match at Horatio Street, on the 29th of September. The last match at this unattractive sounding venue was on the 26th of April, when 'The District' team triumphed by one goal to nil. The terraced houses of Appleby Terrace, and part of Givens Street now cover the site. The next choice of venue required a move away from the area, to North of the River Wear, at Fulwell, and the former home of St.Bedes A.F.C.

ABBS FIELD.

The exact location of Abbs Field, as it was then known, cannot be precisely determined, but it is possibly now the site of the Central Laundry, just to the West of Fulwell Road. This was the first properly enclosed Ground, since Gates were taken here, and for the first time the Club entered the F.A.Cup. But the rising popularity of the team can be gauged from the rent which started at £2-50p per annum, but rose rapidly to £15 after only one season. But even this venue was to be only a temporary base, and after beating Birtley 2-1 at the inaugural match on the 27th of September 1884. Less than two years later, on the 13th of March the final Club game was played at Abbs Field, when St.John's of Middlesbrough were thrashed by six unopposed goals, before a small crowd - the low number no doubt due to the atrocious weather. Several other matches were played after the departure of Sunderland F.C.

A team group of the 1888/89 season. Probably taken within the Ground, (North-east corner) and in front of the Newcastle Road entrance.

NEWCASTLE ROAD.

The Club's fourth move proved to be one with a degree of permanence. The Newcastle Road Ground was just a few hundred metres to the South, and was located just above Crozier Street. A lease on the Ground was obtained from the Thompson sisters - Robert Thompson J.P. was later to take a great interest in the Club and was eventually elected Club President. The annual rent was £15, and although this figure was soon doubled, Mrs.Thompson refunded the first year's rent as a reward for the Club's efforts in keeping the venue in good order! A third pitch length Grandstand was built on the North side of the Ground, with a 1,000 seated capacity, and elsewhere on all four sides open standing terracing was eventually installed. The Ground was fully enclosed, and a sum of £2-50 was spent for the purchase of a Clubhouse.

On the 3rd of April 1886 the first match at the permanent home venue at Newcastle Road was played (a few matches had been played there before) when Darlington were beaten 3-1 before a crowd of around 1,000.

The end of the season home games were completed with matches versus Birtley (six goals shared), Sheffield (before 3,500 spectators), and finally 2,500 attending the Shankhouse Black Watch game. As the years passed, enthusiasm rose, and the best crowd of over 5,000 for the match versus a District Team on the 23rd of February 1887, was easily beaten the following December when 8,000 were present for the 4-2 F.A.Cup victory over Middlesbrough. This win was declared void when Sunderland were expelled from the competition following a protest from the Teeside Club regarding Sunderland playing professional players - the Club were still an amateur organisation. In their efforts to offer ever better facilities, £500 was spent on the Ground during the 1887/88 season, which led to an overall loss of £370, despite £300 of season ticket sales. But at this time dissensions within the Management led to one of the Club's principal founders, James Allen, leaving to form the Sunderland Albion Club at the end of the season.

Sunderland Albion chose the Blue House Field as a home venue, and played the first match there versus Shankhouse Black Watch in May 1888, only two months after their formation. There were now two teams in the town vying for support, but the older Club still managed to attract the lion's share, with attendances generally between five and ten thousand during the 1888/89 season.

An 1897/98 team group in front of the timber Stand at the Newcastle Road Ground.

14,000 were present at Newcastle Road on the 22nd of September to see the Canadian touring side's three goal win, and 18,000 for the 'crunch' match on the 1st of December when the two were in opposition for the first time - a 2-0 victory to the homesters. The Club's attempt to join the Football League for the 1889/90 season failed when they only received two votes, but even so home attendances averaged 6,000 over the year. In 1890 Sunderland were successfully elected to the League, and the gates rose again to around a 7,000 average, with even the pre-season trial attracting 5,000 and this number was doubled for Preston's visit in a friendly match soon after.

The crowds continued to rise as the team took the League by storm (three championships in four years) - 21,000 for the F.A.Cup visit of Preston in January 1892, and 20,000 for the final home League game versus Everton. For the first time figures dipped in the 1895/96 season - an average of around only 5,000 (a poor playing year) - and a similar number one year later when the Club's fortunes hit a 'low', and only a play-off kept the team in the upper division. After their meteoric rise to the top, the Club, with equal speed slumped, and so bad were the finances that doubts were cast on whether they could carry on after the end of the 1896/97 season. But by becoming a Limited Company with a share capital of £5,000, the Club were relieved of such fears. This appears to have driven the team to the heights once again, and on the 23rd of October 1897, a record attendance for a League match at Newcastle Road of 22,000 was present when Aston Villa were the visitors. Meanwhile the predominately Scottish contingent ensconced at Sunderland Albion were unable to match the older team in the town, and after less than five years they went into voluntary liquidation, in August 1892. Great attempts had been made to make the Albion the top team of the town, with substantial developments at the Blue House Ground. But this was all to no avail, since support for the Club dipped dramatically as their near neighbours became such a dominant force in the football World.

At the end of the 1897/98 season the request that Sunderland F.C. should vacate the Newcastle Road must have been received with mixed feelings. Although several highly successful years had been spent there, the Ground was clearly too small to cater for the bigger crowds.

Several improvements were made over the years which increased the capacity of the enclosure, but with it let on only an annual lease - which by now had reached £100 - there was not the incentive to expend even more money. The Thompson sisters could see the commercial advantage in developing the Ground for housing, and so a move was made the short distance to a new venue that became known as Roker Park. The last match at Newcastle Road was played on the 23rd of April, when 11,000 came to see the locals in combat with Nottingham Forest. Five months later, the first game at Roker Park attracted a crowd of over 30,000 (easily a new record number to watch the Club at home).

There remains no trace of the Newcastle Road Ground. The houses of Netherburn Road and Newington Close now lie over the site of what was at one time the best appointed Ground in the North-east; but a short distance to the South-east, the Floodlights of Roker Park are clearly visible.

A painting depicting part of the Newcastle Road Ground in 1895.
(Painted by Thomas M.M. Hemy. By courtesey of Sunderland A.F.C.)

SWANSEA CITY

In the context of this book, Swansea City hardly deserve
a mention! The real roots of the game started in the town
in 1882, with the formation of a Senior Amateur Football
Club. But always in the shadow of the more dominant Rugby
game, it was not many years before this team disbanded.
Swansea Villa also made an attempt to convert the
devotees of the other sport, but they floundered in the
mid 1880's, principally over the difficulty of finding
the Ground rent for the Vetch Field!

The origins of the current Club are difficult to
specifically trace since the Press of the time, together
with the local sportsmen, was obsessed with Rugby, and
very little in the way of Football (Soccer) was
mentioned. It is generally accepted that the current
Football League Club was started in 1900, when a number
of ex-schoolboys, abandoning their Rugby traditions set
about forming a number of Clubs, and which led to the
creation of the successful Swansea and District League.
Around 1909 a number of these still young players got
together with the intention of forming a Senior team. But
finding a home Ground was difficult, and it was not until
three years later that a suitable and regular venue was
found. Until this time a number of open areas were used,
notably the local Recreation Ground, for many of the
District league games.

Eventually the Vetch Field was secured, although this
venue was not new to football, for in the late 19th
Century the Villa Club had used the roughly triangular
shaped sports field (which was first opened for Sport in
1891) for a number of years. But the Ground was hardly
suitable for football as it was not properly grassed, and
Swansea Town's difficulties over the letting were
experienced with the owners, the Gaslight Company. The
site was earmarked for new Plant for the Company, but
eventually in the summer of 1912, the Football Club
received permission to develop it for their own use.

Despite the earlier failures of other teams, a new spirit
was evidenced, when the Club's two trial matches, before
the 1912/13 season, were enthusiastically attended.

The games were played on the Recreation Ground (while work was hurriedly completed at the Vetch), and the second match attracted a crowd of some 2,000. The new Manager, Mr. R. Whittaker had sought suitable Players from a wide area, and from the enthusiasm shown by the locals, it became obvious that there was more support for the round ball version of football than had previously been recognised.

The Club had been fortunate in being elected into the strong Southern League, albeit the Second Division, and the first game at the Vetch Field was played, appropriately, against Cardiff City.

THE CAMBRIA DAILY LEADER, THURSDAY, OCTOBER 17, 1912.

THE VETCH FIELD AS IT WILL BE.

The above is a sketch of the Swansea Town Association Football Ground—the Vetch Field—as it will be. It is, however, intended to proceed with the work by instalments, and, as exclusively announced in the "Leader" last week, the erection of the grand stand, which is on the reader's left, will be the first to be erected. Tenders are out for the erection of a portion of this stand to seat about 1,000, and it will be built in such a way as will allow additions to be made from time to time. The above sketch was made by a "Leader" artist from a drawing by Mr. Benj. Jones, architect and surveyor, Wind-street, Swansea.

An early vision of the Vetch Field.

SWINDON TOWN

It is generally accepted that Swindon Town F.C. first saw
the light of day in 1881, although there are no obvious
written records concerning the team until the 1883/84
season. A 'Swindon Spartans F.C.' were around in 1881,
but they soon disappeared from the football scene, and it
is quite possible that they were the forerunners of the
Town Club.

QUARRY GROUND.

The early 1880's contained purely amateur teams in the
South of the Country, and the Grounds of the vast
majority of Clubs in this area were nothing more than
fields, with perhaps some natural enclosure formed by
trees, and the backs of houses etc. Swindon Town were no
exception, and their first home venue was a field of just
over three acres, situated just to the South of the Bath
Road and to the East of 'The Quarries'. The only entrance
to the Ground was via a lane (now Avenue Road) which ran
between the houses in Bath Road. The Lane turned at right
angles (now Bradford Road) and ran onto Devizes Road,
with this run of the lane forming part of the Northern
boundary of the Club's playing area. The Ground was part
enclosed by virtue of it's location off of the main
roads, and by one side of the quarry, the latter being
some eight metres higher than the pitch. Whereas the
higher elevation would have given a good vantage point
for spectators, this facility also hastened the Club's
departure from the site; a young spectator was injured
when he fell into the quarry, and it was obviously a far
from safe viewing area! At this stage of the development
of the Club it is unlikely that 'gate' money was taken.
The land was owned by Solicitor James Bradford Paul, no
doubt his unusual middle name was given to the later road
of that name. The site of the former Ground has long
since been replaced with housing.

GLOBE FIELD.

It was not long before a move was made a short distance,
to the North of the Bath Road, to the Globe Field. The
venue was hardly an improvement since the field was about
three times larger, and with Eastcott Lane and Landsdown
Road forming the East and South boundaries, it was
probably nothing more than a large open area of land.

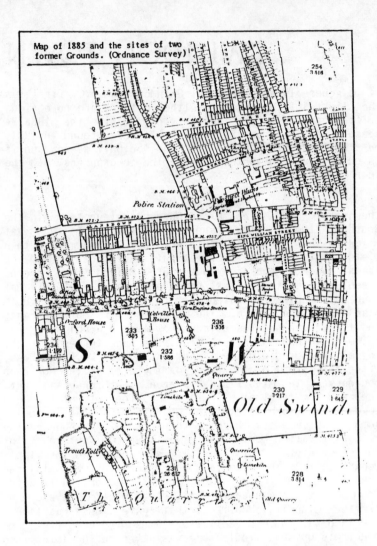

Map of 1885 and the sites of two former Grounds. (Ordnance Survey)

The Club's stay was once again a short one for they moved on in 1884, and by 1900 houses covered the site, with the current Brunswick and Globe Streets bisecting the former field in two directions.

CROFT GROUND.

The third Ground was in close proximity to the previous two, to the East of Devizes Road, where the road and houses of St. Margarets were later built.

On October the 25th the first match was played, versus St.Mark's Young Mens Friendly Society, and won by three goals (plus one disputed) to nil. But the Ground still lacked the creature comforts for spectators and players alike; the former having no cover of any sort, and the latter having to take the long walk from the Fountain Inn where the changing rooms were located.

These frequent moves, with little, if any improvements, were probably justified by virtue of the Club finding Landowners who were prepared to rent out, for reasonable sums, flat patches of land. Professionalism had not reached the South at this time, and therefore running costs were relatively low, as was the income which did not depend on a paying public.

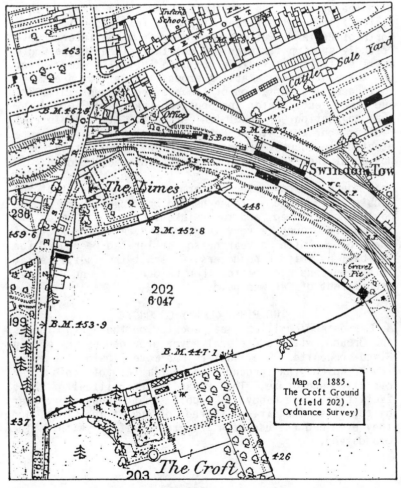

Map of 1885.
The Croft Ground
(field 202).
Ordnance Survey)

It is possible that the Croft Ground (named after the large adjacent house and grounds of the same name), which covered over six acres, was an improvement over the two earlier venues, since the Town played here for eleven years; of course the long stay may have been due to a tolerant Landlord who did not demand an ever increasing rent! During this period the Town first entered the F.A.Cup, in the 1887/88 season, and had unparalleled success in the Wiltshire Senior Cup, which they won for five consecutive years from it's inception in the 1886/87 season. Back in November 1884 the Club were honoured with the Ground being used for the representative game between Wiltshire (who included two Town players) and Oxfordshire - before 'a large number of spectators'.

With the birth of the Football League in 1888, other regionalised competitions rapidly followed suit in the North of England. But the move away from the interminable Friendly and Cup fixtures did not take place in the South until a little later. This new move initially took root in the South-west, starting around the Bristol area, and influenced the formation of the Western League in 1892, and two years later the Southern League was formed, at the suggestion of Woolwich Arsenal. At the initial meeting on the 24th of February 1894, Swindon Town were elected as founder-members and they immediately gave notice of their intention to vacate the Croft Ground.

Gate money was now going to form an important part of the Club's life, and a venue had to be sought where crowds could be attracted, and money taken. A move was made to the County Ground, a very large open area to the North of the Town, which a year or so earlier had been used for football by Swindon Wanderers. At least the facilities at this new venue were better than before, for an initial annual rent of £40 was paid.

THE FIRST COUNTY GROUND.
A Grandstand/Pavilion was located on the North side of the Ground, with additional cover provided by a wooden Stand opposite. The latter was moved inside the cycle track, which ran around the perimeter of this near circular enclosure. The Press, ever critical of their facilities, were happy to report that these were far better than the virtual absence of any at the Croft, and they even had the use of a telegraph office within the Grandstand.

The entrance to the Ground was off the present County Road, located between the Lodge and the County Ground Hotel. A path led directly to the enclosure and wooden stand, entry to which members paid 7/6d. (37p) per season. The main business of the A.G.M. in June 1895, was to re-organise what was in effect a new Football Club. The Club at this time became fully professional, although the total wages Bill in the first season amounted to less than £10 per week.

The first match was played at the County Ground, in September 1895 - a friendly versus Nat Whittaker's XI - and a month later the town made their home debut in the Southern League versus Ilford.

Even then this wasn't the Club's final move, for it was not long before they moved just South of the original area, and established a separate Football Ground, the 'new' County (Football) Ground which remains to this day. A Cricket Ground was then formed on the Football team's earlier pitch; a reversal of the normal trend, when, as so often happened, a Football Club would move onto an established Cricket enclosure! The original County Ground has retained it's original shape, and is still used by the Cricketers to this day.

The Pavilion at the County (Cricket) Ground in 1990. Possibly the same structure that existed when the Town played here around the turn of the century. (Dave Twydell)

TORQUAY UNITED

Football had not taken root in the South-west by the late 19th century, unlike most other areas of the Country, where, by that time it had become a major sport. Devon and Cornwall however had become something of a Rugby stronghold and therefore, when, in 1898 some ex-students of Torquay College decided to form a football club their team was destined to become the first in the town and the immediate area. The first meeting of these enthusiasts took place in May of that year and was later followed by a formal gathering at the Tor Abbey Hotel. It was decided to go ahead with the proposal, and with the help of a local farmer, John Wright, they were accommodated in a field off of Teignmouth Road.

TEIGNMOUTH ROAD.

The venue was nothing more than an undeveloped field of nearly three acres, and although it is doubtful that the Ground was fully enclosed, a gate was taken at the first match which amounted to 5/3d (26p). Such a venture was something of a novelty, and to advise the general public, twelve posters advertising the match were displayed around the town. The game attracted a fair amount of support, but the opposition offered little resistance - Torquay United being at this time the only football Club for some miles - and consisted of nothing more than a 'scratch' team under the grand title of 'The Wanderers' (the same name as early winners of the F.A.Cup). Alderman W.H. Mortimer kicked-off, and the United proceeded to demolish their hapless opponents with a final scoreline of 10-1. But the match was played under very relaxed circumstances, and at half-time rather than handing out the customary lemons for refreshments, a picnic was held which lasted for around twenty minutes!

The agreement was that the Football Club would pay a rent of £5 for the Club's exclusive use from September to March, after which month the team had to play all of their matches away from home, since the field was required for grazing in April. From May the Teignmouth Road venue was used by the Upton Cricket Club, and so impressed were they of their co-occupants first season - they won 17 matches, drew 2 and only lost 3 games - that they joined the Football Club, and for the 1899/1900 season formed the reserve team! Although the field offered nothing for spectators or players alike (save for an old hut which stored the teams basic equipment and the players' coats), the Club were admitted to the East Devon League.

-356-

The footballers were keen and regularly kept fit at
Torquay Gymnasium, which they also used as a
headquarters, but the opposition proved to be too strong
for the United, and by the season's end they finished
bottom of the League. Despite the poor results,
attendances of around 100 became common.

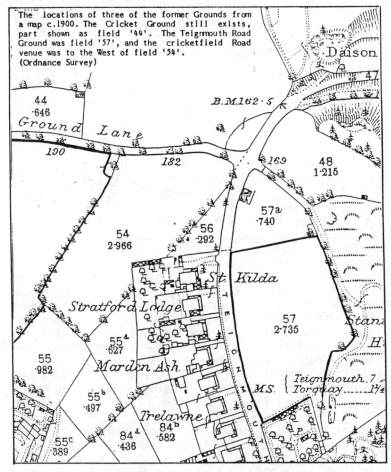

TORQUAY RECREATION GROUND.

With the sport gaining in popularity and the Club ever
enthusiastic, it was decided to move to a properly
enclosed Ground for the 1900/01 season. The Torquay
Recreation Ground became available at a fairly nominal
rental of £5 per annum, providing the Club made
themselves responsible to cut the grass and generally
maintain the Ground.

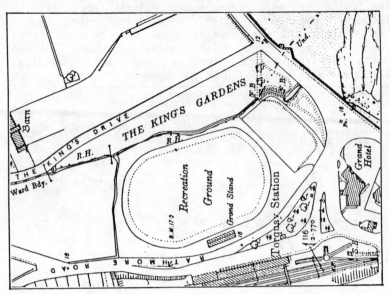

The Torquay Recreation Ground c.1900, now used by the Rugby Club.
(Ordnance Survey)

The Ground had been taken over in May 1888 by the 'Torquay Recreation Ground Ltd.' which set a goal of raising £3,000 in order to substantially develop the venue for sub-letting to sporting bodies. A Grandstand (capacity 250) with dressing rooms under, plus a refreshment bar and cycle track were built, but the Company struggled to survive. By 1900, they folded, and the firm appointed as Liquidators agreed the arrangements with the Football Club. The deal was perhaps not as good as first thought, since the Grandstand had become delapidated and the dressing rooms were virtually unuseable, except for the bathroom.

Alternative dressing-rooms were found by using the large, old refreshment bar; but in bad weather two large coach houses, behind the Grand Hotel, were used instead. At high tides, it was found that the pitch was little better than the facilities around it! A culvert that ran under the length of the playing area frequently became choked up, causing water to cascade out of the top end of the field and saturate the pitch. In these far from ideal surroundings the Club struggled on for five years. Ideally they would have moved elsewhere, but their increasing popularity was not shared by everyone in the town, and no suitable alternatives presented themselves.

The Seated Stand at the Recreation Ground in 1990. This existed during the United's occupation of the Ground. (Dave Twydell)

In 1902, Plymouth Argyle sent a team to Torquay to play a friendly match on a Wednesday afternoon. A record attendance of over 1,000 was present, but those there were disappointed when it was discovered that the professional opposition had only sent their reserve team. The blushes of the locals were in fact saved further, since the homesters lost by ten unopposed goals! During the 1902/03 season the Ground became the property of the town, and with new funds available, a new Grandstand was built on the West side of the ground, in 1904 at a cost of £1,000. With other improvements, the Ground became a desirable venue once again, and at the end of the 1904/05 season the United had to make way for Torquay Athletic Rugby Club, a larger and more respected organisation (football of the round ball variety was still the poor relation of the two games in the town).

CRICKETFIELD ROAD.

The Rugby Club which had been formed in 1875 first played at Cary Park, and in 1881 moved to Warbro Road, the Ground that was destined to later become the Plainmoor home of Torquay United! Now homeless, the footballers found a friend once again in John Wright, who offered them the re-use of the Teignmouth Road venue, or an alternative nearby field which was located to the South of Cricketfield Road.

The Club chose the latter, the lesser of two evils, since
although also offering no manmade facilities, the Ground,
raised several feet above Cricketfield Road, was
virtually enclosed by virtue of a high hedge. The field
was able to contain a 150 yards long by 60 wide pitch,
and at the South end a naturally raised embankment. With
not even basic dressing rooms, and a slope on the field
of supposedly 1:7, the Ground left much to be desired.
The Club tried to get the Local Council to buy the land,
with a view to levelling and other improvements for
re-letting. But within a year the Club knew that this was
not to be for it had been purchased for building houses,
and they knew that their time was limited once again.

TORQUAY CRICKET CLUB GROUND.

During the Club's stay of less than two years, they
entertained Plymouth Argyle for a second match, and put
up a better show than before, and this time against their
opponents first team! The Recreation Ground was used for
the match, and 5,000 spectators attended.

When the time came to move, in 1907, the Club moved to
the other side of Cricketfield Road, and shared the
ground of Torquay Cricket Club (who were later to move in
with the Rugby Club at the Recreation Ground). The
Cricket Club was established in 1851 and the Ground in
the aptly named Cricketfield Road was known as Langways
Meadow. The Ground contained a new and large picturesque
pavilion (with the groundsman's cottage adjoining), plus
two large dressing rooms. The cricketers generously
charged only a nominal rent for the footballers' use. In
the dry weather the pitch was very good, but after rain
it became swampy and, particularly during the Club's
first season there (1907/08), many home games had to be
postponed. During this period the F.A.Amateur Cup was
entered for the first and only time. In a replay, Oxford
City were beaten, before an attendance of over 3,000,
once again at the Recreation Ground, but the Club fell at
the next hurdle.

By 1910, there were three football clubs of note in the
area; Babbacombe - Plymouth and District League,
Ellacombe (who played in the Devon League at the Rugby
Club's former home at Plainmoor), and Torquay United who
were by now in the Torquay and District League. Without a
suitable home venue, it was obvious that the United were
getting nowhere, and an amalgamation between themselves
and Ellacombe, in June 1910, allowed them to move into
the enclosure of their neighbours.

By this date, the United were the Junior member (in status) of the partnership. Plainmoor had by now both a Grandstand and Dressing-rooms, and the first match of the new 'Torquay Town', on the 3rd of September versus St. Austell, attracted an attendance of around 1,000 spectators. From that season Babbacombe ground-shared with the Town Club.

THE GROUNDS TODAY.

The former homes of Torquay United (they later reverted to their former name when they amalgamated with Babbacombe in 1921) are relatively 'rich' in remains. The Teignmouth Road field has long since been developed and now contains a collection of large detached and semi-detached houses; it was situated to the East of Teignmouth Road, just South of the junction with Cricketfield Road (now part covered by Stanaway Park). Conversely the Recreation Ground still exists, almost on the sea-front opposite Corbyn's Beach. The situation is picturesque, and although now larger - the Ground extends northwards to the Rathmore Road and Kings Drive junction - the main playing area is not dissimilar from the early 1900's. On the West side is a Grandstand (extended northwards by the Rugby Club who still occupy the Ground, now in partnership with Torquay Cricket Club), which is probably the original that was built in 1904. The field that was used off Cricketfield Road, was situated almost opposite the current School (to the North) and is now covered principally by the housing of Parkhurst Road. Also nearly opposite this former Ground, and at the junction of Cricketfield and Barton Roads, the old Torquay Cricket Club Ground remains. It has probably changed little over the decades, for the overall area remains the same, and the attractive pavilion - in the North-west corner - is likely to be basically the same as that which was re-built in 1906 (following a fire that destroyed the original).

The Cricket Ground in 1990, and still used for the same purpose. The Pavilion in the background, is in the same position as the original.
(Dave Twydell)

TOTTENHAM HOTSPUR

Harry Hotspur was a Shakespearian character noted for his valour in battle. When the 'Hotspur' football Club was formed, by a group of schoolboys, they chose the name in the hope that they could emulate their hero! The Club first started as a Cricket Club, but it was not long before football was added, as a winter sport. The first home 'Ground' was nothing more than a patch of flat land on the Tottenham Marshes. The Club nearly faded away, but were revived in 1885 by three members of the Club, Messrs. Bushell, Casey and Thompson. These enthusiasts supposedly held Club meetings under a lamp post adjacent to Northumberland Park.

The suffix 'Tottenham' was soon added to 'Hotspur'; notably the latter word is expressed in the singular form rather than the plural, as it is often erroneously referred to. Home made goal posts were stored at Northumberland Park Station, from whence a short walk over the railway lines was made to the Marches which lay to the East of Northumberland Park.

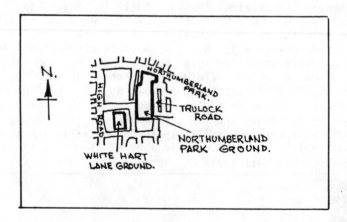

NORTHUMBERLAND PARK:

The ambitious Club made their headquarters at the Red House in the High Road of Tottenham in 1886, and moved to a new Ground, in Northumberland Park, in 1888 where it was possible to make an admission charge.

Four figure crowds had become common on the Marshes where it had not been possible to benefit financially. Records and illustrations of the Northumberland Park Ground are very sparse, but obviously it was enclosed. A small seated Stand was built in 1894 along one side, although at one time this was blown down after a gale! Alongside the Stand there was a narrow raised area for standing spectators, and on the opposite side of the Ground a similar, but wider, area.

Initially the rent was £17 per year, and the Ground was opened with a Reserve game in September 1888, which produced a gate of 85p! The Club adopted professionalism during the 1895/96 season, following a meeting in December. They were accepted as members of the Southern League in the next season, at the end of which they finished fourth. Support for the team continued and it was soon apparent that the Ground was not big enough for the ambitious Club. In 1898, the 'Spurs became a Limited Company.

The 1898/99 season saw the team first make their mark in the F.A.Cup, when after drawing with Newton Heath before a packed crowd at Northumberland Park, they went on to win the replay in Manchester. That same season, the record attendance was produced at the ground when 14,000 crammed into the compact enclosure for a match versus Woolwich Arsenal in April. During the match the roof of a refreshment building collapsed, and although only minor injuries were suffered, it was obvious that the enclosure was just not big enough for such big matches. There were other problems too, for one year earlier the Ground was closed following spectator troubles caused during the fixture with Luton Town!

By now the Club had become one of the best in the South of England, and the 1898/99 season was to become the last at Northumberland Park. They were offered a vacant piece of land that was owned by the Charrington Breweries, and with the greater potential possible from a purpose made Ground, the offer was readily accepted. The first match at the new White Hart Lane Ground (the land was behind the Pub of the same name), attracted a crowd of 5,000 - a typical number that had watched matches at Northumberland Park - when Notts. County appeared for a Friendly encounter. The Stand from the earlier Ground was moved to White Hart Lane, and initially provided the only cover at the new enclosure.

Northumberland Park, until recently, still existed as an open Recreation Ground. It was located behind the Northumberland Arms Public House on Trulock Road, but a school now covers the site. The move from the park was but a very short one, and the site of the former Ground is now dominated by the towering East Stand at White Hart Lane.

January 1899. Spurs versus Newton Heath,
in the F.A.Cup, at the Northumberland Park Ground.

TRANMERE ROVERS

Around the 1870's, the towns in the Wirral area became more populated which, coupled with the development of the railways and the additional time available due to free Saturday afternoons, led to more people following leisure pursuits. The major sports Clubs in the area were Birkenhead Rugby Club, founded in 1871 and Birkenhead Park Cricket Club which came into existance in 1846.

The origins of Tranmere Rovers started in the Summer of 1884, when the members of the two Cricket Clubs of Belmont and Lyndhurst Wanderers called a joint meeting to discuss the formation of a football team. Belmont F.C. came into being, a name which originated from the 'Belmont Lounge' of the Beekeepers Public House which stood opposite the current Prenton Park Ground. The Licensee, William Steele, sub-let three fields in the immediate area, one of which was rented to Belmont Cricket Club, and later also to the Footballers. Most of the members of the new Football Club attended the Sunday School at Wesley Methodist Chapel, and were teetotal – the Beekeepers was a 'dry pub', i.e. alcohol was not served there. Mr. Steele allowed the use of a room in his hostelry for changing, and the Players had a short walk, via the Ground of Tranmere Rugby Club (later to become the first Prenton Park), to their own Ground which was known as 'Steele's Field'.

STEELE'S FIELD.

The new Football Club had immediate success, winning ten of their fifteen fixtures during the 1884/85 season. Matches, although only Friendly encounters, were taken seriously, for training was undertaken on five nights per week at the Ground. In September 1885, at a meeting which was held at Sainty's Cocoa Rooms, it was decided to change the Club name to 'Tranmere Rovers, a title that was more fitting to an organisation with ambition and which referred to a specific and wide area. 'Tranmere Rovers' had previously been used by an unconnected Club some years earlier, when a football team was born out of the Tranmere Rovers Cricket Club in 1881. After one year they dropped the 'Rovers' from their title, and carried on as plain 'Tranmere' until they disbanded in 1888; their home Ground was the currently named Mersey Park.

It was Mr. McGaul, the President of the 'new' Tranmere Rovers - a former member of the same named Cricket Club - who suggested the new title. Tranmere Rovers F.C. played their first match on the 19th of September 1885, drawing 1-1 at Chester Street, the home of Birkenhead Argyle. One week later the initial home match ended in a rout, when Liverpool North End were crushed 10-0 - with three Players of the home Club making up the numbers for the visitors!

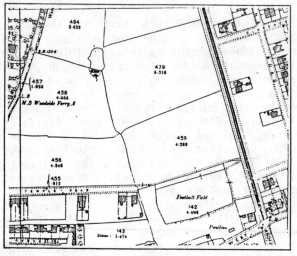

The (Old) Prenton Park Ground in 1899. The adjacent field (no. 459) was the former Steele's Field Ground. Part of the site that became the current Ground is on the bottom right hand edge. (Ordnance Survey)

The Steele's Field Ground was nothing more than a suitably sized pitch, and lacked any facilities. It was far from being ideal since it had a pronounced slope and was poorly drained. It was sited close to the current Temple Road School, fronting Borough Road and between Temple and Parkstone Roads. At the time of the Club's occupation of the Ground, the West side of Borough Road was undeveloped and split into several fields. Temple Road at that time stopped at the West end of the Ground, and a footpath ran parallel with the pitch down Valley (now Borough) Road. The Club remained at this somewhat unsatisfactory venue until the end of the 1886/87 season, at which time they moved to the field next door!

RAVENSHAW'S FIELD OR OLD PRENTON PARK - AND OTHER NAMES!

The move was controversial for Ravenshaw's Field had been
the home of Tranmere Rugby Club. When the Rovers offered
the owners, Tranmere Hall, an annual rent of £5-50p
(considerably more than the Rugby Club was paying), the
oval ball team were ousted from their home. A fence was
erected around the Ground, and cinder paths laid around
the perimeter of the pitch. Later improvements consisted
of dressing rooms and a Pavilion near the South-east
corner of the field. The Club's occupation of Ravenshaw's
Field lasted for 25 years, and by then had become a very
reasonable football enclosure. A 250 seat Grandstand was
erected by the Birkenhead Rugby Union Club in 1902, which
they brought from their previous Ground. The Rugby Club
groundshared with the Rovers from 1902 until they became
defunct four years later; by default the Football Club
inherited the Stand! The popular (North) side later
became covered for the full pitch length, and turnstile
were installed at the entrances. Additional improvements
before the 1910/11 season commenced consisted of an
additional new Stand on the 'popular' side with
accommodation for 700 to 800, which cost £150; to help
pay for the structure admission charges were increased in
this area to 4d. (1½p). Better dressing roomfacilities
were introduced in the Pavilion, plus the installation of
a bath! More protection against the weather in the
reserved Stand was added with an end screen, for which a
6d. (2½p) entry charge was made. At this time a season
ticket cost six shillings (30p).

The name of this second Ground, Ravenshaw's Field, was
taken from Mrs. Ann Ravenshaw, who took over the tenancy
of this and other fields, from Mr. Steele. Over the years
the Ground was also referred to as 'Devonshire Park'
(which is opposite), 'South Road' - the road opposite and
on the other side of Borough Road, and 'Temple Road',
which at this time terminated at the end of Ravenshaw's
Field. Additionally the local Press often made reference
to the 'Borough Road' enclosure, and finally the Ground
was formally renamed 'Prenton Park' in November 1895.
This plethora of names has led to many incorrect
references of upto six different Grounds, but which in
fact, was only one! The later name of 'Prenton Park' adds
to the confusion, since this name was also chosen for the
nearby current home venue of the Club.

Fixture Card for the 1896/97 season. The 'Borough Road Enclosure' is referred to, although this Ground became known as (the first) 'Prenton Park'.

For the 1889/90 season, the Rovers became founder-members of the West Lancashire League, and two years later made their first entry into the F.A.Cup Competition. It was not a very prestigious start into the latter tournament, for they lost their first match by 5-1 to the powerful Northwich Victoria team, and it was not until the 1896/97 season that their first victory in the F.A.Cup was achieved when Warrington St.Elphin's were beaten 5-1 on their own Ground. The Club had a fairly undistinguished record during their days at (old) Prenton Park. The first few seasons in League competition saw the Club play at a modest level, apart from two campaigns in the Lancashire Combination, but the 1899/1900 season became a traumatic one and the Club nearly folded.

Although the (old) Prenton Park Ground was a great improvement over the former home venue, a number of Players were unhappy with the playing surface and the facilities provided. In 1899, a deputation representing the Players requested that the Club should move to the Bedford Park Ground of the former Rock Ferry Club. This was refused and the Players en masse (bar one) formed a breakaway Club under the name of 'Birkenhead F.C.'. This rebel Club only lasted until 1908, but it left the Rovers bereft of Players for the 1899/1900 season, and they only just pulled through.

The (old) Prenton Park headquarters were Groundshared with Cammell Lairds F.C. for two seasons (from 1907), but in 1911, another move was forced upon the Rovers, when continuing developments in the area resulted in plans to build on the site.

Once again the move was only a very short distance, this time to the South side of Prenton Lane West. The new Ground was also, confusingly, titled Prenton Park, a name that was considered somewhat 'upmarket'! The (new) Prenton Park was opened on the 9th of March 1912, when Lancaster were entertained and soundly beaten by eight goals to nil. The low wooden Grandstand from the old Ground was re-erected at (new) Prenton Park, and formed the central portion of the main Stand until its replacement in the 1960's. The (old) Prenton Park venue was located between Prenton Road West and Temple Road, and is now overlain by the Temple Road School.

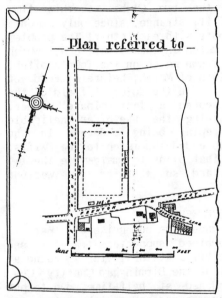

_ Plan referred to _

(Left): The 1912 layout of the (later) Prenton Park, the Stand was moved from the former Ground. (Taken from the original Deeds)

(Below): The main Stand that had been moved from the former Prenton Park in 1912 was demolished in 1968.

WALSALL

It was not long before football had become a popular sport in this area of the Midlands, and by the late 1870's, the local scene was dominated by the Town Club, (founded in 1874 from close connections with the Walsall Cricket Club), and by Walsall Swifts who were formed one year later, as 'Victoria Swifts'. But as early as 1888, the two teams decided to pool their resources and amalgamated, unusually just before the end of the season, in April. The pairing of the two Clubs at this time seemed, on the face of it, strange, since only a month earlier they were in dispute with each other! The problem arose after a semi-final match in the Walsall Cup, which had first resulted in a drawn match on the Town's pitch. One month later, on the 10th of March, before a crowd of over 2,000 the replay - on the adjacent field of the Swifts - the 'homesters' scored a last minute winner. However a dispute regarding the use of an ineligible Swifts man resulted in a replay being ordered. In the final event, the Town Club ceded the match to the Swifts, probably due to the fact that plans to amalgamate the two were already underway, and so a third game was not necessary.

THE CHUCKERY:

The first expected match under the new guise of 'Walsall Town Swifts', saw 500 'combined' supporters travel to see the new Club play Aston Villa at the latter's Ground at Perry Barr, for the Final of the Birmingham Charity Cup. But the game was abandoned at half-time, due to bad light, and when the replay was ordered to take place at Small Heath's Ground, the Walsall team refused to take part, arguing that the re-match should be played at their Chuckery Ground. In the final event the game was never played!

Prior to amalgamation, both teams played at The Chuckery. The Chuckery is an area just to the East of the town centre, and contained a number of football pitch sized fields. On the 6th of March 1888, a meeting was held at the Assembly Room of the Dragon Hotel, when eight members from each Club were elected to form a new combined Committee - and for a half a guinea (52p) subscription, supporters could become Vice-Presidents.

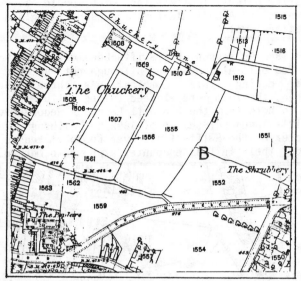

The Grounds at the Chuckery in 1887. Field 1555 was that of the 'Town' Club, while the 'Swifts' occupied 1507. The pavilion in field 1551 (the Cricket Club Ground), was also used by Walsall Town Swifts.
(Ordnance Survey)

It was also decided that the new team colours would be blue and maroon vertical striped shirts, and that for home games, the Town's former pitch would be used. However, in early August - the first proper meeting of Walsall Town Swifts F.C. - the Club's colours were changed to red and white vertical stripes. One of the fields, which had been used by Walsall Cricket Club since the mid-1800's, was complete with pavilion, and this facility was also used by the players of Walsall Town Swifts, whose Ground was immediately adjacent. Lumley Road is now built over the the site of the Football Ground.

In reality the new combined Club did not play their first game until the start of the 1888/89 season. Notably some Clubs were playing their initial matches in the first ever Football League fixtures, although Walsall Town Swifts, a professional team, were not completely left out of any glory. Following their first game of the season (versus Derby St.Lukes on the 8th of September), they played, and beat, Burnley of the Football League two days later. On the 22nd of September, there were over 2,000 present at the Chuckery for the match versus Crewe.

The playing potential within the Club could be gauged when defender Albert Aldridge represented England in an International match.

For the 1889/90 season, the Swifts became founder-members of the Football Alliance, and although not capturing any honours during this Combination's three years of existance, the team were elected (along with the other Clubs) to help form the Football League's Second Division from it's inaugural season of 1892/93. Although Gray was the scorer of the Swifts first ever Football League goal, they lost their initial encounter at home to Darwen.

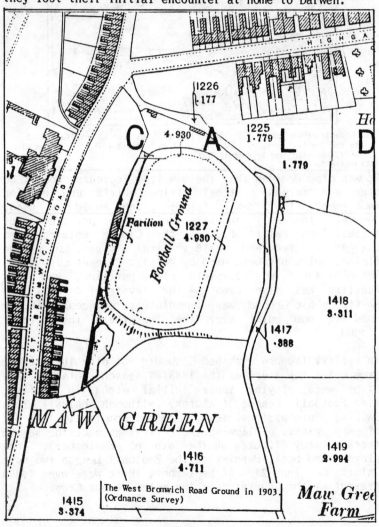

The West Bromwich Road Ground in 1903.
(Ordnance Survey)

Although the Chuckery no doubt offered little comforts to the spectators, the game had become so popular that local residents started complaining about the noise from the Ground on matchdays, and by the end of the season the Club's first move had to be made. The last match at the Chuckery resulted in a 1-1 draw with Sheffield United on the 15th of April.

WEST BROMWICH ROAD FOR THE FIRST TIME:

A purpose built Football Ground was created at West Bromwich Road, on the other side of town. The Ground, which was sited where Grange, East and Haskell Streets now lie, was fully enclosed. Eventually a quarter pitch length Pavilion (Grandstand) was built on the West side, and a small embankment at the Southern end gave standing spectators a better view. But the Ground was not completed in time for the initial fixtures of the 1893/94 season, and so an alternative had to be found. It was not a difficult choice, for just outside of the town boundaries lay Wednesbury Oval. This was the home Ground of the once mighty Wednesbury Old Athletic, and offered an enclosed Ground, although a small pavilion on the site had by then been removed. Two Football League matches were played here - versus Small Heath and Burslem Port Vale - before the first match at West Bromwich Road could be played. On the 23rd of September, Crewe were defeated by 5-1 in the first game at the Swifts new home. The Oval is now an open area of land, and lies off of St. Pauls Road, South of the M6 Motorway. Of particular interest is the probable original North boundary wall of the Ground which once contained several small openings, but which are now bricked up. Doubtless these were initially windows from which tickets were purchased for matches. The Club's support dwindled as they struggled in the League, and the end of the 1894/95 season saw them fail to win sufficient votes in their re-election bid. During the Club's one season in the non-League World the 'Town Swifts' was dropped from their title, and in 1896 they were back in the Second Division of the Football League.

HILARY STREET FOR THE FIRST TIME:

The Club's (initial) occupation of the West Bromwich Road Ground was shortlived, for they celebrated their re-aquaintance with the Football League by moving to the Hilary Street (later named Fellows Park) enclosure. This venue was also known as the Pleck Ground. For some years the Ground - which was finally vacated in 1990 - was fairly sparsely equipped for spectators.

The only entrance was off of Wallows Lane, and this same side had a narrow, 35 yard long Stand. This area of the Ground was partitioned off as a Reserved Enclosure, with at one end, the Officials and Dressing rooms. Elsewhere there was raised, but uncovered banking. Behind the railway end, standing room was impossible for half of the pitch width as it was dominated by the wall of the adjacent Laundry, which remained until 1965.

On the 1st day of September 1896, Glossop North End were entertained, and beaten 4-1, in a friendly encounter, and four days later the first Football League match was played at the new Ground (a two goal win over Burton Wanderers). During the 1896/97 season the Club had the honour of being the first visitors to Villa Park, but financially the Club continued to struggle. Money problems continued to hamper the Club, and at the end of the 1899/1900 season the Club were on the point of folding. The President and the Club Secretary resigned, and it was only the meritous action by the players, who agreed to play for wages based on a shareout of the gate money (less expenses), that allowed the Club to continue. For the next season matches started at the Hilary Street Ground, and the first encounter on the 1st of September was very encouraging, when Barnsley were beaten by 3-0 before a good gate of 3,300 (receipts of £75). Blackpool's visit attracted over 4,000, but after a bright start, it was down to a crowd of only 2,000 for Lincoln's visit in October. A replayed F.A.Cup match with Shrewsbury - midweek - attracted only a few hundred. Even so the Club were at last paying their way, and following a good run of results, a record attendance was expected for the visit of Leicester Fosse on November the 24th. 4,000 spectators paying £95 were present to see the two goal home win, and although most encouraging neither figure constituted a record. Then in early December they were compelled to move back to their earlier West Bromwich Road venue, after being ejected from Hilary Street.

The move was forced upon the Club due to earlier rental arrears and a dispute regarding the ownership of the land - despite the fact that the party in contention was also the Club Chairman!

The boundary wall of the Wednesbury Oval, in 1990.
Walsall's 'home' Ground for two games in the 1893/94 season.
Note the small bricked in openings from
which match tickets were
probably originally sold.
(Dave Twydell)

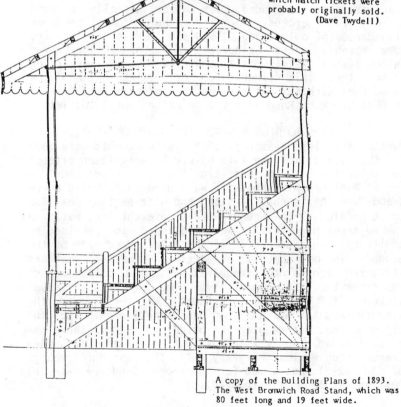

A copy of the Building Plans of 1893.
The West Bromwich Road Stand, which was
80 feet long and 19 feet wide.

TRANSVERSE SECTION

BACK TO WEST BROMWICH ROAD:

The first match at West Bromwich Road, on this second occasion was played against Wellington in the F.A.Cup. Walsall had induced a reversal of the tie by offering £70 to the non-Leaguers (a very high figure), and the attendance of around 4,000 produced gate receipts of a little over £76! The match ended as a resounding six goal victory to the Football League team. There were mixed blessings for the Club and it's supporters at West Bromwich Road, for although the facilities were far superior than those at Hilary Street, the pitch was poorly drained, and access to the Ground was difficult.

The season ended in disaster again as, for the second time, the Club were not re-elected to the Football League. After a high placing in the Midland League one year later, the Club disappointed their followers during the 1902/03 season, and the last games at West Bromwich Road were poorly attended. Over Easter, normally a good period for crowds, the three home games produced attendances of only 2,000, 1,500 and lastly 700 for the home matches versus Hinckley, Gainsborough and Burton United respectively. In all £80 gate money was taken rather than this figure for each match that had been hoped for! Kirkland was the last goalscorer for Walsall at West Bromwich Road in a 2-3 defeat on April the 14th.

BACK TO HILARY STREET (FELLOWS PARK)

During the close season of 1903, arrangements were made for the Club to move back to Hilary Street. In an attempt to at least equal the facilities that had been provided for at West Bromwich Road, it was intended to build a new Grandstand at a cost of £130, and wire netting was also to be erected at the Laundry end to prevent lost balls in the adjacent premises. It was also hoped to provide an additional entrance off of the Hilary Road side of the Ground. In mid-August, pre-season practise matches attracted crowds of around 1,000, and on the 5th of September the first competitive game at Hilary Street kicked off. The Club President, Mr. West, did the honours, and the Walsall Town Band were present for the big occasion. But despite the bright sunny day, there was a poor crowd of only 1,500 present to see the Birmingham League match against Brierley Hill. The entrance charge of 6d. (2½p) was blamed for the poor attendance, and this cost was subsequently reduced.

It was not long before the West Bromwich Road Ground disappeared, to be replaced by terraced housing. The development of Fellows Park during the Club's long stay at the Ground has been fully covered in "The Football Grounds of Great Britain" (Inglis), and the last competitive game there was played on Tuesday the 1st of May 1990, when Rotherham United were the visitors.

Walsall versus Bristol City at Fellows Park 1989.
(Painted by Peter Watson and reproduced by permission of Walsall F.C.)

Fellows Park in 1990.
(Dave Twydell)

WATFORD

Watford Football Club was created in 1898, following the amalgamation of the two senior Clubs in the town, Watford St. Mary's and West Herts. But long before this date another team in the area flourished, by the name of Hertfordshire Rangers. Founded way back in December 1865, the Club originally played at Upper Nascot and later in a field off Langley Road. By 1872, they were a much respected team, and provided the goalkeeper for the England versus Scotland match that year. As the Rangers faded away, Watford Rovers (founded in 1881) took over - for a brief period - the mantle of the town's top team. Their achievements included the winning of the County Cup in 1889. For one season they played home matches at the West Herts. Ground, where they often attracted crowds of around 1,000. Even so, the Rovers were soon on the point of folding, and their members joined the West Herts. Club soon after it's formation.

WEST HERTS. SPORTS GROUND.

The early 1890's saw the creation of a new football team, that were to dominate the scene for some years. In April 1890, the West Herts. Sports Ground was created from eight acres of land on Harwood's Farm, and at a meeting on the 26th of February 1891, West Herts Club and Ground was formed. The lease on the Ground, initially for 21 years, with a further option for the same period at the end of the first, cost £100 per year, a large sum at this time for such an enclosure. The Ground cost £1,200 to build, and included turfing, fencing and erection of a pavilion.

The Ground was, and still is, located to the West of Cassio Road, just off the town centre. The enclosure is very large, and could, if required, comfortably contain two separate football pitches. For the Football Club, a three-sided Ground was created, with the pitch being placed furthest from, and running parallel with, Cassio Road. The pavilion was built centrally on the Western boundary, with entrances and exits on Cassio Road. Narrow covered enclosures, with some seating, were built each side of the pavilion, the latter being used as dressing rooms.

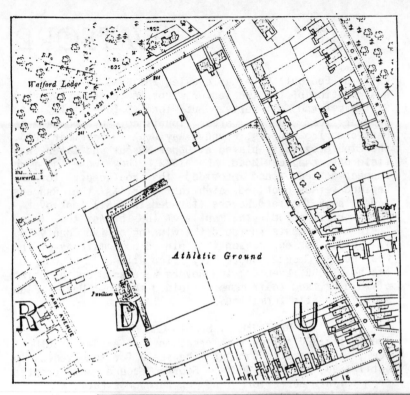

The Football Club were very successful, winning the Hertfordshire Senior Cup in 1891, 1892, 1894 and 1897, and in 1896 joined the Second Division of the Southern League. In their first League season they finished ninth of thirteen, and realising that to compete with the best, they adopted professionalism the next season. The Club's first match, on the 19th of September 1891, was to have been played at home to the 1st Scots Guards but was postponed. "Owing to the occupation of the Goodwin Sands by a party of Russian Bluejackets, and the laying down of torpedoes...", resulted in the unexpected exodus of the Guards to the Front! On October the 3rd the team at last kicked off; Crouch End were demolished with a 14-1 scoreline. The attendance was less than expected, but picked up as the Club continued in this winning way.

(Left): West Herts. Sports Ground in 1914.
(Ordnance Survey)

(Below): West Herts. Sports Ground from Cassiobury Road in 1893.
(Watford Local History Library)

WIGGENHALL ROAD.

Meanwhile another local Club had sprung up (in the early 1890's), Watford St.Mary's, and within a short period they became a match for the older West Herts. team. The Club played in Wiggenhall Road, but the location of the exact field - of many - is difficult to now identify. Suffice to say that it was almost certainly enclosed, since the Football Club took 'gates' at matches (2,000 for Luton's visit in the 1897/98 season), and the pitch had a pronounced slope. Occasionally games were played at other venues, including the Recreation Ground and the West Herts. Sports Ground; a match at the latter attracted a crowd of only 200 for the visit of Chesham in January 1891. Encouraged by their rivals becoming professional (in the Autumn of 1897), the Saints decided to adopt this code, but it soon became apparent that the town could not support two such teams. This change by the West Herts Club became an immediate success, for attendances increased, and the prestigious Friendly game with West Bromwich Albion attracted 2,000 Cassio Road to see the 1-1 draw. This game, on the 30th of April, was the last under the West Herts. name. St. Mary's final appearance was - by coincidence - against the Crouch End team.

WEST HERTS. SPORTS GROUND FOR WATFORD.

As early as 1891, it was not unusual for the West Herts. Club to include St.Mary's players in their line-up! But it was not until 1898 that the two Clubs merged, adopting the more representative name of plain 'Watford F.C.' The two former separate teams often met in friendly matches, the last on the 27th of April 1898. A merger had already been agreed, and there was only between 700 and 800 to see the West Herts. win at home by 2-0. The Wiggenhall Road Ground (where the entrance charge had been 4d - 2p) was abandoned in favour of the Cassio Road enclosure, for the latter offered far more potential. Around this time further Ground developments were made, giving the Club a very acceptable Ground which included cover for some 2,500 spectators. With one side of the pitch already fully developed and roofed, another covered standing enclosure was built that covered the full width of the Northern end. At the other end, and also opposite the pavilion, there were large flat areas, where portable timber terracing gave about five rows of spectators a slight elevation above the pitch. Despite the overall size of the Ground, and the large unoccupied flat areas, there was little more that could be developed since the

Club still shared with the Cricketers. Entrances were still off Cassio Road, and via turnstiles, and the standing charge was 6d. (2½p).

In their first season under the name of 'Watford' the Club finished third in the Southern League, Second Division (London Area - the lower teams split into two sections for this one campaign). They started the season, the first as Watford F.C., at home to Reading Amateurs in front of 1,700 fans on the 3rd of September, and thrashed their visitors with a 8-0 scoreline. One year later the Championship was won, only for the team to struggle in the higher company, until the almost inevitable return to the Second Division in 1903. But by now the Club were in a desperate financial situation, and it was only the personal support of Mr. R.A.Thorpe (Chairman of the local Council) that saw them through, and a return to the higher League once more. In the years upto the First World War the team struggled in the League and the Club got deeper into debt. Fortunately they had the continued backing of Mr. Thorpe, and others after him. In 1909 the Club were reformed and became a Limited Company, and by now the Football Club's rental stood at £50 per year, but even so a very reasonable figure.

The team coming onto the field, and in action in 1915.
(Watford Illustrated Newspaper)

The 1914/15 season brought about a remarkable transformation on the field, with the team capturing the title. However, in keeping with the past performances of the team, attendances were generally well below the numbers attracted to their opponents Grounds. But as the season wore on, the gates improved. In September there were only 1,500 present for the Swindon home match, but by mid-October this figure had risen to over 4,000 for Bristol Rovers visit. The increase was partly due to an influx of servicemen into the area who chose to come to Cassio Road to see a game of football! As War became inevitable, the Ground was also used as a recruiting centre for signing on new soldiers. Matches continued to be played at Cassio Road, and the enclosure was considered to be one of the best in the League; well kept and well drained it was in it's entirety larger than the Lords Cricket Ground, and the Club - who by now had their own large Clubhouse - had, in the past, been welcome tenants.

However, during the period of hostilities, the general public became critical of those non-amateur Clubs who continued playing, and now, after so many years of cordial relations, and following the team's exclusion from the London Combination, the Ground owner, Lady Essex, declined to rent the Ground to the Club, as she was firmly opposed to professional football! With the loss of many subscriptions, no fixtures, no Ground and precious few assets, a halt to playing had to be called, until the 1919/20 season.

The Club meanwhile had found an alternative site for a new Ground, at Vicarage Road, but such plans had to be dismissed due to various governmental refusals for the proposed conversion. Now on the edge of folding completely, Benskins Brewery became the new saviour when they managed to buy the Cassio Road Ground (principally with a view to the Football Club's continued occupation), and so the team were able to continue from where they had left off. The post War season started with tremendous enthusiasm, the first home match attracting a crowd of 3,000 to the Sports Ground. The missing years proved to be no disadvantage to the team, for by the end of the season they only missed out of the Championship on goal average. Crowds rose dramatically, 5,000 for the visit of Norwich, and a record 6,043 (receipts of £283) when they played Southend. 1920 was the year of the mass entry of Southern League Clubs into the new Football League Third Division, and Watford's success, coupled with the desire to be entertained after the years of austerity, continued the hitherto unprecedented interest in the Football Club.

The season ended with Watford finishing sixth in the table, and having rapidly outgrown their Ground! The visit of Luton Town on the 26th of March 1921 produced a new record attendance of 13,000 (match receipts of £782); a number that clearly could be accommodated at Cassio Road, but where many were unable to see no more than a glimpse of the proceedings. A local reporter described the scene; "packed like sardines in a box, in tree-tops, perched on the Stand and the Press box". Additional temporary 'Stands' were used during the season that consisted of Brewery drays and other open waggons, but these hardly fulfilled the needs of spectators and no doubt did not improve the outfield areas of the football pitch! The Club's new Champion, Benskin's Brewery stepped in once again and prolonged and difficult negotiations to purchase the Vicarage Road site were re-opened. After one more season at Cassio Road, the Club finally left after the last game of the 1921/22 season, on April the 29th, which resulted in a single goal victory over Gillingham before 5,000 spectators. Four months later the brand new Vicarage Road Ground was opened when Millwall Athletic played out a goalless draw before a crowd of 8,000.

THE GROUNDS TODAY.

By the outbreak of the First World War, Wiggenhall Road had been built over, and therefore no remains of the former Watford St. Mary's Club Ground are left. Conversely the Cassio Road enclosure is still a large Athletics Ground, even after a century since it's inception. All evidence of the Football Club's occupation have now gone, but the more modern Buildings now on the site are confined to the Western side of the field, as they were during the days of Watford F.C.

Programme cover from the 1919/20 season.

-385-

WEST BROMWICH ALBION

1989: The entrance gates to Dartmouth Park, opposite the site of the Cooper's Hill Ground.
(Dave Twydell)

The West Bromwich Club were founded by a group of young
men from the George Salter's Spring Factory in the town.
Yet although the Club go back to 1879, the team was far
from being the first in the District. In nearby
Wednesbury, there were already the three flourishing
Clubs viz. The Old Athletic, Strollers (formerly 'Town')
and Elwells, the latter a works team. But a Club in West
Bromwich itself was something of a new innovation, such
that the men from Salters had to go to Wednesbury, to the
nearest shop that sold footballs!

In mid-September 1879, the decision was taken to form a
Club, and with the enthusiastic assistance of George
Salter himself, it was not long before these pioneers had
a number of members who were willing to pay a 2d. (1p)
weekly subscription, to cover the cost - not only of a
football - but also for the purchase of a set of
goalposts. Initially the Club were to be called the
'Strollers', but this was soon changed to, the 'Albion'.
This title being derived from a district in West Bromwich
of the same name, where several of the members lived.

COOPER'S HILL AND DARTMOUTH PARK:

The Club's first 'Ground', was nothing more than a roughly triangular shaped piece of waste land, that was located by the side of Beeches Road, and between Treddles Lane and Herbert Street. This venue was known as Cooper's Hill (the back gardens of the houses in Cooper Street formed one boundary); a house of the same name was located in Dartmouth Park, immediately opposite this Ground. But since this venue was also used by the local Cricket team, matches in the early days were also played in the adjacent Dartmouth Park. Although no formal letting arrangements were required, the team usually played on a pitch near the main entrance to the park (just North of Coopers Hill), or further South, and opposite Herbert Street.

The Club's first formally recorded match was played on the 13th of December - in Dartmouth Park - when Black Lake Victoria were beaten by the only goal of the game, in front of some 500 enthusiasts. One week later Bullock's Club were entertained, at Cooper's Hill, and before a crowd of around 1,000, the visitors were soundly beaten by four goals without reply. Both of the Club's home venues were unfenced, and completely lacking in spectator or Player facilities. For changing rooms, the teams initially made use of the Glebe Inn that was situated in nearby Reform Street. Frequent matches were played against the likes of St.Phillips, Hearts of Oak, Christ Church, Smethwick Windmill and Oakfield, but the Albion immediately became a dominant force at the game, and were intent on emulating the superior abilities of Wednesbury Old Athletic and another capable team from further afield, by the name of Aston Villa.

BUNN'S FIELD (THE BIRCHES)

It soon became apparent that the support for the Albion was such that paying spectators could be entertained, for which an enclosed Ground was required. Less than two years after the Club was formed, a nine month lease was taken out, in August 1881, on Bunn's Field, which was located off Walsall Street. Perimeter fencing, to enclose the Ground, was erected by the Club members, and gate money totalling £1-50 per match soon became common. The Ground entrance was opposite Christchurch School, but there were still no facilities for the public, and it was not uncommon for the fans to bring their own planks of wood to stand on, to protect themselves from the often muddy conditions at The Birches (as the Ground became known)!

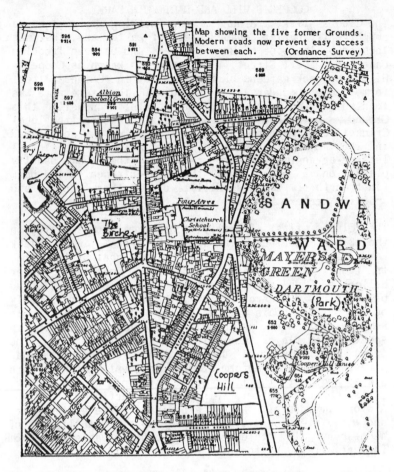

Map showing the five former Grounds. Modern roads now prevent easy access between each. (Ordnance Survey)

For a time the White Hart Public House was used as a Headquarters, which was at the junction of Herbert and Walsall Streets, and was conveniently close to the earlier Cooper's Hill Ground (a short walk from the back of the Pub and over a wall) But the changing facilites were eventually transferred to the Roebuck Inn, at the junction of Walsall Street and New Street. The use of Dartmouth Park was not completely dispensed with, since the the occasional match was played there, notably pre-season matches with Wednesbury Old Athletic.

The Club's first game at the Birches was probably versus Oldbury on the 10th of September 1871, and a good 5-1 victory was to set the standard for the ensuing season, when high scoring wins were to become frequent.

The match attracted a crowd of around 300 and produced match receipts of 15/2d. - 76p! Notable home victories were the twelve goal thumping of Milton (on the 8th of October), 9-1 over Nechells - in December - and a ten goal without reply victory over St.Luke's on the 4th of March. The Club capped a successful year with their progress through to the semi-finals of the Birmingham Cup, a Competition that was first introduced in the 1875/76 season. The Albion's run came to an end with a defeat to the much respected Wednesbury Old Athletic team.

FOUR ACRES:

Support for the successful Albion warranted a better home venue, and the Club were fortunate when they were invited to use the adjacent Four Acres Ground. By now, the Club had emerged as the undisputed top 'town' team, and the Football section of the West Bromwich Dartmouth Cricket Club decided to give up the unequal struggle with the Albion, and let the latter have the use of their well appointed Four Acres Ground during the Winter months. Four Acres was located directly opposite the Birches, on the other side of Walsall Street. The non-uniform shaped Ground, was sandwiched between the rear gardens of the houses to Summer Street and Walsall Street and the boundaries of Christchurch School. The Entrance however was off Seagar Street which ran parallel with Walsall Street. This Ground was the principal venue for the main Sporting events in the town, and although initially having little more than a small Pavilion and a Refreshment Room, the venue was a big improvement over the featureless Birches enclosure.

The only restrictive term of the letting was that the Albion could only play matches on Saturdays and Mondays, and of course they could not overlap with the summer fixtures of the Cricket Club. The tenancy agreement was made in September 1882, and the entrance fee to join the Club was increased to five shillings (25p), with an annual subscription and season tickets, set at half this sum. Yet again the Albion celebrated their first appearance at a new venue with a victory, a ten goal demolition of Stourbridge Standard on the 7th of October. But this highly encouraging start was overshadowed on the 11th of November, when Coseley were humiliated with a 26-0 defeat in the first round of the Birmingham Cup, the Club's biggest ever victory. The Club continued to go from strength to strength, and by the season's end they had recorded a total of 27 wins, 7 draws and only 5 defeats; the goal difference was a staggering 177 for and 60 against. Probably the most significant success was a one goal defeat of Aston Villa.

Improvements were made to Four Acres in the summer of 1883 with an improved pitch enclosure rail (instead of the former rope), wooden duckboards laid on the ground in the Reserved Section, an enlarged and improved Pavilion and a new Ticket Office. Further facilities were later provided by two more Refreshment Rooms and a small open seated Stand adjacent to the Pavilion. The lease for the use of the Ground was extended by a further two years, at an annual rental of £15, in July 1883.

WEST BROMWICH
Albion Football Club
SEASON TICKET
1883-1884

To Admit to all Matches on the
FOUR ACRES,
SITUATE IN SEAGAR STREET.
——
PRICE:—THREE SHILLINGS.

Mr

A Season Ticket
for the Four Acres
Ground which cost 15p.

The Club continued their upward rise in the Football World, and in the 1882/83 season their first major success, when they won the Staffordshire Cup. The highly regarded Aston Villa team were beaten in this cup run, in a replay, after an unruly match at Perry Barr had resulted in a 3-3 draw. The Villa match, in December, attracted a staggering record attendance at Four Acres of 10,447 and match receipts of over £400. Stoke were defeated in the final, when more than 2,000 Albion fans accompanied their team to the Potteries.

By joining the Football Association in the summer of 1883, the Club became eligible to enter for the F.A.Cup. But despite their past successes the first match in this competition resulted in a two goal home defeat by Wednesbury Town - a rare occurence for their colours to be lowered at Four Acres. Good support for the Albion continued, and on Boxing Day a crowd of 3,600 were present for the visit of Preston North End, who were beaten 2-1 in this Friendly match encounter. The Club's second season entry in the F.A.Cup was far more successful than their previous attempt. Junction Street School (Derby) were easily overcome by 7-1 at their opponents Ground, followed by a 4-2 win over arch-rivals Wednesbury Old Athletic. The third round resulted in a goalless draw at Perry Barr, and in the replay - and before another crowd in excess of 10,000 - the Villa team were comfortably defeated by three goals.

A close one goal victory over the Druids (from Wales) was
then achieved, followed by a bye in the 5th round. The
Druids game became a somewhat bizarre affair, for despite
the Referee's insistance, the Welshman refused to take
the field at kick-off time, as they were one Player
short. The Albion nonetheless kicked off against a
non-existant team and recorded a one nil scoreline.
Eventually the visitors decided to make a game of it, but
the Albion scored 'another' goal, and a 1-0 scoreline was
the final official result! This run had taken the team
through to the quarter-finals of the competition, and
they could not have wished for more attractive
opposition, when the Cup-holders - Blackburn Rovers -
came to Four Acres, on the 21st of February 1885.

For the biggest match in the Club's brief history, the
attendance at Four Acres that day reached an enormous
16,393. Additional temporary Stands were added, and
improvised viewing areas were obtained from the rooftops
of the houses in Walsall and Summer Streets. The result
went as expected, a 2 goal win to the visitors. But it
was obvious by now that the Albion had outgrown Four
Acres, and the Club Directors finally settled upon a new
Ground in the Summer of 1885. It was fitting, perhaps,
that the last first team match at the Cricket Ground
should be against the Club's main rivals, the Old
Athletic - on April the 6th. The Albion proved their
contention that they were by now the top-dogs in the
area, with a 3-2 victory.

In the three seasons that the Club had played at Four
Acres, they achieved an enviable home record. Of the 61
games played there only 7 ended in defeat (and 6 drawn),
with a goal difference of 268-56. Included in these
numbers were 22 cup-ties - in four different competitions
- and this record was even more impressive with only two
defeats.

STONEY LANE.

After establishing a Ground Committee within the Club, a
plot of land in Stoney Lane was finally settled on for
the Club's new home venue. It was only a short walk from
all of the Club's previous Grounds, and on the 27th of
October 1885, a seven year tenancy agreement was made, at
an annual rent of £28. The returfed playing pitch
measured 110 by 78 yards, and for the supporters comfort,
an ash footing was laid outside of the playing area.

On the Sandwell Road side, a covered wooden Grandstand provided comfortable viewing for 600, with a further 1,500 accommodated in the two open seating areas each side of the main structure. The seats were no more than wooden planks, and the Stand soon became known affectionately as 'Noah's Ark'. An embankment was built up on the side opposite the Stand, and the wide area at the Stoney Lane end provided space for the Club's supporters to bring in their own Waggonettes and Carts for viewing platforms. Brick Dressing Rooms (with corrugated iron roofs) were built on the Stand side, with - at a later date - a gas water heater for the baths. For all of the spectators benefit, three Refreshment Rooms were located on the Ground. Even though facilities were still somewhat limited, it was an improvement on the former Four Acres venue, although one particular disadvantage was the pronounced pitch slope towards the Stoney Lane end. Fencing and a boundary wall all added up to a grand total cost of £370 for preparing the Ground for the kick-off in September 1885. The progress that the Club had made in just six years since their formation was quite staggering, yet they had not reached their peak!

Spectators entered the Ground principally from the Stoney Lane end, along which tickets were purchased from several payboxes, but as the Club's attendances rose, additional outlets were necessary, from holes in the perimeter wall, from the Plough and Harrow Public House (the Club's headquarters), and - for important Cup-ties - a number of nearby houses. Season tickets cost 2/6d. (12½p) and the normal Ground admission charge was 2p.

The Albion kicked off the 1885/86 season as successfully as they had for the inaugural matches at their previous Grounds, with a convincing victory; 4-1 over Third Lanark Rifle Volunteers from Glasgow, on September the 5th. By the end of the season the Club had achieved far more than they dared hope for, with an appearance in the F.A.Cup Final, the first Club from the Midlands to achieve such a distinction. Although they lost at the last hurdle to Blackburn Rovers (in a replay), perhaps the most satisfying victory was a four goal without reply win over Small Heath Alliance in the semi-finals. By 1888, the Albion achieved a rare distinction with their third year in succession appearance in the Final - losing to their main rivals, Aston Villa, in 1887 - but at last bringing the Cup back to West Bromwich at the third attempt.

The 'Noah's Ark' Stand that was brought from the Stoney Lane Ground.
It was burnt down on the 5th of November 1904!

The Club's stay at Stoney Lane lasted for 15 seasons, during which time they became founder-members of the Football League, and the last game at the Ground was on the 16th of April 1900. In a fitting finale Nottingham Forest were thrashed by eight unopposed goals. Overall, the Club could look back at their Stoney lane days with satisfaction, for in the 350 games played their, only 70 were lost, whilst in the F.A.Cup an undefeated run extended to 14 matches between 1885 and 1893. But these earlier sustained successes of the Club were not to be continued, and attendances at Stoney Lane slumped. The probable record attendance was present during the 1891/92 season when a 'huge crowd' was present for the F.A.Cup quarter-final tie with Blackburn Rovers. But big crowds were rare, except for the visits of the local Clubs, and at the end of that season, when an average attendance of around 6,000 was recorded, gate receipts only totalled £3,864, but the Club's expenditure was around £5,000.

Despite the efforts and facilities provided at the Ground in 1885, little was added to from that time on, and by 1900, the Ground had degenerated to become one of the worst in the First Division! Yet the talk of a proposed move caused much resentment from the supporters who reasoned that should the Club move away from the centralised Stoney Lane enclosure, the Directors would be depriving local tradesmen of revenue, and they would be catering more for Birmingham people rather than for those of West Bromwich. This resentment was a reasonable attitude from the true fans, but the shopkeepers had not come forward to give financial help to the Club when it was sorely needed!

A site near Three Mile Oak - later to become the playing field of West Bromwich Grammar School - was at one time considered, and a deputation claimed that a syndicate was willing to put up £2,000 for ground improvements providing the Directors would take on a new 14 year lease at Stoney Lane. But the Board had made up their minds by the Autumn of 1898 that a move was the best for the revival of the Club's fortunes.

The Directors had been reluctant to spend money on a Ground which was only held on short leases, and in 1900, a 14 year option was taken out, not on the Stoney Lane Ground, but on a 10 acre site, which was to become known as the - now familiar - 'Hawthorns'. It was a gamble that this move would attract the crowds from a bigger catchment area, and was necessary to ensure the Club's survival. Match receipts (often as low as £35) could often not cover the weekly expenditure of around £90; the £500 plus gates for the visits of Aston Villa and the Wolves were all to rare.

The one reminder of Stoney Lane, was the 'Noah's Ark' Stand which was re-built at the Handsworth (East) side of the Hawthorns, but this relic only remained until the 5th of November 1904, when it was burnt down - appropriately - during the night!

THE GROUNDS TODAY.

Nothing remains of the five former Grounds of West Bromwich Albion, and finding the sites is a difficult task with major road improvements, making the short journeys between each, a far from easy task! Some of the roads surrounding the Coopers Hill venue still remain, and the actual location of the (waste) ground is now occupied by the red bricked St.Phillips Church and an adjacent School. Dartmouth Park still exists (opposite, and on the other side of the modern Expressway), but there is, of course no indications of the former football fields of the Albion.

Alfred Street now overlays much of the earlier Beeches Ground, and although still opposite, a somewhat difficult traverse now has to be made to reach the former Four Acres enclosure. Most of this latter Ground is overlain by Park Crescent. Until recent years, the Stoney Lane Ground remained as a patch of wasteland, but bungalows have recently been built there. Probably the only feature to serve as a reminder of the Club's glories in the late 19th Century, is a small estate road, named 'Albion Field Drive'!

WEST HAM UNITED

Professionalism in Essex first came by way of the Old
Castle Swifts Club who during their short career played
on a field at Hermit Road. This was also the venue chosen
by the later Thames Ironworks F.C. As the name would
suggest, the latter team were basically a firm's team
being created by the owner of the largest shipyard on the
Thames, Mr.A.F.Hills. Principally in order to create
harmony with the workers, the Club were founded in 1895.

HERMIT ROAD.

Hermit Road was probably at least partially enclosed - in
view of it's earlier use for professional football and
later for quoits and bowls - but the Ground offered
nothing for the comfort of spectators. Several years of
non-use had left the Ground as a barren waste, and being
virtually grassless it was referred to as a cinder heap!

In these rudimentary conditions the Ironworks - with over
fifty members and a Reserve eleven - played their first
match when a 1-1 draw was fought with the Royal Ordinance
reserve eleven on the 7th of September 1895. Suprisingly
the Club were allowed immediate entry into the F.A.Cup,
although they were thrashed in their first match with a
scoreline of 0-5 by Chatham. The redoubtable Mr. Hills -
before even the Ironworks team had been conceived - had
arranged for an exhibition match under floodlights
between West Bromwich Albion and Woolwich. On the 17th of
September 1894, the Midlands team won the match by one
goal to nil with electric light bulbs suspended from long
poles supplying the illumination and the ball painted
with whitewash. The idea was a great success, despite the
unsteadiness of the lighting, which was to a degree,
remedied the following year when Thames Ironworks beat
Old St. Stephens with a 3-1 victory. To ensure a good
gate canvass screens were erected around the Ground to
provide a more visually secure enclosure. It was obvious
that the new Club were intent on taking the game
seriously, and with the encouragement and financial
backing of Mr.Hills, weekly meetings and training
sessions were held at a schoolroom in Barking Road.

BROWNING ROAD.

After a very satisfactory inaugural season the Club were elected as founder-members to the First Division of the London League. But the Hermit Road enclosure was abandoned for another that was located in Browning Road, just off East Ham High Street. For the short period in this second home the team had difficulty in finding success and consequently interest waned. The probable last encounter at East Ham was the 4-1 victory over Crouch End Vampires on the 3rd of April 1897. Mr.Hills came to the rescue, and at his own expense he paid £2,000 for the construction of a brand new Ground at Canning Town. On the 11th of September 1897, Brentford were the first visitors, in a London League match which the homesters won with the only goal of the game, before a crowd of 1,000. The impressive new venue initially became a successful one for the Club, and by the season's end they were the London League Champions. The first victory in the F.A.Cup was achieved, over Redhill, but their run ended at home to Brighton with a 1-4 scoreline.

THE MEMORIAL GROUND.

The Memorial Ground, as it was named, was an enormous arena, and far bigger than the Club's status at that time merited. The oval shaped playing area was surrounded with an inner running track, and outside of this, a cycle track. On the West side there was a seated and covered Stand whilst opposite uncovered seating areas were provided. Earth embankments were formed at each end, and the claimed capacity was 120,000! This boast would appear to have been an exageration, as was the claim that it was 'good enough to stage the Cup Final!', although it was once earmarked as a potential F.A.Cup semi-final replay venue. As well as football, there were the overall space and facilities for cricket and tennis.

Action from the match versus Plymouth Argyle at the Memorial Ground in 1904.

The Club's rapid rise in stature resulted in them being accepted by the Southern League (Second Division - London), of which they duly became Champions, which led to their elevation to the First Division for the 1899/1900 season. But the relationship of the Club and it's benefactor began to rapidly deteriorate, and a period of financial struggle was on the horizon. Hill became disenchanted with the Club he had created, brought about principally following the inspection of the Club's books by the Football Association in May 1899. It transpired that the Amateur Club - unbeknown to Mr. Hills - had engaged Agents to obtain Players, for which they were fined £25. This slight against the owner's integrity hit him hard for he was a fervent supporter of Amateur football. But for the Ironworks to maintain their place in the Southern League it had become a virtual necessity for them to become Professional.

The 1899/1900 season became little short of disastrous for not only did they finish only one place off of the bottom of the League, but support dwindled. Not only was the team playing in a poor catchment area - they were somewhat removed from the site of their origins - but an attempt at extra income had seen the price of season tickets double in two years, to ten shillings. Further problems occurred with the Ironworks Company buying out a rival organisation, which required extra capital and a trimming of their expenditure. By now the disillusioned Hills was only too willing to disassociate the Company from the loss making Football Club. The Club were now financially on their own, and their formation into a Limited Company was not highly successful for the selling of the 4,000 shares at 50p each was poorly supported.

At this juncture the Club finally removed all ties with their origins and was renamed 'West Ham United'. Hills also wished to make a complete break with the 'new' Hammers, and he offered the use of the Ground to the Amateurs, Clapton Orient. Fortunately for the United they produced a letter to the effect that the Ground was agreed to be for their exclusive use. However, the lease that they had obtained only ran until 1904, and it was obvious that this would not be renewed. After a moderately successful 1901/02 season a small profit was made for the first time, and 500 extra shares were sold. But with another doubling of the price of season tickets, and reduced support, the Club were back into the 'red' one year later, when they showed a loss of £151.

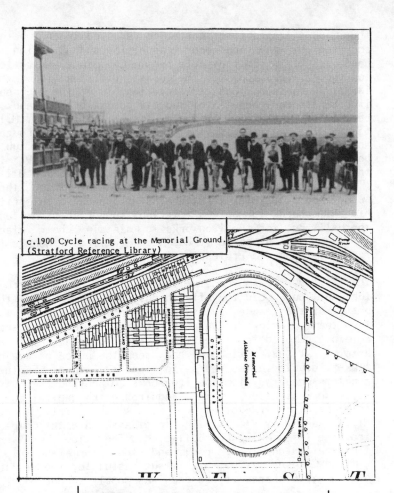

c.1900 Cycle racing at the Memorial Ground.
(Stratford Reference Library)

The Memorial Ground in 1916 (The Club left in 1904)
(Ordnance Survey)

-398-

The last year at the Memorial Ground was an even greater
financial disaster, for the Club lost £793 over the
1903/04 season. The time had now come for an enforced
move of location, and with assets of only £200! The last
game at the Ground was on the 30th of April, when Swindon
Town were the visitors in a Southern League match.

The crowd of between three and four thousand were
somewhat confused during the first half, since both teams
wore very similar playing kits! A change was made at
half-time, but the homesters lost the match by the only
goal of the game. The Memorial Ground provided few happy
memories, despite the 'lucky' horseshoes that were nailed
over the dressing room door!

The Club were in a desperate state, however, in the
unlikely setting of a potato field behind the Elizabethen
mansion of Boleyn Castle, the modern Upton Park Ground
was created. The Club's request for another lease at
Canning Town was refused - probably to nobodys surprise -
but a chance meeting with an official of the Boleyn
Castle School, at a schoolboy match at the Memorial
Ground subsequently led to a suitable agreement.
Fortunately the removal of the Club to a more football
conscious area created sufficient interest for them to
erect a Grandstand in time for the visit of Millwall in
September 1904. The Ground was presumably named after the
nearby Upton Park Club that had existed and thrived in
the area for twenty years from 1866. Two trial matches in
August 1904 produced crowds of over 2,000 and 4,000,
which bode well for the future.

THE GROUNDS TODAY.
All traces of the Browning Road Ground have long since
vanished under the inevitable urban sprawl, although it
is possible that the former Hermit Road Ground is the
current Recreation Ground that is located at the junction
with Bethal Avenue. The location of the Memorial Ground
can be readily identified within the large and currently
entitled 'Memorial Recreation Ground. The former Stadium
portion is currently used by a Rugby Club, and the large
flat playing area remains as do some of the grassed
topped embankments, especially on the North side.

WIMBLEDON

Most of Wimbledon's long lifetime has been spent as an amateur Club, and the early years were in a minor capacity. During those formative years the Club led a nomadic existance that involved several frequent Ground changes.

The Fox and Grapes Public House in 1990. Possibly little changed from when it was used as Dressing rooms for the team in the early 1890's. The second Wimbledon Common Ground was probably at the end of the road. (Dave Twydell)

WIMBLEDON COMMON PITCHES.

The Club were formed in 1889, as 'Wimbledon Old Centrals', from former pupils of the Old Central School in Camp Road, that was located within a small community that lay within the Southern boundaries of Wimbledon Common. For a number of years the Club were no more than a very minor organisation, and therefore records of their early days are very limited. It is known that their first match was played on the 2nd of November 1889, a match that was won 1-0, and was played on the Common. The pitch - for it certainly was no more than a reasonably flat area of boggy grass - was probably in the vicinity of Robin Hood Road, a park road that leads to the Camp Road community. Despite such a low status, there was plenty of enthusiasm, for the playing membership soon totalled around forty members. Seventeen matches were played in the first season (of which six were victories and five were draws), and one year later twenty-three games were played when there were only three defeats. The football was still at a minor level, but a move was made to another location, principally due to the nuisance value (both ways) of balls continually ending up in the nearby carriageway!

Once again it was nothing more than a patch of grass that became the second 'Ground'. The location was close to the original pitch and was probably within the triangular area formed between Rushmere Pond, West Place and another track that led to Camp Road. After initially using a nearby cottage as changing rooms, by 1892 the players made use of the Fox and Grapes Public House which was, and still is, in Camp Road. From 1893 the Headquarters was moved to The Swan, and one year later a significant elevation in status was made when the Club joined the South London League. After a one year stay, the team then played in the Clapham and Herald League, and after a minor and stable existance in the first few years, a period of rapid League and Ground moves was soon to come.

At the 1898 A.G.M. a profit over the season of £18 was reported and one year later the Club's income rose to £40. At this time money was supposedly spent on 'Ground improvements', but in view of the nature of the 'Ground' and the likelihood of charging spectators being most unlikely, it is difficult to see where money was generated (other than from members subscriptions) or what could have been developed at the home venue!

PEPY'S ROAD.
At the annual meeting in August 1901, it was announced that the Club would be moving to a private Ground - and presumably an enclosed one - for the next season. This Ground, which no doubt had no facilities for spectators was at the South end of Pepy's Road and North of the junction with Worple Road West; the nearby Cottenham Park School was used as dressing rooms. By now the Club were able to attract regular support, and for the first time season tickets were sold, with a total of thirty-five for the 1901/02 season.

The 1902/03 season saw the team playing in the Southern Suburban League and after being accepted as a Senior Club two years later, they showed their capabilities with their appearance in the South London Charity Cup Final versus Nunhead in April 1905.

On the first of that month the 'Old Centrals' was formerly dropped from the Club name, and a few months later, as plain 'Wimbledon' they played their first F.A.Amateur Cup game - a 4-2 victory over Eversleigh. The success of the Club continued and they were accepted into the premier F.A. Competition with the initial match resulting in a narrow defeat at home to West Norwood. The following season it has been recorded that the Club played just off of Pepy's Road, however the exact location is not obvious and this could have been one and the same as the venue that had been used since 1901. In any event that period of frequent League changes and Ground moves was upon them.

GRAND DRIVE.

The 1907/08 season saw the team playing at Grand Drive near Raynes Park Station. The area is still fairly open, and this Ground was probably either on the East side of the Drive (currently a large open area of land known as Prince George's Playing Fields) or, more likely, to the West where a Clubhouse was located and presumably the playing area could have been enclosed. Even so this stay only lasted for one year, when a home was found to the West of Merton Hall Road.

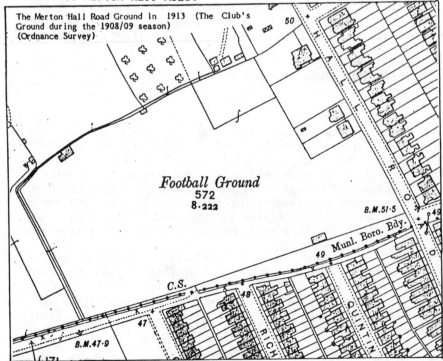

The Merton Hall Road Ground in 1913 (The Club's Ground during the 1908/09 season) (Ordnance Survey)

Football Ground
572
8·222

MERTON HALL ROAD AND MALDEN WANDERERS CRICKET GROUND.

The 1910 O.S. Map records this as a 'Football Ground', but shows very little in the way of facilities for either Players or spectators - only two small buildings which may have been changing rooms. But once again the nomadic existance of Wimbledon F.C. continued for they had moved yet again by the commencement of the 1909/10 season. It was a westward move once again, this time to the Malden Wanderers Cricket Club Ground in Burlington Road, and just South of the current Malden Station. This venue initially seemed ideal, it was conveniently situated, presumably enclosed and the pitch was flat. But whereas the Ground may have been good in the fairly dry summer days, Autumn and Winter rains produced a waterlogged and unplayable surface!

The Club were in a desperate state, as for several years they struggled on the financial front - no doubt the frequent and variable located home Grounds made it difficult to attract regular support. In the summer of 1908 the Club were £20 in debt (a not inconsiderable sum for a fairly minor Amateur organisation), and when the Merton Hall Road Ground was vacated one year later, they were on the point of folding. Later during the 1909/10 season a number of nearby alternative venues were tried, including pitches North of the Station, but by the season's end Wimbledon F.C. were on their last legs. Technically the Club did not fold but announced on the 3rd of September that they would be suspending activities for an undefined period. During this fateful last season the Club had sought help from the local Council, asking only for a suitable roped off pitch, but their pleas went unheard. Meanwhile a new local team was emerging by the name of 'Wimbledon Borough F.C.', a Club created from Council workers.

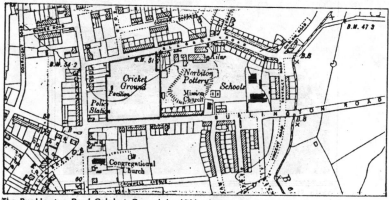

The Burlington Road Cricket Ground in 1911. (Ordnance Survey)

They played their matches at Coppermill Lane, the site
that is now the Wimbledon Greyhound and Speedway Stadium.
After two years of inactivity, 'Wimbledon F.C.'
re-emerged and had talks with the Council team. This led
to the disbanding of the latter, and through an effective
amalgamation of the two organisations a 'new' Wimbledon
F.C. was born. No doubt with the influence that could now
be exerted on the Council, a suitable site was found in
Plough Lane, their current Ground, and the first match
was played there on the 9th of September 1912.

THE GROUNDS TODAY.

For a Club of humble existance during the early years,
their home Grounds were located in many diverse
locations; perhaps it was this factor that led to their
financial problems and probable lack of regular support.
The two pitches on Wimbledon Common cannot of course be
accurately located, although much of the scenery has
changed little over the past century, and the 'Fox and
Grapes' still exists, probably now as it was then. The
Worple Road West enclosure probably had to be abandoned
for the outward urban sprawl, Trewince and Tolverne Roads
now cover the site. Grand Drive is still a very open
area, and just South of Prince George's Playing Fields
the neat little enclosure of Malden Vale F.C. is located.
The former Merton Hall Road Ground, which lies adjacent
to The Chase pedestrian walk, has retained it's basic
shape and is now the sports field for the adjacent
School. The Burlington Road site was, and still is, next
to a Police Station but the former Cricket Ground has now
been built over, as have the football pitches North of
Malden Station.

The South Stand at Plough Lane was purchased from Clapton Orient, and
came from the Millfield Ground in 1923.
(Dave Twydell).

(Courtesy of Wimbledon F.C.)

WOLVERHAMPTON WANDERERS

FOOTBALL.

THE FIRST

GENERAL MEETING

OF THE

GOLDTHORN

FOOTBALL CLUB

Will (by the kind permission of the Vicar) be held at

ST. LUKE'S SCHOOL,

BLAKENHALL,

ON

Friday next, November 10, 1876,

AT 7·30 P.M.

Any Gentleman interested in the game is invited to attend.

Announcement of the meeting which led to the formation of the Club.

Football - the 'round' ball variety - became popular in the town at an early stage in the development of the game. In the mid 1870's, Cricket and Bicycling were by far the most common of sports, although with the foundation of Stafford Road F.C. in 1872, football then began to take a hold in Wolverhampton. This Club was formed by workers of the principal Engineering Company in the town, at their Stafford Road Works. The team had a very rudimentary Ground which was situated in one of the fields at the end of Fox's Lane, and facilities consisted

of no more than basic changing rooms which were located
in a nearby pumping shed. Fox's Lane is still situated to
the North of Wolverhampton, and the fields are still
there, as is a pumping engine house, if not the original,
perhaps at least located in the same place.

The successes of the Works' side provoked the formation
of other Football Clubs, and the origins of the Wolves
team, although somewhat uncertain, appear to have been
created from a number of different Clubs, notably
Blakenhall St.Lukes and Goldthorn Hill. Goldthorn Hill
were the first formed of this pair, in 1876, following a
meeting on the 10th of October. Goldthorn made their
debut on the 13th of January, when they met the Stafford
Road reserves team, at a Ground near the Orphanage; it
was a hard baptism for the newcomers for they lost by
0-8! By 1877, the St.Lukes team had been established,
founded principally by John Baynton and John Brodie, from
the youths that had attended the school of the same name.

GOLDTHORN HILL AND JOHN HARPER'S FIELD.
A Ground in the Goldthorn Hill area (which is within the
Blakenhall district of Wolverhampton) was used, and the
team played their first match, at home, on the 15th of
March. This venue was known as the Old Windmill Field,
and was situated at the end of what is now Grange Road.
This was plainly nothing more than an unenclosed field,
and after two years they moved to John Harper's Field
which was located in Lower Villiers Street, a road that
still exists, and is nearer to the town centre. Once
again it is very unlikely that this 'Ground' was anything
better than an open venue, and was located opposite
Stroud's Niphon Works.

Meanwhile the Stafford Road team were still going strong,
and by 1881 they were frequently attracting crowds of
around 3,000 to their home matches (a match two years
earlier versus Walsall Swifts drew 7,000 to Fox's Lane).
Football was becoming popular countrywide, and many Clubs
sprang up in the Wolverhampton area. However, little was
reported in the local Press, apart from the exploits of
the Stafford Road Club, although in view of St.Lukes
appearance in the Birmingham Cup in the 1880/81 season
(they lost to West Bromwich) - the only Wolverhampton
Club other than Stafford Road to enter the Competition -
the Lower Villier's Street team appear to have been the
more Senior of the 'also rans' in the immediate area.

DUDLEY ROAD.

A further Ground move was made in the Summer of 1881, when the Club transferred to another field, this time located off the Dudley Road. Probably the first match (by St.Lukes) at the new Ground (in the 1881/82 season) was in October when Stourbridge Swifts were defeated by 7-1 before 200 paying spectators. Support generally increased, upto tenfold, for in April 1883, when a single goal defeat was suffered at the hands of Walsall Swifts, there were approximately 2,000 present. But such numbers were not regularly achieved, for the total gate money at the end of that season totalled only £80 although a nominal profit of £1 overall was shown. One year later things were looking bleak, with average crowds of only 1,500, which drastically dipped to only a few hundred for matches in the rain - there was no cover for the fans! On the 27th of October 1883, Long Eaton Rangers were the first visitors to Dudley Road for an F.A.Cup match. The homesters won by 4-1 before a good attendance of 2,000.

The town had more than the it's share of Clubs, all vying for support, and by 1884, the St.Lukes Club, together with Goldthorn Hill (and possibly others) combined to form Wolverhampton Wanderers F.C., a force which was soon to overthrow the might of Stafford Road Works. These two principal Clubs in the town met in a Wrekin Cup-tie at the Wanderers Ground - as formerly occupied by St.Johns - in Dudley Road, in February 1884 (although during the 1884/85 season the Cricket Ground in Blakenhall was also occasionally used). It is open to conjecture on how the new Club's name was evolved. Between them the constituent Clubs had in fact wandered to a fair degree, although the name may have been derived from their famous namesakes - early winners of the F.A.Cup. Alternatively they may have adopted 'Wanderers' from a cricket team of the same name with whom the St.John's Club had once shared a Ground. A good victory in the F.A.Cup was attained during the 1883/84 season, with a home victory over Long Eaton Rangers. The Rangers were a powerful team, undefeated for two seasons, but they were easily dismissed with a 4-1 scoreline, before a crowd of 3,000. There was no giant killing when the Wanderers were beaten in the second round at Wednesbury Old Athletic.

Despite the Wanderers gradual domination of the football scene in the town, it was reckoned that gates in excess of two to three thousand - the norm - were required to make end meet, and despite their rise in stature, the early years were far from prosperous. With the Football League still several years in the future, big gates were few and far between, but the 1885/86 season was to see the Club reach the fourth round of the F.A.Cup, and the financial rewards that went with a good run. Early home victories over Derby St.Lukes (7-0), and a local derby with the fading Stafford Road team (4-2) saw the team through to the third round and another home tie with Walsall Swifts. A 2-1 victory was followed by a visit to West Bromwich Albion, but the homesters (in only their third season in the Competition) won by 3-1, and they went on to become losing finalists. On the 20th of March 1886, Walsall Town were entertained in Wolverhampton in the semi-final of the Walsall Cup. It was not to Dudley Road that the 4,000 spectators flocked, but to the Molineux Grounds. The Grounds were located to the North of the town and were the public Pleasure Grounds of the area, a facility that was duplicated throughout the Country in this era. Recreations included a skating rink, walks and lawns, plus an oval shaped arena for sports. The facilities were limited to a small Grandstand on the Waterloo Road side of the enclosure and slightly raised embankments, but even though limited the Ground was far superior to that at Dudley Road.

A measure of the Club's standing could be judged on the 17th of April, when Preston North End made a rare appearance in the Midlands. Perhaps the Wolves greatest achievement to that date was enacted when the all conquering visitors were vanquished with a 4-1 scoreline before no fewer than 6,000 spectators. But this crowd was dwarfed when Aston Villa visited the town in an F.A.Cup-tie in January 1887, with a massive attendance of around 10,000 - quite probably a record attendance countrywide at that time. When Edinburgh Hibernians were the visitors in April, a crowd of around 2,500 were present to see a 3-2 win by the homesters.

In 1888, the Club were invited to join the Football League in it's inaugural season, and in addition to finishing in 3rd place, they capped a memorable year with their first appearance in the final of the F.A.Cup. But even so the attendances were normally nothing exceptional. The first League match only attracted 2,500 to Dudley Road, despite the visitors being Aston Villa, and other crowds rarely exceeded 4,000. The season's best was 8,600 for the visit of West Bromwich, although the home F.A. cup match versus Sheffield Wednesday on the 2nd of March produced a record gate. The estimated attendance of 10,000 saw the Wanderers triumph by three unopposed goals. On the 23rd of February 1889, Everton became the last visitors to the Dudley Road Ground, at which there was an attendance of 4,000.

Having by now become one of the leading football Clubs in the land, it became obvious that a suitable Ground had to be found. The Dudley Road enclosure was hardly suitable for the Wanderers high standing. Spectator comforts were very sparse, and were limited to a reserve enclosure - which only offered duckboards to protect the feet, for an additional entrance fee - and the only cover consisted of little more than a lean-to shed! The surface of the pitch was uneven and had a pronounced lengthways slope. The Ground was near to the Fighting Cocks Public House, and was South of the junction of Dudley and Knox Roads, and which is now overlain by Wanderers Avenue. Between 1881 and 1899, several matches were played at the Blakenhall Wanderers Cricket Ground, which was located behind the Fighting Cocks Public House.

MOLINEUX.

Important games had been played on several occasions at the Molyneux Grounds - which had previously hosted professional cycle races - and it was towards this venue that the Club's attention was drawn.

The close season of 1889 was a hectic race against time, for the former Pleasure Grounds were dug up, and a brand new Football Ground, with the help of the Northampton Brewery Company, was ready for the first fixture on the 2nd of September. After the Club's F.A.Cup final victory in 1893, the by now built upon Dudley Road Ground honoured the team with two road names; Fallowfield Terrace (where the Cup Final was held), which no longer exists, and Wanderers Avenue.

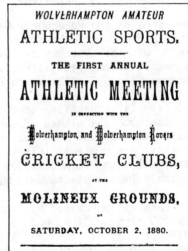

WOLVERHAMPTON AMATEUR
ATHLETIC SPORTS.

THE FIRST ANNUAL

ATHLETIC MEETING

IN CONNECTION WITH THE

Wolverhampton, and Wolverhampton Rovers

CRICKET CLUBS,

AT THE

MOLINEUX GROUNDS,

ON

SATURDAY, OCTOBER 2, 1880.

Molineux was used for other Sports before the Wolves regular occupation.

WREXHAM

North Wales adopted (Soccer) Football much earlier than their Southern counterparts, and this is reflected in reports dating back to 1630 - a sport which at this time was deplored by the Gentry! By the mid-19th century a more recognisable form of the game was being played in the District.

Various dates have been given for the formation of the Club, and at least a forerunner existed in 1870, but 1875 is now recognised as the founding year of the current Wrexham F.C. They are the oldest surviving Football Club in Wales, and indeed one of the oldest in the World.

ACTON PARK AND THE RACECOURSE GROUND.

Records of the early days of the Club are very sketchy, as indeed are the references to the venues which served as home Grounds. Two venues were used, although the exact dates and regularity of the use of each are difficult to accurately ascertain. Certainly the Racecourse Ground regularly featured as the Welsh venue for the early International matches (although the first game was held at Acton Park), and various Wrexham F.C. Players were regularly selected for their National team from soon after the Club's formation.

The area of the Racecourse Ground was, in 1707, known as 'Maes y Flitches', the translation into English being - Field of the Vetches - and therefore has an indirect connection (from its title), with that of the Ground at Swansea City F.C. (The Vetch Field).

But it is generally accepted that the Club's first regular home was within Acton Park. It is safe to say that this 'Ground' was unlikely to be little more than a football pitch within this vast open area, and since the Park extended to nearly 900 acres the exact location is probably impossible to determine.

The Park was purchased by the Wrexham Corporation for £20,500 around the end of the First World War, and by 1920 work had started on transforming the undeveloped land into the network of roads, houses and miscellaneous institutions that are present today.

A Recreation Ground is present in the South-east corner of the current estate, but there is no reason to suppose that this was the site of the Club's Ground.

The first Welsh F.A.Cup Final was held at Acton Park in 1878, and so was a home match for Wrexham when they beat the Druids. The first competitive game of the 1875/76 season (and therefore possibly the first for the Club) was played at the Racecourse Ground, and ended as a scoreless draw with the National Provincial Bank & Insurance Offices; after one hour the match was abandoned due to the incessant rain!

In 1884, the Club took part in a match under floodlights, which was described as; "A Football match at night... the field being illuminated by the electric light". But the match, which was a great success and watched by a crowd of 1,500, was played in a field off Grosvenor Road - another former ground of the Club? Illumination was by way of six, 2,000 candle power lights, but by all accounts there was an uncertainty of light and shade. That same year an incident in a match, when the referee was attacked, led to the Club being temporarily expelled from the Welsh F.A.

There were complaints that the Cricket Club monopolised the Racecourse Ground, which was the preferred venue for football matches, but alternative venues were few and far between, and for some years Acton Park had to suffice for most games. The situation was made worse in 1888, when the Cricket Club declared that the Racecourse Ground could only be used when a paying gate was taken!

This state of affairs continued for some years with most important matches being played at the premier venue, whilst the majority of ordinary Club games took place at Acton Park.

But around the turn of the century, the Racecourse had gradually become the more normal home venue for the Club, and by now the team were attracting sufficient support to merit the use of a properly enclosed Ground. At the A.G.M. in August 1905, the Club announced that match receipts had amounted to £467 over the previous season, with a balance in hand of £199. The Welsh Cup had been won again, this time following a three goal success over Aberdare, at the Racecourse and before a crowd of 6,191 (receipts of £250). The Club had completed a very successful season.

Support had never been higher, and even with an increase in the cost of season tickets, there had been an exceptional number sold. On the 21st of October 1905, the appearance of Aston Villa attracted a record attendance of 6,000, at what by now had become the regular home venue - the Racecourse Ground.

A draw ticket from 1892; at this time the Club's regular Ground was still at Acton Park.

YORK CITY

York City were formed in 1922, although a Senior Club
existed in the Town from early in the 20th Century. The
original York Club, played at Field View, Holgate Road,
and aspired to Senior football when they reformed, and
joined the Northern League for the 1908/09 season. Their
two seasons in this League were not particularly happy
ones, and in 1910 they moved on to the Yorkshire
Combination for a further two years before entering the
Midland League. There they remained until the First World
War, but never re-appeared after the hostilities. The
Ground was reasonably well developed for it had covered
and open Stands.

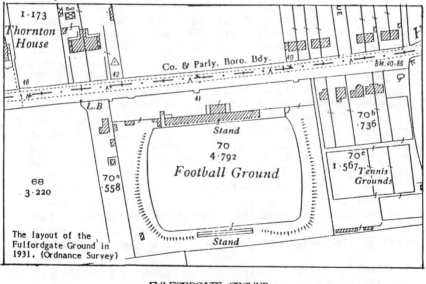

The layout of the
Fulfordgate Ground in
1931. (Ordnance Survey)

FULFORDGATE GROUND.

With the original Club not putting in another appearance,
it wasn't until the 31st of March 1922 that a band of
enthusiasts decided to create another Club. Although the
original meeting, at the Guildhall, attracted 400
enthusiasts it was realised that it would be an uphill
struggle in what at this time was a Rugby stronghold.
Fortunately there was a keen band of fans available to
create a suitable enclosure, and many weeks were spent in
the preparation of a site that was found at Fulford,
located a mile or so South of the City Centre.

By the start of the 1922/23 season it was far from finished, although after the levelling of the pitch area, substantial banking had been formed. This latter exercise led to the members nearly falling foul of the law. The Supporters Club which had been formed, decided to barrow rubble from the sides of nearby Heslington Lane, since they understood that this was to be removed for imminent road widening. But their arbitrary actions were spotted by the Chairman of the Council, who ordered it to be returned. After all of the time and effort expended this was a devastating and daunting prospect, however, the observer was a friend of the Football Club's Vice-Chairman, and after discussions the embankmants were allowed to stay!

A Limited Company was formed with an initial capital of £4,000, and most of the shares were taken up by the working men supporters of the new Club, with payments being made on a weekly basis. By the start of the season the Ground was not ready, and the first few home matches of York City were played at Haxby Road, the Sports Ground of Rowntree and Co. After a trial game before a 1,000 crowd, on August the 26th, a Friendly match was played one week later, when an attendance of 3,000 saw six goals shared with Sheffield Wednesday. The Club had been admitted to the Midland League, quite an achievement since they obviously had no 'track record', and on the 9th of September, Lincoln City were the first visitors in this competition. With an attendance of 4,000, and a victory by 3-2, both achievements lived well up to the hopes of the new found fans. This temporary Ground had a limited seating capacity consisting of three or four unbanked and open rows, but the pitch left a lot to be desired with alternating long grass and bare patches!

Two weeks after the first League match, a friendly game was arranged with nearby Acomb for the initial match at Fulfordgate. Two goals were shared, but after such encouraging earlier support, the attendance of barely 1,500 must have been a big disappointment. But on October the 7th, the visit of Barnsley Reserves for a Midland League game attracted 2,500 fans to the Ground, and no doubt somewhat restored the enthusiasts hopes. There were five hundred more who attended the next home match versus Notts. County Reserves. During this first season various necessities were added; dressing-rooms (with baths) and a near full pitch length seated Grandstand being the priorities.

The Ground was completely enclosed - with several entrances, all off of the Heslington Lane side, and eventually a narrow uncovered Stand about 40 yards long was built on the South side. Elsewhere, spectators had raised banks from which to watch, with a refreshment bar (probably) located in the North-west corner of the Ground.

The Club first entered for the F.A.Cup in their second season, and Castleton and Allerton United were beaten 2-1 in the initial game on the 8th of September 1923.

One year later the Club issued it's first programme which was entitled 'The Citizen', a nomenclature that has remained with the Club throughout its history. During the 1925/26 season, the weekly subscriptions had been largely paid up by the Club's working Class shareholders, but it was to be some years before any real success came to the team on the field. After several indifferent years, apart from progression through to the first round proper of the F.A.Cup in 1929, the Club were somewhat surprisingly elected into the Football League (Division Three North) at the end of

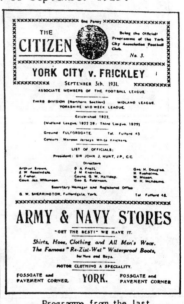

Programme from the last season at Fulfordgate.

that season. Despite the expected difficulties in attracting support the Club had reacted positively throughout their few years of existance, which had started with their first Football League application being made only a few months after their formation in 1922!

Improvements continued at the Ground, with proper terracing behind at least one goal, and cover added to the side opposite the Heslington Lane Stand. The Club's ventures in this higher level were immediately successful for by the end of the 1929/30 season they finished 6th in the League, and made their mark in the F.A.Cup.

(Top): The packed main Stand for the replay with Newcastle United (1929/30 season).
(Bottom): On a snow covered pitch versus Sheffield United (1930/31 season), looking towards the North-west corner.

On the 10th of January they startled the Football World by holding Newcastle United to a 1-1 draw at St.James' Park - the match was played in a blizzard, and the homesters goal was considered by many to be a dubious one! The replay on the following Wednesday attracted unprecedented interest, and all seats were quickly sold, with four or five times as many applications. Entrance on the day cost two shillings (10p) for covered viewing, and half this figure for the open terracing. The gates were closed an hour before the kick-off, which resulted in many of the 700 travelling Newcastle fans being locked out, and a record attendance of 12,583 (Receipts £900) was packed into the compact enclosure.

But there was no repeat performance for the City were narrowly beaten by the odd goal in three. The two games fired the imagination of the York fans, and the following two League games at Fulfordgate attracted high crowds (on Northern section standards), of 5,500 and 6,000.

One year later there was to be a near repeat performance in the F.A.Cup. By reaching the third round again, the Club travelled to Sheffield United, aided by 3,500 fans in the 31,821 crowd. Once again a First Division team was held to a 1-1 draw, and a new record attendance was expected for the replay on the 14th of January. At prices of upto twice those of a year earlier, the match at Fulfordgate was made all ticket, and the final figures showed an attendance of 12,721 (receipts of nearly £1,059). After a scoreless first half, two goals in two minutes took the visitors through to the fourth round. After a poor start in the League, when attendances had dropped to less than 5,000, a recovery was made to place the Club in a final mid-table position. But the Club's future at Fulfordgate was limited, although they were honoured with staging an Amateur International match in November, and an F.A. Amateur Cup semi-final in March 1931.

Although the Club had made such rapid progress, the Ground at Fulfordgate was far from ideal, being located so far from the City centre. Fortunately they owned the Ground, and with the desire for housing in the immediate area, it was a relatively easy step to move their home location. The last League match at Fulfordgate was played on the 28th of April, when their lowest saturday attendance of that season (2,000) came to see the locals thrash Halifax 7-2. One week later Hull City Reserves were beaten 3-1 in the final competitive match, and on the 7th of May, a crowd of under 1,000 were present for a Friendly match with Southport. These poorly attended farewells were a sad end to a Ground that had seen such progress and occasional big matches.

As with their first home, much of the work was undertaken by the supporters in the move to the former Cricket Ground in Bootham Crescent. Many of the Fulfordgate fixtures were dismantled and transported across town in a move which took only three months from start to finish. The new Ground was formerly opened by the Club President, Sir John J.Hunt, on the 31st of August, when a well above (previous) average crowd of 8,106 saw four goals shared with Stockport County.

The Fulfordgate Ground was soon covered by housing, and the only reminder is the street named 'Fulfordgate' that runs North to South, and close to the former West terrace end, and Eastward Avenue at right angles.

Work nears completion at Bootham Crescent in the Summer of 1932. (Yorkshire Herald)

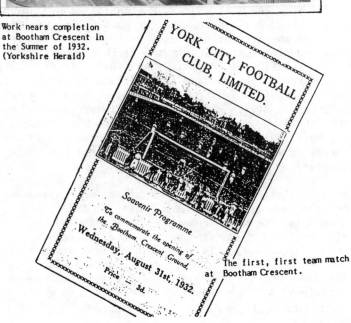

The first, first team match at Bootham Crescent.

With very few exceptions, there is, unfortunately, little left to see
of the former Grounds of the Clubs in the Football League. However,
armed with imagination and this book a number of visits can be most
rewarding. Opinions on which sites are worthy of a visit will vary,
but having been to them all, my choice is as follows:
(In Club - alphabetical - rather than in visit preferential, order).

1 Blackburn Rovers:
    (Alexandra Meadows)
2 Bristol City:
    (St. John's Lane)
3 Bristol Rovers:
    (Eastville - before it finally disappears!)
4 Charlton:
    (The Valley - or will they return?)
5 Chester:
    (Sealand Road - before it is developed)
6 Crewe:
    (Alexandra Athletic Ground)
7 C.Palace.
    (Herne Hill Cycle Track)
8 Doncaster Rovers:
    (The Intake Ground)
9 Halifax Town:
    (The Exley Ground)
10 Hull City:
    (Anlaby Road and The Circle Cricket Ground)
11 Lincoln City:
    (The Guildhall)
12 Millwall:
    (North Greenwich Ground)
13 Norwich City:
    (The Nest & Newmarket Road Grounds)
14 Nottingham:
    (Forest Recreation Ground, The Meadows and Trent Bridge)
15 Oxford United:
    (The Quarry Ground)
16 Port Vale:
    (Cobridge Athletic Ground)
17 Reading:
    (Reading Cricket Ground)
18 Rotherham United:
    (Clifton Lane)
19 Scarborough:
    (Marine Parade Cricket Ground)
20 Southampton:
    (County Cricket Ground)
21 Swindon Town:
    (County Cricket Ground)
22 Torquay United:
    (The Recreation Ground)
23 Walsall:
    (Fellows Park - before it disappears!)
24 Watford:
    (West Herts. Sports Ground)
25 West Ham United:
    The Memorial Ground)

THE REST!:

With all due respect to the following sixteen Clubs, they have no place in this book... they have never changed Grounds!

****

Aldershot:
The Recreation Ground.

Bradford City:
Valley Parade.

Bury:
Gigg Lane.

Chelsea:
Stamford Bridge.

Exeter City:
St.James' Park.

Darlington:
Feethams Ground.

Hartlepool United:
Victoria Park.

Hereford United:
Edgar Street.

Huddersfield Town:
Leeds Road.

Leeds United:
Elland Road.

Liverpool:
Anfield.

Northampton Town:
County Ground.

Peterborough United:
London Road.

Portsmouth:
Fratton Park.

Rochdale:
Spotlands.

Sheffield United:
Bramnall Lane.

****

These final Six Clubs fall into a category which is neither 'have changed' or 'have not changed'!

Burnley:
Burnley Rovers were formed as a Rugby Club c.1875 and played at Calder Vale for a few years. This Club became defunct but was quickly reformed under the same name. In 1881, another rugby team in the town joined forces with the Rovers and became 'Burnley', and also adopted the dribbling code. In 1882, Burnley moved to Turf Moor.

Gillingham:
In the late 19th century this Kentish town was dominated by the Royal Engineers football Club who played at 'Great Lines' which was situated between New Brompton and Chatham. A number of local Clubs also used this open ground, amongst them New Brompton Excelsior. This Club became a Limited Company in June 1893, and purchased a plot of land that was to become known as Priestfield Stadium.

Plymouth Argyle:
Football was promoted in this Devon town by the quest appearances of professional Clubs, around the turn of the century. The Argyle Athletic Club was an amateur Sports Club that had been founded in 1886, and their football matches were played on a number of unspecified open pitches in and around the town. In 1901, the Ground at Home Park that had been formerly used for Rugby matches was leased, and in view of the success of the games against the famous visiting teams to Plymouth, the Club adopted professionalism themselves.

Preston North End:
A football club was created from some cricketers in 1862, who were themselves a split from the earlier Bow Lane Cricket Club. From these early Football enthusiasts, yet another breakaway group eventually formed the Club - Preston North End - in 1867. This new Club appear to have organised themselves on a more formal level for they were able to play on a pitch within the newly constructed Moor Park. An admission charge to matches was not possible and the Club's finances rested on the 2d. (1p) weekly subs. of the members. On several occasions the Club nearly folded due to their lack of funds, but they struggled through, and finally took out a lease on a site, opposite Moor Park - that became the current Deepdale Ground - on the 21st of January 1875. This would appear to make the Ground a contender for the 'longest continuously used Football enclosure by a Senior Club'. However the Club, which in any event probably did not start playing games at their new home until the 1875/76 season, were upto this time a Rugby Club. In fact it was not until 1881, that a proper football (soccer) section was formed, and hence the real Preston North End F.C. emerged.

Stoke City:
Stoke F.C. were founded in 1863 and in their early days played a modified form of Rugby. Around 1875 they first used Sweetings Field (opposite the current Victoria Ground) as a regular home Ground, when an entry charge of 2d (1p) often attracted upto 200 spectators. In 1878 the Club amalgamated with the Stoke Victoria Club and made use of the nearby (new) Athletic Ground which was destined to be renamed the Victoria Ground. It was not until 1925 that 'Stoke City' became the Club's formal name.

Wigan Athletic:
The Club were founded in 1931, but only after a succession of 'Wigans' had tried and failed. The Athletic were not related to the earlier Wigan Borough team that played in the Football League from 1921 until 1931, and who folded in October of that latter year. But one bond that the current Club had with all of their predecessors, i.e. the Wigans - County, United, Town and Borough - was the Ground at Springfield Park.

...On a similar theme, is 'Rejected F.C. ...

'Rejected F.C.': The basic statistics and histories of the ex-League Clubs (those that have resigned or have been voted out of the Football League) are detailed in these two volumes. The days in the League, plus the pre and post League days are included, with separate sections devoted to each Club. There is a good proportion of illustrative material (much of which has not been previously published) including full details of the Grounds and maps for present day locating of the sites. The two books provide the most detailed collective histories of the ex-League Clubs yet published.

Volume 1 (over 350 pages):
Aberdare, Ashington, Bootle, Bradford, Burton (Swifts Wanderers and United), Gateshead/South Shields, Glossop, Loughborough, Nelson, Stalybridge and Workington.

Volume 2 (over 480 pages):
Accrington (and Stanley), Barrow, Darwen, Durham, Gainsborough, Merthyr, Middlesbrough Ironopolis, New Brighton (and Tower), Northwich, Southport and Thames.

The first editions have now sold out, however it is hoped to reprint both volumes. For details (from early 1992) please send a S.A.E.

==

'More.... Defunct F.C.' Follows a similar format to 'Defunct F.C.' (which has sold out and no reprints are planned). 230 pages detailing the histories (written and well illustrated) of six non-League Clubs that no longer exist: Bedford Avenue, Lovell's Athletic, Romford, Rugby Town, Slough Centre and West Stanley. A fascinating insight into these big and lesser known former Clubs.

Copies available from the Author:

Priced: £ 6 - 75.

Plus P/Packing - 95p U.K., £2-00 Europe, £3-00 elsewhere.

~~~~~~

Write to: 12 The Furrows, Harefield, Middx. UB9 6AT.